Kant and the Sciences

For Lorenz Krüger,
who would, I hope, have approved

Kant and the Sciences

Edited by
Eric Watkins

OXFORD
UNIVERSITY PRESS
2001

OXFORD
UNIVERSITY PRESS

Oxford   New York
Athens   Auckland   Bangkok   Bogotá   Buenos Aires   Calcutta
Cape Town   Chennai   Dar es Salaam   Delhi   Florence   Hong Kong   Istanbul
Karachi   Kuala Lumpur   Madrid   Melbourne   Mexico City   Mumbai
Nairobi   Paris   São Paulo   Shanghai   Singapore   Taipei   Tokyo   Toronto   Warsaw

and associated companies in
Berlin   Ibadan

Copyright © 2001 by Oxford University Press, Inc.

Published by Oxford University Press, Inc.
198 Madison Avenue, New York, New York 10016

Oxford is a registered trademark of Oxford University Press

Library of Congress Cataloging-in-Publication Data
Kant and the sciences / edited by Eric Watkins.
p. cm.
Includes bibliographical references and index.
ISBN 0-19-513305-6
1. Sciences—Philosophy.   2. Kant, Immanuel, 1724–1804—Contributions in science.
I. Watkins, Eric, 1964–

Q175.K179 2000
501—dc21   99-087207

1 3 5 7 9 8 6 4 2

Printed in the United States of America
on acid-free paper

Acknowledgments

I would like to thank a number of people for their various contributions to this volume: to all of the contributors, but especially Michael Friedman and Karl Ameriks, for supporting the project so generously throughout its various stages; to Roger Ariew, Richard Burian, Joseph C. Pitt, and Robert Bates as well as the Department of Philosophy, Science and Technology Studies, and the College of Arts and Sciences at Virginia Polytechnic Institute and State University, for helping to host the conference "Kant and the Sciences," at which earlier versions of many of the chapters were delivered; to the Franklin J. Matchette Foundation, for a generous grant for the conference; to the Max Planck Institute for the History of Science in Berlin (especially Wolfgang Lefevre and Falk Wunderlich) for its support of my interests in the scientific context of Kant's philosophy; to Terry Zapata, Clint Jones, Seth Fairbanks, and Joe Hunter, for their help in preparing the manuscript and in organizing many of the details associated with the conference; to Catharine Carlin, Julia Balestracci, and Peter Ohlin, all of Oxford University Press, for their invaluable and friendly assistance throughout the editorial process.

Contents

Contributors

Karl Ameriks is Hank McMahon Professor of Philosophy at the University of Notre Dame.

Martin Carrier is Professor of Philosophy at the Universität Bielefeld.

Michael Friedman is Ruth W. Harris Professor of Arts and Humanities at Indiana University.

Hannah Ginsborg is Associate Professor of Philosophy at the University of California at Berkeley.

Paul Guyer is Florence Murray Professor in the Humanities at the University of Pennsylvania.

Manfred Kuehn is Professor of Philosophy at the Philipps-Universität at Marburg.

Rudolf A. Makkreel is Charles Howard Candler Professor of Philosophy at Emory University.

Thomas Sturm is completing his Ph. D. dissertation in philosophy at the Philipps-Universität Marburg.

Daniel Warren is Associate Professor of Philosophy at the University of California at Berkeley.

Eric Watkins is Associate Professor of Philosophy and a teaching faculty member of the Program of Science and Technology Studies at Virginia Polytechnic Institute and State University (Virginia Tech), currently visiting Associate Professor of Philosophy at Yale University.

Note on Texts and Translations

All quotations from Kant's works (whether they be publications, letters, notes, marginalia, or lecture transcripts) will refer to the volume and page numbers of the Akademie edition, that is, *Kants gesammelte Schriften* ed. Deutsche [formerly Königlich Preussische] Akademie der Wissenschaften, 29 vols. (Berlin: de Gruyter, 1900–), except for quotations from the *Critique of Pure Reason*, which will simply be referred to by A or B and the page number from the first or second edition of this work. (Alexander Baumgarten's *Metaphysica* and Wenceslav Karsten's *Anleitung zur gemeinnützlichen Kenntniß der Natur*, both of which are also reprinted in the Akademie edition, will likewise be referred to by their respective volume and page numbers.) Each contributor indicates in an appropriate note which translations of Kant's works are used. Bibliographic information for all other works is supplied in the notes.

Kant and the Sciences

Introduction

K<small>ANT'S</small> fame in traditional philosophical endeavors (whether it be in epistemology, ethics, or aesthetics) is well documented (by countless articles and monographs on Kant's three great Critiques: *Critique of Pure Reason*, *Critique of Practical Reason*, and *Critique of Judgment*). What has received less positive attention is Kant's significance as a natural philosopher, that is, as one who attempts to incorporate a variety of scientific disciplines and practices into a single philosophical system without violating the integrity of either the various methods and standards of the particular scientific disciplines or the ideals of the discipline whose task it is to unify them, namely philosophy.

Insofar as Kant's philosophy of science has received attention, it has been, with some notable exceptions, mostly negative.[1] The standard criticism of Kant's natural philosophy is that he overemphasizes his own transcendental philosophy by trying to "force" a wide range of diverse scientific practices into a single philosophical mold (whether they fit the mold or not). The criticism holds for physics, it is alleged, because Kant attempts to provide an a priori foundation for a discipline that owes its success to the brilliant, but presumably contingent discoveries of one individual in particular—Isaac Newton. In other words, it is supposed that Kant believes—or his transcendental method implies—that he could have proved the fundamental principles of Newtonian physics, even if Newton had never lived, since his own proofs are completely a priori, that is independent of experience. Yet it is implausible to maintain that Kant could have proved the fundamental principles of Newtonian science without (or prior to) Newton's discoveries. Moreover, it is often thought that Kant simply dismisses disciplines other than physics as nonscientific because they do not satisfy the conditions that physics does. Therefore, since Kant cannot provide a plausible account of either physics or any other scientific discipline, his natural philosophy, it is concluded, is of no special interest.

Despite the diversity of individual theses argued for in this volume, its main purpose is to reexamine more closely Kant's considered attitude toward particular sciences in order to reevaluate Kant's natural philosophy as a whole. For upon closer inspection, it becomes clear that Kant is not only aware of many details of the sciences of his day, but also quite sensitive to the different standards implicit in various scientific practices and their fundamental philosophical presuppositions. Moreover, throughout the course of his career—and despite statements he makes in one particular context, the preface to the *Metaphysical Foundations of Natural Science*—Kant does undertake a sustained attempt at developing a coherent and unified natural philosophy that nevertheless still respects these diverse standards. For example, Kant appreciates and even articulates the special achievements of Newtonian science, but he does not let the special status of physics blind him to the fact that other sciences, such as chemistry, anthropology, and biology, can be scientific in different senses. At the same time, Kant clearly strives to find a single philosophical standpoint, framework, or vocabulary from within which he can unite these various disciplines. Consequently, upon closer scrutiny of Kant's treatment of various sciences one can see that the way in which he engages in philosophical reflection about particular sciences and the unity that binds them together despite their diversity ought not to be immediately dismissed.

This volume attempts to contribute to this reexamination and reevaluation of Kant's account of the sciences in several ways. In chapter 1, Manfred Kuehn sets the proper stage for the remaining essays by delineating the local context of Kant's scientific education. In particular, Kuehn describes each relevant member of the philosophy faculty at the university in Königsberg and what scientific activities each one was engaged in when Kant was a student there, giving us an informed sense of what Kant's scientific training was like. On the basis of this picture, Kuehn then argues that Kant's relationship with one of his teachers, Martin Knutzen (who is often thought to have been Kant's favorite teacher), may have been much more negative or critical than is typically supposed, an evaluation which has important implications especially for our reading of Kant's early works in natural philosophy.

Chapters 2 through 4 articulate at a very general level different possible roles that Kant's transcendental philosophy could play with respect to science. In chapter 2, Karl Ameriks first sets Kant in the broader context of modern philosophy as a whole by suggesting (in contrast to earlier commentators) that Kant not be understood primarily as attempting to (1) defeat skepticism, (2) promote "scientism," or (3) develop a radically new ontology. Ameriks suggests that Kant's philosophy aims rather at taking the claims of common sense at face value and then attempting to mediate between such claims and the claims of science. As Ameriks puts it: Kant sees "philosophy as a systematic articulation of the sphere of conceptual frameworks that mediate between the extremely informal and the highly formal levels of judgment within our complex objective picture of the world."

In chapter 3, Michael Friedman likewise focuses on the task of philosophy as conceived by Kant by considering the relationship between the general metaphysics of the *Critique of Pure Reason* and the special metaphysics of the *Metaphysical Foundations of Natural Science*. Kant claims that what distinguishes the latter from the former is that the latter presupposes an empirical concept, namely the concept of matter, whereas the former does not. Friedman argues that the concept of matter is empirical not in any ordinary sense, but rather in the sense that it requires actual perceptible objects to be given. As it turns out, on Friedman's account, only the system of contingently given, empirical objects of our solar system as described by Newtonian physics satisfies this requirement. This interpretation suggests (in contrast to Ameriks's interpretation) that "experience," whose possibility Kant is exploring in the first *Critique*, is exclusively "scientific experience" and that the task of theoretical philosophy thus lies primarily in understanding the conceptual presuppositions of scientific experience.

In chapter 4, Eric Watkins discusses Kant's acceptance of four principles of rational cosmology, namely the principles of no fate, no chance, no leap, and no gap. Watkins argues that these principles are neither purely analytic nor identical to the epistemological principles of the first *Critique*. Rather, they represent genuine, distinctively ontological principles that underlie the principles of empirical cosmology, which would be discovered empirically. This interpretation would suggest that for Kant philosophy is not governed exclusively (or primarily) by demands stemming from Newtonian science (as Friedman argues) or by attempts at mediating between it and common sense (as Ameriks suggests), but by ontological demands as well.

With these various interpretations of the general task of philosophy with regard to science in mind, one can turn to the remaining essays, which focus on Kant's attitude toward particular sciences. Chapters 5 through 7 focus on physics, which Kant, like many of his contemporaries, considered paradigmatic for other sciences in light of its exceptional rigor, clarity, and support. In chapter 5, Daniel Warren considers Kant's rejection of what Kant calls "mathematical-mechanical" explanations in physics in favor of "metaphysical-dynamical" explanations. In particular, Warren considers Kant's reason for rejecting solidity as a primary feature of bodies. Warren argues that Kant's rejection of solidity is based on his Critical doctrine that we can know only relational properties, whereas solidity is alleged to be an intrinsic or nonrelational property of bodies. Thus, Kant's views on physics (more specifically, on the type of explanation that should be preferred in physics) are driven at least in part by metaphysical considerations from the first *Critique*.

In chapter 6, Martin Carrier focuses on the question of how the masses of bodies are to be determined. Kant suggests that this determination is to be accomplished primarily by considering processes of collision and pressure, that is, specifically mechanical procedures, and by rejecting "dynamical" methods. However, Kant then suggests that one can measure the masses of bodies by means of original attraction (in the form of balances) and, even more strikingly, he describes measurement by means of attraction as being mechanical, even if it is so "only indirectly." Carrier argues that Kant can make good sense of this suggestion by invoking the law of the equality of action and reaction (despite the fact that invoking this law is architectonically awkward insofar as this law appears after Kant's explanation of how mass is to be measured). This shows, contrary to what is often assumed, that Kant is quite adept at developing sophisticated philosophical interpretations of specific empirical scientific practices.

In chapter 7, Eric Watkins compares Kant's laws of mechanics with Newton's laws of motion, noting significant differences between the two. Watkins argues that these differences stem from the fact that Newton's *Principia* was received in an intellectual climate in eighteenth-century Germany dominated by rationalistic (Leibnizian-Wolffian) concerns. Considering this context helps one to understand Kant's position and arguments on a number of crucial issues in physics where Kant differs from Newton, such as the infinite divisibility of matter and action at a distance. Kant's differences from Newton are to be understood not necessarily as unintentional deviations caused by his transcendental or a priori methodology, but rather as intentional modifications undertaken as a result of a different set of concerns and aims.

Chapters 8 and 9 turn to consider "human sciences" in order to determine whether Kant rejects them as uniformly as is commonly maintained, and what his reasoning is in each case. In chapter 8, Thomas Sturm considers Kant's views on the scientific status of psychology. Kant repeatedly divides doctrines of nature into psychology and physics, since there are two kinds of objects of our senses (namely inner and outer), but in the preface to the *Metaphysical Foundations* Kant clearly denies that psychology can be science proper. However, Sturm first argues (philosophically) that Kant's denial of scientific status to psychology is based on a very specific understanding of the kind of mathematizability that is required for science. Sturm then argues (historically) that many of Kant's critical remarks about psychology are in fact directed not against psychology per se, but rather against a particular conception of psychology, namely a conception that goes back to Baumgarten and that was adopted by many psychologists in the eighteenth century, according to which introspection is the sole means of gathering evidence. Although this particular conception of psychology precludes it from being science proper, it is possible that other conceptions of psychology could allow it to be scientific, and even if introspection-based psychology cannot be science "proper," it is clear that for Kant psychology that is not introspection-based, which he would call anthropology, is still a significant factor in our knowledge of the world.

In chapter 9, Rudolf Makkreel explores Kant's views on a wide range of "human sciences," for example, psychology, anthropology, and history. By focusing on the development of Kant's thought throughout his various Anthropology lectures, recently published in volume 24 of the Akademie edition, Makkreel argues that psychology, history, geography, and especially anthropology are sciences in the sense of systematic disciplines that hang together not according to a theoretical idea, but rather according to a *practical* idea of the world-best, and that are guided by reflective rather than determinate judgment. Thus, these disciplines are to be understood not as theoretical natural sciences on a par with physics, but rather as pragmatic cultural sciences, since their aim is to give human beings the kind of knowledge necessary in order to be able to act in the world. In this way, anthropology in particular can become not a formal science, but a "generally useful science." Accordingly, it is clear not only that Kant considers these sciences to be important and scientific in a significant sense, but also that he displays tremendous subtlety and depth in reflecting on and describing the unique features and status of these sciences.

Chapters 10 through 12 consider the sciences of chemistry and biology. In chapter 10, Martin Carrier considers Kant's views on chemistry. As in the case of psychology, in the preface to the *Metaphysical Foundations* Kant claims that chemistry is not a proper science. However, in this case, Kant does not exclude the possibility that it could become a science at some point in the future. Carrier argues that Kant's rejection of chemistry as a science proper is based on his acceptance of one chemical theory in particular, namely a version of Stahl's chemistry of principles, which Carrier presents in detail, especially as it was understood throughout the eighteenth century. Carrier also argues that Kant's acceptance of a Stahlian chemistry of principles provides him with a prime example of the regulative ideals of reason that he introduces at a transcendental level in the first *Critique*. Again, we see that Kant is sensitive to the distinctive explanatory features of a particular science that he is intimately acquainted with, and utilizes these features in filling out his own transcendental philosophy, rather than vice versa.

In chapter 11, Hannah Ginsborg addresses two fundamental questions that Kant's attempt at understanding biology and biological explanation raises. First: What is the role of the concept of purpose in our investigation of organisms, and how does it relate to our failure to explain their origin in mechanical terms? Second: What is it to regard an organism as a purpose, given that we must also regard it as a product of nature? Ginsborg argues that for Kant understanding organisms essentially involves a unique kind of normativity. Again, even if Kant does not consider biology a "proper" science, he nevertheless thinks that we can have knowledge of organisms and, as in the case of chemistry, he even articulates a distinctive philosophical level of knowledge (in the *Critique of Judgment*) in order to be able to incorporate such knowledge into his comprehensive natural philosophy.

In chapter 12, Paul Guyer likewise considers Kant's understanding of organisms, yet Guyer undertakes a developmental approach to the issue, first presenting three different arguments Kant posits in the third *Critique* regarding the kind of explanation organisms require (namely teleological rather than mechanical) and then considering how Kant ultimately seems to find these arguments wanting in the *Opus postumum*. Due to Kant's sustained reflections on how to incorporate teleological explanations of organisms into his natural philosophy toward the end of his career, it would seem, Guyer argues, that it is ultimately only our awareness of the freedom of our own purposiveness that leads us to understand organisms in terms of purposes, which causes a fundamental split between the teleological and mechanical views of nature. In this way Kant can establish an important link between his theoretical and practical philosophy.

Despite all their differences, what these various essays seem to show, taken collectively, is that Kant is by no means a philosopher overly taken with or exclusively committed to the a priori. With respect to physics, it would seem that Kant's differences from Newton are not in fact imposed by his own a priori concerns but rather stem from his attempt at making sense of Newtonian physics where Newton could not. Moreover, Kant does not simply dismiss sciences other than physics as not living up to its standards. In the case of psychology and anthropology Kant is very sensitive to the way in which man is to be studied. In psychology Kant seems to be aware of the limitations of introspection as a means of investigating the mind, and in anthropology he expands his conception of knowledge to include a body of knowledge organized according to a practical rather than a theoretical idea. In chemistry, he incorporates (and possibly even improves upon) Stahl's theory of principles into a broader philosophical framework, and in biology he explores how teleological explanations need to be understood in terms of organisms rather than inert matter and in regulative rather than constitutive fashion. In all of these cases, Kant does not let himself be unduly influenced by either his own transcendental philosophy or the unique status achieved by physics. Rather, he reveals himself throughout as a natural philosopher reflecting in deep and interesting ways on how one might attempt to make sense of a plurality of sciences from a coherent and unified philosophical perspective.

NOTE

1. To cite just one example of many, see S. Körner, *Kant* (London: Cox & Wyman, 1955), 100.

PART I

Historical and Philosophical Context

Kant's Teachers in the Exact Sciences

Manfred Kuehn

KANT'S teachers in what would we would call today "exact science" seem to be for the most part forgotten. Neither Christian Friedrich Ammon (1696–1742), lecturer (*Privatdozent*) in mathematics, nor Conrad Theophil Marquardt, associate professor of mathematics, nor Carl Heinrich Rappolt (1702–53), associate professor of physics, nor even Johann Gottfried Teske (1704–72), professor of physics and supervisor of Kant's doctoral dissertation, are even so much as mentioned by Kant scholars. The only one of Kant's teachers who is better known is Martin Knutzen (1713–51). Indeed, it has become almost dogma of Kant scholarship that Knutzen introduced Kant to Leibnizian-Wolffian metaphysics and Newtonian philosophy, and that the earliest Kant was a follower of Knutzen. Benno Erdmann's argument that Kant's earliest position was, on the whole, identical with that of Knutzen seems to be generally accepted today.[1] Perhaps no one has gone as far as Ernst Cassirer, who claimed that among Kant's teachers "Knutzen alone represented the European ideal of universal science."[2]

This view has initial plausibility. Knutzen was the best known philosopher in Königsberg when Kant studied there. He was a popular and engaging teacher, and Kant's earliest biographers talk mainly about Knutzen when they speak of his teachers. Thus Borowski claimed that Kant "attended his classes in philosophy and mathematics without a pause." He also suggested that Kant primarily relied on Knutzen, who "delineated for him and others the course on which they could become not mere followers, but thinkers in their own right." Borowski claimed further that "Knutzen, a wise judge of heads, found in Kant excellent talents, encouraged him in private conversations, later lent him Newton, and, since Kant liked it, anything else he wanted from his rich library."[3] Christian Jacob Kraus (1753–1807), Kant's student and colleague, observed that Knutzen was the only one "who could have had an influence on his [Kant's] genius," surmising that "what unlocked Kant's genius under Knutzen and led him to the original ideas that he put down in his natural history of the heavens was the comet of 1744 on which Knutzen published a book."[4]

I would like to reexamine Kant's relation to Knutzen in this chapter. To do so, I will concentrate on the work that represents the culmination of Kant's student years, namely his *Thoughts on the True Estimation of the Living Forces and an Evaluation of their Proofs, as they Have Been Given by Herr von Leibniz and other Mechanists in this Dispute, as well as some Preliminary Considerations which Concern Force and Body in General*, which Kant began in 1744 and published in 1747. Starting with a brief sketch of the general intellectual climate at the University of Königsberg in 1740, followed by a short account of the lives and views of his teachers in mathematics and the sciences, I shall make some observations on the nature of Kant's scientific training and then offer suggestions that show why the publication of *Thoughts on the True Estimation* represents a peculiar event that is best explained as an act of rebellion against Knutzen. Finally, I will briefly characterize Kant's philosophical position in his *Thoughts on the True Estimation of the Living Forces*.

1. The State of Philosophy at the University in Königsberg

When Kant entered the university in the winter semester of 1740, great changes were expected in the intellectual life of the university. Frederick William I had died on May 31, 1740, to be succeeded by his son, Frederick II of Prussia. The father was well known for his simple-minded Christian views and his support of the Pietists as allies in reforming Prussia's educational and cultural institutions. At the university in Königsberg, the Pietists were the most influential faction—especially in the schools of theology and philosophy. While the three factions of Pietism, Orthodoxy, and Wolffianism had been locked in fierce battle during the preceding twenty years, the Pietists had spared no effort to eradicate any influence of competing views at the university, and with the support of Frederick William I, they had almost succeeded. Since Frederick II was much more liberal in matters of religion, the enemies of Pietism thought their time had finally arrived. The Orthodox, still influential among the clergy and the professors and city officials aligned with them, were just waiting for an opportunity to pay them back. The Wolffians were also hoping for better times. Having been much maligned at the university, they had been in a tenuous position ever since Christian Gabriel Fischer, professor of natural philosophy, had been banned from Königsberg and all of Prussia in 1725 as a result of Pietist calumnies in Berlin. They had also constantly threatened those who remained Wolffians, even though the king's position toward Wolff had softened.[5] But now it was the Pietists who were scared. Especially their leader Franz Albert Schulz had incurred the wrath of many. He had already predicted that "his head would be cut off within three days of the King's death."[6]

As it turned out, the Pietists had no reason to fear the new king. Though he favored the Wolffians over the Pietists, and though he succeeded where his father had failed, namely in getting Wolff to return to Halle as a professor of law and vice chancellor of the University of Halle, the fears of the Pietists turned out to be exaggerated. The situation in Königsberg did not change suddenly. Frederick II, seemingly more interested in the expansion of Prussian territory than in his intellectual pursuits, left administrative matters more or less as his father had arranged them.

Financially, the University of Königsberg was in dire straits. The ministry in Berlin considered it of secondary importance, compared with the University of Halle. Still, Königsberg was not unimportant. The "Albertina" was one of the two major universities in Prussia, and the only university in Eastern Prussia. While it was not among the largest universities in Germany, it was not one of the smallest either. For most semesters during the eighteenth century, attendance probably hovered between three hundred and five hundred students.[7] It was comparatively successful among the German universities—at least as far as the number of students was concerned. Part of its relative success in attracting students can clearly be attributed to its location. Students wishing to study elsewhere had to travel far. Furthermore, Königsberg also attracted a number of students from the surrounding countries. It was a kind of "international university," with a significant number of Poles, Lithuanians, and other Baltic nationalities in attendance.[8]

The relative isolation of Königsberg also had disadvantages. As late as 1781, Ludwig von Baczko wrote that Prussia was "decried as almost a learned Siberia; and owing to our great distance from Leipzig, the center of the German book-trade, it is natural that we should suffer, since all literary novelties come late to us, and authorship is not favored by facilities of selling books."[9] When Frederick the Great visited Königsberg in 1739—not yet king—he quipped that the city was better suited "to bring up bears than to be an arena of the sciences."[10] Accordingly, not many scholars came to Königsberg with the expressed purpose of teaching at the university, and some who taught there were underqualified. Indeed, in some courses "the teacher was not well acquainted with his science and wanted to learn it by lecturing [*docendo*]."[11] The course offerings were uneven. Some disciplines were not taught at all; others, such as chemistry, natural history, economics, and political science, were not well represented. Mathematics and physics were taught poorly. The experiments that could be performed with the equipment present at the university were rather poor, for instance; and calculus was taught by someone who had no formal training in it. Königsberg was perhaps not atypical in this, but in the natural sciences it was not among the leading universities of Europe or even Germany.

Like all of the Protestant German universities, the Albertina had four schools or *Fakultäten*: theology, philosophy, law, and medicine. Theology was undoubtedly the most important of these. It had the most students. Its teachers received the most secure income, and it was also the most influential of the faculties. The school of philosophy was dominated mostly by theology. Several theologians taught philosophy, and theological concerns motivated most of the philosophical curriculum. Indeed, during the first two thirds of the eighteenth century, philosophy at Königsberg was not much more than the handmaiden of theology.

At the beginning of the century, the orientation of philosophy in Königsberg, like in most Protestant universities, was almost entirely Aristotelian.[12] Descartes and other modern philosophers had little influence. Most philosophy professors were engaged in defending Aristotelianism.[13] But as early as 1715, several philosophers were engaged in trying to find a middle way between traditional Protestant Aristotelianism and some of the more recent philosophical developments. Gottsched reported that during 1714 and 1715 he was taught metaphysics in accordance with Cartesian principles and natural law in accordance with Thomasius.[14] He also claimed that he was exposed to other thinkers, such as Locke and Leclerc, and he said that "the great freedom to philosophize, which was prevalent at the University of Königsberg during my period of study there, has protected me from the slavish way of thinking and teaching that was so common in the dominant philosophical schools."[15] During this period Wolff's philosophy first became important at Königsberg.[16]

By the late thirties, most of the Aristotelians had died. Still, Aristotelianism did not disappear entirely until after the middle of the century. The role it continued to play at the time Kant entered the university should not be underestimated. In any case, the freedom of philosophizing Gottsched had experienced did not last long. Because of a number of strategic appointments by Frederick William I, the Pietists were able to dominate the theological and philosophical faculties from 1725, eradicating completely all Patristic studies and officially preventing Wolffian philosophy from being taught. The Wolffians had to be most circumspect in what they were saying.[17] Lecturing in accordance with Wolffian texts was explicitly prohibited. Wolff's works could not even be purchased.[18]

While no one was able to prevent the Pietists from growing ever stronger between 1725 and 1740, there was a rather unexpected twist in their intellectual outlook around 1732. Buck wrote to Gottsched in August of that year: "You will be very surprised when your brother tells you that the Wolffian philosophy is now imported here by those from Halle themselves, and that they praise it in front of everyone as the best kind. . . . Who would have been able to imagine such a transformation some time ago? Even a year ago it would have appeared to be incredible, if someone had prophesied this."[19] Schulz, who had studied in Halle with both Wolff and Francke and even tried to get the two reconciled before Wolff was banished, had arrived in Königsberg. He thought that there was no contradiction between Wolffian philosophy "properly understood," and Pietism. Schulz's position also represented the current thinking of Frederick William I.

Wolff's philosophy thus became more important in Königsberg again. However, this did not mean a return to free philosophical discussion. The Pietistic apostles may have sounded like Wolff, but they were still apostles. Wolffian philosophy, properly understood, was all right, but not any kind of Wolffianism. Poetry, theater, and other nonreligious diversions were still considered frivolous, worldly, "of the devil," and thus actively discouraged. Everything had to be directed toward the well being of the human soul in accordance with Pietistic principles.

2. KANT'S TEACHERS IN KÖNIGSBERG

These developments had a definite effect on the lives of Kant's teachers in mathematics and natural philosophy and therefore on Kant as well. Some, who would have taught Kant, like Fischer, could not because they had been expelled. Others, who may have been just as worthy or even more worthy than those who were in positions of importance, were less effective because they had to teach subjects they did not want to teach.

Thus Marquardt, a native of Königsberg, who had studied theology in Königsberg and philosophy in Halle, was a strict Wolffian. He had defended his inaugural dissertation on pre-established harmony in Königsberg in 1722, and he was still teaching theology, philosophy, and mathematics when Kant was a student.[20] After 1730 he was an associate professor of mathematics. He also gave lectures in logic and metaphysics until his death in 1749 that are said to have been very popular among the students. He gave his unqualified support to pre-established harmony in the question of the mind–body relation.

During the period under consideration it was more or less universally assumed that only three systems could explain how substances could be related to each other, a question that was of course especially important for understanding the relation of mind and body, which, according to Cartesian principles, were radically different yet still capable of interacting. The first of these systems was the system of physical influx, which held that the change in any substance must be sufficiently and immediately founded in another substance. So, physical influx involved the belief that there really was interaction between mind and body. This position was associated with Aristotle and perhaps somewhat surprisingly also with Locke. The second was occasionalism, which involved the belief that any change in a substance had a corresponding change in another substance, and that both these changes were immediately subordinated to the highest being. According to this position there was no real interaction between substances, there was only co-ordination. This was ascribed to the Cartesians and especially to Malebranche. The third position claimed that both are subordinated to the highest being by two harmonic series of changes. This was called the system of the universal harmony, and it was

Leibniz's position. Wolff himself had come into conflict with the Pietists over just this problem.[21]

Marquardt's views were less guarded than Wolff's. He was much less timid, arguing that all bodily phenomena could be completely explained at the level of bodies. At the same time these phenomena could also be explained at the more fundamental level of the substances because the soul could create all representations on its own. Since God had to create the best of all possible worlds, he had to have established a correspondence between body and soul, or phenomena and substances.[22] Marquardt supplemented his a priori argument with a posteriori arguments, meant both to prove pre-established harmony and to disprove occasionalism and physical influx. As a strict Wolffian, he was even opposed to the Pietism expressed in Wolffian terms that was so popular in Königsberg at the time.[23] Marquardt was persona non grata to the Pietists.

Rappolt was an associate professor of physics. He was the one best qualified to teach the subject at Königsberg, having even studied physics and mathematics in England from 1729 to 1730.[24] His views had been formed mainly by Fischer and other early Wolffians in Königsberg. Indeed, it was Fischer who caused him to abandon his studies in theology and to turn toward physics. He was thus also a Wolffian, though also influenced by British sources. In 1728 he had occasion to write to Gottsched: "Here all science seems to be of no use, and one does not so much consider whether someone has learned something solid as whether someone knows to adapt to the manners of Halle."[25]

Though it is likely that Kant attended the lectures of Marquardt and Rappolt, there is no positive proof. However, we can be sure that Kant was acquainted with the contents of the lectures given by Ammon, Teske, and Knutzen, for we know that he tutored a fellow student in these courses as early as 1741, gave him "books which concerned modern philosophy, and reviewed at least the most difficult parts of all the seminars [the student] took with Ammon, Knutzen, and Teske."[26] He must have attended their lectures during his very first year at the university.

Ammon was a lecturer (*Privatdozent*) in mathematics, who had first been an Aristotelian but had then moved closer to Wolff long before Kant entered the university.[27] His *Lineae primae eruditionis humanae in usum auditorii ductae*, which appeared in 1737, was a short summary of the subjects that students had to master in the philosophical curriculum. He and others used it as a textbook for lectures. More characterized by an eclectic spirit, it was dominated by neither Aristotelianism nor Wolffianism. Kraus did not have a high opinion of Ammon, saying that on the basis of one of Ammon's mathematical tracts he saw, he could only call him a dilettante (*Stümper*).[28] Since Ammon died in 1742 Kant could not have tutored many times for Ammon's courses.

Teske, who received his position as a result of efforts by the Pietists, taught both theoretical and experimental physics.[29] Rappolt had good reason to be angry with him, for Teske was appointed to full professor of physics, even though, being more of a theologian and administrator than a scientist, he had studied physics for less than two years.[30] His position of *Konsistoralrat* made him an important figure in Protestant circles in Königsberg, but it is not clear how this contributed to his scientific views. To say that he was underqualified to teach physics—at least at the beginning of his career—would be no exaggeration.

Still, his courses in experimental physics must have been quite impressive. Borowski speaks highly of him, describing him as a good teacher and person. This is shown as much by Johann Friedrich Lauson's poems about some electrical experiments in his lectures as it is by Herder's high estimation of Teske. He seems to have worked mainly on problems concerning electricity. Using some basic equipment to rather memorable effect, he demonstrated the effects of static electricity. By producing electric charges he created heat, sparks, and flashes, electrified his students, lighted a fire from alcohol and produced a glow in a wire even under water. Lauson's poem does not make not clear precisely what conclusions Teske drew from his experiments, but we know that he thought he had shown that electricity and lightning were of the same nature. He was very interested in the various effects of electricity and how they were related to fire, and he was said to be one of the first who claimed that "electrical fire" was identical with the "material of lightning."[31] Taking great pride that his experiments had shown "how useful it [electricity] was also in the medical sciences"—especially in curing toothaches and other ailments—Teske also collected 243 "physical and mathematical instruments" throughout his life.[32]

Kant was sufficiently attracted by Teske's investigations of electricity and fire to write his thesis for the degree of Magister—entitled "Succinct Exposition of Some Meditations on Fire"—on this topic. Though Teske claimed that he had learned from Kant's dissertation, we may assume that Kant had learned more from Teske's speculations and calculations than Teske learned from Kant.[33] According to some reports, Kant considered the memory of this man "holy"; but, according to Kraus, Kant had "a low opinion of Teske and rightfully so."[34]

The best known and most influential philosopher and scientist at Königsberg was clearly Knutzen, who had studied in Königsberg from 1728 to 1734 with many professors who were still teaching when Kant entered the university. He had been a student of Ammon and Teske, for instance, but he had avoided the Aristotelians. Since none of his teachers knew calculus, he had to learn it on his own. The same was true of algebra, which he learned from Wolff's Latin work on the discipline.[35] In his studies of theology he could rely on A. Wolff and Schulz and other Pietists. In 1732 he was the respondent when the newly arrived Schulz defended his inaugural dissertation. It was characteristically entitled "Of the Agreement of Reason with Faith." Not surprisingly, he became a Pietist in the Schulzian fashion, that is, he followed the Wolffian method, while engaging and criticizing Wolffian philosophy in a serious way. In his dissertation for the Magister degree, he attacked the view that the world may have existed from eternity.[36] For Knutzen, as for any

Lutheran, the world was created by God and had been designed by him with a definite end in mind. It could not possibly be eternal.[37] He developed a new theory, meant to be an alternative to the Leibnizian-Wolffian one. "His pietism belongs in its basic outlook to the great Spener-Francke line."[38]

In 1734, at the age of twenty-one, Knutzen defended his dissertation, "Philosophical Comment on the *commercium* of the Mind with the Body, Explained by Physical Influx." In this work he criticized severely the contents of Wolffian philosophy, but he also expressed his appreciation for the Wolffian approach. But Knutzen was not a Wolffian. His dissertation dealt with the most contentious issue between the Pietists and the Wolffians, namely the question concerning the relation of mind and body. Taking what was essentially an anti-Leibnizian and thus also anti-Wolffian position, he argued that the theories of pre-established harmony and occasionalism were wrong and that the only reasonable theory was that of physical influx.

Knutzen accepted the view that bodies consist of absolutely simple parts. This meant that by the interaction of mind and body, we do not have to understand that two radically different substances interact, but rather that simple elements act on one another. Since physical influx was held by most scholars closely connected with Locke, it would not be entirely inaccurate to say that he defended the Lockean position.

In some ways, Knutzen's philosophical position is more appropriately characterized as being Lockean than Wolffian. In fact, Gottsched accused Knutzen of being too close to Locke in his discussion of sensibility in the earlier work on efficient causality.[39] For Knutzen, just as for Locke, internal and external sensation forms the basis of all knowledge. The principle of contradiction, without the materials given to us in sensation, does not allow us to know anything. At the time of his death he was still working on a translation of Locke's *Of the Conduct of the Human Understanding*.[40] Even Erdmann had to admit that his works "point in the direction of the empiricist skepticism and idealism of English [*sic*] philosophy."[41]

Knutzen appears to have been an engaging teacher. Many former students seem to have been proud that they had studied with him. Hamann's autobiography is often cited as support, for he said: "I was a student of the famous Knutzen in all parts of philosophy, mathematics, and in private lectures on algebra, and I was a member of the physico-theological society that was founded under him, but did not succeed."[42] But this may be rather weak support. His praise of Knutzen is sarcastic, for he goes on to lament that he did not take advantage of the opportunity, and then finds:

> My memory of another academic teacher, who was not as famous, is more pleasant. God permitted it that he lived under depressed, miserable, and obscure circumstances. He was worthy of a better fate. He possessed qualities, which the world does not esteem and therefore does not reward. His

end was as his life: unnoticed. I do not doubt that he is saved. His name was Rappolt; a man who possessed a peculiarly keen judgment concerning natural things and at the same time the consideration, devotion, and humility of a Christian philosopher. He had an exceptional ability to emulate the spirit and the language of the ancients.[43]

The quotation as a whole shows that Hamann himself thought more highly of Rappolt than of Knutzen. Whether Kant's view was similar to Hamann's is not clear because he said nothing about either of them.

When Kant entered the university, Knutzen was a relatively young associate professor, who taught logic and metaphysics. If Borowski was correct in claiming that Kant "attended his classes in philosophy and mathematics without a break," then his weekly schedule during the first semester would have included the following courses by Knutzen: four hours of mathematics, four hours of philosophy, one hour of logic "in outline," as well as exercises in disputation.[44] The second semester would have seen him take a more advanced course in logic, another course in mathematics, in which Knutzen introduced "select minds" to higher mathematics, and again exercises in disputation. In the fourth semester he would have taken practical philosophy, and later rational psychology, natural philosophy, natural law, rhetoric, mnemonics, algebra, and the "Analysis of the Infinite."[45] This means that Kant never attended any lectures by Knutzen on natural science. For this he had to go to Teske's lectures (probably also during his first few semesters). He also went to Ammon's lectures on mathematics and a number of other classes by such people as Rappolt and Marquardt.[46] Even if Knutzen was Kant's favorite professor, he was certainly not the only one who taught him.

But the education Kant received in the lecture rooms was not the only education Kant received. Other events in Königsberg must have been just as important. Thus the notorious Fischer, expelled as a Wolffian in 1725, was allowed to return to Königsberg in 1737. In 1743 a book appeared by an anonymous author with the title *Reasonable Thoughts on Nature by a Christian Friend of God. Who is Nature? That it is Powerless without His Omniscient Limitation. And How through the One, Divisible Power everything in this Word is Possible only in and through the Mediate Causes in Accordance with the Efficacy or Action which Has Been Given to It.* Its author was Fischer.[47] Starting from Wolff and Leibniz, he advocated a point of view that can only be called Spinozistic, thus challenging not only the Pietists, but also the Orthodox. One of the major problems the theologians had with the book was not so much its open Spinozism in general as its specific views on the Holy Trinity, the denial of the doctrine that Christ is both all human and all divine, and many other theological dogmas. After a pastor preached openly against Fischer and his book in a service on New Year's Day, the book created a sensation. Fischer himself was excluded from the Eucharist. He was not allowed to remain the godparent of his grandchild, and he was advised to go to the Reformed Church from then on.[48] The Orthodox had the book banned, but they did not succeed in harming Fischer beyond that. Kant must have taken great interest in the affair.

Another event, perhaps more significant, happened in the following year. Knutzen became famous, or perhaps rather, notorious, as an astronomer beyond Königsberg. In a little noticed work of 1738 he had predicted that a comet that had been observed in 1698 would reappear in the winter of 1744. This prediction was apparently based on calculations that depended on Newton's theory of the course of comets, according to which all of them circle the sun.[49] In 1744, a comet actually did appear, and Knutzen became a great celebrity and the intellectual hero of Königsberg. His success was also noted elsewhere. But soon doubts arose. Euler showed both in letters to Knutzen and in an article that appeared in the very same year that Knutzen's prediction had *not* come "true," that the comet of 1744 was actually *not* identical with the comet of 1698.[50] The course of the comet was of such a nature that it needed "at least four to five hundred years" before it could be seen again.[51]

Knutzen wrote on the comets again in 1744.[52] But his tract was written in part as a response to a certain Johann Heyn, who had argued in an earlier tract, entitled "Attempt of a Consideration of the Comet, the Deluge, and the Prelude of the Final Judgment. In accordance with Astronomical Reasons and the Bible . . ."[53] that the ancient fear of comets as bad omens was well founded. His arguments were largely derived from Whiston's theories. Knutzen objected to this view. For him, just as for Newton and Wolff, comets were just small planets, circling the sun. They traveled a regular course and, even if they were of great interest to the physicist, they did not have to be feared; Heyn therefore had to be viewed as an alarmist and obscurantist. Wanting to attack the fear of comets "in its last stronghold," he vehemently attacked Heyn.[55] The latter responded in kind, accusing Knutzen not only of plagiarism—the prediction had already been made a year earlier in the *Leipziger gelehrte Anzeigen*—but also suggesting that he had not sufficiently proven the identity of the comet of 1698 and 1744. Knutzen and his students seem to have dismissed Heyn's reference to Euler in the same way as they rejected Euler's criticism itself.

Knutzen's understanding of scientific issues and especially his education in mathematics do not seem to have been adequate to the task of advancing the discussion of the more technical aspects of physics. He did not belong to that "small elite" of scientists on the continent who could understand the details of Newtonian physics.[55] His knowledge of calculus was deficient. Relying more on mechanical models than on calculations, he had some general understanding of Newton's *Principia*, but he could not make any original contribution to science. Nor was he interested in drawing a sharp distinction between science on the one hand and metaphysics on the other. Theological and apologetic concerns dictated what they could and could not argue just as much as did scientific ones. Accordingly, he was a rather limited scientist even by eighteenth-century standards.

Kant must have followed all the arguments about the comets with great interest, for he became very interested in the subject matter of comets and his earliest works deal with such matters. These developments must also have led to Kant's disenchantment with his teachers. He may well have realized Knutzen's shortcomings as a practicing scientist through Euler's criticisms. In any case, it is not without interest in this connection that one of the people to whom he sent his first work was Euler. Perhaps it is just as significant that in one of his first essays he dismissed the study of comets as irrelevant to the understanding of the planet Earth.

3. KANT'S INTENTIONS IN THE *TRUE ESTIMATION*

If Kant had followed the more or less common career of a talented student at Königsberg who was pursuing an academic career, after about four years of study he would have begun to write a dissertation in Latin, defended it, and then have assumed the role of a Magister of philosophy. This is what Gottsched did. This was also the course Knutzen took. If Kant had done the same, he would have begun teaching at the university (as well as perhaps at one of the high schools in Königsberg) in 1744.[56] But this is not what happened. Kant did something entirely different. Instead of fulfilling his academic requirements, he wrote a work in German and then left Königsberg to become a private tutor in places that could not advance his scholarly interests very much. Why did Kant fail to present this early work as a dissertation to the university? Why did he, instead of expending his energy on fulfilling an academic requirement that would have allowed him to pursue his interests by teaching the very things he was interested in, choose to write this work? Since he said in the *True Estimation* itself that he wanted to be a scholar, the question must be asked why did he not follow the scholarly course. He certainly could have written the *Living Forces* in Latin. He was confident enough to defend it, but instead he chose to write in German a work that could not advance him institutionally.

Kant does not explicitly say what brought him to write this work, but his preface is an apology of sorts. Admitting that it might be considered presumptuous of him—a completely unknown author—to criticize such famous thinkers as Newton and Leibniz, he argues that such an undertaking, while dangerous in earlier times, is now appropriate. "We may now boldly dare to regard the fame of Newton and Leibniz as nothing whenever it would stand in the way of the discovery of the truth," and we should "obey no other force than that of the understanding" (1:7). Later in the text he says of metaphysics: "Our science, like many others, has indeed reached only the doorway of a genuinely thorough science. It is not difficult to recognize the weakness in many of the things it attempts. One often finds that prejudice is the greatest strength of its proofs" (1:30). Though he mentions neither Teske nor Knutzen, he affirms his belief that "at times it is not without benefit to have a certain noble trust in one's ability" and that to continue on "the broad highway" (1:10) might not be the best approach; Kant goes out of his way to "declare publicly" that he honors and has respect for *"the great masters of our knowledge"* whom he is going to attack in this work (1:13). In a rather uncharacteristic unguarded way he proclaims: "I have already prescribed the route I want to take. I will begin my course and nothing shall prevent me from continuing it" (1:10).

These passages show that Kant saw himself as an independent thinker and that he was confident that he could make an independent contribution to natural philosophy. He was clearly wrong about that. Indirectly, these remarks also tell us what led him to write this work. They address not only the German public as a whole, but also the members of the academy, his colleagues in Königsberg. Still a student of philosophy, he dares to become a participant in a central dispute carried on by some of the most famous philosophers. In a sense, he tells his professors that he is going over their heads, that he is bypassing the discussion within the university, as it were, and that he is asserting his right to be an equal participant in the philosophical and scientific discussion of the period. The tone of defiance that comes through in his introduction suggests that it was not unconnected to the situation that existed in the institution he attended. Thus he talks in the dedication of his "low" status (*Niedrigkeit*), and in the book itself he repeatedly speaks of himself as "common" (*schlecht*). His attack on "the great masters of knowledge," which does not seem to refer only to Leibniz and Newton, and his insistence that nothing will hinder him in achieving his goals, suggest that he was talking not only to the German public, but also to the academic community in Königsberg. At the very least, he seems to have wanted to be noticed.

This raises the question whether Kant did not feel sufficiently appreciated by the members of the philosophical faculty—and perhaps especially by Knutzen. He might have felt that he was not treated in the way he deserved, that his true gifts were not recognized, and that his thesis would have been rejected by those who had to approve it. This may have been the reason he never put it into Latin. If this was so, then it was exactly the opposite of what Borowski reported, namely, it may have been a feeling of not being sufficiently appreciated that led Kant to begin writing his work in 1744 and to publish it in the way in which he did. It may have been more in reaction against Knutzen than inspired by Knutzen.

To be sure, the work shows every sign of coming from the intellectual milieu fostered by Knutzen, but that is what one would expect from anyone who went through this school. But, if anything, the *Estimation of the Living Forces* shows— at least indirectly—that Kant was on his own. The great Knutzen, predictor of the course of comets, was clearly not his mentor in the sense of supporting his further career. There is every reason to believe that Knutzen, if he had found out about Kant's opposition to Pietism, which was already strong at that time, would have had good reasons for disliking Kant or, at the very least, for predicting a dim future for Kant in Königsberg.[57] Yet, just as his prediction about the course of the comet of 1698 was wrong, so his prediction about the course of Kant's career would have been wrong as well. In his old age Kant made clear to one of his biographers that he had tried from his "youth" to be autonomous and independent of everyone so that he "could live for himself and his duty, and not for others. This free independence he declared . . . to be the foundation of all happiness."[58] It was perhaps just this hindrance that Kant needed to develop, or to make up his mind that nothing would prevent him from "taking his course."

A number of facts speak for the conclusion that Knutzen did not appreciate Kant, and Kant did not appreciate Knutzen. First of all, Kant never mentions Knutzen in any of his works. Even his earliest work on the living forces does not contain any explicit reference to Knutzen. Second, while Knutzen recommended a number of his students to others, Kant's name is not among them. Kant's name, for instance, is not to be found among the many students he mentions in his correspondence with Euler as outstanding.[59] This suggests that Knutzen did not regard Kant as one of his best students. Third, Kant is not mentioned in the extensive lists of Knutzen's students given by Knutzen's early biographers. Fourth, there is ample evidence that Knutzen's real favorite was Friedrich Johann Buck (1722–1786), one of his older students, who held review sessions for him and finished his lectures after Knutzen's death in 1751. He also took care of Knutzen's scientific correspondence. Finally, there was not much love lost between Kant and Buck. In fact, Kant ultimately took away the professorship of metaphysics from Buck. Nor did he like another favorite of Knutzen's, one J. Fr. Weitenkampf (1726–??), who entered the university two years after Kant. Knutzen regarded him so highly that he arranged for Weitenkampf to read a speech on how useful academies are for the welfare of nations at the bicentenary of the University of Königsberg in 1744. Knutzen also saw to it that this production was published. It is certainly interesting that Kant, in his *Universal Natural History and Theory of the Heavens*, found it necessary to attack Weitenkampf in a rather pointed fashion. In the long section "On Creation in the Entire Extent of its Infinity in Both Space and Time," he argues not only that though the world had a beginning, it has no end, but he is also concerned with refuting the view that the world cannot be infinite in any sense. Weitenkampf had taken over this view from Knutzen. When Kant argued that Weitenkampf's arguments against the infinity of the world—which was also one of Knutzen's ultimate concerns—prove only that he belongs to those who do not know enough about metaphysics,[60] he was indirectly dismissing Knutzen as well.

4. KANT'S VIEWS IN THE *TRUE ESTIMATION*

Knutzen would have found little to appreciate in the *Living Forces*. It would have been much too Leibnizian for his taste. Kant dealt with one of the central disputes in German natural philosophy during the early part of the eighteenth century, namely the problem of the measurement of force. Late in the previous century, Leibniz had opposed the Cartesian theory, which he saw as an attempt to explain all of nature by what he called "dead force," by differentiating between this "dead force" and a "living force" (*vis viva*). This distinction was connected with the difference between the Cartesian and the Leibnizian account of the world. Whereas the Cartesians believed that "the nature of body consisted of inert mass [*massa*] alone," Leibniz argued that something else needed to be postulated to account for the phenomena.[61] Saying he did not care whether this principle was called "form," "entelechy," or "force," he claimed that this force was central for understanding motion. The Cartesians were wrong in equating a body's moving force with the momentum or with the product that results from multiplying the quantity of motion, or the speed, with the weight of the body. He argued that there was an important difference between speed and force, and that more than twice the force must be present to give something twice the speed, and that living force equals actually mv^2 (where m = mass and v = velocity). This theory of how force is measured thus has deep roots within Leibnizian metaphysics. Newtonians, who were not interested in such hypotheses, also opted for an account of moving force in terms of "momentum" rather than "living force." And the dispute between Cartesians, Leibnizians, and Newtonians was fierce. What was the true measure of force? Was it Descartes's and Newton's momentum or Leibniz's "living force"?

Euler's *Mechanica sive motus scientia* of 1736 had already moved the question to a different plane. He formulated and solved the problems of physics in a strictly mathematical way. It is not clear whether Kant, as a student of Knutzen whose mathematical skills were probably not up to the task of understanding Euler's *Mechanica*, knew this work then. In any case, he framed the problem in rather metaphysical terms, and he wanted to mediate between the different parties. Both are wrong. Neither party can describe all of nature. The Leibnizians have perhaps the most severe problems. Mathematics proves them wrong. "It allows no other measure of force than the old *Cartesian* one" (1:139). The mathematical definition of body allows only external relations between bodies as far as mechanics is concerned. And most of the book is concerned with showing that the Leibnizian arguments against this position are insufficient. But, in a surprising turn of argument, Kant argues in the third part of the book, "which presents a new estimation of the living forces as the true measure of force in nature," that the mathematical definition of body is not necessarily the only or the correct definition of physical bodies.[62] The axioms of mathematics may exclude certain characteristics of bodies that bodies of nature may nevertheless really possess. He argues that they may well contain an internal principle that causes them to exert force, or to "increase within itself the force that has been awakened in it by the cause of an external motion" (1:140). The motion caused by such an internal principle is a "free motion," i.e., a motion whose speed always remains the same. The measure of the speed of bodies in free or infinite motion is living force. The measure of all other motions is momentum. What is important to Kant is that living force is possible only if there are free motions (1:151). But we cannot prove that there are free motions. We can only assume them as a hypothesis. Therefore, the theory of living forces is also only a hypothesis, and this is—Kant points out—all that Leibniz meant to say in the *Théodicée*.[63] Kant's new theory turns out to be a defense and modification of Leibniz's theory of living forces. It is a return to Leibniz.

Though Kant also accepts physical influx as the correct account of certain kinds of motions, he insists that physical influx cannot explain all of reality. It is essentially restricted to account for external causality. The internal principles of substances obey different laws. God and pre-established harmony are required to keep the internal and external forces in harmony. What consequences does this have for our understanding of a passage that occurs very early in the book, and that is often used to show that Kant was an influxionist? In this passage Kant claims that "a certain sharp minded author was hindered by nothing more to make perfect the triumph of physical influx over pre-established harmony than by this small confusion of concepts, from which one can easily extract oneself as soon as one pays attention to it" (1:21).[64] First, this passage is clearly somewhat sarcastic. It is only a small confusion that prevents perfect triumph. If the "sharp minded author" is indeed Knutzen—as most commentators seem to suppose it is—then this is a put-down. There is no reason to suppose that Kant really believed that physical influx would ever triumph over pre-established harmony in the way Knutzen believed it could, i.e., by replacing it. What Kant says is quite compatible with the view that it was a perfect triumph in one area, namely as far as dead force and external causality is concerned, not as far as the systematic account of the whole is concerned.

The doctrine of living forces was connected with the theory of monads. Leibniz believed that a completely materialistic or mechanistic explanation of phenomena is impossible and therefore posited form, entelechy, or force as the internal principle of substances. Kant clearly bought into this. When he differentiates between mathematical bodies and natural bodies, and when he assigns an internal force to a natural body that enables it to have free motion, he seems simply to follow Leibniz. But he is not. Rather, he is following, or rather explicating, Baumgarten, a Wolffian who moved closer to Leibniz than Wolff himself intended to do, and who defended pre-established harmony against physical influx.[65] Though some of his observations are meant to modify Leibniz's view, these modifications are not of a fundamental nature. In fact, Kant claims that, if he had more time, he would show that his theory can do justice to Leibniz's "theory of universal order and harmony," which has been made so "praiseworthy" by Leibniz's view of living forces. Indeed, he claims that he has "some sketches" in which he is doing precisely that (1:171). Kant seems to say explicitly that he accepts the Leibnizian theory of pre-established harmony. Indeed, his "new system" may be understood as giving a new foundation for this Leibnizian doctrine. Kant's pre-established harmony is different from that of Leibniz in that what is pre-established is not just the internal states of substances, but both the internal states *and* the external interactions, and that the external interactions of the substances are of primary importance for establishing a world. Michael Friedman claims that "Kant attempts to revise the Leibniz-Wolffian monadology in light of Newtonian physics," that his "primary notion of active force is not that of an internal principle," but "that of an action exerted by one substance on another substance," and that Kant in this way has "imported Newton's second law of motion into the very heart of the monadology."[66] But Kant remains a Leibnizian in this very crucial respect: the order of the world is pre-established and the internal principles of substances are in harmony with their external relations. Erdmann claimed, in a similar way against Baumgarten, that his pre-established harmony is different from Leibniz because he holds that monads can act on each other. This is certainly true. But this does not mean that his theory is one of physical influx. Just like Kant, Baumgarten believes that external influences (what he calls "real influx") awaken an inner principle of the monad that ultimately explains the action ("ideal influx"). And he must admit that Baumgarten's "ideal influx" is identical to the theory of pre-established harmony. Erdmann's claim that Baumgarten had "completely abandoned" Leibniz's theory seems to me to rest on his failure to take seriously the "phenomenal" character of real influx in Baumgarten (and Kant). Ideal influx provides the foundation of real influx. It may be true that substances are really connected by their mutual relations, and not just virtually by pre-established harmony, but there is nevertheless harmony. It is just not virtual or ideal, but real. To Knutzen, that probably would have made matters worse.

The theory of pre-established harmony was for deep theological reasons unacceptable to Knutzen and the other Pietists in Königsberg. It seemed to them to conflict with a belief in the freedom of the will and to lead to a thorough determinism and fatalism. In so far as Kant is trying do justice to Leibniz's "theory of universal order and harmony," which has been made so "praiseworthy" by Leibniz's view of living forces, Knutzen must have rejected Kant's view. There was no room for bargaining here. Kant was advocating an unacceptable position. Indeed, in some ways, his position in the *Living Forces* is as close to the views of Marquardt or Rappolt as it is to the Pietistic position. He wanted to have it both ways. I doubt that Knutzen or anyone else in the Pietistic faction was open-minded enough to overlook this departure from the party line, even if they would have been able to forgive the quip about the small confusion of a sharp minded author. To use Wolffian principles was one thing, but to endorse the theory of pre-established harmony quite another. The book may thus be viewed as an act of defiance. Kant rejected one of the major tenets of his teacher. It is an expression of his "opposition to pietism," and it could not "pass" the scrutiny of the Pietists, which is probably part of the explanation of why his book could not become a doctoral thesis and why he felt he had to leave Königsberg.

Kant returned only after Knutzen was dead, and he proceeded to write a rather uncontroversial dissertation on fire with Teske. But, as if to remind those in the know, he also published his *Universal History of Nature and Theory of the Heavens.* The cloak of anonymity would have been thin in Königsberg. In any case, his disputations as a young lecturer left little doubt where he stood: not so much with Knutzen and the Pietists as with Marquardt and Rappolt. Adopting the textbooks of Baumgarten, the most Leibnizian among the Wolffians, would have raised even more eyebrows among the Pietists.

NOTES

This chapter is based on the second chapter of my Kant biography that will appear from Cambridge University Press in the near future. All translations are mine.

1. Benno Erdmann, *Martin Knutzen und seine Zeit. Ein Beitrag zur Geschichte der Wolf-fischen Schule und insbesondere zur Entwicklungsgeschichte Kants* (Leipzig, 1876; reprint, Hildesheim: Gerstenberg, 1973).
2. Ernst Cassirer, *Kant's Life and Thought,* trans. James Haden, introduction by Stefan Körner (New Haven: Yale University Press, 1981), 25.
3. Ludwig Ernst Borowski, *Darstellung des Leben und Charakters Immanuel Kants* (Königsberg, 1804). I use Siegfried Drescher, ed., *Wer war Kant. Drei zeitgenössische Biographien von Ludwig Ernst Borowski, Reinhold Bernhard Jachmann und E. A. Ch. Wasianski* (Pfullingen: Neske, 1974), 37, 39, 50, 85, 92.
4. Rudolph Reicke, *Kantiana. Beiträge zu Immanuel Kants Leben und Schriften* (Königsberg: Th. Theile's Buchhandlung, 1860), 7.
5. The result was an order by the king issued on November 15, 1725, which commanded Fischer to leave Königsberg within twenty-four hours and Prussia within forty-eight because "he had dared in his classes to dishonorably defame some of the professors newly appointed by the king, and because he already had earlier followed and defended the evil principle of Professor Wolff who has been removed from Halle." Erich Riedesel, *Pietismus und Orthodoxie in Ostpreußen. Auf Grund des Briefwechsels von G. F. Rogall und F. A Schultz's mit den Halleschen Pietisten* (Königsber: Ost-Europa Verlag, 1937), 39. See also Paul Konschel, "Christian Gabriel Fischer, ein Gesinnungs und Leidensgenosse Christian Wolffs in Königsberg," *Altpreussische Monatsschrift* 53 (1916): 416–44.
6. Carl Hinrichs, *Preußentum und Pietismus* (Göttingen: Vandenhoeck and Ruprecht, 1971), 281. Some time later he reported: "Here the noise increases daily. Now even the rabble begins to get involved. Thus for some weeks I can hardly walk the street safely. In the evening I cannot leave the house at all."
7. Karl Vorländer, *Immanuel Kant: Der Mann und das Werk,* 2 vols. Zweite, erweiterte Auflage. Mit einem Beitrag "Kants Opus postumum" von Wolfgang Ritzel. Unter Mitarbeit von Konrad Kopper, ed. Rudolf Malter (Hamburg: Felix Meiner), 1:49. Vorländer claims that in 1744 there were 591 theologians, 428 law students, and 13 medical students.
8. Compare Stavenhagen, *Kant und Königsberg* (Göttingen: Deuerlichsche Verlagsbuchhandlung, 1949), 13.
9. Baczko, according to J. H. W. Stuckenberg, *The Life of Immanuel Kant* (London: Macmillan, 1882), 38.

10. Vorländer, *Immanuel Kant*, 1:48.

11. Hippel, according to Vorländer, *Immanuel Kant*, 1:48.

12. Erdmann, *Knutzen*, 13.

13. See Georg Chr. Pisanski, *Entwurf einer preussischen Literärgeschichte* (Hartung: Königsberg, 1886), 519.

14. Erdmann, *Knutzen*, 13. (Compare Pisanski, *Entwurf einer preussischen Literärgeschichte*, 523, who says that others testified to this as well.)

15. Erdmann, *Knutzen*, 18.

16. Pisanski, *Entwurf einer preussischen Literärgeschichte*, 553.

17. Riedesel, *Pietismus und Orthodoxie in Ostpreußen. Auf Grund des Briefwechsels von G. F. Rogall und F. A. Schultz mit den Hallenschen Pietisten* (Königsberg: Ost-Europa Verlag, 1937), 38.

18. Paul Konschel, *Der junge Hamann nach seinen Briefen im Rahmen der lokalen Kirchengeschichte* (Königsberg, 1915), 5.

19. Erdmann, *Knutzen*, 21.

20. The title of the dissertation was "De harmonia praestabilitata inter animam et corpus, amplissima facultate philosophica consentiente," *pro receptione* in eandem, publice disseret M. Conradus Theophilus Marquardt, respondente Joh. Christoph. Bohlio, Reg. pruss. anno MDCCXXII d. xxii april ab hora VIII ad XII in auditorio philosophico (Königsberg, 1722).

21. Wolff had endorsed Leibniz's theory of pre-established harmony in his *Reasonable Thoughts of God, the World and the Soul of Human Beings as well as of All Things in General* of 1720 not as absolute truth but as the most reasonable hypothesis, saying that his discussion of the human soul had led him "against his expectations" to the Leibnizian position. He never endorsed pre-established harmony but was attacked by the Pietists for favoring it. They argued that universal harmony contradicted the freedom of the will required by Christian faith.

22. See Erdmann, *Knutzen*, 68.

23. Langhansen, a theologian who also taught mathematics and physics.

24. Rappolt also taught English and philosophy and held lectures on Pope, which by all accounts were very successful. In 1741 he gave a lecture on Pope, and in 1742 he announced two courses on him. See Erdmann, *Knutzen*, 140, 149n.

25. Konschel, *Der junge Hamann*, 26–27n. Lindner, one of Kant's friends, learned English from him. Hamann was close to Rappolt, who may also have first introduced Pope and other British authors to Kant.

26. Reicke, *Kantiana*, 48–51, Malter, *Immanuel Kant in Rede und Gespräch* (Hamburg: Felix Meiner, 1990) 18.

27. Erdmann, *Knutzen*, 14n.

28. Reicke, *Kantiana*, 7.

29. Riedesel, *Pietismus und Orthodoxie in Ostpreußen*, 43.

30. Konschel, "Christian Gabriel Fischer," 433.

31. Johann Friedrich Lauson, *Erster Versuch in Gedichten, nebst einer Vorrede von der sogenannten extemporal Poesie, und einem Anhange von Gedichten aus dem Stegreif* (Königsberg: Driest, 1753) and *Zweyter Versuch in Gedichten, nebst einer Vorrede von den Schicksalen der heutigen Poesie, und einem Anhange von Gedichten aus dem Stegreif* (Königsberg: Driest, 1754). Herder, who studied in Königsberg in the early 1760s, also took courses with Teske. His notes show that his lectures in physics were most important to Herder. See W. Dobbek,

J. Herders Jugendzeit in Mohrungen und Königsberg, 1744–1764 (Würzburg: Holzener Verlag, 1961), 94.

32. Pisanski, *Entwurf einer preussischen Literärgeschichte,* 546, 548.

33. Borowski, *Leben,* 39; Vorländer, *Immanuel Kant,* 1:50.

34. Borowski, *Leben,* 87.

35. See Johann Friedrich Buck, *Lebensbeschreibungen derer verstorbenen preußischen Mathematiker* (Königsberg and Leipzig, 1764). See also J. Chr. Strodtman, "Martin Knutzen," *Geschichte der jetztlebenden Gelehrten* 9 (1746): 75–76.

36. He defended this thesis in 1733.

37. See Erdmann, *Knutzen,* 52; see also Pisanski, *Entwurf einer preussischen Literärgeschichte,* 30. Knutzen's writings were successful beyond Königsberg. In 1745 he republished his inaugural dissertation under the title *System of Efficient Causality (Systema causarum efficientium),* and in 1747 he published *Elements of Rational Psychology or Logic Demonstrated in the Method of General and Special Mathematics.*

38. Riedesel, *Pietismus und Orthodoxie in Ostpreußen,* 97. Knutzen's philosophical agenda was not entirely defined by his opposition to, and modification of, Wolffian philosophy. His interests ranged much further. In 1740, the year Kant entered the university, he published a work written in German called *Philosophical Proof of the Truth of Christianity* that became the most successful of his works. It was perhaps also his most characteristic work, defending Christianity against Deism, and especially against Toland, Chubb, and Tindal. It first appeared as a series of articles in the *Königsberger Intelligenzblätter.* It was reissued several times. The 4th edition (Königsberg: Hartung) appeared in 1747. The title reads *Philosophischer Beweiß von der Wahrheit der christlichen Religion, darinnen die Nothwendigkeit einer geoffenbarten Religion insgemein, und die Wahrheit oder Gewißheit der Christlichen insbesondere, aus ungezweifelten Gründen der Vernunft nach mathematischer Lehrart dargethan und behauptet wird.*

39. Erdmann, *Knutzen,* 112; Gottsched, *Neuer Büchersaal* 4: 3, 241.

40. See Heiner Klemme, *Die Schule Kants* (Hamburg: Felix Meiner, 1994), 40n. Also Alois Winter, "Selbstdenken, Antinomien, Schranken. Zum Einfluss des späten Locke auf die Philosophie Kants," in *Eklektik, Selbstdenken, Mündigkeit,* ed. N. Hinske (Hamburg: Felix Meiner Verlag, 1986), 1: 27–66.

41. Erdmann, *Knutzen,* 110.

42. Hamann, *Brevier,* 19. Several others talked about Knutzen in similar terms. See also Borowski, *Leben,* 38, and Erdmann, *Knutzen,* 6, as well as Waschkies, *Physik und Physikotheologie des jungen Kant. Die Vorgeschichte seiner allgemeinen Weltgeschichte und Theorie des Himmels* (Amsterdam: Gruner, 1987), 310.

43. Johann Georg Hamann, "Gedanken über meinen Lebenslauf," in *Johann Georg Hamann Londoner Schriften,* ed. Oswald Beyer and Bernd Weißhuhn (Munich: C. H. Beck Verlag, 1993), 321.

44. Borowski, *Leben,* 37, 39, 50, 85.

45. Borowski, *Leben,* 23.

46. Borowski, *Leben,* 39.

47. Riedesel, *Pietismus und Orthodoxie in Ostpreußen,* 142; Erdmann, *Knutzen,* 44.

48. Konschel, "Christian Gabriel Fischer," 437.

49. Hans-Joachim Waschkies, *Physik und Physikotheologie,* 296–347.

50. See Waschhkies, *Physik und Physikotheologie,* 310.

51. Waschkies, *Physik und Physikotheologie*, 310 (Euler, Beantwortung verschiedener Fragen, 67–68).

52. *Rational Thoughts on the Comets, in which is Examined and Represented their Nature and their Character as well as the Causes of their Motion, and at the same Time Given a Short Description of the Noteworthy Comet of this Year* (1744).

53. It appeared in Berlin and Leipzig in 1742 with a preface by Gottsched. He also published a translation of Maupertuis's "Lettre sur la comète" with a letter.

54. Waschkies, *Physik und Physikotheologie*, 335.

55. Waschkies, *Physik und Physikotheologie*, 345.

56. The degree of "Magister" is at the very least equivalent to that of today's Ph.D.

57. The information that Kant did not study theology "because he was opposed to pietism" comes from Reicke, *Kantiana*, 7.

58. Borowski, *Leben*, 157.

59. Waschkies, *Physik und Physikotheologie*, 20n.

60. 1:309n. He belongs to the "*Metaphysikkundigeren*," but not the "*Metaphysikkundigen*." Compare Waschkies, *Physik und Physikotheologie*, 461n., 462.

61. G.W. Leibniz, *Philosophical Essays*, ed. and trans. R. Ariew and D. Garber (Indianapolis: Hackett Publishing, 1989), 123.

62. 1:139 (the phrase represents the subtitle of part III).

63. 1:152. Kant refers to this work.

64. See Eric Watkins, "Kant's Theory of Physical Influx," *Archiv für Geschichte der Philosophie* 77 (1995): 285–324, 289.

65. Baumgarten, *Metaphysica*, §294 (17:91), §§210–23 (17:70–76), especially §220 (17:74). But compare also Erdmann, *Knutzen*, 95–96.

66. It is likely that he would have rejected even at that time the idea that the universal harmony was pre-established. Michael Friedman, *Kant and the Exact Sciences* (Cambridge: Harvard University Press, 1992), 5. I agree with all of this. Susan Meld Shell, *The Embodiment of Reason* (Chicago: University of Chicago Press, 1996), 10–30, has a nice summary of Kant's position in the *Living Forces*, which, according to her, "is flatly at odds with the claims of the Leibniz-Wolffian school," 28. In the most significant points concerning what she describes as "cognitive dualism," Kant is rather close to Gottsched, his philosophical predecessor in Königsberg. The best account of the problem of physical influx and its relation to Leibnizian-Wolffian philosophy is still Gerd Fabian, *Beitrag zur Geschichte des Leib-Seele Problems (Lehre von der prästabilierten Harmonie-und vom psychophysischem Parallelismus in der Leibniz-Wolffschen Schule)* (Langensalza: Hermann Beyer & Söhne, 1925). The book deserves to be better known.

2

Kant on Science and Common Knowledge

Karl Ameriks

I want to have only a piece of the system of the whole of human cognitions, namely the science of the highest principles, and such a project is modest.

Kant, Metaphysik Mrongovius, *29:748*

T HE relationship between Kant's philosophy and modern science continues to be the object of fruitful studies that concern issues of considerable exegetical and technical complexity. At a more general level, however, I believe that there remain some basic and relatively simple issues that have not yet been given adequate attention, and that may profit from a perspective that takes a somewhat more distant view than one tends to find in much Kant scholarship. I have in mind a constellation of problems having to do with the basic *form* of the Critical philosophy, its peculiar place in philosophical *history*, and the metaphilosophical problem of the *methodological* status of philosophy itself vis-à-vis what is called science.

I will begin with a preliminary section that offers a sketch of the peculiar problem of the standing, within the overall framework of Kant's philosophy, of all types of knowledge that, like philosophy itself, fall *in between* the extremes of rudimentary "common knowledge" and exact scientific knowledge. Against this backdrop, I will go over again, in more detail in the second and main section, the historical context of Kant's answer to the specific question of the scientific status of his own philosophy. This section will focus on comparing Kant's conception of the key requirement of *systematicity* with other very influential conceptions of it right before and after him. Throughout, I will be arguing for a way of looking at Kant's philosophy that takes its claim to "modesty" seriously, and that can thereby defend it as an especially appropriate model in our own time for approaching the crucial and often neglected issue of the role that philosophy can play as a *mediator*, rather than a guarantor, of common knowledge and science.

1. PRELIMINARY OVERVIEW

The introductory observations of the first section fall into three brief subsections: (1.1) a reminder of some basic options within the era of modern philosophy, (1.2) a preliminary proposal about how to situate Kant's transcendental philosophy with regard to these options, and (1.3) an elucidation of an important new problem—the problem of "in between knowledge"—that arose for this era and generated a complex Kantian response.

1.1. Three Options

Any very brief characterization of the whole period of modern philosophy obviously must be understood to have many implicit qualifications. Without any claim to originality, I propose that the most helpful place to start in determining what is *distinctive* about modern philosophy is to focus on the remarkable phenomenon of *modern* science, and specifically on the new disciplines that arose with the Galilean revolution and the development of the exact science of Newtonian physics. This development by no means determined only one sort of possible philosophical reaction. I see three main lines of reaction especially worth distinguishing: *skepticism*, *scientism*, and classical modern *systematic metaphysics*. The first two lines were encouraged by the very sharp contrast that arose between the highly theoretical and counter-intuitive "scientific image" of modern physics, and the range of other widespread options, especially the "manifest image" of common sense, the entrenched so-called common sense of the Aristotelian tradition, and the claims of primitive and radical empiricism.[1]

1.1.1. It is well known that the multiplicity of these images and the striking contrasts between them, combined with other cultural developments at this time (for example, momentous religious conflicts and the new availability of ancient texts), generated a deep and influential concern with skepticism.[2] Even when, as in Descartes, the skeptical position was not at all presented in order to be endorsed, it hounded the modern era, at the very least until Hume—and precisely because the very rigor of modern thought disclosed more and more difficulties in finding philosophical responses to it that did not beg the question. For my purposes, even philosophers who themselves are not at all skeptics can be seen as belonging to this group as long as they take—as so many still do (e.g., Stroud, Rorty, and Cavell)—the central function of philosophy as such, at least up to now, to be nothing less than a discovery of, or an endless discussion about, the refutation of skepticism.

1.1.2. A second, "scientistic" option, which grew ever more popular in the aftermath of Hume, was to turn away from the frustrating issue of skepticism while accepting a sharp contrast between modern science and other images of reality, and then to take this contrast to signify nothing other than the sheer error of all nonscientific perspectives. On this option, philosophy becomes "scientism" when it goes beyond an intense but limited concern with science and the philosophy of science, and it embraces the radical view that responsible philosophy is *nothing other than* philosophy of science. "Scientism" was not a project well worked out in Kant's own time, but it took on a dominant position soon thereafter in the positivist programs that viewed philosophy as little more than a codification of technical knowledge accepted largely without question from ideal images of on-going scientific disciplines.[3]

1.1.3. Familiar as these options have become, especially in our own time, most of *classical* modern philosophy seems to have taken a third and quite different course. In rationalism and empiricism alike—in Descartes, Leibniz, Spinoza, as in Berkeley and (much of) Hume and Mill, among others—what one finds is not *primarily* a direct development of skepticism nor anything like a proto-Quinean scientistic physicalism. What one finds is rather the construction of intricate and massive "systems of the world," each set out with many of the *formal* features of the new highly systematic sciences of the Newtonian era, but with ontologies—for example, of monads or other special substances, or all-encompassing impressions—determined ultimately by philosophers alone, and ultimately in considerable contrast to the "furniture" that the scientists of the era took themselves to be discussing. Only with the decline of phenomenalism (and of traditional idealism), and the growing anarchy of metaphilosophical developments after the Second World War, has this remarkable option moved away from the center of the philosophical stage.

1.2. Kant's Transcendental Option

Where does Kant's philosophy fit in among these options? One could *try* to align it with any one of the three paths that have been noted, namely, the battle with skepticism, or the articulation of modern science, or the development of a pure philosophical ontology. In fact, many contemporary Kant interpretations have fixed on one or the other of the first two approaches, that is, the extremes of taking Kant to be basically a respondent to the skeptic (cf. Strawson, Wolff) or an apologist for the Newtonian science of his time (Körner and after). I have often argued against these popular interpretive strategies,[4] and I would contend more positively now that it is most useful to think of Kant's transcendental approach as introducing a unique *fourth* basic option in response to the fundamental challenge set by the rise of modern science.

Like other options here, the Kantian transcendental option accepts as its starting point a *sharp apparent* contrast between common sense and modern science. However, what Kant goes on to propose is that, instead of focusing on trying to establish with certainty—against skepticism—that the objects of common sense exist, let alone that they have philosophical dominance, or, in contrast, on explaining that it is only the theoretical discoveries of science that determine what is objective, one can rather work primarily to determine a *positive* and balanced *philosophical* relation *between* the distinct frameworks of our manifest and scientific images.

This is, I believe, how the basic propositions of Kant's first *Critique* can best be understood. That book defends principles involving philosophical concepts, such as causality and substance, that can be taken, in different ways, as necessary framework presuppositions relevant *both* for ordinary empirical judgments—so that we can, for example, properly understand that a boat is moving a certain way, in objective space and time, only if we place it in relation to some general and "transcendentally" necessary principles of experience—as well as for the fundamental axioms of modern physics, as Kant goes on to try to show in detail in his *Metaphysical Foundations of Natural Science*. Kant's investigations can be seen as trying, among other things, to clarify the basic meaning and metaphysical presuppositions of Newtonian axioms, and yet, since his investigations first provide a general ground for causality, they do not—unlike "scientism"—simply take the objective truth of the scientific principles themselves as an absolute first premise. On this strategy, one also does not aim basically at refining a special philosophical ontology for the natural world (there are complications here, for I would not deny that Kant has some important ontological concerns, and even is committed to more than what is "natural"), that is, a "new system"—to repeat a Leibnizian phrase that Kant echoed in his own early career—that competes with the entities posited by science itself. Instead, one tries to explain how the peculiar objects of modern science can cohere with the ordinary sensible judgments that we make, as well as with whatever general metaphysical commitments turn out to be unavoidable for us. In the end, particular statements about houses and boats are to be considered as backed up by reference to items that are instances of general laws covering in an exact way all sorts of theoretical entities, entities that one is not expected even to be *able* to perceive directly—as Kant notes with respect to small particles and magnetic fields.[5] The whole framework of these entities can be taken not to replace but just to provide a precise ground of explanation for—while also remaining epistemically dependent upon—the "common knowledge"[6] or everyday judgments that we make about the macro-objects of ordinary perception.

Kant calls his philosophy "transcendental" here because it speaks primarily not about objects as such but about our a priori *knowledge* of objects, that is, about the general principles that seem necessary if we are to have any empirical knowledge at all—and that are *also* claimed to be necessary for the new exact mathematical sciences that are taken to underlie all such knowledge. For example, transcendental philosophy does not itself supply a geometrical specification of objects, but it does argue for principles that "make intelligible"[7] an a priori link between geometrical science and the objects of experience. In this way Kant's philosophy is unique in focusing on a level "in between" the domains of ordinary empirical judgment and theoretical science. While it accepts both domains as legitimate, it takes neither as absolute by itself but rather aims to articulate the philosophical principles they need to share in order to be jointly understandable and acceptable.

Scientific theory, elementary common knowledge, and philosophical interpretation are thus all intertwined in a process of reflective equilibrium.

1.3. The Problem of the Status of Kant's Option

1.3.1. Whatever the immediate attractions of this Kantian option, there is an obvious new problem that must be faced by all philosophies that take very seriously the precise theoretical perspective of modern science. The problem is that, even if we were to go so far as to assume an easy fit between experience and one exact scientific framework of mathematics and physics—an assumption obviously much more questionable now than in 1781—there remains a cluster of prestigious disciplines that do not seem limited to that austere framework. There are, for example, the disciplines of psychology, of chemistry and biology, of anthropology and history ("social science"), and also, somewhere along the line, the assertions of fields such as aesthetics and philosophy itself. In all these areas, highly respected authorities claim to have attained considerable knowledge, and yet the judgments that constitute their disciplines obviously cannot in any plausible way be translated or directly transformed into the language of either actual physics or elementary common sense—or even the constitutive principles of Kant's mediating Transcendental Analytic.

1.3.2. For a long time the most influential philosophical way of reacting to this difficulty was dominated by the positivist presumption that there is no deep significance in holding on to the autonomy of domains less exact than physics, or—in the case of the tradition from Hume to Mill and Mach—than a psychological theory of sensations designed precisely to model the latest physics. To be sure, for various heuristic and practical purposes, disciplines other than physics (and its exact correlates) might be allowed to continue, but the common presumption was that they gained their ultimate theoretical value solely from their eventual foundation (whether or not it could ever be achieved in a "reduction") in a truly "hard" foundational science. When the laws of physics came to be taken in a less mechanistic and more dynamic manner, or for a time were even transposed into psychological laws, this only underscored rather than undercut the hegemony of the form of modern physics. Descartes's philosophical disinterest in manifest empirical qualities such as color (regarded as too "confused" to be a "true" idea in the ultimate science) was an indication of the attitude that was to be typical of most scientific philosophers throughout the modern period. In the end, the account of the domain of commonsense judgments, and of all disciplines that were not expressed with the exactness of physics, was little more than a matter of pragmatics and a theory of error. (This kind of attitude can still be seen in current accounts, for example in philosophies of mind that take explanations couched in commonsense language to have the status of nothing more than a scientifically immature and ultimately irrelevant "folk psychology.")

1.3.3. There are endless complications in this story, but for our purposes the first point to note is that initially *Kant's* own account can *seem* to fall right into this general dismissive pattern of modern philosophy. But the crucial second point to note here is that Kant's approach is actually quite distinctive and has aspects that make it both worse and much better than the typical modern system. On the one hand, there is the embarrassing fact that sometimes Kant is extreme about an allegiance to physics and physics alone. His textbook concerning natural science explicitly excludes all psychology (and intentionally ignores history) and even chemistry (because he did not see then that it had developed its own precise quantitative explanations[8]) from the domain of genuine science, and thus he appears to turn his back on the remarkable rise of two of the major cognitive developments of his time. On the other hand, and more importantly, it is clear that as Kant moved beyond the core principles of the understanding in the Transcendental Analytic even in his first *Critique*, he focused more and more on special non-mathematical ideas of reason (and, at first, he suggests something like such ideas for systematic features of even physics as well) that he argued we also need in order to make intelligible the vast realm of common claims about our environment that we cannot hope to demonstrate from physics alone—since, as he puts it, there could *never* be "a Newton" for even "a blade of grass."[9]

Thus, at the same time that Kant criticized claims made on behalf of the rigor of fields such as psychology and chemistry, he still argued that they are governed by fundamental, and not merely empirical, "regulative" principles that we should never expect to be replaced by the constitutive claims of any physics that humans could actually develop. It is important to see that Kant always insisted on an *objective* place for such principles, even for disciplines that he came to criticize strongly precisely with regard to their *exact* scientific status. In Kant's schoolbook tradition, psychology, for example, was presented confidently as a science, in both empirical and rational forms, just as, in what appear to be older parts of the first *Critique*, Kant himself speaks of a distinct "physiological" science of mind fully parallel to that of body.[10] By the time of the *Metaphysical Foundations* (preface), however, he clearly denied that psychology was a genuine science—and yet he never took back his claim that its "idea" of "unity" provides a basic regulative principle that *we must* always use when *objectively investigating* the mind as such. He insisted that we reason in an entirely proper and inevitable fashion here, profitably organizing our common knowledge, as long as we do not inflate this idea of the mind's unity—even of the "necessary unity of apperception"—into a certain ontological claim at *either* the level of nature or beyond.

A similar perspective can be found in Kant's remarks on the other disciplines that fall "in between" elementary common sense and physics and also the constitutive transcendental principles underlying both domains. Psychology is hardly the only example here; the *Critique of Judgment* is focused largely on the claim that biology is forever to be governed by a regulative idea of purposiveness. At the same time that Kant restricts all *constitutive* claims about organisms as purposive, he also insists that in "reflectively" judging about them, as we constantly must as the finite rational beings that we are, we cannot progress otherwise than by thinking in purposive terms, by seeing them "as if" they have a unity that is a ground and not only an effect of their parts. For anthropology and history Kant introduces the similar—although only similar—idea of a "pragmatic" or moral purposiveness that provides for a distinctive unity in the study of human beings. Just as, for all that we "really know," blind mechanism and not genuine purposiveness might be the ultimate truth about living beings as such, so too an amoral structure and pointless end might be the ultimate truth about the history of the human race—and yet in neither case, supposedly, can a rational human judge "really think" in such terms. In the case of human history, we even realize that the purposive structures we are most interested in are generated not so much from heuristic *scientific* considerations as from hope in a destiny pleasing our own noblest ambitions—and yet for Kant this remains a common and thoroughly *rational* hope, a moral belief answering to a general interest that is even more compelling than that of scientific systematicity. Not surprisingly, notes from Kant's metaphysics lectures even contain a statement that such "moral belief is as unshakable as the greatest speculative certainty, indeed even firmer" (29:778).

Kantian aesthetic theory can be seen as one more development along this line, a line where pure ideas such as unity, purposiveness, and morality are presented as rationally inescapable in very specific contexts even while their "non-constitutive" status is repeatedly noted. For Kant, a naturally beautiful object is to be thought of as "purposive *without* a purpose" (i.e., precisely as not designed beforehand, and yet as especially "fitting" our faculties), and as "disinterestedly" pleasing, that is, apart from merely sensuous or moral grounds—and yet[11] such an object is still to be taken as truly purposive *for all of us* and pleasing in a pure way. My main point here is that this claim, whatever its limitations—and whatever the general difficulties in all talk of "merely regulative" principles—is clearly taken by Kant to have a "universal" standing, a claim on all other humans as such, that is about as "solid" in its own way as assertions in other "in between" fields such as psychology or even biology, where one also proceeds in making legitimate and nontrivial public claims about the sensible world that are not fully exact or clearly ontologically absolute.

1.3.4. If so much might be claimed in a highly disputed field such as aesthetics, it would seem only fair to preserve at least an equal dignity for the claims of philosophy itself. But on what basis? Kant denies that philosophy can model itself on quantitative disciplines, and he also draws attention to the fact that its central discipline, metaphysics, does not express even an informal "common knowledge" but rather appears to be a "battlefield of endless controversies" (Aviii).

In order to see in what sense Kant could still believe that philosophy, which itself is neither an exact science nor a mere part of "common knowledge" or a harmonious tradition, can nonetheless amount to knowledge and even "come forth" as a science, we must turn now, in a second part of these considerations, to consider in more detail how Kant thought that the Critical philosophy, and it alone, manages to satisfy in an exemplary fashion the key condition of science in a *general* sense, namely *systematicity*. This will be a complicated story, because Kantian systematicity, precisely when it is most charitably understood, can seem at first to be devastatingly modest—and yet, I will argue, this very modesty will turn out to be its saving grace, and what allows Kant's work to remain uniquely relevant to this day for the thematization of the relation of philosophy and science.

2. Kant's Answer: Philosophy as a Modest Science

2.1. *Kant on Philosophy and System*

Kant claimed his philosophy was scientific, in a broad and crucial sense, because it was so truly systematic that it alone restored the rigor to philosophy that Wolff was to be praised for at least seeking (Bxxxvii). This claim was quickly and energetically disputed, but to the very end Kant wrote with uncompromising insistence about the satisfactory systematic character of his own work. Against suggestions by Fichte and others that he had fallen short in any way in this regard, Kant protested vehemently:

> [T]he assumption that I have intended to publish only a *propaedeutic* to transcendental philosophy and not the actual system of this philosophy is incomprehensible to me. Such an intention never occurred to me, since I took the completeness of pure philosophy within the *Critique of Pure Reason* to be the best indication of the truth of my work.[12]

Yet the clear fact is that by his own standards Kant never actually presented a "complete" philosophy. In a letter to Jakob of September 11, 1787, he explained in a brief outline what a "short system of metaphysics" might look like,[13] but he did not publish such a system himself. He often claimed[14] that the first *Critique* could be completed easily enough in an explicit system (in its "material part") that would take the two-part form of a metaphysics of nature and a metaphysics of morals, that is, a systematic theoretical philosophy and a systematic practical philosophy. But although toward the end of his career Kant did finish a volume called *The Metaphysics of Morals* (1797), that book always remained very much overshadowed by his interjection of the *Groundwork of the Metaphysics of Morals* (1785) and of the second and third *Critique*, works that approached moral issues in ways not foreseen in his first Critical remarks on a system.[15] Moreover, Kant never even published a metaphysics of nature, and this failure goes much deeper than his not getting around to supplementing the *Metaphysical Foundations of Natural Science* (1786)—his theoretical parallel to the *Groundwork*—with a completed "transition" to a full philosophy of physics in his *Opus postumum*. The most startling fact is that Kant never made it to writing out a theoretical metaphysical system, not even something in the short outline form that he recommended to Jakob. And yet he lectured year after year on this subject, clearly presenting it as his favorite and as the compendium of theoretical philosophy as such.[16]

If Kant had published a general metaphysics textbook, the most basic systematic issue that one would hope to find explained would be that of the unity of his work, and of precisely how the metaphysics of nature and of morals are to be related. He repeatedly claims that what distinguishes science as such is that it is a study that has a unity of principles, rather than being a mere aggregate of claims. Philosophy is distinguished from natural science simply by its offering an explanation (and not merely an employment) of a priori and not only empirical principles. For Kant, both philosophy and natural science are sciences, and they are also both said to belong to philosophy in a broad sense, since they each systematically employ reason, in the one case merely for objects of experience, in the other case in such a way that this restriction is not a matter of definition.[17]

Does the lack of a fully unified and articulated Kantian system signify only an absence of incidental detail, or does it mean, as many readers have felt, that there are fundamental flaws in his whole approach to systematicity and his whole understanding of philosophy as a science? Kant himself remained extremely confident and concluded his repudiation of Fichte by reiterating that the first *Critique* had accomplished basically all that is needed:

> [T]he critical philosophy must remain confident of its irresistible propensity to satisfy the theoretical as well as the moral, practical purposes of reason, confident that no change of opinions, no touching up or reconstruction into some other form is in store for it; the system of the *Critique* rests on a fully secured foundation, established forever, it will be essential too for the noblest ends of mankind in all future ages.[18]

These are strong words, but the fact remains that the way that Kant's "foundation" grounds the two branches of his system is not worked out anywhere in detail; the *Critique of Pure Reason* says little about practical reason, and the second *Critique* says little about theoretical reason. The third *Critique* then makes matters only more complicated by providing not a mere unification in retrospect but rather a new threefold division of faculties: understanding, judgment, and reason. By multiplying faculties, Kant would seem to be only multiplying divisions and problems, rather than providing a straightforward account of what gives his philosophy a true unity. To understand Kant's most effective answer to this worry—and to avoid losing the forest in the trees—I propose that it is better not to get entangled in his complex terminological rearrangements, but rather to step back again to consider in more detail the broader context of Kant's work, in order to see how the basic issues in his era determine what lies behind all the special concern with a "system."

2.2. For Others, Why a System? *(Representationalism versus Skepticism)*

Quite apart from Kant, a natural beginning would be to think that systematicity is at best an ideal, not a requirement of knowledge in general or of philosophical knowledge in particular. If one starts with some relatively simple things that one obviously seems to know, it is natural to try to relate these to other cognitions that one may have. But one can't be expected at once to know everything, or even what is most relevant, so one can hardly start with a full system or outline of knowledge, or even with the certainty that all will be able to be brought into such a system. And yet the major philosophers that Kant was most familiar with, the great modern master thinkers, all clearly worked with the aim of erecting a system and took this systematic orientation to be virtually self-evident. As was noted earlier, empiricists as well as rationalists all presumed that the human mind and its operations comprise a systematically connected whole. Whether the subjective basis be innate ideas or sensible impressions, whether the objective correlates be physical structures and metaphysical grounds or mere psychological propensities and reliable constructs, and whether the claimed results be phrased in terms of absolute certainty or probability, what classical modern philosophy produces, time and time again, is a confident reconstruction of a *new comprehensive system* that both common life and technical disciplines are taken to require and to be incapable of articulating themselves.

A major inspiration for this assumption is not difficult to find: The giants of the scientific revolution, figures such as Galileo, Descartes, and Newton, managed to discover what is a *real* system, the basic components of an exact and truly universal physics that provided a way of thinking that was to be a paradigm for all later research. The strong systematicity of their works was striking from the start; the general laws that they contained, and the way that they were combined to explain many very different kinds of phenomena, were crucial to their initial formulation in precise mathematical "systems of the world." But if modern science already has a systematic explanation *in nuce* of the world, there would seem to be no basic need to duplicate things with special philosophical furniture. Hence, one might well expect that the evident success of these scientific systems would have meant the immediate demise of philosophy as a major discipline, or perhaps its return to something more in the form of rhetoric. What actually happened, however, is that philosophy experienced a remarkable expansion and flowering, with Descartes influencing everyone else by working out not only a new physics but also a "foundation" for it, with epistemological considerations and ontological components that are presented explicitly as not part of either "working" science or common knowledge.

This development was sketched earlier, but without raising the crucial and often neglected question that can be put off no longer: What was the *point* of all this ingenuity?

One might regard the philosophical accounts as mere ideological ploys—desperate attempts to keep medieval interests alive by other means—or instead, and more purely, as just a legitimate scholarly addendum, as providing an abstract fine-tuning of basic terms, for example, of how "thing" and "action" might be understood now in their most general senses. This can be an interesting enterprise in its own right, and practices of this kind persist in our day. And yet there is a world of difference that is easy to recognize here: Whereas current writers on subjects such as formal semantics or action theory almost always aim their clarifications only at other specialists, without expecting to have any dramatic influence on the world at large, or even the academy in general, the original moderns surely presumed that an awful lot was hanging on what they were doing.

This presumption was not a matter of an unrealistic sense of self-importance; it had an understandable explanation in a number of developments of the time, and in particular in the very success of the new science. The presence of this new paradigm of knowledge generated the acute question of what to do with the old views that were not part of it, that is, of what to make not only of religion, ethics, and scholastic philosophy, but also of elementary common sense and the whole range of notions developed in long-standing and prestigious disciplines that were not organized like the new fundamental and quantitative sciences. In addition to the plurality of respected but apparently mutually incompatible views that had to be sorted out here, there was, as noted earlier, also a dramatic rise in the stock of radical skepticism, abetted by the perplexing nature of the more abstract notions of the new science itself, and the constant desire to find for philosophy a certainty at least as persuasive as that of its fellow abstract discipline, the flourishing paradigm of mathematics.[19]

In this context there arose what was not merely a loose and general discussion about how to relate the "manifest" and the "scientific images"; rather, there arose one especially influential strategy, the dominant and so-called Cartesian move of isolating a privileged sphere, a set of foundational representations—be they clear and distinct ideas or sense data (or, later, noeses of primordial intentionality, or forms of language)—from which the claims of both prescientific and scientific experience could be evaluated and reconstructed. The key idea here, the main "point" behind the systematicity of most classical modern philosophies, was the thought that a special philosophical discourse about a *system of representations* would provide the only coherent and fully responsible way of meeting skepticism while also incorporating the achievements of modern science. In this way, the third basic modern option discussed earlier can be understood as taking on a form—systematic representational metaphysics—that is designed precisely to meet the concerns of the first two options, skepticism and science. But this thought led to a dead end, because what really gave skepticism its greatest strength was the ironic fact that the very representational tools that modern philosophers turned to as a certain foundation (be it sense data, ideas, words, or associations), in order to find something immune from doubt, created an abyss of uncertainty between those tools and the separate objects that they were supposed to help us reach.[20]

Modern philosophy thus seemed condemned to two opposite but equally unappealing options. One option is to accept (or endlessly dispute) the challenge of skepticism and to try to save the claims of science only by integrating them within an internal system of representations—but then, unfortunately, to deny thereby their original meaning as claims that transcend what is already within the common knowledge of mere natural belief (hence the standard objections to Berkeley and positivism). The other option is to accept modern science itself as absolute, as naturalism has done with more and more popularity recently,[21] and not to worry that this leaves traditional philosophy as well as common sense, taken as special sources of truth, reduced rather to confusion, error, and irrelevance.

2.3. Kant's System: Not versus Skepticism, But for Common Knowledge

If we try now to locate Kant within these alternatives, it is all too tempting and common to see him, as, for example, Richard Rorty has done, as but one more failed version of the representationalist option[22]—and precisely because of Kant's strong interest in system. For many readers, the Kantian system, with its massive transcendental idealist architectonic, has appeared to be but one more desperate attempt to construct a modern pseudo-object, a literally fabricated philosopher's world, lying in an unneeded nowhere land between the informalities of common life and the strict claims of science itself. Even if one brackets the troublesome issue of Kant's metaphysical commitments, it remains hard from the start for most philosophers to accept any of Kant's complex apparatus because it still seems not even capable of responding to the challenge of skepticism without falling back into what is only a more complicated rearrangement of the old internal and inadequate tools of representationalism.

These are familiar complaints, and no doubt there are many grounds in Kant's own language for condemning his system because of the problems that arise on the standard story. Nonetheless, as I have indicated, there may be a quite different way to understand his basic strategy, a transcendental approach that escapes these objections. This alternative interpretation can now be developed further by explaining just how it contrasts with the original and still common reaction to Kant.

Practically before the ink was dry on Kant's Critical work, the suspicion arose that for all his talk of a system, his own philosophy was not systematic in any satisfactory sense, and this for precisely the reasons that (a) it only exacerbated rather than alleviated the challenge of *skepticism,* and (b) it lacked basic *unity* because it divided the world, the self, and philosophy into untenable strict dualisms such as the phenomenal and the noumenal, the sensible and the rational, the theoretical and the practical. These issues dominate the worries not only of many current writers but also of Kant's first influential critics: G. E. Schulze, F. H. Jacobi, and J. G. Fichte—and even of his first major advocate, K. L. Reinhold, who soon insisted that Kant's system had to be revised radically, so that it could be brought into an adequately "firm" and "broad" shape.[23]

Schulze and his successors in the late eighteenth century, just like Strawson and Stroud in our century, generated an atmosphere in which the measure of Kantian philosophy tends at first to be nothing other than how well it can defeat skepticism's challenge. It is as if Critical philosophy is all an obscure enterprise unless it can be formulated as a transcendental "objectivity argument" that ideally turns the very tools of Cartesianism against itself and shows that mere self-consciousness absolutely requires physical objects.[24] This is an old issue in the Kant literature, and here I will do little more than gesture to earlier work in which I and others have contended that, despite numerous complications, the intentions of the first *Critique,* and even of the legendary Refutation of Idealism, can actually be understood better by abstracting from any such claim to defeat radical skepticism on its own terms.[25] This is not at all to say that there are no intriguing new responses to skepticism that can be teased out of *suggestions* in Kant's texts. The contention of the moment is only that seeking knock-down arguments on this issue need not be assumed to fit best with the literal intent or main value of the Critical philosophy, especially in the context of its relation to science. Behind this contention is also the ever-more confirmed suspicion (which is of course still controversial) that radical skepticism is a position that no one is going to be able to defeat with a compelling theoretical argument,[26] and so it is not a significant failing if a specific philosopher such as Kant has no such argument either.

If we look back at the prime concern of modern skepticism, the problem of proving the existence of physical objects, it should be clear enough how this particular problem became *acute* in the era immediately preceding Kant. Not only did reflections on modern physics undermine naive presumptions of common sense (especially as infected by Aristotelianism or other outdated traditions) about the intrinsic *nature* of specific kinds of external objects (e.g., about their color or force); they also eventually undercut all assumptions about any insight into the form of causal connections—and without such insight there can be no certain path at all from our perceptions to whatever external ground they may have, however systematically they might be organized. Kant was especially familiar with this problem from the lively disputes among his teachers concerning issues such as the doctrine of pre-established harmony,[27] and from early on he expressed a commonsense attitude toward it that I take to be a crucial and underappreciated indication of his general methodology. He remarked that on such issues even philosophers should simply accept what I have been calling "common knowledge," that is, what all normal people really do believe—in this case, in a plurality of finite interacting things—and move on from there.[28] This might seem like a horribly deflationary approach, one that would put him back in the ranks of the crude "popular philosophers" whom he generally castigated. But such objections overlook other crucial differences and presuppose that Kant must be read as a representational foundationalist, as someone who takes private inner ideas as the absolute given and assumes that philosophy must rebuild a world from the start out of such components. I do not see Kant as ever committed to such a premise, but it is not necessary to try to prove that view here. There are countless exegetical complexities involved, and it is enough for immediate purposes if a nonrepresentationalist reading can be offered that at least seems to fit many aspects of Kant's texts here, and that opens a different and fruitful way to approach his basic philosophical project.

In favor of reading Kant as a representationalist, there are, to be sure, facts such as his very frequent use of the term "representation" and his general preoccupation with many problems that come straight out of the Descartes to Hume tradition. But there are harmless ways to explain these facts, and it is at least equally obvious that Kant initiated a very striking departure from the common practice of beginning arguments from an elementary basis of mere "representations" in the typical modern pre-Kantian sense, for example, private images or sense data. While Kant did not deny the existence of such "data," he premised his arguments on a higher level of consciousness not adequately explored by his predecessors. In focusing on "experience" (*Erfahrung*) in the sense of putatively warranted empirical *judgment*, Kant made a decisive methodological break with all philosophies that insisted on beginning with simple ideas or impressions. Unlike impressions, judgments are not atomic entities that merely exist or fail to exist; they are already structured cognitive wholes, with essential semantic and normative features. In their paradigmatic form in Kant's texts, they are originally oriented toward external objects, as in the "judgment of experience," "bodies are heavy" (B142).

A traditional representationalist might object that if Kant is starting with "common knowledge" judgments in this sense, then all the interesting questions are already being begged (see section 2.4). But the Kantian transcendental reply is that from this level on there remain a host of significant and genuine questions, for example, the questions at the heart of the *Critique*: Supposing that there are legitimate empirical judgments, can we make sense of ordinary practices of justifying these without eventually invoking any formal limits, any a priori principles that would order them systematically? In the general spirit of the sciences of his time, Kant was sure that, with his doctrine of forms of judgment and its related table of the categories, he had discovered substantive and final answers here. Most philosophers now would prefer a more flexible and historical notion of "the a priori,"[29] but as long as it still appears worthwhile to explore some kind of answers here of a broadly Kantian type (helpful answers such as, e.g., those that Michael Friedman has shown that the Carnapian tradition produced in our own time[30]), some kind of formal constraints for knowledge at least as we can envisage it now, then the underlying idea of the Kantian system can maintain its value as a basic option. In place of leaving us with only radical subjectivism or radical naturalism—and all their limitations—and instead of resting content merely with common sense or technical disciplines alone, the Kantian hypothesis of a layer of structured formal principles can serve as a useful mediator between ordinary life and exact science. Principles such as causality (whose precise meaning needs to be refined over time, of course) can be argued, for example, to function both as necessary conditions for particular empirical judgments and as framework postulates for specific higher sciences, and in this way the whole fabric of our knowledge can take on a much more coherent sense for us as its major intertwining threads are revealed.

This general strategy can be filled out further by noting that Kant's own principles are not a mere contingent array, but rather are linked to each other in a thoroughly systematic fashion in which the very structure of judgment itself provides a constant "clue."[31] Kant's approach is systematic in a multiple sense because it claims a necessary and tightly connected framework that provides philosophical principles which bridge the extremes of common and scientific judgments, while also implying similar although somewhat looser structures within each of the spheres of common and scientific judgments themselves, structures that parallel the architectonic of the philosophical principles. For example, the relations between Kant's specific principles of substance, cause, and interaction correspond in multiple ways to relations between both weaker "everyday" uses of these concepts, and also stronger, scientifically determined employments of them. This general notion of a nesting of types of systematicity can be worth exploring even if one allows that Kant himself went overboard in his confidence about the specific systematic structures that he thought he had established. Obviously, it is very hard for us now to accept the alleged certainty, unrevisability, and extraordinary range of content of his transcendental claims. But such problems are common to modern philosophy and should not blind us to the heart of Kant's achievement, the opening up of a plausible role for philosophy as a systematic articulation of the sphere of conceptual frameworks that mediate between the extremely informal and the highly formal levels of judgment within our complex objective picture of the world. The crucial point about Kant's enthusiastic talk about a philosophical "system" is simply that he understood that more is possible—and desired by us now—than a simple reliance on a chaos of popular truths or an absolutized set of quantitative theories. Part and parcel of this stress on systematicity is Kant's rejection of foundationalism and naive representationalism: he understood, and argued more influentially than anyone else, that knowledge is anything but a "mirror of nature," a matter of isolated tokens magically picturing transcendent correlates;[32] it is a web of judgments, tied together by an order of conceptual "knots" that hold up over and over again in all kinds of arguments. It is no accident that concepts such as space, time, and causality, which structure everyday life systematically, also take on a fundamental role in the higher sciences. Practically any account that thematizes the relation between these concepts in an organized but nonreductionist manner—and thus contrasts with prior modern philosophies—can qualify as Kantian in an extended sense.

Kant's own interest in philosophical systematicity goes far beyond a few analogies, and it is by no means limited to the well-known discussion of specific regulative principles near the end of the first *Critique* and developed throughout the third *Critique*. On a Critical view, philosophy itself has a fundamental systematicity already in its basic transcendental structure, which contains three main steps: (1) an exposition of a commonly accepted basis, (2) a set of ordered immediate derivations from that basis, and then (3) a determination of the nature of the range and domain of these derivations.[33] The first of these steps consists in explaining that we have experience, that is, episodes subject to a "principle" of judgment[34] and thus to a specifiable logical structure needed by any sensible beings who can make claims that aim to be true. The second step, the layer of particular deductions, takes the form in Kant's work of a sequence of ordered transcendental arguments, that is, deductions that concern space, time, categories, and principles that each already presume some kind of objective knowledge, for which necessary epistemic conditions are then offered. In his third basic step, Kant tries to determine the full range of possible a priori knowledge, and to explain exactly where principles of reason become theoretically ungrounded when they lack an objective transcendental role. A final aspect of this step (and a very important one, not to be conflated with the others), which can be abstracted from for now, is to give a metaphysical interpretation of the meaning of the whole domain of experience that has been transcendentally explored. For Kant this amounts to an endorsement of the specific doctrine of transcendental idealism as the only metaphysics that consistently helps "make intelligible"[35] all that we already know.

I have formulated this account with an implicit orientation toward the structure of the first *Critique*, and the "theoretical" common knowledge that starts from elementary empirical judgments about spatiotemporal objects. But the notion of common knowledge can be naturally expanded, and was so expanded by Kant, to include what he took to be even more evident claims in other fields, especially ethics. There too one finds, for example in the three-part structure of the *Groundwork*, an initial exposition of what is taken to be a set of common or "popular" examples of moral judgment, followed by a regressive argument for underlying pure principles, and then a concluding reference to at least the outline of a unified metaphysics that would anchor these principles in Kant's general system. A parallel reconstruction could be given of Kant's discussion of aesthetic judgments, which also begins from a set of features presumed to be common in typical aesthetic judgments, then moves on to general principles about pure activities of the mind, and concludes with a discussion of relevant features of the metaphysical system in which these are to be understood as embedded.

While a system with all these features may strike us as overly ambitious, what I want to draw attention to is how, in comparison to many other approaches, there still is a remarkable modesty that marks even the detailed Kantian notion of a philosophic system. Note that there is no insistence on an absolute certainty for the basis. The "experience" that we start with is not metaphysically necessary, and it is not even claimed to be epistemically irresistible—skeptics could opt out of the discussion and not accept that there are any such warranted judgments. Note secondly that the derivations do not claim an absolute necessity, and Kant is perfectly willing to allow that various basic aspects of experience remain inexplicable primitives; we just do work with space, time, and the forms of judgment, and there are no more basic entities—Leibnizian monads, Spinozoan substance, Humean impressions, and so on—from which these commonsense notions are taken to be even in principle derivable. For Kant there is no discoverable single "root" faculty, nor is there a single top-down procedure for all truth, such as Leibnizian analysis. Thirdly, note that there are substantive limits that are stressed even in the account of the scope of Kant's system, both in its negative claims about what constitutive unifying principles of reason can be found, and also in its general metaphysical thesis that our theoretical knowledge is restricted because of transcendental idealism. In the third *Critique* especially, Kant emphasizes that although there is a "regulative" injunction to seek to tie together all of our actual knowledge into an overarching natural science, in principle we can never expect to claim that this science will reach a point of absolute completeness. Similarly, whatever transcendental idealism exactly means, Kant stresses that it is not an account that even purports to give any positive "explanation" of how we come to have the basic powers of mind that we exhibit.

What all this shows is that while, on the one hand, Kant departs from the level of mere common sense by constructing a complex philosophical system, the system that he actually outlines, like the general idea of philosophical systematicity that he promotes, intentionally contains several clear limits, all linked back to a respect for common sense, and thus it still amounts to what can, after all, be called a position of "modest" systematicity. Unlike his predecessors, Kant does not set up a detailed ontology that contrasts with science itself, nor does he raise epistemological demands to unrealistic levels.

2.4. Kant's Immediate Successors: Contrasting Reactions to Modesty

The contrast between Kant and his immediate successors (Reinhold, Fichte) also illustrates this point, for they were still preoccupied by the problem of skepticism and deeply disturbed precisely by the limits of Kant's system. In the place of Kant's hypothetical basis of experience, his conditional argument for the categories, and his notion of a "formal" idealism that still allowed meaningful claims about something beyond human sensibility, they repeatedly called for an absolutely certain basis, an absolutely necessary set of derivations, and a truly exhaustive (global and constitutive, rather than partial and regulative) interpretation of the scope of experience.[36]

It is quite striking that this very feature of Kant's work, its relative modesty, was in fact well appreciated by some of Kant's genuine but surprisingly rare early followers. It was at Jena in the late 1780s and early 1790s that Kant's work first received intensive study, not only through the reviews of the *Allgemeine Literatur Zeitung*, the efforts of C. C. Schmid and his *Kant Wörterbuch*, and the installments of Reinhold's extremely popular (in all senses) *Briefe über die Kantische Philosophie*, but also in the discussions that took place in the circle of Friedrich Niethammer. Niethammer is perhaps best known for his later support of Hegel, but in his early years in Jena he was connected with early romantic figures such as Novalis, who delighted in undermining systematic pretensions. Niethammer was especially close to two sober Kant enthusiasts, Johann Benjamin Erhard and Franz von Herbert, who were immediately and vividly disturbed by the first attempts of Reinhold and Fichte to replace orthodox Kantianism with a radical foundational system that would supposedly be absolutely certain at its base and absolutely unified by reason in its extent. In the lead article of his new *Philosophisches Journal*, Niethammer focused precisely "On the demands of common sense to philosophy,"[37] and he even used the dilemmas of foundationalism to argue for the view that "the claims of common sense have to be regarded as the supreme criterion of all truth in our knowledge."[38] He does not take this approach to be in conflict with all presentations of philosophy as a "science"; his point is simply, against the new foundationalist philosophers, that, precisely for sensible scientific purposes, philosophy need not (and cannot successfully) try to start from any basis better than common knowledge. Niethammer also notes explicitly that Kant's philosophy takes as its starting point the "general main fact, that there is experience."[39] Niethammer stresses that from such a point one can move "only" to hypothetical substantive claims, but he realizes that it would be a misunderstanding of both philosophy and science to take this fact as a devastating obstacle—since in fact the "hypothesis" that is started from is inevitably and commonly shared. Both philosophy and science can thrive even if the a priori principles that they introduce or use do not have a connection with the premise of experience that has anything more than a discursive, that is, nonintuitive and fallible, certainty.

2.5. Apologetics

Underlying Kant's own approach here is a general and important methodological feature that needs to be made explicit, namely the acceptance of what can be called a fundamentally "apologetic" role for philosophy. One way to develop a philosophy might be, to use Strawson's words, to present a "revisionary" metaphysics,[40] that is, to introduce a philosophical construction that is meant to displace the commitments of ordinary people and ongoing disciplines. But especially after his early "Rousseau experience," Kant was loath to call into question, or demand some esoteric original ground for, the commitments of reason found implicitly in the simplest person, for example, even a Savoyard vicar.[41] Yet he also knew that those commitments had been severely challenged by modern developments, scientific and philosophical, and that many had come to think that once modern people become reflective at all, it must be difficult for them to feel truly rational while holding on to such ordinary beliefs as common ethics and even the core of popular religion. To meet this challenge, Kant came to realize that all he needed was not a theoretical account of how the metaphysics of ethics and religion work in detail, but only an apology, a story of how the best examination of all the latest options of metaphysics and science—and a thorough exploration of all their own perplexities—shows that there is still room for (what he took to be) our most important common beliefs. He also went on to insist that he had proven there was no way that the core content of these beliefs could ever be shown to be impossible. This claim, like much of his talk about philosophical "certainty," was more than what was strictly needed, as was his extra belief that various alternative philosophies, such as materialism, were not only dubious or uncertain but definitely false. There was often some overconfident "overkill" in Kant's formulations, but we can bracket this again and still extract from his work an attractive apologetic strategy that gives philosophy the modest negative role of primarily defending modern agents simply against philosophy itself—and its ever growing alienating effects, including challenges to the very notion of science as a crucial and distinctive form of knowing. This strategy nicely supplements the modest positive and systematic role for philosophy discussed earlier, its unique function of providing a structured account of how all our different levels of knowledge hang together.[42]

The fact that there remain, no doubt, many difficulties in Kant's specific arguments should not blind us to the general point that, unlike the other moderns and their followers, he managed to outline a task for philosophy that allows it to take on a systematic and therefore scientific form in precisely the modest sense that is alone realistic today. In sum: Can philosophy itself be scientific, and is Kant's philosophy truly scientific? Of course, as long as one allows that philosophy and science must involve a relation to common knowledge, and not only exact knowledge.

NOTES

For suggestions on these topics, I would like to express my appreciation to the participants at the Virginia Tech conference, and especially Eric Watkins, as well as to Don Howard and my other colleagues at Notre Dame, for their comments on a version of the chapter.

1. These images are emphasized in W. Sellars's very Kantian and aptly titled volume, *Science, Perception, and Reality* (London: Kegan Paul, 1963).

2. See, e.g., R. Popkin, *The History of Skepticism from Erasmus to Descartes* (New York: Harper, 1964), and E. Curley, *Descartes Against the Skeptics* (Cambridge: Harvard University Press, 1978).

3. A sophisticated variation of this view is critically discussed in Michael Friedman's presidential address, "Philosophical Naturalism," *Proceedings and Addresses of the American Philosophical Association* 71 (1997): 7–21.

4. See my "Kant's Transcendental Deduction as a Regressive Argument," *Kant-Studien* 69 (1978): 273–87. This is not to deny that of course Kant was highly concerned with the Humean skepticism specifically about "reason."

5. Kant, *Critique of Pure Reason*, A226/B273. Quotations of this work are from the Norman Kemp Smith translation (London: Macmillan, 1929). Translations from transcripts from Kant's lectures on metaphysics will be from Immanuel Kant *Lectures on Metaphysics*, ed. and trans. Karl Ameriks and Steve Naragon (Cambridge: Cambridge University Press, 1997).

6. One should keep in mind that I will be using "knowledge" with the meaning that Kant's *Erkenntnis* and *Erfahrung* has, that is, unlike the standard English philosophical use of "knowledge," it signifies only a kind of "cognitive state" that involves a grounded or putative truth claim, but not necessarily an actual truth.

7. *Critique*, B41; cf. A11/B25. I am not presuming that Kant's argument here is persuasive.

8. See M. Friedman, *Kant and the Exact Sciences* (Cambridge: Harvard University Press, 1992), esp. chap. 5.III.

9. *Critique of Judgment*, §75. Joachim Waschkies has drawn my attention to the fact that Kant is intentionally choosing a very simple form of "Kraut" here, since it was a commonplace of the period to comment on the intricate structure of more complex plants, e.g., cabbage.

10. Cf. A846/B874.

11. See the discussion and references in my "On Paul Guyer's 'Kant and the Experience of Freedom,'" *Philosophy and Phenomenological Research* 55 (1995): 361–67.

12. Kant, April 7, 1799, open letter against the *Wissenschaftslehre*, in *Kant: Philosophical Correspondence: 1755–1799*, trans. A. Zweig (Chicago: University of Chicago Press, 1967), 254 (12:370–71).

13. Zweig, *Philosophical Correspondence*, 125.

14. E.g., A12/B26.

15. See further discussion of this point at the end of chap. 1 of my *Kant and the Fate of Autonomy: Essays on the Appropriation of the Critical Philosophy* (forthcoming).

16. See the editors' introduction to *Lectures on Metaphysics*, and the preface to the new and revised edition of my *Kant's Theory of Mind* (Oxford: Clarendon Press, 1982; 2nd ed., 2000).

17. See, e.g., 29:750.

18. Zweig, *Philosophical Correspondence*, 254.

19. See, e.g., work cited in n. 2, and J. B. Schneewind, *The Invention of Autonomy* (Cambridge: Cambridge University Press, 1997).

20. See Hegel's classic critique in the beginning of his introduction to the *Phenomenology of Spirit*.

21. Quine has been most influential here. But see the fine Kantian counterattack by Michael Friedman, in his "Philosophical Naturalism," and "Exorcising the Philosophical Tradition," *Philosophical Review* 105 (1996): 427–67; and also Michael Friedman and Graham Bird,

"Kantian Themes in Contemporary Philosophy," *Proceedings of the Aristotelian Society*, suppl. Vol. 72 (1998): 131–51. Bird's position is even closer to mine than Friedman's, since it keeps more distance between Kant and philosophy of science, and emphasizes a dimension of experience similar to what I have been calling "common knowledge."

22. See Richard Rorty, "Strawson's Objectivity Argument," *Review of Metaphysics* 24 (1970): 207–44, and *Philosophy and the Mirror of Nature* (Princeton: Princeton University Press, 1979).

23. See my "Kant, Fichte, and Short Arguments to Idealism," *Archiv für Geschichte der Philosophie* 72 (1990): 63–85.

24. See P. F. Strawson's classic, *The Bounds of Sense* (London: Methuen, 1966), chap. 2.II. Many recent versions of the strategy can be found, e.g., in Q. Cassam, *Self and World* (Oxford: Oxford University Press, 1996).

25. See n. 4 above, and my "Recent Work on Kant's Theoretical Philosophy," *American Philosophical Quarterly* 19 (1982): 1–24; *Kant's Theory of Mind*, chap. III.C.

26. Here I have been influenced by the work of A. Brueckner and R. Fogelin.

27. See E. Watkins, "Kant's Theory of Physical Influx," *Archiv für Geschichte der Philosophie* 77 (1995): 285–324, and "The Development of Physical Influx in Early 18th Century Germany: Gottsched, Knutzen, and Crusius," *Review of Metaphysics* 49 (1995): 295–339.

28. I have been struck especially by the Moorean point made at Metaphysik Herder: "finden sich in der Folge Säzze die dem Sens commun widersprechen, so prüfe man alle vorhergegangene Beweise" ("if one finds propositions that contradict common sense, one should test all prior arguments") (28:6).

29. See Philip Kitcher's "flexible Kantian" account along this line, "The Unity of Science and the Unity of Nature," in *Kant and Contemporary Epistemology*, ed. P. Parrini (Dordrecht: Kluwer, 1994), 331–47.

30. See again Friedman, "Philosophical Naturalism."

31. See B. Longuenesse's work on Kant's table of judgments as a systematic clue to the whole structure of the *Critique*, in *Kant and the Capacity to Judge* (Princeton: Princeton University Press, 1998); and Reinhard Brandt, *The Table of Judgments: Critique of Pure Reason A 67–76, B 92–101*, North American Kant Society Studies in Philosophy, vol. 4, trans. E. Watkins (Atascadero, CA: Ridgeview, 1995).

32. An appreciation for this side of Kant's work is one of the values of McDowell's *Mind and World* (Cambridge: Harvard University Press, 1994), the title and idea of which can be taken as a variation on C. I. Lewis's classic and Kantian *Mind and the World Order* (1929). I am not claiming that Kant's talk of rules and synthesis fully explains the mysteries of intentionality. But it is a start that has at least made us sensitive to the limits of earlier and cruder theories. See also G. Prauss, *Erscheinung bei Kant* (Berlin: de Gruyter, 1971), and McDowell's Woodbridge lectures, "Having the World in View: Sellars, Kant, and Intentionality," *Journal of Philosophy* 95 (1998): 431–91.

33. See, for example, the typical heading of *Critique*, introduction, sec. 3: "Philosophy stands in need of a science which shall determine the possibility, the principles, and the extent of all *a priori* knowledge" (A2/B6).

34. See already the first preface to the *Critique* on "the common principle," by which "the inventory of all our possessions through pure reason is systematically arranged" (Axx).

35. This expression comes from the Transcendental Aesthetic's first grounded assertion of transcendental idealism at B41.

36. See again my "Kant, Fichte, and Short Arguments to Idealism," and *Kant and the Fate of Autonomy*.

37. Friedrich Niethammer, "Von den Ansprüchen des gemeinen Verstandes an die Philosophie," *Philosophisches Journal* 1 (1795): 1–45. See especially the compressed discussion of this and related issues by Manfred Frank, "Philosophical Foundations of Early Romanticism," in *The Modern Subject*, ed. K. Ameriks and D. Sturma (Albany: SUNY Press, 1995), 65–85; and the extended discussion (959 pages) in *Unendliche Annäherung: Die Anfänge der philosophischen Frühromantik* (Frankfurt: Suhrkamp, 1997), esp. 439, which cites and discusses the letter of Herbert (with an afterword by Erhard) to Niethammer, May 6, 1794. After hearing Fichte's own preview of the *Wissenschaftslehre* in Zürich, Herbert declared himself the "unreconcilable enemy of all so-called first principles in philosophy." Herbert goes on to stress that Kant himself based his philosophy on presumed commonsense judgments (especially concerning morality), and he bids Niethammer simply to use his special talent to give Kant's philosophy a clear exposition and to remain "a simple teacher and reader of the *Critique of Pure Reason*." See *Friedrich Immanuel Niethammer: Korrespondenz mit dem Herbert-und Erhard-Kreis*, ed. Wilhelm Baum (Vienna: Turia + Kant, 1995), 76; Fichte, *Züricher Vorlesungen über den Begriff der Wissenschaftslehre: Februar, 1794*, ed. Erich Fuchs (Neuried: Ars Una, 1996); Marcelo Stamm, "Prinzipien und System: Rezeptionsmodelle der Wissenschaftslehre Fichtes 1794," *Fichte-Studien* 9 (1995): 215–40; *Immanuel Carl Diez, Briefwechsel und Kantische Schriften*, ed. D. Henrich (Stuttgart: Klett-Cotta, 1997); and my *Kant and the Fate of Autonomy*.

38. Niethammer, "Von den Ansprüchen," 32.

39. Niethammer, "Von den Ansprüchen," 23. It is important to keep in mind again that "experience" here is *Erfahrung*, which is precisely not a mere sense datum but an empirical judgment, a putative common knowledge claim. Cf. Herbert's letter to Erhard, October 7, 1794: "Kant's entire system can be expressed in the hypothetical proposition, 'If experience is, then . . . ' That experience is, is thereby presupposed, postulated, or however one calls it. Now if a skeptic were dumb and shameless enough to say, 'But is there experience?' there is really no answer for such a type other than a beating" (cited in Frank, *Unendliche Annäherung*, 507).

40. P. F. Strawson, *Individuals: An Essay in Descriptive Metaphysics* (London: Methuen, 1959).

41. Kant, 20:44. Kant developed a similar answer for other forms of presumed knowledge, such as mathematics, which seemed at least not as vulnerable in the public mind to philosophical undermining by problems at the foundation. He used this fact as a wedge against figures such as Hume, arguing that if a Humean would only admit the simple mathematical propositions that everyone else already concedes, then enough of an apparatus would ultimately have to be conceded to be able to underwrite other more contested a priori claims.

42. Is all this inherently "conservative"? No, there can be revolutionary scientific and social developments that seep into popular consciousness in such a way that theoreticians can mobilize them for the purpose of philosophically undermining repressive ideologies—as Kant did, for example, in his influential work as a liberating Enlightenment writer.

3

Matter and Motion in the Metaphysical Foundations *and the First* Critique

The Empirical Concept of Matter and the Categories

Michael Friedman

T HE *Metaphysical Foundations of Natural Science* is intended to be a "realization" of the more general system of transcendental principles of the first *Critique* that provides "examples (cases *in concreto*)" for the concepts and principles of the latter. In this way, the concepts and principles of transcendental philosophy are further specified so as, in particular, to yield pure principles of natural science. In connection with the category of substance and the First Analogy, for example, the concept of substance is realized in terms of the quantity of matter, and the principle of the permanence of substance is realized in terms of a conservation law for this quantity. What Kant calls "special metaphysics"—here the metaphysical doctrine of body—thereby supplies "sense and meaning" to the exceedingly abstract and relatively indeterminate system of "general metaphysics" or transcendental philosophy, without which the latter would remain a "mere form of thought."[1]

The bridge between the two systems, between general metaphysics and special metaphysics, is what Kant calls "the empirical concept of matter" (4:470). For it is by adding this concept to the more abstract and general concepts and principles of transcendental philosophy that we then obtain the concepts and principles of special metaphysics—the metaphysical doctrine of body—from the former. In the case of the category and principle of substance, for example, in order to obtain the conservation of matter from the First Analogy it is necessary "only to verify what substance is to be in matter." Since matter is "the movable in space," and since "the aggregate of movables external to one another is the quantity of substance [in matter]," it follows that the total quantity of such movables is necessarily conserved—although, to be sure, they remain entirely free to separate from one another and thereby change their overall arrangement in space.[2]

This much is relatively clear and uncontroversial. But when it comes to saying more precisely what the content of the concept of matter is, explaining in what sense this concept is empirical, and articulating the precise relationship between this concept and the pure concepts or categories of the first *Critique*, we are immediately plunged into what appear to be insuperable difficulties.

First of all, what is the content of the concept of matter, and how is it possible nonetheless to extract a priori knowledge from such an admittedly empirical concept? In the preface to the *Metaphysical Foundations* Kant introduces the idea of a *special* metaphysics of nature as that which

> concerns itself with a particular nature of this or that kind of things, for which an empirical concept is given, but still in such a manner that, outside of what lies in this concept, no other empirical principle is used for its cognition (for example, it takes the empirical concept of matter or of a thinking being as its basis, and it seeks that sphere of cognition of which reason is capable *a priori* concerning these objects), and here such a science must still always be called a metaphysics of nature, namely, of corporeal or of thinking nature. However, [in this second case] it is then not a general, but a *special* metaphysical natural science (physics or psychology), in which the above transcendental principles are applied to the two species of objects of our senses (4:470).

And, in the first *Critique*, Kant addresses the question of how a priori knowledge can thereby be forthcoming as follows:

> How can I expect an *a priori* cognition, and thus a metaphysics, of objects in so far as they are given to our senses, and therefore given *a posteriori*? . . . The answer is: we take no more from experience than what is necessary to *give* us an object—of either outer or inner sense. The former takes place through the mere concept of matter (impenetrable, lifeless extension), the latter through the concept of a thinking being (in the empirical inner representation: I think) (A847–48/B875–76).

We know a priori that there are two general types of objects of our senses: objects of inner sense and objects of outer sense. The concept of matter, it appears, is simply that of an arbitrary object of outer sense—the concept of an object in space. And, in this sense, its content then appears to be entirely a priori.[3]

This suggestion seems to be confirmed—and indeed even strengthened—in the next paragraph of the *Metaphysical Foundations*, where the idea of a priori knowledge in this connection is further articulated:

> To cognize something *a priori* means to cognize it from its mere possibility. But the possibility of determinate natural things cannot be cognized from their mere concepts; for from these the possibility of the thought (that it does not contradict itself) can certainly be cognized, but not the possibility of the object, as a natural thing that can be given outside the thought (as

existing). Hence, in order to cognize the possibility of determinate natural things, and thus to cognize them *a priori*, it is still required that the *intuition* corresponding to the concept be given *a priori*, that is, that the concept be constructed (4:470).

Kant appears to be saying that we obtain a priori knowledge from the concept of matter precisely by *constructing* this concept in pure intuition. Thus, not only is the content of this concept given wholly a priori, but objects corresponding to it can also be given wholly a priori—that is, by mathematical construction.[4] The sense in which the concept of matter is actually empirical may now appear entirely to evaporate.

The idea that the concept of matter is not really empirical after all appears to be further supported, finally, by the way in which Kant describes the relationship between the special metaphysics of corporeal nature and the general metaphysics of the first *Critique*:

It is also indeed very remarkable (but cannot be expounded in detail here) that general metaphysics, in all instances where it requires examples (intuitions) in order to provide meaning for its pure concepts of the understanding, must always take them from the general doctrine of body, and thus from the form and principles of outer intuition; and, if these are not exhibited completely, it gropes uncertainly and unsteadily among mere meaningless concepts. This is the source of the well known disputes, or at least obscurity, in the questions concerning the possibility of a conflict of realities, of intensive magnitude, and so on, in which the understanding is taught only by examples from corporeal nature what the conditions are under which such concepts can alone have objective reality, that is, meaning and truth (4:478).

Here Kant seems to be saying that without the special metaphysics of corporeal nature the pure categories of transcendental philosophy would not yet have objective reality—a suggestion that looks particularly plausible when this passage is compared to a parallel passage added to the second edition of the *Critique*:

It is even more remarkable, however, that, in order to understand the possibility of things in accordance with the categories, and thus to verify the *objective reality* of the latter, we require not merely intuitions, but always even *outer intuitions*. If, for example, we take the pure concepts of *relation*, we find, first, that in order to supply something *permanent* in intuition corresponding to the concept of *substance* (and thereby to verify the objective reality of this concept), we require an intuition *in space* (of matter), because space alone is determined as permanent, but time, and thus everything in inner sense, continually flows (B291).

It appears, then, that we need the concept of matter to demonstrate the objective reality of the categories.[5] So this concept can hardly be an empirical concept in any ordinary sense of the term.

Something has gone terribly wrong here. It is perhaps not so problematic if the concept of matter is not really an empirical concept in the ordinary sense of the term. For it is clear beyond the shadow of a doubt that Kant takes this concept to be a source of a priori knowledge. It would be intolerable, however, if it turned out that we needed the special metaphysics of corporeal nature to demonstrate the objective reality of the categories. For this would entirely erase the distinction between general metaphysics or transcendental philosophy and special metaphysics. The task of demonstrating the objective reality of the categories is already supposed to be completed in the main argument—the Transcendental Deduction—of the first *Critique*. If special metaphysics is required for *this* task then it must belong, contrary to Kant's completely explicit intentions, to transcendental philosophy. Moreover, it would also be intolerable, as we shall see below, if we could demonstrate the objective reality of Kant's concept of matter by mathematical construction, or, even worse, if we could demonstrate the objective reality of the categories in this way. So let us now try to untangle these questions step by step.

First of all, if the content of the concept of matter were simply that of an object of outer sense in general, then it would be entirely unclear how this concept differed from a pure a priori concept. How, in particular, would it differ from the concept of "the *real* in space," which Kant introduces in the Anticipations of Perception (A173/B215)? This latter concept belongs to the categories of quality and is thus a pure a priori concept (reality plus space, as it were); and, for precisely this reason, Kant emphasizes explicitly that no *empirical* concepts are involved: "I may not here call [the *real* in space] impenetrability or weight, for these are empirical concepts" (A173/B215). But we know from the *Metaphysical Foundations* that precisely these concepts—impenetrability and weight—are essential constituents of the empirical concept of matter and, as such, are manifestations of the fundamental forces of repulsion and attraction respectively. Repulsion belongs immediately (analytically) to the concept of matter itself; attraction is added to it (synthetically) by inferences (4:509). Accordingly, Kant explains the concept of matter as follows: as "impenetrable, lifeless extension" (A848/B876); as that concept which contains the concepts "of *motion*, of *impenetrability* (on which the empirical concept of matter is based), of *inertia*, and so on" (4:295); and as that concept which includes the concepts "of motion, of the filling of space, of inertia, etc." (4:472). Hence, the empirical concept of matter differs from the mere concept of something real in space in virtue of precisely the circumstance that the (empirical) concept of impenetrability belongs to the former but not to the latter.[6]

Second, with respect to the concept of impenetrability itself, Kant makes a central distinction between two types of impenetrability and two different concepts of matter that may arise thereby. On the one hand, there is a "mere mathematical concept of impenetrability (which presupposes no moving forces as originally inherent in matter)," in accordance with which "matter as matter resists all penetration utterly and with absolute necessity" (4:502). And from this concept of matter there arises "the mathematical-mechanical mode of explanation" (4:524) or "the mechanical natural philosophy," which aims to explain the specific variety of matters "by the constitution and composition of their smallest parts, as machines," that is, by "*atoms* and the *void*" (4:532). On the other hand, however, there is also a dynamical concept of impenetrability, which Kant himself defends. "According to our discussion," he says, "impenetrability rests on a physical basis; for expanding force first makes matter itself possible, as an extended thing filling its space" (4:502). In accordance with this concept, "everything real in the objects of the outer senses, which is not merely a determination of space (place, extension, and figure), must be viewed as moving force" (4:523), and there thereby arises "the metaphysical-dynamical mode of explanation" (4:525) or "the dynamical natural philosophy" (4:532). Therefore, in order to obtain Kant's particular concept of matter, we must first add the concept of impenetrability to the mere concept of the real in space, and then, in addition, the much more specific concept of what Kant calls relative or *dynamical* impenetrability.

Third, when Kant sets up a comparison between the mathematical and dynamical concepts of matter, it emerges that the former concept has at least *one* advantage. The possibility of the dynamical concept cannot be comprehended or demonstrated a priori, because the possibility of fundamental forces cannot be comprehended a priori. In the mathematical-mechanical mode of explanation, however, we use only purely geometrical concepts, such as extension, figure, and the void, without presupposing any fundamental forces. In this case, therefore, we can give an a priori proof of possibility, "because the possibility of figures, and also of void interstices, can be verified with mathematical evidence" (4:525). But, in the case of the dynamical concept of matter, the situation is entirely different: "by contrast, if the material itself is transformed into fundamental forces . . . , we lack all means for *constructing* this concept of matter, and presenting what we thought universally as possible in intuition" (4:525). Thus the dynamical concept of matter, in sharp contrast to the mathematical concept, can by no means be constructed in pure intuition.

More generally, only pure mathematical concepts can be constructed in pure intuition and thereby be shown to be really possible. In the Postulates of Empirical Thought Kant makes an explicit distinction between empirical concepts, which are "extracted (*erborgt*) from experience," and pure concepts, on which, "as *a priori* conditions, experience in general (the form thereof) rests" (A220/B267). The concept of a triangle, for example, can be constructed a priori in space, and, because "space is a formal *a priori* condition of outer experience," this construction is sufficient to demonstrate the real possibility of this concept (A223–24/B271). In the case of empirical concepts, by contrast, their "possibility can only be gathered from their actuality in experience" (A223/B270). This holds, in particular, for "concepts of substances, of forces, of interactions": "If one wanted to fashion [such concepts], without borrowing the example of their connection from experience itself, then one would find oneself among mere phantoms of the brain, with absolutely no criterion at all of their possibility" (A222/B269). Therefore, we can only exhibit the real possibility of the two fundamental forces constituting Kant's dynamical concept of matter by perceiving their actuality in experience itself: "no law of either attractive or repulsive force may be risked on *a priori* conjectures; rather, everything, even universal attraction as the cause of weight, must be inferred, together with its laws, from data of experience" (4:534). And it is in precisely this way, in fact, that empirical concepts are essentially different from pure mathematical concepts in regard to their real possibility.[7]

There is a parallel yet additional distinction, finally, between the pure concepts of the understanding—and thus the pure concept of an object of experience in general—and pure mathematical concepts. In the Discipline of Pure Reason Kant explains this distinction as follows:

> Now an *a priori* concept (a non-empirical concept) either already contains a pure intuition in itself, and in this case it can be constructed, or it contains nothing but the synthesis of possible intuitions that are not given *a priori*, and in this case we can indeed judge by means of it in a synthetic and *a priori* manner, but only discursively in accordance with concepts, and never intuitively by the construction of the concept (A719–20/B747–48).

Consequently,

> the *a priori* synthetic cognition of [the concept of a *thing* in general] can therefore supply nothing further than the mere rule of synthesis of that which perception may yield *a posteriori*, but never the *a priori* intuition of the real object, because this must necessarily be empirical. Synthetic propositions that extend to things in general, whose intuition can by no means be given *a priori* . . . contain merely the rule, in accordance with which a certain synthetic unity of that which cannot be intuitively represented *a priori* (perception) is to be empirically sought (A720–21/B748–49).

The objects corresponding to the pure concepts of the understanding—and thus to the pure concept of an object of experience in general—can never be given a priori by mathematical construction. On the contrary, they can only be given a posteriori by means of sensible and empirical perception. Such objects are in principle *empirical* objects.

It does not follow, however, that the real possibility or objective reality of the pure concepts of the understanding is itself empirical. For the objective reality of these concepts does not consist in their having corresponding objects. It consists in precisely the circumstance, rather, that they contain the a priori conditions in virtue of which experience of objects of perception—however the latter may be given—is first possible. In the Postulates of Empirical Thought, Kant writes:

> Only in the circumstance, therefore, that [pure concepts of the understanding] express *a priori* the relations of perceptions in every experience, do we cognize their objective reality, that is, their transcendental truth. We certainly do this, moreover, independently of experience, but not independently of all reference to the form of an experience in general, and to the synthetic unity in which alone objects can be empirically known (A221–22/ B269).

The pure concepts of the understanding thus contain only the form in accordance with which the empirical objects of perception must be experienced, if objective experience of these objects is possible at all. But the pure concepts of the understanding cannot supply these objects themselves. They supply only the *rule* by which we must *search out* the appearances, in order thereby to find, where possible, the objects of experience. And it is in precisely this way, and no other, that the pure concepts of the understanding acquire their own real possibility and objective reality.

What, then, is the relationship between the objective reality of the categories, on the one side, and that of the empirical concept of matter and the associated general doctrine of body, on the other? In the passage from the preface to the *Metaphysical Foundations* cited above (4:478), Kant asserts that "general metaphysics, in all instances where it requires examples (intuitions) in order to provide meaning for its pure concepts of the understanding, must always take them from the general doctrine of body," so that "a separated metaphysics of corporeal nature does excellent and indispensable service for *general* metaphysics, in that the former furnishes examples (instances *in concreto*) in which to realize the concepts and propositions of the latter (properly speaking, transcendental philosophy), that is, to give a mere form of thought sense and meaning." Hence, the only concrete instances we have that satisfy or realize the pure concepts and principles of the understanding are those provided by the special metaphysics of nature of the *Metaphysical Foundations*.[8] And these, according to what we have just seen above, are necessarily *empirical* objects given in perception.

So what exactly are these objects? I do not have room to argue this here, but I believe that the system of empirically given spatio-temporal objects corresponding to the Kantian concept of matter consists of the solar system together with the other heavenly bodies (including the sublunary region around the earth), as this system of bodies is described by Newtonian physics.[9] If this system were not given to us in perception, then we would have no basis whatsoever for "extracting" the fundamental forces of attraction and repulsion "from data of experience." Therefore, if this system were not given to us in perception, the empirical concept of matter would have no actual object corresponding to it—and thus no objective reality. For, as we have seen, Kant's dynamical concept of matter, in sharp contrast to the opposing purely mathematical concept favored by the "mathematical-mechanical mode of explanation," cannot be constructed in pure intuition and, accordingly, can only acquire a corresponding object in experience.

Now precisely the same system, as Kant suggests in our passage from the preface, is also the only actual system of objects or "example *in concreto*" known to us corresponding to transcendental philosophy in general. In particular, it is the only system of objects known to us in which the concepts and principles of the pure understanding are fully and precisely realized. Only here do we have an empirically given system of "substances, forces, and interactions," our knowledge of which is in fact rigorously made possible by a combination of transcendental and mathematical knowledge—that is, by a priori knowledge. For only here can we use geometry together with the Newtonian laws of motion actually to ground our empirical knowledge of perceptual objects. Nevertheless, although this system is the only instance known to us of the transcendental concept of an object of experience in general, it is by no means the only possible such instance. For the content of the transcendental concept of an object of experience in general is much more abstract, and much less determinate than that of the empirical concept of matter. Kant's dynamical concept of matter depicts a world of material, lifeless substances that interact with one another by the fundamental forces of attraction and repulsion and thereby mutually alter their states of motion. The transcendental concept of an object of experience in general, by contrast, depicts an otherwise entirely indeterminate system of substances in space, living as well as lifeless, that alter their states—whatever these may be—only by means of entirely undetermined forces and interactions. In this way, and in particular, Kant can now leave it entirely open how the future course of natural science may advance beyond Newtonian physics through the discovery of *new* substances, forces, and interactions.

This last feature of the pure concepts of the understanding—their much greater generality in comparison with the empirical concept of matter—further elucidates the sense in which their objective reality, as opposed to that of both empirical concepts and pure mathematical concepts, is not dependent on the existence of any particular given concrete instances. For these concepts obtain their objective reality rather from the circumstance that they express the a priori conditions under which alone objective experience of *any* empirical object whatsoever is possible. Accordingly, the characteristic function of the pure concepts of the understanding is precisely to ground the spatiotemporal unity of *any and all* empirical objects that may be given to us. Kant explains this point as follows in the case of the concept of causality:

By means of the concept of cause I actually proceed from the empirical concept of an event (where something happens)—not, however, to the intuition that exhibits the concept of cause *in concreto*, but rather to the condition of time in general, which may be found in experience in accordance with the concept of cause. I thus proceed according to concepts, and I cannot proceed by the construction of concepts, because the concept is a rule of synthesis of perceptions, which are not pure intuitions, and thus cannot be *a priori given* (A722/B750n).

The pure concepts of the understanding (the concepts of general metaphysics) do not express mathematical but rather metaphysical conditions, "drawn from the essence of the thinking faculty itself" (4:472). An a priori proof of their objective reality, as opposed to such a proof for a mathematical concept, can therefore not proceed by the a priori exhibition of any particular object. What can be exhibited, once again, is only the form or rule of time-determination in general underlying all *possible* empirically given objects.

Let us now return, with these points in mind, to the two parallel passages in which Kant explains how the objective reality of the categories depends on "the form and principles of outer intuition"—the one from the preface to the *Metaphysical Foundations*, the other from the General Remark to the System of Principles added to the second edition of the *Critique*. The first point to notice is that in the latter passage, unlike the former, Kant does not actually mention the empirical concept of matter and the general doctrine of body. He does not explicitly appeal to the special metaphysics of corporeal nature. After saying, as we already saw, that the objective reality of the category of substance requires "an intuition *in space* (of matter)," Kant rather continues as follows:

Second, in order to exhibit *alteration*, as the intuition corresponding to the concept of *causality*, we must take motion, as alteration in space, for the example. Indeed, it is even the case that we can make alteration intuitive to ourselves solely in this way, as no pure understanding can conceive its possibility. Alteration is combination of contradictorily opposed determinations in the existence of one and the same thing. How it may now be possible that an opposed state follows from a given state of the same thing is not only inconceivable to any reason without example, but is not even understandable without intuition—and this intuition is the motion of a point in space, whose existence in different places (as a sequence of opposed determinations) alone makes alteration intuitive to us in the first place. For, in order that we may afterwards make even inner alterations intuitive, we must make time, as the form of inner sense, intelligible figuratively as a line—and inner alteration by the drawing of this line (motion), and thus the successive existence of our self in different states by outer intuition. The essential reason for this is that all alteration presupposes something permanent in intuition, in order even to be perceived as alteration, but in inner sense no permanent intuition whatsoever is to be found (B291–92).

Here Kant gives a completely explicit example of an intuition in outer sense required for verifying the objective reality of the categories. But this is an example in *pure* intuition: the motion of a point in space.

Moreover, the same idea of a "figurative" representation of time in terms of the motion of a point in space plays a prominent role in §24 of the second-edition Transcendental Deduction, entitled "on the application of the categories to objects of the senses in general." After introducing the notion of "figurative synthesis" (*synthesis speciosa*) or "transcendental synthesis of the imagination," characterized as "an action of the understanding on sensibility and its first application to objects of an intuition possible for us (and at the same time the ground of all other applications)" (see B150–52), Kant goes on to illustrate this notion as follows:

> We always observe [the transcendental activity of the imagination] in ourselves. We can think no line without *drawing* it in thought, no circle without *describing* it, . . . ; and we cannot represent time itself without attending, in the *drawing* of a straight line (which is to be the outer figurative representation of time), merely to the action of synthesis of the manifold, through which we successively determine inner sense, and thereby attend to the succession of this determination in it. Motion, as action of the subject (not as determination of an object*), and thus the synthesis of the manifold in space—when we abstract from the latter and attend merely to the action by which we determine *inner* sense in accordance with its form—[such motion] even first produces the concept of succession (B154–55).

A crucial step in the Transcendental Deduction of the categories—the demonstration of how the unity of apperception is applied to sensibility so as to convert inner sense into a "*determinate* intuition . . . , which is only possible through the consciousness of the determination of the manifold by the transcendental action of the imagination (synthetic influence of the understanding on inner sense), which I have called figurative synthesis" (B154)—therefore proceeds precisely by the pure representation of motion.

In the footnote to this passage, however, Kant makes a fundamental distinction between two very different ways of considering the concept of motion:

> *Motion of an *object* in space does not belong in a pure science and thus not in geometry. For, that something is movable cannot be cognized *a priori* but only through experience. But motion, as the *describing* of a space, is a pure act of successive synthesis of the manifold in outer intuition in general through the productive imagination, and it belongs not only to geometry, but even to transcendental philosophy (B155n).

Motion as the describing of a space takes place in *pure* intuition: It is the motion of a mere mathematical point belonging, in the first instance, to pure geometry, but also, via its role in the figurative representation of time, to transcendental philosophy. By contrast, the motion of an actual object in space—that is, an empirical object—takes place in empirical intuition; and motion understood in this sense cannot, as Kant says, belong to a pure science; it can belong neither to geometry nor to transcendental philosophy.

It is striking, then, that a parallel distinction is present at the very beginning of the *Metaphysical Foundations*. After stating, in explication 1 of the first chapter, or Phoronomy, that "*matter* is the movable in space," Kant explains, in the first remark to this explication, that motion is here considered as that of a mere mathematical point:

> Since in phoronomy nothing is to be at issue except motion, no other property is here ascribed to the *subject* of motion, namely, matter, aside from *movability*. It can itself so far, therefore, also be considered as a point, and one abstracts in phoronomy from all inner constitution, and therefore also from the quantity of the movable, and concerns oneself only with motion and what can be considered as quantity in motion (speed and direction) (4:480).

In the second remark, however, Kant immediately introduces a quite different mode of consideration:

> If I am to explicate the concept of matter, not through a predicate that belongs to it itself as object, but only by relation to that cognitive faculty in which the representation can first of all be given to me, then every *object of the outer senses* is matter, and this would be the merely metaphysical explication thereof. Space, however, would be merely the form of all outer sensible intuition. . . . *Matter*, as opposed to *form*, would be that in the outer intuition which is an object of sensation, and thus the properly empirical element of sensible and outer intuition, because it can in no way be given *a priori*. In all experience something must be sensed, and that is the real of sensible intuition, and therefore the space in which we are to arrange our experience of motion must also be sensible—that is, it must be designated through what can be sensed—and this, as the totality of all objects of experience, and itself an object of experience, is called *empirical space* (4:481).

With respect to empirical space, moreover, as opposed to the pure form of outer sensible intuition, motion can certainly not be considered as an a priori concept:

> Since the *movability* of an object in space cannot be cognized *a priori*, and without instruction through experience, I could not, for precisely this reason, enumerate it under the pure concepts of the understanding in the

> *Critique of Pure Reason*; and . . . this concept, as empirical, could only find
> a place in a natural science, as applied metaphysics, which concerns itself
> with a concept given through experience, although in accordance with *a
> priori* principles (4:482).

Comparing the wording here with that in the footnote to B155, it is clear, I believe,
that precisely the same distinction is at work in both texts.[10]

Thus, the *Metaphysical Foundations* is brought into a priori connection, as it
were, with the transcendental philosophy of the *Critique* by means of a *transition*
from the pure concept of motion, as the describing of space in pure intuition, to
the empirical concept of motion, as the determination of an object in space in
empirical intuition. The first representation indeed plays a central role in the deduction of the objective reality of the categories. Nevertheless, it does not provide
actual objects corresponding to the categories, for these, as we have seen, must be
empirical objects. What it provides, rather, are *schemata* for the categories, where

> the schema of a pure concept of the understanding is something that can
> by no means be brought into an image, but is rather only the pure synthesis,
> according to a rule of unity by concepts in general, which the category
> expresses. And it is a transcendental product of the imagination that con-
> cerns the determination of inner sense in general, in accordance with con-
> ditions of its form (time), with respect to all representations, in so far as
> they are to cohere *a priori* in a concept according to the unity of appercep-
> tion (A142/B181).

This first schematization of the categories by means of the describing of space in
pure intuition, as "an action of the understanding on sensibility and its first application to objects of an intuition possible for us (and at the same time the ground
of all other applications)," then serves as such a ground precisely by securing the
basis in the understanding for mathematical construction in intuition and also,
and at the same time, for the concepts of alteration and succession. In particular,
the motion of a point involved in the drawing of a straight line yields a representation of *rectilinear inertial motion*—the privileged state of force-free motion serving as the foundation for all modern physics and thus for "pure natural science."
In finding an actual domain of concrete objects corresponding to the demands of
the categories, the understanding then has the task of *applying* these representations—those given by mathematical construction and the pure representation of
rectilinear inertia—so as to *seek out* a system of empirical objects whose behavior
can actually be described by them.

In applying the representation of motion to empirical objects, however, a fundamental problem immediately arises. In the fourth chapter or Phenomenology of
the *Metaphysical Foundations* Kant explains that "the movable, as such a thing,
becomes an object of experience, when a certain *object* (here a material thing) is

thought as *determined* with respect to the *predicate* of motion" (4:554). But in such a determination motion is always considered in relation to one or another given empirical space: As we change the empirical space relative to which the object is considered (as we change what we now call the reference frame), the predicate of motion as applied to this object is constantly changing as well.[11] How, then, is an objective and determinate predication here possible? The remainder of the Phenomenology chapter outlines a procedure whereby "all motion and rest [is] reduced to absolute space, if the appearance thereof is to be transformed into a determinate concept of experience (which unites all appearances)" (4:560). This procedure, as I have argued elsewhere, is modeled on Newton's argument in book III of the *Principia* for inferring the true or absolute motions in the solar system from the relative or apparent motions.[12] For Newton, the argument terminates in the center of mass frame of the solar system—a frame fixed very close to the center of the sun. For Kant, however, the procedure is to be indefinitely extended beyond this point: to the center of mass of the Milky Way galaxy, to the center of mass of a system of galaxies containing the Milky Way, to the center of mass of a system of such systems, and so on ad infinitum. And it is in this sense that the concept of absolute space, for Kant, is in the end "a necessary concept of reason, and thus nothing but a mere *idea*" (4:559).

The Kantian procedure for inferring the true motions from the apparent, and thus for making "the movable in so far as it, as such a thing, is an object of experience" first possible (4:554), is based, as is the Newtonian argument, on the application of geometry and the laws of motion (especially the third law of motion, the equality of action and reaction) to the appearances presented to us by the solar system from our vantage point here on the earth. And an essential ingredient in this procedure, of course, is the theory of universal gravitation, which is simultaneously inferred along with the true motions themselves. Since "the *action* of the universal attraction immediately exerted by each matter on all matters, and at all distances, is called *gravitation*" (4:518), it is clear that Kant's fundamental force of attraction is also given to us along with the same procedure. Moreover, although the role of Kant's fundamental force of repulsion in this procedure is not quite so transparent, it is clear that the *reflection of light* from the other heavenly bodies is what first makes it possible for us to perceive their relative positions (and thus relative motions) around us—a circumstance that Kant himself explicitly emphasizes in the Third Analogy (A213/B260). Kant seems to have this circumstance also in mind when explaining the complementary roles of attraction and repulsion in an important remark in the *Metaphysical Foundations* (4:509–510). For it is only by means of "that property whereby it fills space" that the determinate figure, quantity, and position of a [heavenly] body can first "strike our senses" and thereby underwrite "the first application of our concepts of *quantity* to matter, through which it first becomes possible for us to transform our outer perceptions into the empirical concept of a matter, as object in general."

A system of objects realizing the categories thereby emerges step by step, as the outcome of a kind of constructive procedure. The pure concepts of the understanding, independently of sensibility, provide us with the idea of a unified world of mutually interacting substances, bound together, and thereby constituting a single world, precisely by means of such interactions. And this idea, which is already fully expressed in the pre-Critical writings, is clearly modeled on, although also much more abstract and general than, the Newtonian system of universal gravitation.[13] In schematizing this idea in terms of the forms of sensibility, a process that is of course characteristic of the Critical period, we then obtain the idea of a system of substances in space, interacting with one another and thereby changing their states in time via some or another, otherwise entirely indeterminate forces. Moreover, since this process of schematization essentially involves the pure intuition of space, wherein the substances in question are arranged about us, as it were, and through which, accordingly, both they and we continually interact and move, the pure representation of motion, which makes both geometrical construction and the fundamental principle of mathematical physics (the law of rectilinear inertia) first possible, is also necessarily applicable to the world of substances in space as an object of experience in general.[14] In this way, in particular, we obtain a basis for a priori knowledge of such objects that is *both* metaphysical *and* mathematical. Nevertheless, in applying such an a priori basis to actual objects of experience, by starting from our particular vantage point and then working our way out, as it were, toward a fully objective description of this world, we find that a second, essentially empirical representation of motion, that of the motion of an object relative to one or another *empirical* space (material reference frame), is also required. And this circumstance leads to the problem of distinguishing true from apparent motion—a problem which is only solved, once again, by the Newtonian system of universal gravitation, and therefore, in accordance with this system, by the two particular fundamental forces of attraction and repulsion. The empirical concept of matter, a representation having one foot in the a priori basis for empirical knowledge provided by a combination of metaphysics (that is, *general* metaphysics) and mathematics, and the other foot in the necessary conditions for the application of this a priori basis to the actual objects of perception we in fact find arranged about us (the system of heavenly bodies), thus emerges naturally as the solution to *Kant's* problem.

The system of heavenly bodies described by Newtonian universal gravitation thereby confers objective reality on the empirical concept of matter, and it is precisely the need for actual perceptually given instances here that makes this concept a genuinely *empirical* one. By contrast, although the same system of heavenly bodies is also the only system so far known to us in which the pure concepts of the understanding are actually fully realized in experience, we cannot conclude, in addition, that it also confers objective reality on these concepts. For the role of the categories, as we have seen, is to provide the a priori conditions that make possible *any and all* objects of experience, including all those objects of experience not yet accounted for by universal gravitation (those essentially involving chemical phenomena, electric and magnetic phenomena, thermal phenomena, biological phenomena, and so on)—objects that will only receive their proper a priori grounding as empirical natural science continually advances beyond Newtonian physics. Finally, since the a priori basis for such grounding nonetheless remains identically one and the same throughout the indefinitely extended continual advance of our knowledge—and is given precisely, in fact, by the a priori schematization of the categories in pure intuition—it is just this a priori schematization, and not any particular empirically given objects made possible thereby, that, in the end, confers objective reality on the categories.

NOTES

I am indebted to discussions with and comments from Konstantin Pollok, during our work together on the Kantian conception of motion in connection with his essay, "Kant's Critical Concepts of Motion." I am particularly indebted to both Pollok and Daniel Sutherland for help with the notes and references. I would also like to acknowledge helpful comments from Daniel Warren on a previous draft.

1. All quotations here are from the preface to the *Metaphysical Foundations* and, in particular, from 4:478. All translations are mine.
2. All quotations here pertaining to substance and the quantity of matter are from 4:541–42.
3. The view that the content of the concept of matter is a priori, and that it designates simply an arbitrary object of outer sense, is represented especially by P. Plaass, *Kants Theorie der Naturwissenschaft* (Göttingen: Vandenhoeck and Ruprecht, 1965), translated as *Kant's Theory of Natural Science* (Dordrecht: Kluwer, 1994). For Plaass, whereas the content of the concept is a priori, its objective reality can only be given empirically—by the fact that there are in fact objects of outer sense. A similar view is represented by M. Washburn, "The Second Edition of the Critique: Toward an Understanding of Its Nature and Genesis," *Kant-Studien* 66 (1975): 277–90, who holds, apparently following Plaass, that the concept of matter is empirical only in that experience is needed to show that it is nonempty.
4. That the concept of matter can be mathematically constructed in pure intuition is explicitly asserted by Washburn, "The Second Edition," 290; he also asserts, accordingly, that the real possibility and objective reality of the concept can thereby be demonstrated a priori (289, n. 41). Washburn does not explain how this is supposed to be consistent with the idea that experience is needed to show that the concept is nonempty.
5. That the concept of matter, and the project of the *Metaphysical Foundations*, is needed to demonstrate the objective reality of the categories, is a central thesis of E. Förster, "Is There 'A Gap' in Kant's Critical System?" *Journal for the History of Philosophy* 25 (1987): 533–55. According to Förster, the *Metaphysical Foundations* was written precisely to fill this yawning "gap" in the Critical system, and it was Kant's later conviction that the *Metaphysical Foundations* also fails that led to the so-called "transition" project of the *Opus postumum*. For a different view of the transition project and the "gap" it was intended to fill see my *Kant and the Exact Sciences* (Cambridge: Harvard University Press, 1992), chap. 5.

6. Contrary to Plaass, then, it appears that the *content* of the concept of matter is clearly empirical: It explicitly includes (as a partial concept) the empirical concept of impenetrability and is precisely thereby distinguished from the pure a priori concept of something real in space.

7. Thus, I do not see how the content of the concept of matter can be a priori while, at the same time, the question of its objective reality or real possibility is empirical (compare notes 3, 4, and 6). Kant's discussion of (real) possibility in the Postulates of Empirical Thought leaves room for only two types of concepts: a priori concepts and empirical concepts. The real possibility of the latter "can only be gathered from their actuality in experience," whereas that of the former "can only occur [in so far as they are] formal and objective conditions of an experience in general" (A223/B271).

8. Kant further asserts in this same passage that "the understanding is taught only by examples from corporeal nature what the conditions are under which such concepts can alone have objective reality—that is, meaning and truth" (4:478). This does not mean, in my view, that only the objects of corporeal nature provide objective reality for the categories, but rather that without the objects of corporeal nature (the only actual instances or examples of the categories known to us) we would have no idea what the conditions for the objective reality of the categories actually are—which conditions, however, are themselves much more general than those of corporeal nature (see below).

9. See my *Kant and the Exact Sciences*, chaps. 3 and 4, and "Causal Laws and the Foundations of Natural Science," in *The Cambridge Companion to Kant*, ed. Paul Guyer (Cambridge: Cambridge University Press, 1992), 161–99.

10. A few pages later in the Phoronomy Kant elucidates the mere motion of a mathematical point involved in the first remark to explication 1 as follows (4:489): "In phoronomy, since I am acquainted with matter through no other property but its movability, and may thus consider it only as a point, motion can only be considered as the *describing of a space*. However, I do this in such a way that I attend not only, as in geometry, to the space described but also to the time in which, and thus to the speed with which, a point describes the space." Thus I cannot follow Plaass (*Kants Theorie*, §5.2) when he entirely disassociates the "describing of a space" at B155n from the concept of motion of the *Metaphysical Foundations*— and, in particular, from the phoronomical concept. This same disassociation is evident in K. Cramer's otherwise very rich account of the concept of motion, in *Nicht-reine synthetische Urteile a priori* (Heidelberg: Carl Winter, 1985), where the discussion of B155n in chapter 3 considers only "the motion of an object in space" and omits the describing of a space, whereas the discussion of phoronomical motion in chapter 4 similarly fails to consider the parallel passage at 4:489. Yet I am also unable to follow K. Gloy, *Die Kantische Theorie der Naturwissenschaft* (Berlin: de Gruyter, 1976), who, by giving exclusive emphasis to the a priori concept of motion as the describing of a space (see especially §16), fails to consider the explicitly empirical elements introduced in the second remark to explication 1 of the Phoronomy.

11. This same problem is the main theme of the second remark to explication 1 of the Phoronomy considered above; and thus it is precisely here, in my view, that the crucial transition from a pure to an empirical representation of motion takes place (compare note 10).

12. See the references cited in note 9.

13. That Newtonian universal gravitation consistently provides Kant with his model for a fully realized system of substances coexisting in space—and thus for the fundamental meta-

physical concepts of substance, force, and interaction—is sufficient to explain, in my view, why the preface to the *Metaphysical Foundations* insists that without the metaphysics of corporeal nature even general metaphysics or transcendental philosophy would be empty. But this does not mean, once again, that only the objects of corporeal nature can provide objective reality for the categories. Compare note 8.

14. For the connection between motion (of the subject) in space and specifically *geometrical* construction see my "Geometry, Construction, and Intuition in Kant and his Successors," in *Between Logic and Intuition: Essays in Honor of Charles Parsons*, ed. G. Scher and R. Tieszen (Cambridge: Cambridge University Press, 2000).

4

Kant on Rational Cosmology

Eric Watkins

KANT'S views on rational cosmology[1] have not received a great deal of attention for a variety of reasons.[2] One likely reason is that Kant does not seem to place any special emphasis on rational cosmology in his Critical publications, given that he neither uses it as a standard technical term[3] nor designates it in any consistent fashion as one of the main branches of metaphysics.[4] Further, one might think that Kant's attitude toward rational cosmology is similar to his attitude toward rational psychology and rational theology insofar as he considers these disciplines to be primarily dogmatic. The main reason in virtue of which rational psychology's and rational theology's arguments must be fallacious (i.e., it must be illegitimate to assert synthetic claims merely on the basis of an analysis of a given concept) would seem to apply to rational cosmology as well. Insofar as the Antinomies are supposed to reveal the contradictions into which reason is inevitably drawn when it attempts to determine the fundamental features of the world, the Antinomies, too, might naturally be interpreted as showing that rational cosmology is entirely dialectical and thus has no positive consequences for Kant's own natural philosophy. Finally, Kant's acceptance of a broadly Newtonian dynamical and mechanical physics[5] leads many to focus on Kant's relation to Newton, implicitly assuming that his adherence to fundamentally Newtonian principles would preclude the possibility that an essentially Wolffian rational cosmology might have a significant influence on Kant.

In this chapter I argue that Kant's views on rational cosmology play a surprisingly important role in his overall philosophical system. To this end, I first briefly explain the fundamental aspects and principles of rational cosmology as it was understood by Baumgarten. I then explore how Kant develops four principles of rational cosmology that stem either directly or indirectly from Baumgarten. I conclude by considering how Kant's views on rational cosmology fit into his Critical philosophy as developed in the *Critique of Pure Reason*. The thesis I defend in this final section is that Kant's four cosmological principles are related in close ways to his Principles of Pure Understanding. Thus, Kant's views on rational cosmology form a crucial, independent part of his theoretical philosophy. This implies that the Critical turn does not consist in a wholesale rejection of ontological issues in favor of epistemological ones, and it also implies that Kant's attitude toward rational cosmology is significantly different from that toward rational psychology and rational theology insofar as the former plays a positive, constitutive role that the latter two do not seem to. But first we must briefly consider the proper historical context for these issues, namely Alexander Baumgarten's *Metaphysica*.

1. RATIONAL COSMOLOGY IN BAUMGARTEN

Baumgarten's *Metaphysica*, which Kant used as a textbook for several decades, divides metaphysics into four branches: ontology, rational cosmology, psychology, and theology. Each section begins with a definition of the relevant object (being in general, the world, the soul, and God) and then analytically derives a variety of principles from more fundamental, ultimately self-evident principles, such as the principles of contradiction and sufficient reason.[6] Baumgarten's discussion of cosmology divides into three main chapters. The first chapter introduces the notion of the world, with sections explaining both positive and negative concepts of the world. The second chapter considers the parts of the world, treating both the simples out of which the world is composed and the composites they thereby form. The third chapter discusses the perfection of the world, with sections on the idea of the perfection of the world and on the means for its perfection. Throughout these chapters, Baumgarten discusses a wide range of important issues. For example, his treatment of the perfection of the world considers the three theories of causality widely disputed in the seventeenth and eighteenth centuries, namely, pre-established harmony, occasionalism, and physical influx, as well as the nature and possibility of miracles. In various other passages he discusses egoism, materialism, idealism, atomism, and corpuscularianism. He also attempts to prove that there can be no change in the world without motion (§415) and, though he does not mention Newton or Huygens, he argues for the law of the equality of action and reaction (§412) after first proving that action cannot occur without reaction (§410).[7]

But rather than focusing on these topics (which deserve discussions of their own), let us turn to the chapter on the concept of the world where Baumgarten introduces the following set of cosmological principles, which govern all events in the world:

> §382. Fate is the necessity of events in the world. Fate from the absolute necessity of the world is Spinozistic and is not a being, §361, 105, to be assumed either in this or in any other world, §354, 58.

§383. An event in the world of which the sufficient reason is unknown is chance. Pure chance, for which there is no sufficient reason, is impossible, §22, and is to be assumed neither in this nor in any other world, §354, 58. §386. An event without a proximate sufficient reason is an absolute leap. An event without an ordinary proximate sufficient reason is a relative leap. §387. What exists without any proximate sufficient reason, §27, exists through pure chance, §22, 383, such an absolute leap is impossible, §386, 284, and is to be assumed in neither this nor any other world, §354, 58 (17: 107–108).

Accordingly, Baumgarten presents three cosmological principles that are commonly referred to in abbreviated form as the principles of no fate (*non datur fatum*), no chance (*non datur casus*), and no leap (*non datur saltus*), which is sometimes also referred to as the law of continuity (*lex continui*).[8] To these three principles, Kant will add a fourth principle, closely related to the law of continuity, namely the principle of no gap (*non datur hiatus/abyssus*).

2. Kant on the Four Cosmological Principles

What is remarkable about these cosmological principles and what shall require detailed explanation is the fact that Kant *accepts* all four principles in his Critical period (though the precise sense in which he accepts them may differ significantly from Baumgarten's). After the Third Postulate of Empirical Thought (following the Refutation of Idealism), Kant states:

> The proposition that nothing happens through blind chance (*in mundo non datur casus*) is an a priori law of nature; likewise the proposition that no necessity in nature is blind, but is rather conditioned, consequently understandable necessity (*non datur fatum*). . . . The principle of continuity forbade any leap in the series of appearances (alterations) (*in mundo non datur saltus*), but also any gap or cleft between two appearances in the sum of all empirical intuitions in space (*non datur hiatus*) (A228–29/B280–81).

Because Kant's explanation of these principles in the first *Critique* is so brief (presumably due to the fact that he can simply assume that his eighteenth century audience is sufficiently familiar with these principles), we must look to other sources in order to be able to explain this passage, i.e., to explain how Kant can accept what might appear to be dogmatic principles in his Critical period.

The best sources for Kant's views on traditional metaphysical topics are the transcripts from his metaphysics lectures, since, instead of focusing on an independent and autonomous project as the first *Critique* does, they react more or less directly to specific claims advanced by either Baumgarten or others in the Wolffian tradition. Accordingly, we shall turn to the various cosmology lecture transcripts to consider Kant's discussion of each of these principles, starting with fate and chance.

2.1. Fate and Chance

Kant's discussion of the principle of no fate is, in one important sense, uniform throughout his metaphysics lectures, for he consistently rejects fate.[9] More significant, however, is Kant's discussion of the different kinds of fate and his reasons for rejecting fate. For he distinguishes (with some textual basis in Baumgarten) between absolute fate and conditional fate (28:663). Absolute fate, which he sometimes also calls blind destiny, occurs when the necessity of the relevant event(s) is absolute, while conditional fate involves merely conditional necessity. The idea underlying this distinction is not Leibniz's distinction between God's antecedent and consequent will,[10] but rather the idea that conditional necessity is a necessity that is based on a ground, cause, or law of some sort, whereas absolute necessity is a necessity that has no ground, cause, or law that necessitates the event. Given this distinction, Kant's basis for rejecting absolute fate is expressed most clearly in a passage in the Metaphysics Mrongovius lectures (1782–83):

> Of that, that something should be without any grounds and causes, and yet be necessary, we have not the slightest concept. For we find nothing at all contradictory in this, that something would also not have happened. To want to explain something by destiny is nonsensical, for calling upon destiny just means that I cannot explain something (29:926).[11]

In this passage, Kant seems to be raising two separate objections to absolute fate or destiny. The first objection is that the necessity of absolute fate lacks justification or grounding. Something is necessary if its denial involves a contradiction. But denying an event that is allegedly the result of absolute fate does not involve a contradiction because, as Hume famously points out, the denial of any particular event (i.e., a matter of fact) can never involve a contradiction. Further, since absolute fate precludes any ground, cause, or law, no ground, cause, or law can be used to generate a contradiction. Because no contradiction can be generated, the necessity involved in absolute fate cannot be justified as well. The second objection is that absolute fate, even if it were somehow justified, would violate valid principles of explanation. In an earlier passage (from the Metaphysics Herder lectures [1762–64]) Kant explains that nature and freedom alone "are the two explanatory grounds of our understanding" (28:200) and that explanations that do not appeal to these two grounds "serve only as a cushion for ignorance, and deprive the understanding of all use" (28:200). Similarly in a passage from the Metaphysics Mrongovius lectures: "Destinies are deviations from maxims. . . . Destinies conflict with the interest of reason. For if I accept them, then I must renounce the use of reason" (29:

925–26). Accordingly, we must appeal either to nature (in the form of the laws of nature) or freedom (in the form of maxims or the laws of practical reason) in order to provide satisfactory explanations.[12]

Of course, Kant's endorsement of explanatory appeals to freedom is limited by significant constraints.[13] The main constraint is that no nonmoral or physical event can be explained by means of freedom, a point Kant makes explicitly in the Metaphysics Mrongovius lectures: "When we do something, insofar as it proceeds from physical causes, we must explain it from the laws of nature and not from spontaneity, otherwise we would come to intelligible grounds which belong to the noumenal world; and that would be passing over into another genus, that takes place only in moral relations" (29:926). At the same time, as Kant's Third Antinomy demonstrates, explanations based solely on the laws of nature are necessarily incomplete. Interestingly enough, Kant makes this point as early as the L1 lectures (from the mid 1770s): "The necessity of nature cannot be the explanatory ground of everything; the first ground of origination must happen through freedom, because nothing but freedom can furnish a ground of origination" (28:200).

The fundamental point of Kant's discussion of fate in his metaphysics lectures is that one cannot accept events as necessary unless one can identify a ground that our understanding can comprehend. As it turns out, the only grounds our understanding can comprehend are derived from nature or freedom, and grounds of freedom can be invoked only under certain conditions. Thus, the only kind of necessity that could be unconditionally endorsed would be one based on the laws of nature. Since absolute fate or destiny asserts a necessity that appeals neither to such laws nor even to freedom (insofar as Kant sees destiny as a deviation from maxims), Kant rejects fate as unintelligible.

This account, based on Kant's lecture transcripts, is consistent with Kant's brief rejection of fate in the first *Critique*, which similarly invokes the laws of nature. After making the preliminary point that necessity applies not to the existence of things or substances but rather to that of their states, Kant notes:

> Thus it is not the existence of things (substances) but of their state of which alone we can cognize the necessity, and moreover only from other states, which are given in perception, in accordance with empirical laws of causality. From this it follows that the criterion of necessity lies solely in the law of possible experience that everything that happens is determined *a priori* through its cause in appearance. Hence we cognize the necessity only of *effects* in nature, the causes of which are given to us, and the mark of necessity in existence does not reach beyond the field of possible experience. . . . Necessity therefore concerns only the relations of appearances in accordance with the dynamical law of causality, and the possibility grounded upon it of inferring *a priori* from some given existence (a cause) to another

existence (the effect). Everything that happens is hypothetically necessary (A227–28/B279–80).

In short, since (1) necessity applies only to states and (2) the laws of nature dictate necessity only for the relation between states, the only necessity we can cognize is hypothetical, i.e., we can know that state B is necessary only if both state A and a law of nature asserting 'if A, then B' are given. Further, this necessity must be internal to nature, i.e., state A must be one that we can cognize in nature. But if the sense of necessity at issue is hypothetical and internal to nature, there can be no absolute fate or destiny, which necessarily appeals beyond nature (and, for that matter, beyond freedom as well).

Kant's discussion of chance parallels his treatment of fate in many ways, although (or precisely because) the position to be excluded in this case is the direct opposite of fate.[14] For the merely conditional necessity established by the arguments that exclude fate is still a necessity based on the laws of nature. Accordingly, it rules out events that have no necessity or cause whatsoever, that is, chance.

Kant's fullest explanation of his rejection of chance is developed in his L1 lectures. He explains blind chance or accident as follows: "Blind accident is an event which is contingent, and indeed, that the contingency takes place in every regard. But something can be contingent in one regard and necessary in another regard; only that which is contingent in *every* regard is a blind accident. . . . If I assume a blind accident, something contingent absolutely and in every regard, then it is an exception to all laws and all grounds" (28:199–200). The idea Kant is expressing here is that if something were truly to occur by chance (in the strict sense of the word), it would be absolutely contingent. But since "every ground determines its consequence necessarily" (28:41), such an occurrence would lack entirely a ground or cause. Given the principle of sufficient reason, it is clear that chance cannot occur.

2.2. Gaps

Kant does not explicitly refer to the principle of no gap in his published work until his Critical period and, in line with this fact, it does not appear in the metaphysics lectures until the Metaphysics Mrongovius lectures (1782–83). At this point Kant also explicitly orders the four cosmological principles according to the headings of his table of judgments/categories. The principle of no leap is related to quality, no gap to quantity, no chance to relation, and no fate to modality.[16] Kant's assignment of each of these principles to a categorial heading provides a plausible explanation for the addition of the law of no gap. Only if there are four cosmological principles can one be assigned to each heading, and it would be natural (at least for Kant) to think that the world would have quantitative, qualitative, relational (i.e., causal), and modal features and thus that the world must be determinable in some fundamental way with respect to each feature. Kant provides a partial explanation of his particular assignments in two cases. He suggests that the principle of no chance falls under the heading of relation since, as we saw in the previous section, chance is excluded by causal considerations which are expressed in the relational categories of causality and community. One might think that the strong parallels between fate and chance would imply that fate too would fall under the heading of relation. Kant argues, however, that fate belongs to modality insofar as it adds "to the causal determination the concept of necessity" (A228/B281).

What Kant means by a gap is empty space or empty time, and he distinguishes between empty space and time within the world from empty space and time without, since in some cases his arguments are different for each. In the Metaphysics Mrongovius lectures his main argument against empty space and time outside the world is based on the familiar point that we cannot comprehend or know such a space or time given that they lie outside any possible experience. Further, since the sensible world has no determinate boundaries and knowledge of such boundaries would be required in order to know that any empty space or time is outside the world, we can never know space or time as *extra mundanum*.

His argument against empty space and time within the world is fourfold. First, like empty space and time outside the world, they cannot be an object of experience; we could have, in principle, no evidence for them.[16] Second, Kant presents an argument against them based on an analysis of change. The claim is that they would be inconsistent with change. "For if a body merely moved in an empty space, then nothing would be altered, neither in itself nor outside it. There would thus have happened no alteration at all" (29:922). In short, the motion of a body in an empty space or time (where motion is understood as change of place) would, *per impossibile*, not involve any change, since the body that is changing its state with respect to empty space or time is changing its state with respect to nothing, that is, it is not in fact changing its state. Third, if two (presumably spatiotemporal) objects in the world were separated by empty space or time, then they would be separated causally, but, given Kant's definition of the world,[17] these things would not belong to the same world, which is contrary to the initial assumption (as well as to Kant's Critical claim that there is only one space and time). Kant's final argument is that a gap would entail a leap,[18] but since, as we shall see below, leaps are not possible, neither are gaps. It is to leaps that we now turn.

2.3. Leaps and the Law of Continuity

Kant's views on the law of continuity are by far the most complex and most interesting. Kant defines leaps and continua by noting that a leap "is an immediate sequence of two states wholly unconnected with each other, without passing through the states that are between them" (29:863), whereas a quantity is continuous if "one cannot determine in and for itself how many parts are in it. Continuity is thus the absolute indeterminability of the parts in the whole" (28:200). Continuity has this feature in virtue of the fact that for any continuous quantity there are always further points or moments between any two points or moments; two points or moments are never immediately next to each other if they are points or moments of a continuous magnitude.

As early as the Herder lectures (1762–64) Kant distinguishes between logical, mathematical, and physical versions of this law.[19] Kant understands logical continuity to mean that whatever applies to something having a certain magnitude will also apply to it if it has any other degree of that magnitude (28:41).[20] One of Kant's examples is that of a body in motion. If a body is in motion, whatever quantity one attributes to it (e.g., extension) will also be applicable to it when it is at rest (i.e., if it has a vanishingly small degree of motion) (28:662). Kant seems to accept such a version of the law of continuity, though without giving any explicit argument for it.

Kant understands the physical law of continuity to apply to kinds or species of things and to imply that "no kind or species is so closely related to another that another intermediate kind or intermediate species might not be able to occur between them" (29:921). One typical version of this law states that all beings are ordered continuously according to their degree of perfection.[21] If God is to create the best possible world, then he must create as much being as possible with the greatest amount of diversity. If God cannot create two beings with the same degree of perfection,[22] then creating the best possible world implies creating one being for every possible degree of perfection, that is, an infinity of beings, each with a different degree of perfection. In this way, there would be a continuum of beings from the very least to the very greatest (excepting God, who lies outside the series). Kant does not think that any such version of the law of continuity can be proved (29:921–22). In fact, in the Dohna lectures (1792–93) Kant argues against it on the grounds that "it is a mere chimera, for if we are talking about things, then there is no necessary ground of connection for it at all" (28:662). Similarly, in the L1 lectures Kant states: "If creatures exist there must still be a space between one and the other creature, in which there is no infinite degree of intermediate creatures; thus the physical law of continuity is only *comparative*" (28:205).

It is what Kant calls the mathematical law of continuity, however, that is of greatest interest, not only because it "is the first law of nature, whose necessity can be comprehended *a priori*" (28:203) but also because it applies to a wide variety of important topics: (a) both extensive and intensive magnitudes, (b) composition, and (c) alteration or change. Consider first intensive and extensive magnitudes. Kant applies the law of continuity to extensive and intensive magnitudes by noting that between zero and any particular quantum there are an infinite number of intermediate degrees. This law clearly holds for extensive magnitudes such as space and time, since they are obviously continuous quanta,[23] but it also holds for intensive magnitudes such as the real in space and time insofar as it is a quantum. As Kant notes in the Metaphysics Mrongovius lectures: "For internally the real is the sensations, externally that which corresponds to them. But sensation has a degree and an infinite multitude of degrees" (29:862). Kant illustrates this point with the example of bodies. "Each body has extensive magnitude insofar as it is in space and in time, and also intensive magnitude or a degree of reality. No bodies are so closely related to one another that the difference between them could not be still smaller" (29:863). Kant's point here is that in the mere comparison of any quantities (whether extensive or intensive magnitudes) any differences must be related as continuous magnitudes.

Kant also applies the law of continuity to composition in the Metaphysics Mrongovius lectures as follows: "With respect to quanta, the simple is zero. From that to the quantum are infinitely many parts. A thing thus consists not of finite degrees, also not of finite parts, for that would be an infinite given, but rather the regression in division is infinite" (29:862–63). In other words, the law of continuity implies that the world is not composed of simples, a view that directly contradicts the monadologist's position.[24] The monadologist's position is that since the (spatio-temporal) world is a composite, it must ultimately consist of (either finitely or infinitely many) simple parts. Kant objects that the world cannot consist of simple parts given an appropriate understanding of continuity. For spatial parts cannot be simple (on account of the infinite divisibility of space), and spatial simples, that is, points, cannot constitute a spatially extended world, since such a world has a quantum that cannot be attained through the addition of (even infinitely many) points,[25] given that the magnitude of a simple point is zero.[26]

In the L1 lectures Kant qualifies his claim that there are no simples in appearances by noting: "There is indeed something simple, that is, a point in space and a moment in time; but those are not parts of space and of time; for otherwise one could think of them before space and time. But now I think a moment in time and a point in space; thus, they are determinations and not parts" (28:204). In other words, there may be simples in the world, but they are not *parts* of the world, that is, they do not *compose* the world. Rather, they are mere determinations, limits, or boundaries of what is not simple (28:201).[27] He then continues his line of reasoning in the L1 lectures as follows:

> But are substances nonetheless simple? Of course! But when I see bodies, then I see no substances, but rather appearances. I also cannot at all perceive the substances, for no being, other than the creator alone, can perceive the substances of another thing. . . . Although all experiences happen through the senses; thus, we can still anticipate appearances through the understanding, and comprehend *a priori* the conditions of objects (28:204).

In this passage Kant seems to be claiming that bodies qua appearances do not consist of substances; rather, substances exist only in the noumenal world.[28] However, Kant will change his position on this point in his Critical period. For Kant comes to argue that the concept of substance, which is thought through the understanding, must apply to objects given through the senses. But since objects of the senses cannot be simple, Kant must revise his conception of substance by giving up the Leibnizian requirement that being must have true unity, that is, simplicity.

Another significant application of the law of continuity is to alteration or change. This law states simply that all change is continuous, that is, if an object changes from one state to another, it must successively pass through all of the continuous states that lie between these two states. Kant's position on the continuity of change in the first *Critique* might seem to be ambiguous. On the one hand, he seems to accept this law in the Second Analogy when he concludes: "That is, now, the law of the continuity of all alteration, the ground of which is this: That neither time nor appearance in time consists of smallest parts, and that nevertheless in its alteration the state of a thing passes through all these parts, as elements, to its second state" (A209/B254). Similarly, in the Anticipations of Perception Kant notes: "The proposition that all alteration (transition of a thing from one state into another) is also continuous could be proved here easily and with mathematical self-evidence" (A171/B213). On the other hand, there is also textual evidence that seems to contradict this view. For the passage just quoted from the Anticipations of Perception continues:

. . . if the causality of an alteration in general, did not lie entirely beyond the boundaries of a transcendental philosophy and presuppose empirical principles. For the understanding gives us no inkling *a priori* that a cause is possible which alters the state of things, i.e., determines them to the opposite of a certain given state, not merely because it simply does not give us insight into the possibility of this (for this insight is lacking to us in many *a priori* cognitions) but rather because alterability concerns only certain determinations of appearances, about which experience alone can teach us, while their cause is to be found in the unalterable. But since we have before us here nothing that we can use except the pure fundamental concepts of all possible experience, in which there must be nothing at all empirical, we cannot anticipate general natural science, which is built upon certain fundamental experiences, without injuring the unity of the system (A171–72/B213).[29]

In this passage Kant is expressing reservations about the law of continuity, apparently based on the idea that "experience alone" can provide us with knowledge of the continuity or discontinuity of the changes that appearances undergo.

Fortunately, Kant's metaphysics lectures clarify his position on precisely this point. First, the metaphysics lectures eliminate any doubt about whether Kant accepts or rejects the law of the continuity of change. For Kant provides an explicit justification of the law of the continuity of change in a wide range of lectures. Consider, for example, the following passage from the L1 lectures:

Every state[30] has two limits (*terminos*): from which (*a quo*) and to which (*ad quem*). Each of these states is in a particular distinct moment. With each transition the thing is in two moments distinct from one another. The moment in which the thing is in the one state is distinct from the moment in which the thing arrives in the other state. But between two moments there is a time, just as between two points a space. Thus the transition happens in time; for in the moments in which it moves from A to B there is a time in which it is neither in A nor in B. But in this time it is in the mutation, in the transition. Thus a thing never goes immediately from one state into the other, but rather through all intermediate states, and thereby the alteration of the state of a thing is possible. The differences of the states all have a magnitude, and in this magnitude is continuity (28:201).[31]

The main idea here is that due to the continuity of time there will always be a period of time between the two states that represent the starting and ending points of a change, and it is during this period of time that the transition through all of the intermediate states that lie continuously between the starting and ending points must occur.

Now one might object that this argument begs the question by simply assuming that the intermediate states must all be gone through.[32] Why is it not possible for an object to change its state from, say, A to D without going through B and C?[33] While Kant does not explicitly formulate this objection, he makes two points that provide resources for a response. First, he seems to advance the following line of argument. In virtue of the infinite divisibility of time one can identify intermediary moments that lie between the moments in which the object is in states A and D. Now, the object must be in some state during these moments. The natural option is that the object is in states B and C during the intermediary moments. This option seems even more natural (perhaps natural enough to seem compelling) if one considers how this possibility would apply to the case of motion—which is Kant's primary instance of change.[34] If a body is said to move along a line segment from point A to point D, it is very natural to assume that it does so by passing through points B and C (which lie between points A and D). If it did not pass through points B and C, then it must simply have passed out of existence when it 'left' point A and then popped back into existence when it 'arrived' at point D. Obviously, bodies do not move in such a fashion.[35] Therefore, they must pass through all intermediate points when they change from one state to another.

Second, Kant seems to appeal to a claim that is based on an analysis of the concept of a leap. In the Dohna lectures, after introducing the law of continuity, Kant notes that a "leap is the immediate connection of a conditioned (of a consequence) with a distant ground without an intermediate ground [*Grund ohne Zwischengrund*]—[which is] a contradiction" (28:662). The idea is that it is simply a contradiction to claim that A conditions D without A being connected to D either immediately or mediately (that is, through intermediate grounds). Now A cannot ground D immediately because A is, by definition, a distant ground. But A cannot ground D through intermediates such as B and C, since intermediate grounds are excluded. Yet if A cannot ground D either immediately or mediately, then it cannot ground D at all, which contradicts the claim that A (qua distant ground) is connected with D (qua conditioned). Kant might hope to invoke this analytic claim by arguing that since there are infinitely many degrees between any two states (say, A and D), any ground that explains why the object in question comes to be in state D from state A must also be able to explain the transition from state A to state D, that is, must be able to explain how the object "moved" from state A to state D through all of the intermediate states. If one were to accept a leap, one would be accepting a ground explaining why the object comes to be in state D from state A that did not also explain how the object "moved" through all of the intermediate states. Since such a ground is impossible, all change must be continuous.[36]

Kant applies the law of the continuity of change to a variety of particular instances. With respect to physics, for example, Kant argues that the law applies both to speed and direction.[37] It also applies to the construction of geometrical figures, where Kant refers to Kästner's discussion of the issue, and to optics, where Kant cites Newton's account of refraction as an instance of the law. Kant even suggests that it holds true of our conscious states (an example of an intensive magnitude): "If there are obscure representations in my soul, then it must seek to make the representations ever clearer until they finally obtain an adequate degree of clarity" (29:864).

All this evidence from Kant's metaphysics lectures suggests that he accepts the law of the continuity of change. But how is Kant's acceptance of this law to be reconciled with his statement (quoted above) that only experience could determine the truth of this law? In the Dohna lectures, Kant explains that "we always make leaps, for we cannot possibly cognize the infinite intermediate states" (28:662). From this remark it is clear that the point behind the reservations Kant expresses in the first *Critique* is that we do not immediately perceive all the intermediate states that an object goes through in changing from one state to another. The law of continuity expresses an ontological, not an epistemological claim: There is a continuous series of intermediate states that lie between the initial and terminal states of a changing object. This claim in no way implies that we know all the intermediate states. The only way to know these intermediate states is by consulting what is given to us in experience; it is not possible to infer any precise information about these states solely from the initial and terminal states. In this way Kant can assert the law of the continuity of change as an ontological principle without threatening his epistemological doctrine that knowledge requires experience.

3. Rational Cosmology and the Critical Kant

To summarize briefly what has been established in Kant's discussions of the principles of no fate, no chance, no gap, and no leap in his metaphysics lectures: It is now clear that Kant not only accepts these four principles of rational cosmology, but also presents a number of arguments for them and applies them in a wide variety of contexts. The issue that must still be addressed, however, is how these principles (along with the arguments Kant provides for them) relate to Kant's position as it is presented in the first *Critique*.

One might initially have been tempted to think that any principles forming part of rational cosmology are for that reason simply dogmatic remainders from Kant's pre-Critical period that he would (or at least should) reject in his Critical period.[39] That is, one might have thought that these four cosmological principles were applicable only to the noumenal world and as such could not constitute knowledge in the full sense of the first *Critique*, since they could be, at best, analytic principles derived from a nonempirical concept of the world. However, in light of our discussion above, such an attitude toward both rational cosmology in general and these four principles in particular seems much less attractive. For not only are these four principles endorsed throughout the Critical period (e.g., in the Mrongovius and Dohna lectures), but they also do not appear to be dogmatic. Further, in the K3 lectures (1794–95) Kant explicitly states with uncharacteristic clarity that they can be established for the *phenomenal* world:

> The world is thus a substantial whole which is not part of another. . . . Now if one thinks the world as noumenon, then it is nothing further than an absolute whole of substances; but one is also not in the position a priori to determine further what it might have as properties or determinations. But if one thinks the world as phenomenon, therefore the things in space and time as their real relations, in which they must stand opposed to each other, then the following four principles can be established, under which the determinations of the world must be thought: [in the world there is no (1) abyss, (2) leap, (3) chance (blind accident), fate (blind necessity) *in mundo non datur* (1) *abyssus*, (2) *saltus*, (3) *casus* (. . .), *fatum* (. . .)] (29:1006).

This brief passage is highly suggestive about Kant's understanding of rational cosmology and of how the four cosmological principles fit into rational cosmology as a whole. Kant initially defines the world in such a manner that its most general features will hold for any world whatsoever (that is, for both the phenomenal and noumenal worlds). Accordingly, the world is "a substantial whole that is not part of another."[39] He also distinguishes between the matter and the form of the world in such a way that the matter is substance and the form mutual interaction. (In this way, the form of the world binds the matter together in such a way that we can speak of a single world with a plurality of elements in it.) After noting the principal traits that can be attributed to any world whatsoever (that is, merely in virtue of being a world), he then distinguishes between the noumenal and phenomenal worlds, specifying what further traits will hold for each. Accordingly, although he expresses skepticism in this passage about the possibility of determining any further features of the noumenal world, numerous other passages make it clear that more can be said: for example, that its substances must be finite in number and simple in nature. Similarly, Kant understands the phenomenal world to consist of infinitely many substances that are not simple in nature. Given this general understanding of the structure of rational cosmology, this passage clearly indicates that the four cosmological principles are to be understood as principles that pertain specifically to the phenomenal world and are thus not dogmatic principles that apply to the noumenal world.

One might still object, however, that the four cosmological principles are, if not dogmatic remainders from his pre-Critical period, then at least merely analytic principles and, in virtue of being principles that concern the negative concept of the world as well, do not really add any significant content to what the first *Critique* establishes. The first point to note is that the fact that Kant's four cosmological principles concern the negative concept of the world does not imply that they are analytic, just as the negative aspect of the claim that God does not exist does not imply that it is analytic. For, as an existential claim, it is clearly synthetic. Further, as we saw above, many of the arguments Kant develops for these principles were not based solely on an analysis of the concepts involved, but rather involved other significant principles (e.g., epistemological and ontological considerations).

Since these principles are neither dogmatic nor analytic, it is natural to consider what relationship holds between these principles (or rational cosmology in general) and the Principles of Pure Understanding, given that the latter, like the former, are synthetic and apply to the phenomenal world. I would suggest that one can discern at least a loose correlation between these four principles and the Principles of Pure Understanding (beyond Kant's claim that the four principles correspond to the four headings of the table of judgments/categories). The Axioms of Intuition and the Anticipations of Perception are complementary components of the law of continuity, since the Axioms of Intuition establish continuity for "all intuitions" (B202) (in the form of their extensive magnitudes), while the Anticipations of Perception do the same for "the real, which is an object of the sensation" (B207) (in the form of its intensive magnitude). The Anticipations of Perception also imply as an indirect consequence the principle of no gap (cf. A172/B214). The Second and Third Analogies, which, when taken together, establish the ubiquity of reciprocal causality in the world, correspond roughly to the principles of no fate and no chance and express the form of the world, at least taken in its generic sense.[40] The First Analogy establishes the matter of the world (namely substance). Thus, all of the Principles of Pure Understanding that determine content (i.e., all except the Postulates of Empirical Thought)[41] can be linked to various aspects of Kant's concept of the world as it is expressed in rational cosmology—including the four principles that concern the negative aspect of our concept of the sensible world.

Although no closer, systematic connection seems to obtain between the four principles of rational cosmology and the Principles of Pure Understanding, a comparison of the two sets of principles will reveal important implications for our understanding of Kant's Critical philosophy as a whole. One relevant difference between these two sets of principles is that the four cosmological principles are broadly ontological in character, while the Principles of Pure Understanding seem to stress epistemological features of our experience (especially in the second edition of the first *Critique*). The form of the world, as dictated by rational cosmology, must consist of a reciprocal causal relation among substances, whereas the Third Analogy claims that one must apply the *category* of community (i.e. mutual interaction) in order to *know* the objective coexistence of substances. One might be tempted to understand this difference in such a way that the epistemological aspect of the Principles of Pure Understanding excludes any ontological conditions (that would be expressed by rational cosmology). For the exclusively epistemological character of the Principles of Pure Understanding might be understood as following necessarily from Kant's central claim in the first *Critique* that the conditions of the possibility of experience are the conditions of the possibility of objects of experience (A158/B197). However, taking Kant's principles of rational cosmology seriously constitutes important evidence against such an understanding. For the fact that these two sets of principles stress different features in no way implies that they are incompatible. And the claim that the conditions of the possibility of experience are the conditions of the possibility of objects of experience need not be understood as asserting that epistemological conditions are the *only* kind of conditions to which objects of experience are subject. That is, while it stresses that objects of experience are in fact subject to epistemological conditions, it in no way implies that other, for example, ontological conditions must be either irrelevant or misplaced.

Given what has been established above with respect to Kant's understanding of rational cosmology, one can see more clearly than before how epistemological factors are not only compatible with, but actually dovetail nicely with ontological ones (despite their diversity). At the most general level, one can note that for Kant experience requires an object of experience, namely the (sensible) world (or, as he sometimes calls it, nature[42]). In other words, experience must be experience *of* something. In this sense, experience, an epistemological notion, requires an object of experience, which is broadly ontological in character.[43]

One specific way to see the ontological character of at least some of the constraints placed on an object of experience according to Kant is to consider what underlies the principle of continuity as it applies to change. If only epistemological features were involved in his argument for this principle, then the continuity of time (which is a crucial premise in his argument for the continuity of change) would have to be inferred from the fact that time is, for example, an a priori intuition or a form of intuition. However, it seems much more plausible to think that the continuity of time is simply a primitive ontological feature of the sensible world. Accordingly, it would seem that the principle of the continuity of change is an ontological principle that is derived from a more fundamental, but equally ontological principle.

One can also consider the argument of the Third Analogy as yet further support for the claim that ontological considerations about the world complement rather than conflict with the epistemological considerations prominent in the first *Critique*'s Principles of Pure Understanding. One crucial premise in the argument of the Third Analogy is that a substance cannot determine its own place in time. This premise is required in order to be able to infer the reciprocal nature of mutual interaction, since the necessity of such interaction can be established only if one excludes the possibility that one substance could determine the place in time of both another substance and itself. While one might want to suggest that epistemological features of time-determination justify this premise, it seems more natural to think that it is based on ontological conditions pertaining to activity and substantiality (and their relation to time).[44]

Further, there are no positive reasons to think that ontological principles are in principle incompatible with the epistemological principles of the first *Critique*. Now if ontological principles placed constraints on objects that were inconsistent with what could be experienced by human beings (or by any being with space and time as sensible forms of intuition and the categories as discursive forms of thought), then it is true that such principles would be incompatible with epistemological principles. However, there is no reason to think that the principles enunciated within rational cosmology are of that sort. Indeed, as we have seen above, Kant gives us a variety of specific reasons for thinking that human beings can experience the world as it is explained within rational cosmology.

In light of this result, it is clear that the essence of the Critical turn (should there be one at all) is not, as is sometimes thought, the rejection of dogmatic ontological principles in favor of purely epistemological ones, but rather the subtle way in which ontological and epistemological considerations complement each other in the establishment of Kant's Critical system. Such an understanding of the Critical turn has the added advantage of putting one in a position to make sense of the continuities that one finds on many issues between Kant's pre-Critical and Critical periods, continuities that are otherwise either problematic or embarrassing.

It also reveals that Kant's attitude toward rational cosmology is significantly different from that toward rational theology and rational psychology. For in neither of these areas of metaphysics do we find ontological principles that relate in such a close fashion to epistemological principles such as the Principles of Pure Understanding (though the relationship between rational psychology and Kant's own transcendental psychology as established in, for example, the Transcendental Deduction may constitute an important exception to this general claim).[45] Rather, the principles of rational theology and rational psychology are primarily (though perhaps not exclusively) analytical principles that follow from the definition of God or the soul and apply mainly to the noumenal world insofar as we attempt to think it. In rational cosmology, however, the fact that Kant both accepts and argues for these four cosmological principles as elements of a positive doctrine of the phenomenal world is significant and, as I hope to have shown, important for our understanding of Kant's theoretical philosophy.

NOTES

I would like to thank the audience members at the conference "Kant and the Sciences" held at Virginia Tech, March 6–8, 1998, for their valuable comments. In particular, I would like to thank Michael Friedman, Karl Ameriks, and Paul Guyer for their comments on an earlier version of the chapter. In the following, translations from the *Critique of Pure Reason* will be from *Critique of Pure Reason*, trans. and ed. Paul Guyer and Allen Wood (Cambridge: Cambridge University Press, 1998). Translations from Kant's metaphysics transcripts will be from *Lectures on Metaphysics*, trans. and ed. Karl Ameriks and Steve Naragon (Cambridge: Cambridge University Press, 1997). Translations from Baumgarten's *Metaphysica* are mine.

1. I use the term "rational cosmology" to indicate cosmology that "borrows its principles not from experience, but rather from pure reason" (28:195), a "cosmology of pure reason" (29:956), or the metaphysics of "the entirety of nature or of the world" (29:754). Of course Kant's concern with what one might naturally call "empirical cosmology," namely his cosmogony as developed in his *Universal Natural History and Theory of the Heavens, or Essay on the Constitution and Mechanical Origin of the Entire Universe, treated in accordance with Newtonian Principles* (1755) is well known.

2. Exceptions to this claim are Karl Ameriks's "The Critique of Metaphysics: Kant and Traditional Ontology," in *The Cambridge Companion to Kant*, ed. Paul Guyer (Cambridge: Cambridge University Press, 1992), 249–79, and my "Kant's Theory of Physical Influx," *Archiv für Geschichte der Philosophie* 77 (1995): 285–324.

3. However, Kant does use the term repeatedly in his metaphysics lectures. See note 1.

4. Within the Wolffian tradition, it is traditionally one of the three or four branches of theoretical metaphysics, which also includes ontology, psychology, and rational (i.e. natural) theology. Naturally, when Kant lectures on metaphysics using Baumgarten's *Metaphysica*, he follows this division and does divide up (theoretical) metaphysics into psychology, rational (or natural) theology, rational cosmology, and at times either ontology or rational physics (29:754–55).

5. Especially in the *Metaphysical Foundations of Natural Science* and *New Theory of the Heavens*.

6. Kant seems to endorse this general conception of the principles of rational cosmology in the Metaphysics Mrongovius lectures when he remarks: "Little is presented of the intelligible world [*mundo intelligibili*] since we can cognize little more of it through the understanding than what follows from the definition [of the world]" (29:850).

7. For a fuller discussion of which of Newton's laws of motion were discussed and provided with nonempirical justifications, cf. my "The Laws of Motion from Newton to Kant,"

Perspectives on Science 5 (1997): 311–48. Baumgarten's proof of the law of the equality of action and reaction is most similar to Johann Peter Reusch's (*Systema Metaphysicum*, Jena, 1735).

8. One finds the law of continuity stated explicitly by, e.g., Georg Bilfinger, *Dilucidationes Philosophicae de Deo, anima humana, mundo, et generalibus rerum affectionibus* (1723; reprinted as Abt. 3, Bd. 18 of Christian Wolff's *Gesammelte Werke* [Hildesheim: Olms, 1982]), 168–74.

9. Cf. 28:199 ("All phenomena in the world do not exist by fate"), 29:925 and 28:663 ("There is no fate in the world"), and, very briefly, at 29:1006.

10. Cf. Leibniz's letters to Arnauld (*G. W. Leibniz: Philosophical Essays*, ed. and trans. R. Ariew and D. Garber [Indianapolis: Hackett Publishing, 1989], 69–70).

11. I should note that Kant sometimes seems to think that absolute necessity stems from "the highest cause" (28:200), i.e., God.

12. The same arguments apply if absolute necessity (and thus absolute fate) stems from God, for Kant repeatedly stresses that it is not appropriate to appeal to God instead of physical causes in explaining any event.

13. Kant explicitly restricts the role of freedom, at least in his Critical period.

14. In the L1 lectures, Kant treats fate and chance jointly, because they are both blind (i.e., blind necessity and blind accident) and it is precisely their blindness that makes them "contrary to reason" (28:199).

15. Kant suggests such a correspondence in the first *Critique* when he says: "We could easily represent the order of these four propositions (*in mundo non datur hiatus, non datur saltus, non datur casus, non datur fatum*) in accordance with the order of the categories, just like all principles of transcendental origin, and show each its position, but the already practiced reader will do this for himself or easily discover the clue to it" (A229/B282).

16. Kant's argument for this claim is to be found in his Anticipations of Perception.

17. We shall consider Kant's account of the world in his metaphysics lectures in more detail later.

18. See 29:922–23.

19. Again, Kant makes such a distinction throughout his metaphysics lectures (up through Metaphysics Dohna, 1792–93).

20. The main idea is that differences in degree do not bring about differences in kind.

21. Leibniz would seem to hold such a version. In the Herder lectures Kant seems to understand the physical law differently as pertaining to how beings attempt to perfect themselves (see 28:42).

22. The Principle of the Identity of Indiscernibles might be taken to exclude this possibility.

23. One limitation of Kant's argument here is that it is difficult to see that *every* extensive magnitude must be continuous. For being an extensive magnitude implies merely that the properties of the whole are determined by the properties of its parts. Thus, the very definition of an extensive magnitude does not imply that its parts could not be finite and discrete. However, Kant's concern with extensive magnitudes reaches no further than spatiotemporal magnitude and this case is clear.

24. Kant's justification of simples is found not in the Metaphysics Herder, but rather in the Metaphysics L1.

25. Obviously, Kant's thoughts on this issue are more complicated than this isolated passage can reveal. For example, see his pre-Critical *Physical Monadology* (1756) and his Critical *Metaphysical Foundations of Natural Science* (1786).

26. Kant also expresses the argument as follows: "no appearance can consist in the simple, because from the simple to matter there would be a sudden transition to something which is distinguished from it generically [*in genere*]" (29:863). The idea is that there is a qualitative difference between zero and other quantities, because adding zero to itself will never produce a finite (nonzero) quantity. Kant makes the latter connection more explicitly in the following passage: "The world cannot consist of monads, for with respect to quanta the simple is a null. But the transition from null to a quantum is a leap. I can put together as many simples as I want, but they will never become a quantum" (29:921).

27. At 28:202–203 Kant presents an extended argument showing that any appearance cannot consist of simple parts based on the fact that all appearances are in time, which is a continuous magnitude.

28. Accordingly, Kant's position in the L1 lectures is not identical to that of either his inaugural dissertation (which maintains phenomenal substances) or his first *Critique*.

29. Kant then immediately adds: "Nevertheless, we are not lacking proofs of the great influence that our principle has in anticipating perceptions" (A172/B213).

30. I would suggest that Kant intends "change" rather than "state."

31. Three brief remarks are in order here. First, the argument is obviously based in important ways on time. Kant recognizes this fact in several passages (e.g., 28:202). Second, Kant presents a very similar argument a few lines later at 28:202–203. The notable difference is that in this later passage Kant seems to emphasize that this argument will work for all objects because all objects must be given in time through the form of inner sense. Third, Kant suggests a similar argument at 29:863–64 and in the Second Analogy at A208/B253–54.

32. One might object to the very positing of intermediate states. However, given Kant's argument above (namely that the mere comparison of magnitudes, whether extensive or intensive, necessarily reveals continuity), it is clear that there must be infinitely many possible intermediate states.

33. Using letters to represent states is misleading insofar as letters are discrete in ways that states are not supposed to be.

34. Kant considers such a case at 28:201: "If something could transfer from one location to another without running through all intermediate locations, then this would be a change of place through a leap. But no thing goes immediately from one location to another except through all intermediate locations; it must go through the infinitely many parts of space."

35. Kant sometimes calls such a transition a leap, but if one takes the metaphor seriously, even leaping suggests that there is a continuous line in space from the takeoff spot to the landing spot. The picture underlying the idea of a leap is something like the following. A body simply moves from state A to state D in one discrete change. At one moment of time it is in state A and at the next moment of time it is in state D, having leapt from A to D without going through B and C. However, the continuous nature of time (and perhaps space) shows that such a picture is in fact incoherent. The problem is of course that given the continuous nature of time no two moments of time are immediately next to each other and thus one cannot say that it is in state A at one moment and then at D in the very next moment. Given that it cannot be in state A and state D at the same moment of time (change presupposes contradictory predicates), they must be in these states at different moments of time. Given that they are different moments of time, there are moments between the moments in which the body leaves A and enters D, and in these moments they must be in some kind of state, namely the intermediary ones.

Of course, Kant still has not really given any compelling reason to think that they must be in the intermediary states other than the fact that bodies do in fact seem to move that way. Another problem with the argument lies in its status. For in the body example it is ambiguous for the purposes of the argument whether the fact that bodies do not move by leaps is supposed to be supported empirically or nonempirically. If the support is empirical, then Kant can hardly claim (as he does) that the law of continuity can be proved a priori. If the support is supposed to be nonempirical, then even after the above analysis, it is difficult to see that there is really an analytic connection, unless the second line of argument is successful.

36. Though Kant does seem to suggest such an argument, it is far from clear that it is not plagued by a serious defect. Even if one grants that there can be no leaps in the order of grounds, it does not immediately follow that there could not be leaps in the order of states. And since grounds are required by states (rather than vice versa), it is far from clear that denying leaps in the former requires the denial of leaps in the latter.

37. It applies to speed as follows: "If a body is brought from rest into motion, then it goes through all of the smallest degrees of speed up to the highest degree of speed with which it has power, and if it is again brought to rest: then this happens through smaller degrees of speed" (28:41–42). (Cf. 28:203 for a very similar passage.) Kant applies it to direction at 29: 921 and 28:203.

38. For example, if one were to accept the patchwork theory, the passage in the Postulates of Empirical Thought in which Kant endorses these principles would be an older passage that Kant should have omitted.

39. See, e.g., 29:849 and 28:657.

40. For a fuller discussion of Kant's concept of the world, see my "Kant's Theory of Physical Influx."

41. Even in the case of the Postulates of Empirical Thought, Kant suggests in one passage that the principle of no fate might be correlated with modality (and thus, indirectly, with the Postulates of Empirical Thought).

42. Cf. A418–19/B446–47 for Kant's Critical explanation of the relation between world and nature.

43. It is clear that I do not understand ontological to be equivalent to noumenal.

44. For a more detailed reconstruction of Kant's argument in the Third Analogy, cf. my "Kant's Third Analogy of Experience," *Kant-Studien* 88 (1997): 406–441.

45. See Karl Ameriks, *Kant's Theory of Mind* (Oxford: Oxford University Press, 1982), for an extended defense of the view that Kant's attitude toward rational psychology is much more positive than is traditionally allowed.

PART II

Physics

5

Kant's Dynamics

Daniel Warren

A GREAT deal of the philosophy of the seventeenth and eighteenth centuries can be seen as an attempt to come to terms with the new science that supplanted the conception of the physical world inherited from Aristotle. It is a characteristic strength of Aristotle's system that his physics is so closely interwoven with his views about the world generally and our place in it, that is, with his metaphysics. His physics could not simply be replaced by another, leaving the metaphysics intact. So, the new, more mathematically conceived physics put great strain on the view of the world that emphasized metaphysical notions like power, activity, and purpose.

Furthermore, there was a significant shift within the development of the new science, which made this tension even more acute. There was an earlier "mechanistic" phase in which all phenomena were to be explained exclusively in terms of properties like the size, shape, and motion of bodies, properties that were thought to have particular clarity.[1] But this was followed by the introduction of a "dynamical" physics, advanced in different ways by both Leibniz and Newton, which laid great weight on notions of force or power. The idea of a body exerting a force or possessing a power, however, was particularly problematic. To many, the use of such an idea seemed like a pernicious return to Aristotelianism, a move capable of endangering all the clarity and explanatory power that the new science had attained. To others—Leibniz, for example—the appeal to the concept of a force or power was a vindication of some of the central features of the Aristotelian picture, which had been too hastily repudiated. To Kant, the use of such concepts in natural philosophy seemed a great leap forward, which, at least in the kind of physics he saw as starting with Newton, could be made without carrying along a lot of Scholastic baggage. "The dynamical mode of explanation," says Kant, is at work "when certain basic powers are assumed from which the phenomena are derived" (29:935).[2] He goes on to say that "this was first discovered by Newton and is more satisfactory and complete than the former," that is, than the mechanical mode of explanation. (See also 28:211 and 28:665.) Kant was thinking in particular of Newton's introduction of an attractive power. However, Kant thought that this "dynamical mode of explanation" in its Newtonian form could be applied even more broadly than Newton himself applied it. It could afford us a better understanding even of some of the features of matter that were most central to the mechanistic approach, namely matter's impenetrability or solidity—and this is what I will be concentrating on in this chapter. Kant's advocacy of a dynamical treatment of impenetrability is often regarded as a move toward a more Leibnizian picture, but one of the points I wish to emphasize is the extent to which it reflects a generalization of an insight that Kant would have regarded as fundamentally Newtonian in character. This focus on the contrast between mechanical and dynamical approaches, as applied to impenetrability, will also serve to bring out Kant's views about a more fundamental shift in the conception of matter's most basic properties, and in the explanatory projects in which they figure.

1. Explanatory Projects and Primary Qualities

The rise of the mechanistic approach in natural philosophy was tied to the developing idea of a distinguished set of properties called "primary qualities." In Locke's work, for example, the notion of a primary quality plays a central role, and he counts the properties of "solidity, extension, figure and mobility," among others, as having this special status. We often think of primary qualities as contrasted to properties that involve an essential reference to something subjective, like powers to produce sensations of certain sorts. But in fact Locke contrasts them to powers more generally—not only to powers to produce changes in a perceiving subject, but also powers to produce observable changes in other *objects*, for example, the sun's power to blanch wax, or the power of fire to liquify lead. (See Locke's *Essay*, book II, chap. VIII, esp. §§10, 23, 26.) The primary qualities, however, are *not* conceived of as causal powers. Rather, the powers that an object has are thought of as based in its primary qualities—these powers are as far as possible to be explained in terms of them. By appealing to a thing's primary qualities, we characterize a thing apart from its relations to others, or more particularly, apart from its causal relations to others. And this is certainly crucial to the explanatory role they are meant to play vis-à-vis causal powers. For to explain a causal power is to explain how an object can produce effects of the appropriate kind. And if we are to provide an explanation of how an object can enter into such causal relations, we cannot simply say, again, that it has a power to do so. Perhaps we could explain a power in terms of other powers. But if we go no farther than that, we will have to grant that the operations of these other powers are no better understood. Thus, at least according to this traditional doctrine of primary qualities, if we are to understand the operation of a power, we must ultimately explain it in terms of properties that are not thought of as powers. In this way the primary qualities were accorded a primacy in our understanding of the relations, in particular of the causal relations among things.

Now, I am going to be focusing on matter's "space-filling" property—that property of matter by which filled space was distinguished from empty space. Locke called this property "solidity," and he counted it as one of the primary qualities. Moreover, if I am right about the special role Locke means primary qualities to play in explanation, it will make sense to think that when Locke makes an explanatory appeal to solidity, he does not take himself to be simply making an appeal to another causal power. And in this, the proponents of the mechanist approach, as Kant will describe it, are clearly in agreement with Locke. Rather, solidity was regarded as the kind of property which, along with shape, size, and motion, allows us to characterize an object apart from its possible causal relations, and thus (to the extent that it is possible for us) to *explain* the operation of causal powers.

Kant, however, in defending what he calls the "dynamical" approach, wants us to think about matter's space-filling property in a very different way. In the first *Critique*, Kant says that we must seek the character of matter "in all the effects which it exercises" (A277/B333), and at another place in the same section of the *Critique* he says: "We are acquainted with substance in space only through forces which are active in this or that space, either bringing other objects to it (attraction), or preventing them penetrating into it (repulsion and impenetrability)" (A265/B321). These quotations are from passages in which Kant is defending a more general doctrine, namely the doctrine that we know only the relational features of things, never their inner determinations. Kant's view as specifically applied to space-filling is that we must characterize the space-filling property of a thing not in abstraction from, but rather *in terms of* its possible causal relations with other things. As far as its role in our knowledge is concerned, the whole content of characterizing something as having this property is given through its relations to its possible effects, or through a law governing these effects—in the same way that we might say that the content of ascribing a power of attraction to, say, the sun is exhausted by giving the inverse-square law of gravitational attraction which says that bodies around the sun will change their state of motion depending on their distance from the sun and on the mass of the sun. Kant wants to bring about a shift in the way we think about the fundamental properties figuring in our best explanations of what happens in the sensible world, that is, he wants to bring about a shift in the way we think about primary qualities. Instead of conceiving of them as *contrasted* to causal powers, we are meant to see that the set of primary qualities includes causal powers as essential and ineliminable members. Moreover, this necessarily rules out certain kinds of explanatory ambitions. For if the content of ascribing a particular quality to something is simply that it has a power to produce effects of a certain sort, then no explanatory insight is provided by saying that objects with this property produce effects of that sort. At some fundamental level, we will have to renounce the project of explaining how something with certain primary qualities produces such and such effects. But Kant was sufficiently impressed by what *could* be done by Newton's assumption of an attractive power that he could regard it as paradigmatic of a basis for scientific explanation, rather than as something in need of a more fundamental explanation that did not appeal to causal powers.

2. Mechanical and Dynamical Conceptions: The Incompressibility of Matter

Kant contrasts the two accounts of impenetrability, or solidity, in the second chapter of the *Metaphysical Foundations of Natural Science* [*MFNS*].[3] Kant presents the *MFNS* as an application of the doctrines of the *Critique* to the special case of the concept of matter. And in the second chapter of the *MFNS*, Kant treats the concept of matter with respect to the categories of quality, and he takes the property of impenetrability, or solidity, to fall under the category of reality (the first of the categories of quality) in that it is that feature by which filled space is distinguished from space that is empty. Kant contrasts the two accounts of space-filling in the course of distinguishing two very general conceptions of matter, which he calls the "mathematico-mechanical" conception, on the one hand, and the "metaphysico-dynamical" on the other. (I will often refer to the former simply as the "mechanical" conception and the latter as the "dynamical".) To begin with, I just want to give a relatively superficial characterization of the contrast. In doing this I will be able to spell out two ways in which the mechanist's property of solidity is not to be counted as something given in sensibility. Later I will discuss what I believe to be the significance of this contrast for Kant at a more fundamental level. Now, as I just mentioned, the second chapter of the *MFNS* is concerned with that property by which filled and empty space are distinguished. This space-filling property is to be understood as being that property in virtue of which a thing excludes others from its space. Noting that what constitutes a given thing's space can change in a variety of ways (the thing can move, it can change shape, etc.), we can give the idea a more specific content by saying that it is that property in virtue of which a thing is resistant to compression, i.e., resistant to a decrease in its *volume*. And the term "impenetrable," as used in this context, should be understood in the very same sense, rather than as meaning, for example, hardness. The mechanical and the dynamical conceptions of matter constitute two ways of explaining what it is for something to fill space, thus two ways of explaining what it is for something to be impenetrable, or resistant to compression.

Kant usually associates the mechanistic conception with atomism, that is, an account of matter on which it is made up of perfectly hard, and therefore indivisible, particles of various shapes and sizes. But the most important element of the mechanistic conception, as far as the second chapter's explicit focus on the space-filling property is concerned, can be isolated and treated separately from the full commitments of atomism, and this element is the account of matter's impenetrability.[4] On the mechanical conception, a homogeneous piece of matter was thought of as completely incompressible, i.e., as unyielding to surrounding pressure, no matter how great. The mechanist's matter was said to have "absolute" impenetrability. Any compression of a body would have to be due to the reduction of the amount of empty space it contains—like compressing a sponge. Once you eliminate all the empty space, no more compression whatsoever is possible. Variations in the density of bodies are explained, on the mechanist conception, in terms of the relative amounts of filled and empty space they contain.

The dynamical conception, on the other hand, presents a rather different picture of the impenetrability of matter and of the variation in its density. On the dynamical conception, a given region of space is said to be filled on account of a force—a repulsive force—which is associated with that region. And, for Kant, this will mean that a region is said to be filled on account of the effects, i.e. the changes in motion, which are produced in other bodies which impinge on that region. Insofar as it is possible for these changes in the impinging body's motion to occur at a greater or a lesser rate, we can conceive of the space as endowed with a greater or a lesser repulsive power. And thus we can think of the space as filled to a greater or lesser degree. So on this conception, impenetrability is a matter of more or less, in contrast to the mechanist conception, where it is all or none. The dynamical view, as Kant spells it out, also entails that since a region of filled space is composed of smaller regions, each of which is itself filled, the parts of a body will exert a repulsive force on one another. And since, according to Kant, this force has a finite degree, every body will compress, at least to a certain extent, under a sufficiently great degree of externally applied pressure. The compression of matter will be analogous in certain ways to the compression of an elastic spring. The mechanistic conception, by contrast, attributes to matter an impenetrability that is, in a certain sense, greater than any finite degree. Matter, for the dynamist, is "relatively," rather than "absolutely," impenetrable, as it is for the mechanist. On the dynamical conception, a body fills a space in the way an elastic medium does. Kant thought that a body could fill space homogeneously—without containing any empty spaces—and that it could be compressed in such a way that each part occupied a correspondingly smaller space and thus exerted a correspondingly greater force on the parts which neighbor it. The body's space-filling property is termed its "original elasticity." In a similar way, differences in the density of bodies could be accounted for without appealing to empty spaces the body encloses, as was necessary on the mechanical conception.

Some conclusions can already be drawn at this point. The principle of the Anticipations of Perception—namely the principle that the real (those properties falling under the category of reality) in appearance has an intensive magnitude, that is, a degree—cannot be what rules out the mechanistic conception of space-filling. Indeed, the rhetorical thrust of that section of the *Critique* is that the assumption of absolute all-or-none impenetrability is not *forced* on us, that there is an alternative to it, an alternative according to which space can be filled completely (i.e., without empty spaces) but in varying degrees. The Anticipations establish that such an alternative is a real possibility,[5] but not, I believe, that it is or must be the case. It is worth pursuing the question of why it does not establish this, that is, why the Anticipations do not show that space-filling must be a matter of degree, ruling out the all-or-none conception of space-filling advocated by the mechanist. The argument of the Anticipations proceeds by way of establishing the claim that all sensation has an intensive magnitude, that is, a degree. So, to get clearer on our question, consider a situation in which we attempt to compress a body, e.g., by placing it between our hands and then trying to press them together. And now compare the sensation of impenetrability that would be produced if the body were absolutely impenetrable (as the mechanists claim) with that produced if it is only relatively impenetrable (in accordance with the dynamical account). Would there be a difference that would show an inconsistency between the former and what the Anticipations section claims about the character of our sensations? Clearly not, for in both cases—whether the body was absolutely impenetrable or only relatively so—the *sensations* would have a finite degree, an intensive magnitude, which would simply depend on how hard we were pressing with our hands. The Anticipations argue that our sensations must have a degree, and neither case poses a problem on that account.

But then a further question arises. And that is whether, by means of this sensation, the space-filling property (the "real") in the object is presented to us in empirical intuition. If so, it would be presented to us as having a corresponding degree. In general, we can say that the character of mechanical impenetrability in no way rules out the claim that all the sensations it produces have a finite degree. What becomes clear is that absolute impenetrability (which in effect has an infinitely great degree of impenetrability) is not something we can represent in an object by means of sensation at all. In this sense, it is not a property that can be given in sensibility. That is, even if absolute impenetrability is regarded as the space-filling property, and thus as falling under the category of reality, still it would not be something that could be presented to us through the sensation-component of an empirical intuition. We can construe the Anticipations as claiming that properties falling under the category of reality, insofar as they are given in sensibility, have a degree. But what is being denied here is that absolute impenetrability is, in the appropriate sense, "given in sensibility."

Perhaps we could say that, in the case of absolute impenetrability, what really corresponds to a sensation having a certain degree is the force the body exerts on the hand, for that force does have a corresponding degree. But the point is that, on the mechanistic account, the property of space-filling (impenetrability) does not determine what degree of force is delivered; the character of this property is fixed and is independent of the force the body delivers to the hands, and, for that matter, it is also independent of the force which the hands apply to the body. On the dynamical account, by contrast, the force exerted by the body corresponds to the degree of space-filling (the degree of impenetrability). And this depends, as in the case of an elastic spring, on the degree of compression.

In both cases, differences in the force delivered to the hands correspond to differences in the force applied by them. But there is an asymmetry in that the dynamical conception provides for corresponding differences in the space-filling property of the interposed body, and it is precisely these differences that are captured in sensibility, specifically in the intensive magnitude or degree of the sensation of impenetrability. Relative impenetrability is precisely the kind of property that can, at least in principle, be presented to us through the sensation-component of empirical intuition.

3. MECHANICAL AND DYNAMICAL CONCEPTIONS: THE INTERACTION OF BODIES

I have just been laying out a basic element of the contrast between the mechanistic and the dynamic conceptions of matter, that element being the different accounts of matter's impenetrability. I now want to say something about the differing accounts of the *interaction* of bodies under the two conceptions of matter. To do this it will be useful to consider the natural philosophy of an actual adherent of a roughly mathematico-mechanistic approach—J. H. Lambert. Lambert is one of the few mechanists Kant mentioned by name in the *MFNS* as a proponent of the view of space-filling he was opposing (4:497–98).

I said that, for a proponent of the dynamic conception, matter fills space in virtue of being endowed with a force—a power of repulsion. On the other hand, Lambert, in accordance with Kant's characterization of the mechanist, explicitly *distinguished* a body's having a force from its property of filling space—the property that Lambert (like Locke before him) called its "solidity."[6] On either conception, a (moving) force is just a power to produce a motion. From the mechanist's standpoint, a body has a force insofar as it is in motion, and this goes beyond the simple contrast between filled and empty space. A body in motion has a force that we can perceive, for example, if we try to stop it. That is, it has a force that it exercises upon impact. The degree of this force will depend on the speed that it has. In typical mechanistic interactions, one body, in virtue of having a certain motion, exerts a force when it collides with another body. And, in this conception, it is on account of the first body's having this force that it causes a change in the state of motion of the second. A body at rest may also be regarded as having a force on account of which the motion of a body colliding with it is changed. (This will be characterized as a force of inertia.)[7] But whether the body is moving or at rest, its having a force (a power to produce motions) goes beyond the contrast between filled and empty space. In the mechanist's picture, what is being denied is that a body has a force just in virtue of being solid, just in virtue of excluding others from its space. Nevertheless, the mechanistic account of collision also assigns an indispensable role to solidity. For, the exertion of the force associated with motion requires that both bodies be solid and therefore fill space. Otherwise, the bodies would pass right through one another. So even though a body's solidity is not conceived of as a force, it is an essential part of the account of how changes in motion are produced. In other words, according to a mechanist like Lambert, the force an extended thing has in virtue of its motion could never be exercised in an interaction with another unless both already filled their respective spaces.

For a dynamist like Kant, by contrast, the property by which filled and empty space are distinguished is *itself* a force. Just in virtue of having this space-filling property, a body is a cause of changes in the motion of neighboring bodies. It is endowed with a repulsive force.[8] On the dynamical conception, the communication of motion in a collision between two bodies is thought of as occurring on account of a repulsive force between them. That is, during the entire period in which the two bodies are interacting, it is as if there were a compressed spring between them. This spring force which a body exerts on another body impinging on it, and which acts for as long as they are in contact, is responsible for the change of motion, that is, the recoil, of the impinging body. And here, in *contrast* to the mechanistic conception, the force which causes this change of motion in other bodies is the very same property on account of which we say that a region of space is filled at all. The idea of a repulsive force which can be ascribed to bodies merely insofar as they fill space has as its model the Newtonian conception of attractive force, at least as Kant interprets it. For a body can be thought of as endowed with attractive force independent of its state of rest or motion, and thus, in drawing on this model, Kant goes beyond the conceptions of powers to produce motion that the mechanist has most centrally in mind. In thinking about the interactions of bodies, we can treat attractive and repulsive forces analogously: we can regard the attractive force or the repulsive force (as the case may be) as responsible for the respective changes of motion in the interacting bodies.

There is a further point I still wish to make about the mechanistic conception, which has to do with the relation between the character of solidity and the effects produced in collisions. It is that we cannot attribute the mechanistic or absolute impenetrability to an object on the basis of the effects produced in collision. For the effects brought about by absolute impenetrability will be, so to speak, infinitely great accelerations, which occur at the moment at which the bodies are in contact. That is, when two *absolutely* impenetrable bodies collide, there is a finite change in velocity in an infinitely short period of time. But the existence of such a discontinuous change of state can never be confirmed by observation. One might determine the state of motion at one moment and then again at a later moment, but one could only say that the change occurred sometime during the interval between the two times. One could say that there was an acceleration greater than or equal to the minimum compatible with that change of motion occurring in that time interval. But from such observations one could never be in a position to say that there was an infinite acceleration.[9] And so one could never be in a position to say that the impenetrability of a body was absolute. In this way, the content of ascribing absolute impenetrability can be seen to outrun all possible observable consequences. This provides a further sense in which absolute impenetrability is not given in sensibility. In this sense and the one elaborated earlier, we can understand Kant's claim in *MFNS* (4:525) that, in relying on the notion of absolute impenetrability, the mechanistic approach lays an "empty concept" at its foundation.[10]

4. Conceiving Matter According to Its Inner Determinations

Now, what, at a more fundamental level, is at stake for Kant in the distinction between these two conceptions of matter? I want to suggest that Kant's reservations about the mechanistic conception stem from the fact that he thinks the mechanist is attempting to characterize matter as it is apart from its relations to others, specifically, apart from its causal relations to others. And this is in conflict with Kant's doctrine, mentioned earlier, that all we know of things are their relational features, not their inner determinations—when this doctrine is applied to a property like space-filling. Moreover, the unknowability of inner determinations is, for Kant, closely tied to the idea that we cannot know things in themselves, for as I understand Kant's view on this, any attempt to characterize something through its inner determinations is an attempt to characterize it as it is in itself.[11]

Kant discusses the contrast between the two conceptions throughout the second chapter of his *MFNS*. But he begins the chapter with the odd proposition that "matter fills a space, not by its mere existence, but by a special moving force" (5: 497). It seems odd that filling space by mere existence should be put forward as the alternative to filling space in virtue of a force. What kind of a view could Kant have in mind as proposing such an alternative, and what is his objection to it? And if, as Kant says, filling space is a matter of its *impenetrability*, what could it even *mean* to say that matter fills space by its mere existence?

I want to address this last question first. What could it mean to say that matter fills space by its mere existence? I think there is a lot more packed into the expression "by its mere existence" and that there is a lot more in the idea of what may or may not follow from a thing's "mere existence" than is evident on the surface. The expression comes up in very closely related contexts in Kant's inaugural dissertation of 1770 and in the earlier *Nova Dilucidatio* (1755). In these works Kant says that the mutual causal relations of distinct things do not follow from and cannot be understood by reference to the "mere existence" of the things involved. And in the *MFNS* we are also trying to characterize a property in terms of which we are to understand something's relations with others—here, its resistance to other bodies tending to penetrate into its space.

In the *Nova Dilucidatio* version of the proposition concerned with the possible basis of reciprocal causal interaction, Kant begins with the claim that "finite substances by their mere existence are unrelated" (1:412–13). A bit later, he writes, "the mutual relations of these things do not follow simply because God founded their existence," and then, "merely on the basis of its existence there is no relation and obviously no interaction." And in summing up, Kant says: "Therefore the mere existence of substances is obviously inadequate as a basis for mutual interaction and a relation of determinations" (1:414), and "no substance of any kind has the power of determining other substances, distinct from itself, by means of that which belongs to it internally" (1:415).[12] These passages suggest that, insofar as God simply "founds the existence" of some thing, certain features of the thing do not necessarily obtain of it, while certain others do. And the latter set of features, those which follow from the "mere existence" of the thing, are those which follow from "that which belongs to it internally," that is, from the inner determinations of the thing. Following from "the mere existence" of the thing is very closely related to, if not equivalent to, following from the thing's inner determinations.

In a corresponding discussion in the inaugural dissertation, he says:

> Given a plurality of substances, a principle of possible mutual interaction is not given by their mere existence; something more is required from which their mutual relations may be understood. Through their mere subsistence they do not necessarily refer to anything else, except perhaps to their cause [i.e., the cause of their mere existence] (2:407).

It should be noted that Kant seems to be using the expressions "by their mere existence" and "by their mere subsistence" interchangeably. This helps us to see what Kant has in mind in the *MFNS* proposition being discussed, where he chooses the term "substance" as a gloss on the expression "everything which exists" when stating the view he means to be opposing, namely, that "solidity must be assumed in everything which exists (substance)" (4:497).

It is not surprising that there is this tie to the idea of subsistence, given what was noted above in relation to the *Nova Dilucidatio* passage. For, traditionally, substance was understood as something that was independent of all other (finite) things. And in the rationalist conception that Kant was drawing on, this meant that something is understood, as substance, in terms of the determinations it has apart from its relations to other (finite) things. These are the inner rather than the relational determinations of a thing. And insofar as they are the determinations with which God endows a thing just in creating it, they are the determinations it has "by its mere existence." Moreover, Kant clearly means to exclude from these inner determinations any *powers* the thing might have for entering into causal interactions with other things, since it is precisely Kant's point that the basis for such interactions cannot be understood "by means of that which belongs to it internally."[13]

So in the earlier works it is made a lot clearer that to understand something in terms of its mere existence is to understand it as it is apart from all of its relations to other things. Moreover, this way of presenting the problem of causal interaction is not limited to works of the pre-Critical period. In the General Note to the System of the Principles, added in the B-edition of the *Critique*, Kant puts the difficulty of understanding causal interaction between one thing and others in precisely the same terms. How are we to think it possible, he asks,

> that because there is something in the one there must also in the others be something *which is not to be understood solely from the existence of these others*? For this is what is required in order that there be community [i.e., mutual causal interaction]; community is not conceivable as holding between things each of which, *through its subsistence*, stands in complete isolation (B292–93, my emphasis).

There are, it should be noted, certain differences between Kant's aims in these three passages on interaction, on the one hand, and in the *MFNS* proposition about space-filling, on the other. The discussion of causal interaction is more general and more fundamental, in that it is part of an account of our grounds for thinking in terms of causal relations at all. It involves both a positive and a negative aspect. The positive account changes as Kant's views take on their mature form, but the negative point, that these grounds are not to be found among the determinations a thing has "by its mere existence," is common to all three of these discussions. The *MFNS* proposition takes the possibility of causal interaction to have already been established (as part of the "Critical" philosophy presented in the first *Critique*). It is concerned with a particular case. And we can see that, along with claiming that the space-filling property of a thing must be understood as a causal power ("moving force"), what this proposition is intended to do is reiterate the corresponding negative point, namely, that this property *cannot* be understood in terms of the "mere existence" of the thing, that is, in terms of its inner determinations.

5. THE MECHANISTIC VIEW: KANT'S ELABORATIONS AND OBJECTIONS

Now let us return to the first of the two questions I raised earlier. When Kant denies, in the first proposition of the Dynamics chapter of the *MFNS*, that matter fills space "by its mere existence," what kind of a view about matter does he mean to be rejecting, and what is his objection to the view? I want to suggest that Kant in fact has the views of Lambert and other proponents of the mathematico-mechanical approach in mind. For, in the observation Kant attaches to the proposition I have been discussing, he starts by explicitly criticizing "Lambert and others" (4:497) and then goes on to characterize their view as that of "the mathematician" (4:498). Kant begins the observation by saying that they maintained that solidity must be assumed in everything that exists in space. This immediate reference to "existence in space" is the observation's tie-in to the ideas at work in the proposition to which this observation is attached. Specifically it is the tie-in to the idea of the properties something has "by its mere existence" (namely, inner properties) which I discussed in the last section. The view Kant is criticizing in the observation is precisely the kind of view that he is rejecting in the proposition to which it is appended. When Kant denies that matter fills space "by its mere existence," he is ruling out—and in this context he probably has it foremost in his mind to rule out—the mechanist's view of the space-filling property (solidity). The mathematico-mechanical approach, as Kant is interpreting it, holds that solidity is a feature something has "by its mere existence," that is, a feature something has apart from its relations to others, and specifically, apart from its causal relations to others.

Kant then continues his characterization of the view he is criticizing. It is, for Kant, an extremely significant part of that view that it includes an account of the necessity with which a body prevents the intrusion of others into its space. Kant says, "according to their [Lambert's and others'] concepts, the presence of something real in space must by its very concept carry with it this resistance and hence does so according to the principle of contradiction."[14] For Kant, the emphasis on what can be known from concepts, i.e., from the principle of contradiction, is characteristic of the view he is opposing. What Kant finds objectionable in this view is the idea that a body's resistance to the intrusion of neighboring bodies follows logically from, and in this way can be understood and explained in terms of, its solidity or space-filling property, as the mechanists have construed it— namely, as a property something has by its mere existence, and thus, apart from that thing's relations to others.

According to the dynamical conception, by contrast, the notion of space-filling involves the ascription of a repulsive force. And the content of such an ascription is given by reference to the causal relations that thing can bear to others, that is, through a law which governs the effects, following the model of the inverse square law in the case of Newtonian attraction. To say that something fills a space is to say that it can produce effects of a certain sort. By contrast, Kant feels that there is something misguided in the mechanists' claim to explain the resistance to the intrusion of other bodies by appeal to absolute impenetrability. For if the concept of something real in space (as they construe it) contains the concept of its resistance, then it is, as Kant puts it, simply a contradiction if approaching bodies do not recoil from it. But, according to Kant, this is to misrepresent the kind of explanation that is appropriate here. Matter, he says, does not resist penetration with "absolute necessity"; rather, it rests on a "physical ground" (4:502). The relation between the presence of a given body and the recoil of other bodies is a *causal* relation, and as Kant emphasizes in many ways, causal necessity can never be understood as a kind of logical necessity; it cannot be understood through the law of contradiction (or, equivalently, through what he calls the "law of identity"). To be sure, as Kant himself points out (4:498), once we attribute a (repulsive) causal power to something present in a space, then it certainly follows by the law of contradiction that an impinging body must be deflected by it. But saying *that* gives us no insight into the character of the causal link and *its* necessity. And it certainly does not succeed in reducing *that* necessity to a logical one.

Kant is making the same general point in his pre-Critical essay on negative magnitudes (1763), when arguing that real grounds cannot be understood as logical grounds:

> How should I understand that because something is, something else is? A logical consequence is only really posited because it is identical with the ground. . . . But the will of God contains the real ground of the existence of the world. The divine will is something, the existent world is a wholly different thing. And yet the one posits the other. . . . Of two bodies situated on a straight line, the one A is in movement, the other, B, in rest. The movement of A is one thing, that of B something else, and yet, by the one, the other is posited. Now, analyze the concept of the divine will as much as you please, you will never encounter an existent world, as if it were contained and posited by identity. It is the same in the other cases (2:202–203).

Now comes the crucial point:

> I will not be put off with the words, "cause and effect," "force," and "action." For, if I already regard something as a cause of something, or ascribe to it the concept of a force, then I have already thought in it the relation of real ground to consequence, and then it is easy to see the positing of the consequent according to the law of identity. For example, through the all-mighty will of God, one can distinctly understand the resistance of the world. But here, "might" signifies that something is God, through which other things are posited. Yet this word already denotes the relation of a real ground to the consequences which I wished to be explained. . . . How, through the motion of one body, is that of another destroyed? . . . If I presuppose the impenetrability which stands in real opposition with any force which strives to penetrate the space which the body occupies, then I can already understand the destruction of the motions. But thereby I have reduced one real opposition to another (2:203).

Kant's idea here is as follows. We do not understand how something brings about the effects that necessarily follow upon it. It certainly does not follow by the principle of contradiction. But it also gets us nowhere to include the concept of a particular causal power in the very notion of the thing, even though deriving a contradiction from the denial of the effect would then be trivial. In such a strategy we merely shift our ignorance from one place to another. If there was a question about a necessary connection to begin with, there must remain a doubt about the nature and possibility of the corresponding property, that is, the corresponding causal power. The problem with the causal relation was that its necessity cannot be understood through the law of contradiction. And *that* necessity, the necessity of the connection, for example, between the presence of the one object and the deflection of others, is no *more* intelligible when we attribute a force or power to the body. In a full explanation of the deflection, we will still have to appeal to a causal connection somewhere along the way. And when we attribute a causal power to an object, we are presupposing a causal law, namely, that, whenever and wherever the object is present, incoming objects will be deflected (with an acceleration dependent on its degree of compression). If the causal connection has not been made fully intelligible, then neither has the nature and possibility of the corresponding causal power.[15]

The mechanists conceive of space-filling, or solidity, as a property a body has apart from its relations to others. And, like those who assign a fundamental explanatory role to primary qualities understood in the traditional sense, they conceive of this property as the kind of thing that could *explain* why the body has the effects it has on other things—for example, why their motion changes in certain ways. The mechanists do not regard solidity as a power, but rather as a property meant to explain the operation of powers. And for this reason the content of ascribing the property of solidity could not simply be given through the law governing its effects.

Earlier, I stressed the fact that the mechanists' "absolute" impenetrability is not a property we can ascribe to a thing in virtue of its observable consequences. We do not ascribe it to a thing on account of that thing's possible causal relations at all. As discussed earlier, Kant will regard such ascriptions with suspicion. But from the mechanists' point of view, *given their explanatory project*, such ascriptions *must* be regarded as permissible. It is not that this explanatory project necessarily requires that impenetrability be of an all-or-none variety. Rather, the point is that such a project, by its nature, must already have granted the admissibility of properties requiring a non-relational characterization, of which absolute impenetrability is an example. In particular, it must already have been prepared to deny that the permissibility of introducing such a property requires that it be characterizable through its relations to its observable consequences.[16]

6. Comprehending the Possibility of a Natural Force

One thing that I have just been saying is that Kant has doubts about whether we can make intelligible to ourselves the possibility of something's having a causal power or force. These worries are particularly prominent in certain of Kant's pre-Critical writings, namely, the 1763 *Essay on Negative Magnitudes* (2:202–204) and the 1766 *Dreams of a Spirit-Seer* (2:322). Now it is well known that with the advent of the Critical period, Kant articulates questions about the validity of the concept of causality, and, in the Transcendental Deduction and the Analogies, attempts to show the legitimacy of that concept and, I take it, of the concept of a causal power or force as well. Yet, those considerations do not (nor, I believe, are meant to) fully address the doubts Kant expressed in the pre-Critical writings. For he will make the same points, in almost the same terms, during the Critical period. Kant writes in the *MFNS* that, "in the case of fundamental forces, their possibility can never be comprehended [*eingesehen*]" (4:524–25), and this kind of remark comes up a number of times in that work.

However, we need to look more generally at what would be involved in "comprehending" the possibility of a causal power or force. What does it mean to comprehend how a natural force is possible? Some help in answering this question comes from the following remark, also from the *MFNS*: "That the possibility of fundamental forces should be made conceivable is a completely impossible demand; for they are called fundamental forces precisely because they cannot be derived from any other forces, i.e., they cannot be conceived" (4:513). This suggests the following picture. If it can be shown how a force can be explained in terms of more basic forces, then we have (to that extent) come to understand how this force is possible. In explaining it, we would have to show how its effects are just those that would be expected from the more basic forces when they are combined and arranged in a certain way. It is in this sense that one can be said to "comprehend" how a body can have that (less basic) force. That is, we will have shown how something endowed with the more basic forces can produce precisely the set of effects attributed to the force being explained.

However, as far as the *fundamental* forces are concerned, as Kant repeatedly emphasizes, we cannot understand how *they* are possible. We cannot have any deeper understanding of how a body endowed with a fundamental force produces its characteristic effects. Thus, unlike the case of the derived forces, where such deeper understanding is available, with the fundamental forces we can have no insight into how they are possible.[17]

Kant writes that "all natural philosophy consists in the reduction of natural forces apparently diverse to a smaller number of forces and powers sufficient for the explanation of the former. But this reduction continues only to the fundamental forces, beyond which our reason cannot go" (4:534). Kant is describing an explanatory regress. With each step backwards, the effects attributed to a causal power are being explained—moreover, they are being explained in a way that is nonvacuous. For Kant, the content of ascribing a force to an object is given by the rule governing the effects it can produce. The causal power is thus characterized by its relation to its possible effects. Now, so characterized, such a force might be capable of explanation in terms of more basic forces. This would be a matter of accounting for the rule governing the effects of the former force in terms of the rules governing the effects of the more basic forces when arranged or combined in a given way. And although the more basic forces, too, are characterized by reference to a rule governing *their* effects, we have been able to say something genuinely explanatory about how the force we were originally examining produces its characteristic effects. We have been able to say something beyond the vacuous claim that it just is the power to produce such effects. By carrying such an explanatory regress as far as possible we would approach a characterization of the forces in terms of forces which are fundamental.[18]

But what could even count as a *possible* answer, when what we want to know is how a *fundamental* force is possible, that is, when we want to know how an object endowed with such a force produces the corresponding effects? I want to suggest that one possible way of interpreting this question—the way the mechanists interpret it—is that we are asking for a characterization of the object in terms of its inner determinations, and thus, as I understand it, as it is in itself. We are asking for a characterization that is capable of explaining the operation of this power. We want to understand, given such a characterization of the object, how the effects are produced. More specifically, we want to characterize the object apart from its relations to its possible or actual effects in others. We want to know how such an object might be constituted if it is to have such effects. Only *that* could give us the further understanding of these effects that is being sought after. For, if we are aiming to give an *informative* explanation of how an object produces a given kind of effect, we cannot *simply* characterize the object as having the power to produce such effects. Yet, because the power in question is fundamental, we cannot explain it as we did in other cases, i.e., we cannot simply aim to account for the rule governing the effects of the power in terms of the rules governing the effects of more basic powers when arranged or combined in a given way. There are no more basic powers to appeal to, so we will need to appeal to properties of a quite different character. What we are seeking is a characterization of the object in terms of its primary qualities, traditionally conceived, that is, as properties that are not themselves powers, but rather are intended to explain them. This would be a way of bringing to an end the explanatory regress in which we sought an ever deeper comprehension of the possibility of a given causal power. In asking how an object is to be constituted if it is to produce the effects associated with a *fundamental* causal power, we are asking for the inner determinations of the object, determinations in terms of which the power to enter into certain relations is to be explained. Yet, according to Kant, such a characterization is not *available* to us, given his view that all our knowledge is of the relational features of things, never of their inner determinations. And even if we *did* come upon such characterizations, we still could not see why these features of the object *necessitated* the occurrence of the effects.

In Kant's view, the mechanists deny both of these points. They employ a characterization of the objects apart from their relations to others, and they claim to see why the effects must be produced *given* this characterization. The mechanists, in other words, claim to give us just what we wanted when we were asking how a fundamental force like repulsion is possible. They claim to characterize a thing in terms of properties it has "by its mere existence," in terms of its inner determinations, and they claim to account for a body's resistance in terms of them. But Kant's view is that they seem to do so only by misconceiving a causal connection as a logical connection.

Now, where is Kant left at this point? He will want to say that, in ascribing a fundamental force to an object, we characterize the object in terms of its relations, that is, in terms of its relations to its possible effects in others, where these effects are described in terms of a rule that governs them. Moreover, he will claim, we can have no explanatory insight whatsoever into *how* these effects are produced, or, equivalently, into *how* the fundamental force is possible. And any demand that we come to know how these effects are produced involves a claim to be able to know things in terms of their inner properties, a claim to be able to know things apart from their relations to others. And such a demand is therefore illegitimate.

In conclusion, I want to indicate a connection between these considerations and Kant's treatment of one of the central problems in the development of the new science, namely the problem of gravitational attraction acting at a distance. When gravitational attraction was introduced by Newton, one purported source of dissatisfaction with it was that it was not really explanatory. The complaint was that it merely gave a mathematical rule governing certain effects, namely, accelerations, which occur in bodies in the presence of an attracting body. But, the complaint goes, that does not show how this body *produces* these accelerations. What was wanted was some kind of *mechanism* by which the effects were produced, e.g., an account in terms of vortices in a surrounding ether. It was felt that only a mechanistic explanation could afford us real insight into how the acceleration of the planets resulted from the presence of a massive body like the sun. Mechanistic explanation was regarded as a standard of intelligibility.

It is precisely this idea that Kant was attempting to undermine. For an appeal to a fundamental force—namely repulsive force—was required to explain even the interactions that were regarded as paradigms of mechanical interaction. And we no more understand how repulsive forces produce their effects than we understand how attractive forces produce theirs. If a fundamental irreducible attractive force is thought to be incomprehensible, we have no reason to regard the mechanisms that might be offered to explain attraction as ultimately any *more* comprehensible.[19] With regard to its intelligibility, a fundamental attractive force is no less admissible than a fundamental repulsive force. Those who were dissatisfied with the introduction of attractive force misinterpreted the character of our ignorance about how attraction occurred. Kant, as we have seen, can assimilate it to a much broader philosophical view about what we can know, namely the idea that all we know are the relational features of things, never their inner determinations. But the mechanists must see it simply as a lacuna in our understanding of nature. They must see in it a question that is unanswered, but which is perfectly intelligible to us—how something with such and such an inner constitution produces such and such motions. The question, according to the mechanists, is of a sort that is answerable in principle. It is just the sort of question they think mechanistic explanations deal with. But Kant, I think, would see in such questions an attempt to go beyond the bounds of human understanding. In fact, a characteristic strength of Kant's defense of a broadly Newtonian physics is the way in which he links it to a systematic account of the limits of our knowledge. When we rule out all explanations which appeal to a mediating mechanism, for example when we posit an attractive force which acts *immediately* over a distance, this will seem to the mechanist to be an irremediable gap *within* empirical knowledge. And the mechanists will see no reason in principle to renounce their ambition to understand even how attraction occurs. Kant's project, I have suggested, was to show why such ambitions and the ideal of knowledge and explanation implicit in them were misguided.

NOTES

I wish to thank John Carriero, Michael Friedman, and Hannah Ginsborg for extremely helpful discussions and comments on earlier drafts.

1. Many mechanists, for example, Locke, also included a property they called "solidity." This will be central to the discussion that follows.

2. In quotations from the *Critique of Pure Reason*, I have followed the translation of Norman Kemp Smith. In quotations from the *Nova Dilucidatio*, I have followed the translation by John A. Reuscher, found in *Kant's Latin Writings*, ed. L.W. Beck (New York: Peter Lang, 1986), 57–106. In quotations from the inaugural dissertation, I have followed the translation of John Handyside as revised by L.W. Beck, in *Kant's Latin Writings*, 145– 88. The translations of quotations from the *Essay on Negative Magnitudes* are my own. In quotations from the *Metaphysical Foundations of Natural Science*, I have followed the translation by James W. Ellington, found in Immanuel Kant, *Philosophy of Material Nature* (Indianapolis: Hackett Publishing, 1985). In quotations from the *Lectures on Metaphysics*, I have followed the translation by Karl Ameriks and Steve Naragon, found in Immanuel Kant, *Lectures on Metaphysics*, ed. Karl Ameriks and Steve Naragon (Cambridge: Cambridge University Press, 1997).

3. I discuss certain aspects of this contrast in more depth in chap. 3 of my "Reality and Impenetrability in Kant's Philosophy of Nature" (Ph.D. diss., Harvard University, 1994), forthcoming from Garland Publishing.

4. The mechanistic conception of space-filling does not itself entail atomism. We can imagine a picture of matter according to which it is incompressible in the way the mechanistic conception requires, and yet divisible ad infinitum, and thus perfectly fluid all the way down.

5. This way of putting the point, i.e., that the Anticipations establish the "real possibility" of this alternative, was suggested to me by Michael Friedman, who has emphasized the role that philosophy can play in legitimizing certain scientific proposals as genuine *possibilities*, even if on its own it does not establish that some particular one among them is the correct one.

6. Here I draw on Lambert's *Neues Organon* (1764), Alethiologie, chap. 2, and his *Anlage zur Architektonic* (1771), chap. 3, found in Johann Heinrich Lambert, *Philosophische Schriften*, ed. Hans-Werner Arndt (Hildesheim: Georg Olms, 1965), vols. 1 and 3.

7. Kant, too, has a place in his physics for a mechanistic conception of force. He allows that a body in motion has a power to produce motions in others, which it exercises on impact with them. This mechanistic notion of force, unlike the dynamical notion, does not have as its model a Newtonian idea of attractive force. Rather than rejecting the mechanist's forces, what Kant does is to embed them within a characterization of the bodies, as endowed with dynamical forces (like attraction and repulsion), which bodies have independent of their state of motion or rest. However, these mechanistic forces, insofar as Kant allows for them, are restricted to bodies in motion. What Kant *does* reject (from 1758 on, at least) is the idea of inertia as a force, and the idea that bodies even at rest are endowed with such a *vis inertiae*. But what is added by Kant is a notion of a privileged reference frame, that of the center of mass of the bodies under consideration, and it is by reference to this frame that the motion which is relevant to determining the mechanical force of a body is to be assessed. So instead of thinking of the collision of a moving body with another at rest as involving a force due to the motion of the first and an inertial force associated with the second, Kant will ascribe to each of them a (mechanistic) force due to motion, but motion that is relative to a different reference frame, namely, to the center-of-mass frame. Given the way Kant thinks about the mechanistic picture, he will be able to say that a body has a (mechanistic) force only insofar as it is in motion (with respect to the center-of-mass frame), and that solidity, unlike (mechanistic) force, is a property a body has independently of its state of motion—indeed, it is a property a body has even if it is considered to be at rest.

8. Perhaps, from Kant's standpoint, the sense in which the mechanist's solidity is not to be conceived as a matter of having a repulsive force—even an *infinitely strong* repulsive force acting only on contact—is to be seen in the fact that, on the mechanist conception, the presence of another body in proximity or even in contact with the given body is not, all else being equal, sufficient for any change of motion of either. There is no tendency for them to move away from one another. They can simply sit there, even sit there in contact with one another. Nor is there any need on the mechanist's conception to bring in a countervailing force (e.g., attraction) to explain why they can sit there without any change of motion. In this way, one can better see the sense in which the exclusion of the other body is not being conceived on the model of a force. Similarly, if one thinks about the solid *parts* of a body that neighbor each other or are in contact, they do not, on the mechanistic conception, repel one another. On the mechanistic conception, there is no tendency of a

solid body, insofar as it is made up of solid parts, to expand, as there is on the dynamical conception. (Kant's particular conception of finite repulsive forces allows for sustained continuous action, even though they act only on contact. This is because contact can be maintained even as the repulsive force has its effect, for the repelling body can itself expand in the process.)

9. It is important to note here that Kant seems to assume that the occurrence of a continuous change *can* be confirmed in experience. It is worth asking what kind of warrant he has for this assumption. It seems likely that the concept of a continuous alteration is like the concept of cause and effect in certain ways. That is, Kant might regard our use of the concept of continuous alteration as *legitimate* even though the correctness of applying it is never based on observations alone. Perhaps the justification of this concept is to be thought of as a part of the work of the Analogies. The concept of continuous alteration might be regarded as playing a role in time determination, but instead of focusing on the successiveness of temporal moments, this argument might in some way concern their continuity.

10. This reflection also suggests an answer to the following question. If the Anticipations do not rule out the mechanistic conception of impenetrability, then which, if any, of Kant's Critical doctrines *do*? Kant argues for the continuity of all alteration at the end of the Second Analogy (A207–11/B252–56). As Kant characterizes it, the argument depends on the claim that time is continuous, i.e., that it is made of parts none of which is the smallest. However, the nature of the argument is extremely obscure, and there seem to be several versions of the argument, which appear very different from one another. The claim that all alteration is continuous certainly *entails* the rejection of the mechanistic conception of space-filling. But it is not clear that this means that Kant's argument for this claim constitutes an argument for rejecting the mechanist conception. For at least one version of the argument seems to include an assumption ("Now every alteration has a cause which evinces its causality in the whole time in which the alteration takes place" [A208/B253]), which may itself be tantamount to that conclusion, which would make it question-begging, as far as establishing this point is concerned. It is not clear whether other versions of the argument are or are not free of such an assumption. At one point in the Second Analogy Kant says that "only in appearances can we empirically cognize this continuity in the connection of times" (A199/B244). Perhaps here Kant is claiming that the continuity of alteration is a condition on "time-determination," where the temporal property being "determined" is its continuity. (This suggests a parallel to the main argument of the Second Analogy, which claims that the causal rule-governedness of appearances is a condition on time-determination—in the sense that it is a condition on making judgments concerning the temporal successiveness of appearances. But it is not clear what the parallel spelling out of "condition on time-determination" would be in the case of temporal continuity. If it were simply spelled out as "a condition on making judgments concerning the temporal continuity of appearances," it is not clear that an argument parallel to the successiveness argument could be carried out. At a minimum, there is this disanalogy: The latter argument relies on the contrast between appearances that are successive [the ship example] and those that are not [the house example]. But in the case of continuity, one of the contrasting terms is precisely what is being ruled out.) Whatever the precise character of the argument, it seems clear that Kant means it to rule out the kind of discontinuous change of motion entailed by the mechanist's conception of absolute impenetrability. However, my focus here will not be on this argument, but rather on the way Kant characterizes the contrast between mechanistic and dy-

namical conceptions of impenetrability in the second chapter of the *MFNS*. This will, I believe, give us a fuller sense of what kind of error the mechanists are making, and of why they are led to make it.

11. This is not to suggest that in attempting to characterize something through its inner determinations, we are necessarily attempting to characterize it as something that is non-spatial and nontemporal; rather the point is that, if we are trying to characterize some *aspect* (e.g., the solidity) of a thing by means of inner determinations, then we are claiming to represent that aspect, and (possibly) to know that aspect, in a way that could be appropriate only if we were capable of representing and knowing things as they are in themselves. I discuss at length the connection between determinations and things in themselves in chap. 2 of *Reality and Impenetrability in Kant's Philosophy of Nature*.

12. In this last quotation, I rely on Walford's translation, which is in this instance much closer to the Latin than Reuscher's, and is in agreement with the translation by England.

13. Thus, in this context, we characterize a thing by means of its inner determinations insofar as we abstract, not just from a thing's actual relations to others, but from its possible relations as well.

14. I think it is worth mentioning, on Lambert's behalf, that Kant does not seem to be correctly representing Lambert's position here. Lambert's view is that the notions of "existence in space" and of "solidity" must be thought together, that to separate them in thought is, in some sense, to violate conditions of "thinkability." But on Lambert's view, these latter conditions are explicitly distinguished from conditions deriving from conceptual analysis or the principle of contradiction. However, it remains obscure what precisely Lambert's distinctive notion of conditions of thinkability amounts to. Kant appears to be substituting his own conception of conditions of thinkability, i.e., the conditions deriving from conceptual analysis and the principle of contradiction, which is the only coherent conception of such conditions he thinks is available. In part, I draw on L.W. Beck's *Early German Philosophy* (Cambridge: Harvard University Press, 1969), 404–406, as a source on Lambert's general views described in this note.

15. In order to understand Kant's attack on "Lambert and others," who maintained that "solidity must be assumed in everything that exists (substance), at least in the external sensible world," it is extremely helpful to consider a broader formulation of the view he is opposing. In particular, the "absolute necessity" with which the mechanists thought bodies resisted penetration, can admit of interpretations other than analyticity. And this will better enable us to see the force of Kant's denial that matter fills space "by its mere existence." A good example of the idea Kant is rejecting is suggested by a passage from Locke. It is a passage in which Locke, pursuing a rather metaphysical vein, discusses the identity and diversity of the three basic sorts of substances: God, finite intelligences, and bodies (*Essay*, book II, chap. 27, §2). He writes:

> [C]ould two bodies be at the same place at the same time, then those two parcels of matter must be one and the same, take them great or little; nay all bodies must be one and the same. For, by the same reason that two particles of matter may be in one place, all bodies may be in one place; which, when it can be supposed, takes away the distinction of identity and diversity of one and more, and renders it ridiculous. But it being a contradiction that two or more should be one, identity and diversity are relations and ways of comparing well founded, and of use to the understanding.

(I take the last sentence to mean: But [on account of] it[s] being a contradiction that two or more should be one, [and therefore, its being impossible,] identity and diversity are relations and ways of comparing [which are] well founded, and of use to the understanding.)

What I wish to focus on in this passage is the idea that two bodies cannot be in the same place at the same time because otherwise they would not be two bodies, but one. For this is supposed to be an account of why bodies must *exclude* one another. If one body could penetrate another, they would cease to be "distinct existences." Thus, it is their character as substances, i.e., as persisting distinct existences, that is purported to explain why bodies must exclude each other from their spaces. Were one body to pass through another, there would be a time during which there was only one body rather than two, and therefore they could not both be said to persist. (I assume that persistence was taken to entail identity, i.e., that Parfit-style approaches are not under consideration.)

This view presents the property of impenetrability as a feature required by an essentially metaphysical consideration, i.e., the idea that the existence or nonexistence of genuine (mundane) substances is independent of their (intramundane) relations. Bodies, on this view, can be said to resist penetration with "absolute" necessity. ("Lambert and others," on Kant's account of them, can be considered as presenting the special case in which absolute necessity is interpreted as logical or conceptual necessity.) Kant's reaction to this view, like his reaction to that of "Lambert and others," is that it is misguided as an explanation of impenetrability. Knowing that a body's existence has the necessary independence appropriate to a substance cannot explain why changes in the motions of impinging bodies must occur, *unless* we also ascribe a causal power (viz., a moving force) to it. In saying why the something's state of motion *had* to change as it impinged on another, we must appeal to a *causal* necessity. What is being opposed is a view according to which the deflection of an approaching body *must* occur, just because it is an independent existence (substance) that is involved.

When Kant denies that matter fills space "by its mere existence," we can regard him as excluding also this possibility. For earlier on I indicated the close connection between what Kant means by the features a thing has "by its mere existence," and what is true of it just in virtue of its character as substance, i.e., a part of the character it has apart from its relations to other things. It is in terms of this character that we can conceive what it was that God created when he made a thing whose existence is independent of all other (finite) things, and, in particular, is independent of its interactions with them. There is an essential contrast, Kant is suggesting, between giving an account in terms of properties a thing is conceived as having "by its mere existence," on the one hand, and in terms of the fundamental forces it is endowed with, on the other. It is this contrast that forms the philosophically most important core of the difference between the mathematico-mechanical and the metaphysico-dynamical approaches to natural philosophy, or, rather, between the basic resources each draws upon.

It might be objected that the requirements associated with being a substance have a role to play in explaining why the motion of an impinging body must change, even if we admit the need that a causal power be involved. For we might say only that the substance-requirements explain why a body *must have* a causal power of a certain sort (viz., a repulsive moving force). That is, bodies must have a repulsive moving force if they are to persist as distinct existences during the course of collision interactions. And to that extent the substance-requirements play a role in explaining why a deflection *had* to occur.

I see no reason why Kant would have to be opposed to such a suggestion in principle. His point is only that a body's deflection of something impinging upon it, and thus, its resistance, cannot be explained *without* appealing to specifically causal connections. And questions about the intelligibility of this relation may remain and may need to be addressed. I think what is fundamental to Kant's worry here is that we not confuse two different kinds of necessity. It is one thing to say that a substance *must* have a causal power of a certain sort. The sense of necessity relevant here is not causal. But when we ask why a certain thing's motion changed as it impinged on another, Kant takes it that we are asking why it *had* to change, where the kind of necessity at stake is causal.

16. One of the disadvantages of the mechanical approach, on Kant's view, is that it burdens us with the task of "building a world *merely according to fancy* out of fulness and emptiness" (4:524, my emphasis); it must "allow the imagination more freedom in the field of philosophy—and indeed allow this freedom as a rightful claim—than can be consistent with the caution of philosophy" (4:525); it "give[s] far too much freedom to the imagination to supply by fiction the lack of intrinsic knowledge of nature" (4:532). Kant also says that the dynamical mode of explication is "far more suited and more favorable to experimental philosophy," whereas the mechanical approach, by contrast, involves "the freedom of assuming empty intermediate spaces and fundamental particles of determinate shapes, neither of which can be discovered and determined by any experiment" (4:533). These kinds of passages are especially emphasized by Philip Kitcher in his "Kant's Philosophy of Science" in *Self and Nature in Kant's Philosophy*, ed. A. Wood (Ithaca: Cornell University Press, 1984). I believe that they fit well with the line I have been pursuing, namely that we must seek the character of matter "in all the effects which it exercises" (A277/B333). (This quotation is taken from the Amphiboly passages, where Kant is arguing that we only know the relational features of things.) We characterize what is present in a region of space by means of a rule governing its effects, rather than by speculations about the (all too many) possible distributions of particles of different shapes that might be the cause of these effects. However, my sense is that at least some of the passages about the mechanical approach that have been cited here are specifically focussed on problems associated with the atomistic aspect of the mechanistic approach. My focus has been on what I believe to be a more basic aspect of the mechanical conception, i.e., the conception of the "space-filling" property, what Kant calls "absolute" in contrast to "relative" impenetrability. (As I emphasized in note 4, these two aspects are, in principle, separable.)

17. Kant is perhaps making a very closely related point at the very end of the *Essay on Negative Magnitudes* (2:204), when he says: "That concept [the concept of a real ground] can probably be reduced by means of analysis to simple concepts of real grounds, albeit in such a fashion that in the end all our cognitions of this relation reduce to simple, unanalysable concepts of real grounds, *the relation of which to their consequences cannot be rendered distinct at all*" (my emphasis).

18. I do not believe that the arguments of the *MFNS*—specifically, the arguments of the Dynamics chapter—should be regarded as having brought us to the completion of this explanatory regress. The *MFNS* claims to establish that there must be fundamental attractive forces and that there must be fundamental repulsive forces, and that these forces have certain basic properties. But it does not really claim to establish the corresponding force laws, and *that* is what is crucial in completing the explanatory regress. (Moreover, I am not convinced that the *MFNS* should even be regarded as establishing how many fundamental forces—

taking this to mean: how many fundamental force laws—there are, beyond having established that there must be at least two.)

19. Note that this is distinct from the claim that attraction *cannot* be explained by means of repulsive forces acting through contact. This requires a distinct argument, which Kant claims to provide. The point I am making is that, for Kant, the appeal to a fundamental attractive force is not in any way intrinsically unsatisfactory. In other words, the intelligibility of nature does not *require* that attraction be explained mechanistically (by appeal to vortices, and so on).

6

Kant's Mechanical Determination of *Matter in the* Metaphysical Foundations of Natural Science

Martin Carrier

I_N his *Metaphysical Foundations of Natural Science* Kant set himself the task of demonstrating that the "pure part" of natural science was apodictically certain.[1] The method he employed for this purpose was to apply the forms of intuition and the categories he had elaborated in the *Critique of Pure Reason* to the more specific problem of analyzing the cognition of matter as the "movable in space." The forms of intuition and the categories are supposed to be constitutive of every process of gaining empirical knowledge. By applying them to the more restricted domain of the knowledge of matter, a more substantial characterization of the relevant "conditions of the possibility of cognition" should be feasible. By elaborating the transcendental conditions of the cognition of matter in an a priori manner, the concept of matter is intended to become suitable for the application to experience. In this way, the pure part of physics is identified.

I focus on the third chapter of the *Metaphysical Foundations*, the Mechanics chapter, which is devoted to the application of the "categories of relation." The objective is to clarify—in a transcendental way—the relationship between different parts of matter and, in particular, the transfer of motion between them. That is, the problem concerns the capacity of moved matter to "impart this motion to another matter" (4:536). The forces that are influential in these "mechanical" processes cannot straightforwardly be identified with the forces in the Dynamics chapter. "Dynamic" forces are responsible for the material filling of space and are not essentially connected to the motion of matter (4:536). "Dynamic" forces primarily act within matter, "mechanical" forces between parts of matter.

The capacity to impart or communicate motion goes back to a "moving force." Like each chapter, the Mechanics chapter begins by giving an explication of the concept of matter. Explication 1 specifies matter as "the movable in so far as it as such has moving force" (4:536, translation amended). In the associated note Kant explains that the communication of motion by "pressure" and "collision" is primarily at issue and that, consequently, repulsive forces are most relevant. Kant mentions processes such as the acceleration of bodies by the release of suspended elastic springs or by their collision with other bodies. By contrast, the forces of attraction, and, in particular, the gravitational interaction between the earth and celestial bodies, are accorded only secondary importance (4:537).

However, it will become clear that Kant does not actually ascribe only marginal significance to gravitation in this context, but rather grants it a leading role in the determination of the quantity of matter. In fact, this is quite legitimate within the framework of Kant's approach. Gravitation is not only efficacious within matter and constitutive for its filling of space but also acts between different parts of matter. Propositions 7 and 8 of the Dynamics chapter state that the influence of the "original attraction" extends through empty space to infinite distances, and, consequently, to other parts of matter (4:512, 516). In this vein, gravitation is included in the set of mechanically relevant influences: It is counted among the factors that serve "the communication of motion by attraction" (4:537).[2]

Explication 2 adds two more important mechanical characteristics of matter. First: "The quantity of matter is the quantity of the movable in a certain space" (4:537, translation amended) and is called *mass*. Second: The "quantity of motion" is determined by the mass and the velocity of the corresponding body (4:537).[3] In modern terminology, the quantity of motion is the linear momentum p, which is represented by the product of mass m and velocity v ($p = mv$). Incidentally, Newton gives an identical definition of the quantity of motion in the *Principia*.[4]

In addition to these two explications, the Mechanics chapter essentially contains four propositions: (1) the specification of mass measurement, (2) the law of the conservation of mass, (3) the principle of inertia, and (4) the law of the equality of action and reaction. These propositions are supposed to capture the essence of Newtonian mechanics; but not all of them are actually identical with their Newtonian counterparts.[5] Propositions 2 through 4 are thought to be derived from an application of the categories of relation to the "movable in space": The conservation of mass arises from the category of substance; inertia stems from the category of causality; and the principle of action and reaction emerges from the category of interaction (4:551). No category is given for establishing proposition 1 on mass measurement.

A striking deviation from Newton's *Principia* consists in the absence of Newton's second law. According to this law, each acceleration of a body, or as Newton puts it, its "change of motion," is proportional to an impressed force. Kant does not assign a proposition to this fundamental law of Newtonian mechanics. To be sure, there are passages in the *Metaphysical Foundations* that might be viewed as alluding to the law in an obscure fashion, so it is not missing entirely. But this passing and ambiguous allusion is a far cry from an explicit statement, let alone evidence that Kant regarded it as one of the chief principles of the theory.

I single out proposition 1 on the determination of the quantity of matter for more extensive treatment. What I shall try to do, in particular, is to reconstruct the procedure Kant specifies for this purpose. Kant's intention is to ground the determination of mass on the moving force that matter possesses by virtue of its motion and that moving bodies display by setting other bodies in motion (4:536). This *motive force*, that is, the moving force resulting from motion, constitutes one of the topical foci of the entire Mechanics chapter. Note that a motive force is a special form of a moving force. It is a moving force that acts by virtue of a body's motion. The systematic issue bearing on mechanical mass measurement concerns the role of gravitation as compared to processes that qualify as mechanical in the more restricted sense of "pressure and impact." I intend to show that Kant invokes gravity for the purpose of determining the quantity of matter mechanically and that he relies on terrestrial procedures. Kant's crucial step is to take terrestrial weighing as the determination of a body's mass from this body's own motive force.

1. MEASURING MASS VALUES BY COMPARING MOMENTA

It is the objective of proposition 1 to make the concept of the quantity of matter suitable for the application to experience. In order to obtain a "determinate concept," values for the quantity need to be given. "For the determinate concept of a quantity is only possible through the construction of the quantum" (4:538). The construction of a quantitative concept (a quantity) requires the construction of its quantitative features (the quantum). This is achieved in various ways, depending on the case at hand. The construction of the fundamental forces demands the derivation of the dependence of the intensity on distance. As for the quantity of matter, the "construction of the quantum" requires the determination of its quantitative characteristics, which in turn necessitates the specification of a measurement procedure. This is the challenge addressed by proposition 1 and its accompanying explanations. Proposition 1 reads: "The quantity of matter can be estimated in comparison with *every* other matter only by its quantity of motion at a given speed" (4:537, translation amended). That is, the evaluation of mass is derived from the linear momentum at a given speed, i.e., $m = p/v$. This procedure is said to be the only one that is universally applicable.

In Kant's view it is the so-called "fundamental principle of general mechanics," which guarantees that mass can be reliably measured by motion. According to this principle, a body's motive force at a given speed depends exclusively on the body's quantity of matter (4:539–40). This means that a body's capacity to transfer a part of its own motion to another body depends only on these bodies' mass values and not on further properties (such as density or chemical nature). The momentum of a body determines the moving force it can exert by virtue of its motion (4:538).

This approach implies measuring mass values by comparing values of momenta at equal speeds. "The quantity of the movable in space is the quantity of matter; but this quantity of matter (the amount of the movable) *manifests itself* in experience only by the quantity of motion at equal speed (e.g., by equilibrium)" (4:

540, translation amended). The phrase "manifests itself in experience" indicates reference to measurements. The condition of equal speeds says, then, that only under this condition are momentum and mass proportional to one another. "For only this amount of the movable can at the same speed give a difference in the quantity of motion" (4:540–41, translation amended). The significance of the requirement of equal speeds becomes clear against the traditional background of representing the connection between two quantities as a proportional variation. In this framework, the dependence of a quantity on two others is expressed by saying that the first quantity is proportional to the second if the third is constant. In the *Principia*, proportionalities figure prominently, and Newton likewise presents a multiple dependence in precisely this way.[6] Equations were seldom used in the eighteenth century. On this interpretation, Kant's reference to equal speeds is nothing but a way, typical of the period, to capture the dependence of a quantity on two others. However, Kant's wording might also contain an obscure reference to the balance. I return to this issue later (see sec. 3).

Kant explicitly notes that his approach might at first sight appear to suffer from circularity. According to explication 2, momentum is determined by mass, whereas according to proposition 1, the reverse holds (4:540). In order to resolve this apparent circle, Kant places emphasis on the distinction between the *explication* of a concept, on the one hand, and the procedures involved in its *application* to experience, on the other. The explication proceeds from the mass as the quantity of the movable in space; this concept is invoked for an explication of linear momentum. In terms of systematic order, momentum follows mass. However, momenta are used for determining mass values empirically. In terms of measurement, mass follows momentum. The relationship between mass and momentum is of a different conceptual nature in each direction, and this is why no circle emerges (4:540).[7]

However, even with this clarification it is far from obvious how Kant wished to perform the relevant measurements. If it is granted that the measurement of speeds involves no particular difficulty, one is left with the challenge of measuring momenta. And what makes this challenge demanding is the requirement not to resort to mass values taken from other sources. After all, the procedure is supposed to afford reliable mass values in the first place. It is tempting to draw on the conservation of momentum in collision processes. As mentioned above, Kant singles out "pressure and impact" as particularly suitable for characterizing matter by its motive force (4:537). In a collision of two bodies with mass values m_1 and m_2 at velocities v_1 and v_2 before impact and v_1' and v_2' afterward, conservation of momentum yields: $m_1 v_1 + m_2 v_2 = m_1 v_1' + m_2 v_2'$. It follows: $m_1 \Delta v_1 = m_2 \Delta v_2$, which leads to $m_1 : m_2 = \Delta v_2 : \Delta v_1$. Conservation of momentum yields that the mass ratio of two colliding bodies equals the inverse ratio of their corresponding velocity changes, so that the former ratio can be inferred by measuring the latter. However, there is no textual evidence whatsoever that Kant had a procedure of this sort in mind. This means that Kant never specifies a procedure for measuring mass that actually relies on collisions. So it remains unclear, at this juncture, how the momentum values are to be gained that are subsequently to be used for determining mass values.

2. MASS EVALUATIONS AND THE ACTION OF FORCES

However the evaluation of mass by comparing momenta is to be performed precisely, Kant emphasizes that this procedure is the only one that is *universally* applicable. This claim is justified by rejecting alternative procedures. It is based, in particular, on Kant's refusal to invoke the original forces of matter, as discussed in the Dynamics chapter, for a mechanical determination of the quantity of matter. "There is yet to be noted that the quantity of matter is the *quantity of substance* in the movable and, consequently, not the magnitude of a certain quality of matter (of repulsion or attraction, which are cited in dynamics)" (4:540). That is to say, the assessment of the quantity of matter in mechanical respect is to be based on the corresponding body's "moving force" (4:536). Evaluating a body's mass mechanically requires recourse to this body's force of its *own* motion (4:541). Kant's point is that this condition is violated if attractive forces are invoked, or so it seems. The underlying argument is to be construed as follows. Measuring a body's mass by relying on forces proceeds by determining the mass of body *A* by ascertaining the effect of its forces on body *B*. This effect manifests itself in the motion of *B*. Consequently, this procedure does not involve estimating the quantity of a body by relying on the motive force of this body itself and is for this reason disqualified as a mechanical procedure. However, shortly we shall see that Kant reintroduces gravitation as an appropriate basis for mass measurement and thus revokes the exclusion of forces in general as a means for determining the quantity of matter mechanically.

Kant places heavy emphasis on the condition that each mechanical construction of the quantity of matter is to be based on the motive force of the body whose quantity is to be determined. Mechanics deals with the moving force a body can exert through its own motion (538.29–32). This is the reason for singling out the approach sketched by proposition 1 as the *only* universally reliable one: Differences in mass (meaning: mass ratios) are to be obtained by differences in the quantities of motion (meaning: momentum ratios) at equal speeds:

> Therefore matter can neither directly nor indirectly be validly estimated in comparison with every *other* matter as long as one abstracts from its own motion. Consequently, there remains no other universally valid measure of the matter than the quantity of its motion. But in this the difference of the motion, which rests on the different quantities of the matters, can only be

given when the speed is assumed to be equal among the compared matters (4:538, translation amended).

The general exclusion of forces as a basis of mass measurement and the exclusive reliance on momentum ratios apparently rules out weighing as an adequate measuring procedure. Given Kant's argument, as sketched so far, one would expect that Kant rejects weighing as unsound. Arguments to this effect can easily be conceived. One might object to using a spring balance by pointing out that it measures weight rather than mass and that the relationship between the two depends on the particulars of the gravitational field present. For instance, a mass of 1 kilogram weighs 9.8 N on earth, 1.5 N on the surface of the moon, and is weightless in a terrestrial orbit. Accordingly, Kant could have argued that the inference from weight to mass is dependent on the specific circumstances realized and that weighing thus fails to furnish trustworthy results in general.

But Kant does not in fact argue this way. Rather, his claim is that, in general, the intensity of forces is dependent on the particulars of the situation. A "small part of air," for instance, may be more or less elastic (4:541). This is to say, the internal moving forces of matter may vary with the specific properties of the bodies involved and the constraints of the situation. For this reason they are not necessarily proportional to mass and thus fail to license any reliable inference to the mass values of these bodies. But Kant hastens to restrict the import of this objection significantly. As he argues, the proviso regarding the specific efficacy of forces does not apply to the original forces; in particular, it does not apply to universal gravitation (4:541). Gravitation demonstrably acts proportional to mass and thus provides an appropriate basis for determining mass values. Consequently, weighing is a legitimate procedure for measuring the quantity of matter.

> Nevertheless, *original attraction* as the cause of universal gravitation can indeed provide a measure of the quantity of matter and its substance (as it actually happens in the comparison of matter by weighing), although there seems to be laid at the foundation here not the own motion of the attracting matter but a dynamical measure, namely, attractive force (4:541, translation amended).

The conclusion suggests that Kant regards weighing as a "dynamic" procedure, that is, one appealing to original forces rather than motive forces.

But this construal would be mistaken. In fact, Kant considers weighing as a "mechanical" procedure, that is, as one taking recourse to the weighed body's motive force. The key to a proper reconstruction of weighing lies in taking the reciprocal equality of gravitational forces into account. In weighing, the earth and the weighed body reciprocally communicate motion to each other, which is proportional to their mass.

> But in the case of this force, the action [is] . . . proportional to the number of the parts. Because of this fact, the attracting body also imparts the speed of its own motion to itself (by means of the resistance of the attracted body). This speed is directly proportional, in equivalent external circumstances, to the number of the attracting body's parts; because of this the estimation takes place here, as a matter of fact, mechanically, although only indirectly so (4:541, translation amended).

Kant's argument is to be reconstructed as follows. To be sure, it is true in principle—as the aforementioned objection entails—that the gravitational force of body *A* is proportional to the mass of *A* but produces motion in the body *B*. However, due to the reciprocal equality of gravitational forces, *A*'s force on *B* coincides with *B*'s force of the same intensity on *A*. And this latter force produces motion in *A*. On the whole, then, the gravitational force of *A* is proportional to the mass of *A*, it results in the motion of *A*, and it endows *A* with a motive force. The gravitational force of a body generates a motive force in this very body that is proportional to its mass value. Thus, it is the principle of the equality of action and reaction that connects gravitation with the motive force. For this reason, weighing provides a "mechanical," not a "dynamic" measure of mass. It follows that using a balance—in contrast to other means for measuring mass—is actually not rejected but reconstrued as "mechanical"—if "only indirectly so." Weighing is supposed to be based on the determination of the relevant body's motive force. This shows that Kant does not actually obtain his mass values from collision processes but from employing scales.

3. KANT'S REQUIREMENT OF EQUAL SPEEDS

In one of the passages already quoted Kant demands that the empirical comparison of quantities of matter be performed at equal speeds of the bodies involved. "The quantity of the movable in space . . . *manifests itself* in experience only by the quantity of motion at equal speed (e.g., by equilibrium)" (4:540; see sec. 1). In light of the preceding discussion, Kant's reference to equilibrium can be understood as an allusion to the balance. But the condition of equal speeds was interpreted earlier as implying a reference to proportional relations rather than equations: The mass values of two bodies can be inferred directly from their momenta only if their speeds coincide (see sec. 1). However, if one adopts the view that weighing was Kant's first choice for obtaining mass values, it suggests applying the condition of equal speeds to the balance as well. At first glance, there is no sensible way to do so. It is true, in the equilibrium states of spring and equal-arm balance alike, all relevant speeds are zero, that is, equal. But this interpretation of the equality condition is too trivial to be plausible.

I suggest that Kant's condition of equal speeds is intended to express the requirement of equal *accelerations,* or equal *changes of speed.* Cast in this way the condition is equivalent to the proportionality of inertial and gravitational mass, and it means that this proportionality is a presupposition for employing scales for measuring mass. The plausibility of this construal hinges quite obviously on the fact that Kant uses the term "speed" to refer to accelerations. Passages to this effect can certainly be located. In one of the statements already quoted Kant says that in gravitational interaction "the attracting body also imparts the speed of its own motion to itself (by means of the resistance of the attracted body). This speed is directly proportional, in equivalent external circumstances, to the number of the attracting body's parts" (4:541, translation amended). Taken literally, the sentence says that in gravitational interaction speed is proportional to mass. By contrast, Newtonian mechanics has it that acceleration is proportional to mass. This suggests reading Kant's term "speed" as referring to accelerations.

More indications to this effect are found in student notes of Kant's lectures on physics. In the copy of a physics lecture of 1776, called *Berliner Physik* after the place where it was found, Kant explains the free fall of bodies. As he says, "all bodies fall at equal speeds if we abstract from the resistance of the air" (29:80–81). And quite analogously one reads in the *Danziger Physik* of 1785, which originates from the period in which the *Metaphysical Foundations* was composed: "Gravity means the speed at which a body falls; it is the same among all (bodies)" (29:142). Since it should be assumed that Kant knew that free fall is accelerated, and he explicitly recognizes this fact in the *Opus postumum* (21:405–406), these statements clearly indicate Kant's use of "speed" for acceleration.

Actually, the *Danziger Physik* also contains the condition of equal speeds and elaborates it further:

> Since the bodies attain equal speeds by reason of gravity, the bodies exhibit the same ratio as the quantities of matter. In weighing we only see where their moving force is. We say: They are of equal quantity if their moving forces are equal. The moving forces exhibit the same ratio as the quantities if the speeds are equal. And since this is the case, the moving forces exhibit the same ratio as the quantities. Galileo was the first to find that the speeds are equal; the ancients were not aware of this. This was confirmed by the air pump. If the speeds are equal, weighing indicates the quantities of matter according to their proportion. Otherwise it does not, since weighing only shows the proportion of the moving forces (29:142).

In this passage Kant directly addresses the relationship between weighing, moving force, and equality of speeds. He emphasizes that weighing by itself only measures the "moving forces," that is, weight, and goes on to explain that weight is proportional to the quantity of matter, that is, mass—provided that the "speeds" coincide; provided, that is, that gravity endows all bodies with "equal speeds." It was discovered by Galileo and confirmed by the air pump, as Kant argues, that this condition is actually satisfied.

To repeat, Kant was certainly aware of the fact that the velocity of freely falling bodies does not remain the same. It is thus tempting to assume that Kant somewhat carelessly employs the term "speed" for "change of speed" or "acceleration." In fact, Newton himself states in the *Principia* that in a vacuum on earth different bodies, such as a "bit of fine down and a piece of solid gold descend with equal velocity."[8] This wording contrasts with the usual formulation of the law of free fall, which invokes equal accelerations. It is true, equal accelerations from rest imply equal speeds at each instant; the speeds of two bodies falling alongside one another indeed coincide. So what Newton says is not literally wrong; but it is misleading. Plausibly enough, he simply abbreviated "change of speed" to "speed"—just as Kant did a century later.

On this construal, Kant's condition of the equality of speeds expresses the universality of the acceleration of freely falling bodies. Given this interpretation, the upshot of the just-quoted paragraph from the *Danziger Physik* is that weighing indicates mass values reliably only on the condition that the gravitational acceleration of all bodies agrees. By contrast, if gravitational acceleration depended on the size of the bodies or their chemical nature, mass values could not be determined using a balance. In sum, what Kant explains here is that mass measurements with the balance presuppose that weight W is proportional to mass m, which in turn requires that the earth's acceleration g is constant ($W = mg$).

This passage from the *Danziger Physik* provides a clue for elucidating the analogous passage from the *Metaphysical Foundations*. Plausibly enough, the equal-speeds requirement in the latter work also refers to the universality of acceleration in free fall. Construed this way, Kant's condition is completely appropriate. If it were violated, gravitational acceleration would depend on the specifics of the relevant body, and weighing would fail to furnish adequate mass values.

4. WEIGHING AS INVOLVING THE COMMUNICATION OF MOTION

I wish to reconstruct Kant's account of weighing in more detail by applying his argument to the example of the spring balance. Two features are relevant here. The first concerns the reason that the spring balance provides a reliable route to mass values; the second justifies Kant's interpretation of weighing as a mechanical procedure in his sense. As to the first issue, the suitability of the spring balance for measuring mass goes back to the universal equality of the earth's acceleration. The spring balance measures the weight of the relevant body in the first place. But since weight is related to mass via the earth's acceleration, and since the latter agrees for all bodies, the measured weight is a dependable indication of the body's mass. As I argued above, Kant is aware of this condition; he refers to it by his requirement of equal speeds. That is, Kant realizes that the universality of the earth's acceleration is needed for the inference from weight to mass (see sec. 3).

Further, the equilibrium state of the spring balance is determined by the equality between the downward force of gravity and the upward elastic force of the spring. Before reaching this equilibrium state, the body is accelerated by the gravitational attraction of the earth. The earth generates motion in the body and thus causes the elongation of the spring. It is this acquired speed or acceleration, along with the spring's elastic constant, that determines the equilibrium elongation and thus the measured mass value. This consideration shows that measuring mass with the spring balance involves setting the weighed body in motion by the force of gravitation. In the spring balance the "speed of [the body's] own motion" (4:541) indeed features prominently.

In spite of the fact that the spring balance indicates weights in the instrument's equilibrium state, which is distinguished by its lack of motion, the procedure essentially involves recourse to motion. The same applies to the equal-arm balance although the situation is more intricate. After all, it is quite possible that the device would remain in equilibrium during the entire process of weighing so that the speeds of the bodies involved would continually vanish. Still, the reconstruction of the spring balance can be applied to the equal-arm balance if a counterfactual proviso is adduced: The significant feature is the *capacity* of gravity to set the weighed bodies in motion. It is true, there is no motion in the equilibrium state. But the equilibrium state indicates the equality of weights only on account of the fact that motions are induced in all nonequilibrium states. In a terrestrial orbit, that is, with gravitational attraction counterbalanced, each position of the arms represents equilibrium. No motion is induced and the device is of no use. Only if bodies of unequal mass engender motion, will the equal-arm balance be an appropriate means for measuring mass. For this reason, mass measurement with the equal-arm balance is performed via gravitation-induced motions of the weighed bodies.

So far, so good. But this account still fails to accord a place to the principle of action and reaction. The mass of the weighed body is assessed by invoking the motion induced in it through the gravitational attraction of the earth. A body's mass is thus estimated by its own motion. We are not dealing with a situation of the type that was rejected as inadequate before; with a situation, that is, in which the force of body *A* generates motion in *B* which is used for the determination of the mass of *A*. The earth exerts its gravitational influence on the weighed body, but this influence is not used for measuring the mass of the earth. It is rather employed for assessing the mass of the body moved by its attractive influence. Accordingly, there appears to be no need to draw on the principle of action and

Mechanical Determination of Matter in Metaphysical Foundations   127

reaction to characterize weighing as a mechanical procedure. It relies on the motion of the weighed body anyway.

However, the crux is that this reconstruction does not invoke the motive force of the weighed body. This force expresses the capacity of a body to communicate its motion to another body (see sec. 2). But this feature is completely absent in the picture drawn so far. The weighed body is subject to an external force but does not seem to impart its motion to any other body. This is where the principle of action and reaction enters the framework. The challenge is to determine a body's mass on its basis. For one thing, this can be achieved by relying on collision processes. The latter involve a reciprocal communication of motion that is suitable for determining the pertinent mass values (see sec. 1). For another, a slightly elaborated analysis of weighing using a spring balance shows that this principle is likewise operative here. Owing to the reciprocity of action and reaction, the weighed body is not only attracted by the earth, but it also attracts the latter. Leaving the spring's elastic force out of consideration for a moment, the earth and the weighed body induce the same changes of momentum $m \Delta v$ in one another. On account of this equality, the changes in the speeds of the body and of the earth are inversely proportional to their respective mass values. That is, $\Delta v_{body} : \Delta v_{earth} = m_{earth} : m_{body}$. A relatively large speed is induced in the body with a comparatively small mass. It is the ratio of the speeds acquired during this reciprocal gravitational action that indicates the ratio of the relevant mass values.

This analysis of weighing brings motive forces into the picture. The weighed body attracts the earth gravitationally and in virtue of this body's mass. It thereby imparts motion to the earth. Due to the principle of action and reaction, the earth acts back on the weighed body with a force of the same intensity and thereby generates motion in the weighed body. This motion goes back to the gravitational attraction the body exerts on the earth and is for this reason proportional to the body's mass. On the whole, then, the weighed body, via a detour through the earth's attraction, sets itself in motion. Within this framework, the mass of a body, by virtue of its gravitational influence on another body, communicates motion to itself.

I take it that this is the picture Kant is aiming at by characterizing weighing by the feature that "the attracting body also imparts the speed of its own motion to itself (by means of the resistance of the attracted body)" (4:541) (see sec. 2). In order to qualify as a "mechanical" procedure in Kant's terminological sense, it is not sufficient that the empirical determination proceed from the motion of the corresponding body. It also has to draw on the body's motive force, that is, on its capacity to communicate its own motion to bodies. In collision processes, mass is estimated by a body's ability to impart its own motion to other, impinging bodies. In weighing, mass is measured by a body's capacity to communicate motion to itself—using the mediation of another body and relying on the principle of action and reaction. The moving force of gravitation, which the weighed body eventually exercises, creates a motive force in this body itself. Weighing qualifies as a "mechanical" procedure because it involves the weighed body's motive force and not only its motion. And it has to resort to the reaction of another body and is for this reason "only indirectly" (4:541) mechanical.

Within the framework of this interpretation, motion and motive force are to be distinguished conceptually in spite of the fact that, in modern terms, both are represented by linear momentum. Motive force expresses a particular dispositional feature of a moving body, namely, the capacity to induce changes in the motion of other bodies by means of its own motion. In collision processes the motive force of body A alters the motion of body B; and the motive force of B changes the motion of A. Although both terms refer to momentum, the activity of generating change is captured only by the term "motive force."

The distinction of the balance as the preferred procedure for determining the quantity of matter has important conceptual ramifications. In his "fundamental principle of general mechanics" Kant stresses that the basis for obtaining mass from considering motion consists in the fact that a body's motive force at a given speed exclusively depends on mass (4:539–40). The factor responsible for the transfer of motion in collision processes is "inertial mass," expressing the resistance to accelerations. However, the reliability of the balance rests on the fact that gravitational attraction at a given distance likewise depends exclusively on mass. But in this context, the relevant factor is "gravitational mass," indicating the intensity of gravitational attraction. Kant is well aware of the difference between the two quantities (see B215). The whole account implies, then, that the adequacy of the balance as a method for measuring the quantity that also manifests itself in collision processes, or in a body's motive force, depends on the fact that inertial and gravitational mass are proportional to one another.

The systematic bearing of this result is that it helps resolve a possible incoherence in Kant's approach. The "mechanical" explication of matter places momentum and motive force in the crucial position. It follows that inertial mass is the systematically primary quantity so that it should conceptually precede gravitational mass. However, the Dynamics chapter of the *Metaphysical Foundations* elaborates the claim that gravitation is among the constitutive forces of matter and that its proportionality to mass can be proven. Accordingly, mass should be ascertained by gravitational attraction in the first place, implying that gravitational mass should conceptually precede inertial mass.[9] In the framework of the suggested interpretation of Kant's views on weighing, this incoherence is removed. Measuring mass via gravitational attraction eventually amounts to evaluating *motion* and *motive force*, as brought about by this attraction. That is, assessing gravitational mass relies on determining inertial mass. Conversely, the only procedure for estimating "the force in a body's own motion" that Kant explicitly discusses is weighing. That is, measuring inertial mass involves estimating gravitational mass. Systematically speaking, the conflict between the primacy of inertial and gravitational mass is resolved by the fact that the two are determined jointly.

Consequently, Kant remains in accordance with the *Metaphysical Foundations* when he refers to weighing as the only legitimate procedure for measuring mass values in his *Opus postumum*. As he says regarding the quantity of matter:

> It can only be measured by weighing, i.e., by compression of an elastic matter (e.g., a steel spring) or, and chiefly, by means of a balance (with lever-arms of equal length). The weight, which indicates this quantity of matter, is a pressure, which the matter exercises due to the fact that earth, as a cosmic body, attracts it (21:408).

Therefore, spring and equal-arm balance are the "only" suitable instruments for obtaining mass values. The exclusive route to estimating the quantity of matter leads through gravitational mass—whose measurement in turn involves assessing inertial mass.

5. MASS MEASUREMENT IN THE FRAMEWORK OF THE *METAPHYSICAL FOUNDATIONS*

According to this construal, Kant elaborates two methods for determining the quantity of matter. The first compares mass values by measuring momenta at equal speeds. Some of the characteristics Kant ascribes to this approach suggest that collision processes are the focus, and such processes would qualify as an appropriate means to the desired end (see sec. 1). However, Kant does not pursue this line any further and draws on weighing instead. His objective is to reconstruct weighing as a "mechanical" method. This is done by showing, first, that weighing involves recourse to the weighed body's own motion. Using gravitational motion as an indication of mass requires the universality of gravitational acceleration, which is captured by the condition of "equal speeds." Weighing constitutes an appropriate procedure for measuring mass because inertial and gravitational mass are proportional to one another so that the gravitational accelerations of all bodies agree. Second, one needs to demonstrate that weighing actually invokes the body's capacity to communicate its motion. This is achieved by drawing on the principle of action and reaction, according to which weighing involves a reciprocal transfer of motion. The weighed body imparts motion to itself, relying on the assistance of the gravitational attraction of the earth (see sec. 4).

However, this interpretation implies that Kant's approach is afflicted with a reciprocal dependence between estimating the quantity of matter and constructing the communication of motion. The crux of Kant's method for measuring mass is the reciprocal equality of the gravitational forces between two bodies (see secs. 2 and 4). However, this equality only follows from Newton's principle of the equality of action and reaction that Kant intends to capture by his proposition 4. Yet, in fact, Kant's action-and-reaction principle is more specific than its Newtonian counterpart and, in particular, makes use of the center-of-mass frame of reference of the interacting bodies. It amounts to momentum conservation in center-of-mass frames. Kant's action-and-reaction principle says that in each transfer of motion (or "action") a "reaction" occurs and that the quantities of motion of the interacting bodies coincide. The construction of the communication of motion requires that the momenta involved be equal and opposite (4:547–48).[10] This condition is satisfied only in the center-of-mass frame of the bodies involved. The center-of-mass frame is given by the condition that the sum of the momenta vanish. For two bodies this implies that the quantities of motion are equal and opposite. Kant's action-and-reaction principle is valid in Newtonian mechanics, to be sure, but is restricted to center-of-mass frames. Its Newtonian analog, by contrast, refers to the change of momentum and holds in each inertial frame.[11]

The difficulty that emerges against the backdrop of this discussion is that, in general, the characterization of the center-of-mass frame demands knowledge of the mass values of the relevant bodies. Kant is clearly aware of this demand (4: 546, 4:547). For this reason, the applicability of Kant's action-and-reaction principle—if not its validity—requires that mass values be available. However, mass values gained from "moving forces" can be obtained only by applying this principle. It underlies the reciprocity of gravitational attraction and accordingly transforms weighing into a "mechanical" method (see secs. 2 and 4).[12] This feature creates a reciprocal dependence that distorts the linear architectonics of the *Metaphysical Foundations*. It deserves emphasis that this reciprocal dependence does not amount to a vicious circle. The validity of the action-and-reaction principle is guaranteed by the category of interaction (4:551); the principle is not in need of empirical verification. But only the latter undertaking would require reliable mass values. Systematically speaking, one might begin with a transcendental justification of the action-and-reaction principle and pass on to grounding mass measurement on it by the use of scales.

Although Kant's own approach does not run into a vicious circularity, the architectonics of the *Metaphysical Foundations* is impaired nevertheless. The drawback is that Kant's method for determining the quantity of matter does not stand on its own. First, it primarily rests on the original force of "dynamics" and applies only derivatively to a body's motive force. Second, interpreting weighing as a mechanical procedure must draw on the principle of action and reaction, which is introduced only at a later stage. Taking the liberty of giving Kant some advice, I suggest he should have started with the transcendental derivation of his action-and-reaction principle, that is, with proposition 4 of the Mechanics chapter. This proposition amounts to momentum conservation in center-of-mass frames; it would have allowed for the determination of mass values from collision processes (rather than from weighing). One could make use of perfectly inelastic collisions for the sake of identifying the center-of-mass frame of the colliding bodies without prior knowledge of their mass values. In this frame the two bodies are at rest after the collision (as Kant is well aware; 4:546). The ratio of the relevant velocity changes gives the pertinent mass ratio. This means that the transcendental grounding of the action-and-reaction principle would suffice for establishing mass measurement using collision processes. Proposition 1 would be superfluous on this approach; mass measurement would rest on proposition 4 instead.

An important advantage of this suggestion is that it allows one to drop proposition 1 as the only proposition in the Mechanics chapter without a transcendental foundation. The estimation of the quantity of matter would rather be based on the principle of action and reaction and the associated category of interaction. An additional conceptual advantage of this recourse to collisions is that mass measurements would rely directly on the communication of motion and the bodies' own motive forces. There would be no need for the (somewhat cumbersome) reinterpretation of gravitational attraction as a "mechanical" process (see secs. 2 and 4). Adopting this path to the quantity of matter would have streamlined considerably the architectonics of the Mechanics chapter.

6. TERRESTRIAL VERSUS CELESTIAL MASS MEASUREMENTS

My interpretation of Kant's procedure for measuring mass shifts terrestrial methods to center stage: The evaluation of the quantity of matter is achieved primarily by employing scales. This emphasis on earth-based methods squares well with the general thrust of the Mechanics chapter. In the general introduction to the chapter Kant sketches its terrestrial focus and explains that cosmic attraction is left out of consideration.

> One will forgive me for not further mentioning here the communication of motion by attraction (e.g., if a comet of stronger attractive power than the earth might in passing by the earth drag the earth after itself), but only mentioning the agency of repulsive forces, such as agency by pressure . . . or impact (4:537, translation amended).

According to these remarks, the scope of the Mechanics chapter is largely focused on the communication of motion among bodies on earth.

By contrast, Michael Friedman places Kant's method for measuring mass in an astronomical context. According to his reconstruction, it is the action of gravitation in the solar system that affords the basis for Kant's evaluation of the quantity of matter. Friedman's claim is that the relevant Kantian explanations belong to the Dynamics rather than to the Mechanics chapter, and that the method Kant favors relies on the "essentiality" of gravitation. Mass can be evaluated only if gravitational attraction is considered an essential property of matter. Consequently, this essentiality is a condition of the possibility of applying the concept of the quantity of matter to experience. This fact establishes the transcendental significance of the essentiality condition.[13]

Friedman's reconstruction proceeds from a passage in the Dynamics chapter in which Kant chides Newton for his lack of consistency. In refusing to regard gravitation as essential to matter, Newton is "at variance with himself. For he absolutely could not say that the attractive forces of two planets, e.g., Jupiter and Saturn, which they manifest at equal distances of their satellites (whose mass is unknown), are proportional to the quantity of matter of these heavenly bodies, unless he assumed that they merely as matter, and hence according to a universal property of the same, attracted other matter" (4:515). It is not contentious to say (as Friedman does too) that a chief objective of this paragraph is to underscore the view that the universality of gravitation entails its essentiality. But Friedman intends to ground further reaching claims on it. The salient point is that Kant associates the intensity of the attractive forces among the planets with their quantities of matter. Friedman's hypothesis is that Kant held gravitation to be universal and essential because this is the only way to make measurements of planetary mass possible.[14]

The argument proceeds from an analysis of the attractive forces between Jupiter and its satellites, Saturn and its satellites, and Jupiter and Saturn themselves. It follows from an application of Newtonian mechanics to this situation that the mass values of the planets can be derived from the gravitational acceleration of their satellites—provided one assumes the action of gravitation between the planets themselves. That is, the measurement of the mass values of Jupiter and Saturn requires that their gravitational influence is supposed to extend beyond their respective satellites. In order to evaluate the quantity of matter of these planets one needs to demand that their gravitational action reaches further than to their immediate vicinity and spreads out to other planets as well.[15] This is where the transcendental significance of the universality and essentiality of gravitation comes in. Only if it is assumed that gravitation is an essential property of matter and hence universal, will planetary mass values be determinable empirically; that is, only on that condition is it possible to apply the concept of the quantity of matter to experience. It follows that the essentiality of gravitation is a condition of the possibility of applying the concept of matter to experience.

Friedman's reconstruction is highly ingenious indeed. Kant's reference to the satellites of Jupiter and Saturn and his claim that the dependence of gravitation on mass may be shown by considering this configuration make it plausible that Kant actually envisaged an argument of the kind Friedman expounds. However, the contentious issue concerns the question of whether Kant really circumscribes his preferred method for measuring mass in this passage. Two textual findings militate against this construal. First, the quoted passage contains no explicit reference to mass measurement. Kant explains the conceptual foundation of the proportionality of gravitational attraction to mass—which is the essentiality of gravitation. The problem of determining mass values is in no way addressed (except for the quoted remark in brackets that the mass of the satellites is unknown). Second, if one assumes that Kant regards the essentiality of gravitation as a condition of the possibility of evaluating mass, or the mass of planets at least, then it is hard to understand why he explicitly leaves planetary attraction out of consideration when he turns to the problem of measuring mass in the Mechanics chapter (see earlier). In sum, in discussing the essentiality of gravitation Kant fails even to mention the problem of determining mass values, while in addressing the measurement problem, he does not even faintly allude to the essentiality issue. This is difficult to square with Friedman's interpretation that Kant considers the essentiality of gravitation as the transcendental foundation of mass measurement.

My interpretation agrees with Friedman's reconstruction in imputing to Kant the view that gravitation provides the foundation of mass measurement. The difference merely concerns the question of whether this measurement is based on terrestrial or astronomical effects of gravitation. However, this difference possesses some systematic import. Only if Kant appeals to astronomical methods for measuring mass values can the essentiality of gravitation be traced back to the significance of gravitation for estimating the quantity of matter. The reliability of terrestrial weighing does not rely on any such principle. It rather rests on the *fact*, "discovered by Galileo and confirmed by the air pump," that all bodies are accelerated at the same rate. Incidentally, Friedman's Newtonian analysis of the Jupiter–Saturn system also invokes the principle of action and reaction. Consequently, his astronomical approach to the quantity of matter suffers from the same architectonic weakness as the terrestrial one. I am prepared to grant that Kant's argument, as reconstructed along Friedman's lines, is subtle and brilliant. The drawback, however, is that the textual evidence in its favor is somewhat scarce. Friedman's reconstruction says how Kant could have improved his argument or how he should have argued rather than how he actually did argue.

7. CONCLUSION

In spite of the seemingly remote details addressed here, the underlying issue is by no means marginal. Matter as the "movable in space" is the fundamental concept of the entire *Metaphysical Foundations*; the book is devoted to elucidating the characteristics and the significance of this notion. Against this background, the determination or "construction" of the quantity of matter is an important endeavor. It is of transcendental relevance that some route to the determination of the quantity of matter can be outlined. Kant acknowledges this demand by enunciating proposition 1 of the Mechanics chapter and by appending sketches of suitable measuring procedures such as weighing. It goes without saying that specific measuring instruments (such as the spring balance) contain too many purely empirical features to allow for a transcendental explanation. The more detailed accounts of particular measuring instruments, as given here, were intended to provide examples for the determination of the quantity of matter. The spring balance is not a condition of the possibility of making matter subject to scientific knowledge, but weighing in general is. To elaborate a determinate concept of the quantity of matter its quantitative features must be specified. This is what connects Kant's consideration of mass measurement with the overarching epistemological project pursued in the *Metaphysical Foundations*.

Further, the difficulty of understanding the relevant Kantian passages is that they appear to involve considerable twists and turns. Kant's opening move is that the mechanical determination of the quantity of matter has to rely on momentum and a body's own motive force. But this approach is broken off abruptly—or so it seems—and weighing is resorted to instead. The interpretation proposed here is intended to remove this apparent incoherence by showing that for Kant both methods are of the same kind in the relevant respect. Appearances to the contrary notwithstanding, collision processes and weighing are equally suitable for determining the quantity of matter mechanically, that is, by recourse to the corresponding body's motive force. So, after all, there are no twists and turns; proposition 1 actually matches the accompanying explications and notes. From the perspective of the Mechanics chapter, invoking collisions and employing scales at bottom amount to the same procedure. Consequently, Kant's argument is in fact coherent—though not the best imaginable.

NOTES

I am grateful to Michael Friedman and Eric Watkins for valuable suggestions that were helpful for improving the argument.

1. All translations from the *Metaphysical Foundations* are from Immanuel Kant, *Philosophy of Material Nature*, trans. James W. Ellington (Indianapolis: Hackett Publishing, 1985). Translations from the *Opus postumum* are from *Opus postumum*, trans. and ed. Eckart Förster (Cambridge: Cambridge University Press, 1993). Translations from the *Critique of Pure Reason* are from *Critique of Pure Reason*, trans. N. Kemp Smith (New York: St. Martin's Press, 1929). All other translations are mine.

2. The same holds analogously for the second "original force," namely, repulsion. Repulsion is introduced as the physical cause of the impenetrability of bodies. By means of this force, a body resists the penetration of another body (4:497). A resistance of this sort is a relational feature, not a monadic property. Repulsion makes impinging bodies recoil; it thus contributes to the communication of motion and qualifies as "mechanical" in this sense (4:536). On the other hand, repulsion does so only derivatively. Its constitutive property is to make matter possible that fills space to a determinate degree. The defining characteristics of repulsion and attraction alike concern their action within matter, not between different parts of matter.

3. Kant's precise wording is that the quantity of motion is "estimated" (*geschätzt*) by drawing on mass and velocity. Kant usually employs the verb "to estimate" so as to refer to

empirical evaluation or measurement. However, this usage is confusing when compared with a later passage where the given explication is supposed to constitute a definition rather than a measuring procedure (4:540). Kant should have employed concepts like "to determine" here: The quantity of motion is "determined" by the mass, and the mass is "estimated" by the quantity of motion. I shall return to this problem later (see sec. 1).

4. *Mathematical Principles of Natural Philosophy*, trans. A. Motte and F. Cajori (Berkeley: University of California Press, 1962), 1.

5. See my "Kant's Relational Theory of Absolute Space," *Kant-Studien* 83 (1992): 399–416, esp. 409.

6. Newton, *Principia*, 411.

7. For this reason it is infelicitous that Kant uses the same verb, *schätzen*, for characterizing each direction of the relation in his initial introduction of the concepts of mass and momentum (4:537) (see n. 3).

8. Newton, *Principia*, 543.

9. I erroneously stressed the incoherence between the two views in my "Kants Theorie der Materie und ihre Wirkung auf die zeitgenössische Chemie," *Kant-Studien* 81 (1990): 170–210, esp. 190–91.

10. See Carrier, "Kant's Relational Theory of Absolute Space," 405–407.

11. Ibid., 409.

12. It might be objected that Newton's, and not Kant's, version of the principle of action and reaction was applied to the analysis of weighing in secs. 2 and 4. But in this context the difference between the two is immaterial. First, in a spring balance the weighed body is accelerated from rest so that its gravitationally induced momentum change equals its eventual momentum value. Momentum changes coincide with momenta. Second, the center-of-mass frame of the earth and the weighed body, as required by the Kantian approach, virtually concurs with the earth. And the latter (approximately) constitutes the inertial frame in which a Newtonian analysis is to be performed. So, the conceptual difference between the two versions of the principle is inconsequential as to reconstructing weighing.

13. See Michael Friedman, "The Metaphysical Foundations of Science," in *Kant's Philosophy of Physical Science. Metaphysische Anfangsgründe der Naturwissenschaft 1786–1986*, ed. R.E. Butts (Dordrecht: Reidel, 1986), 25–60, esp. 45–46, 51.

14. Ibid., 46, 50.

15. Ibid., 46–51.

7

Kant's Justification of the Laws of Mechanics

Eric Watkins

I_T is often noted that Kant attempts to justify Newtonian science in general and Newtonian mechanics in particular in his *Metaphysical Foundations of Natural Science* (1786). While numerous questions and difficulties arise in attempting to explain either the nature or the details of such a justification,[1] in this chapter I focus on only one specific difficulty that arises in the context of Kant's justification of the laws of mechanics in particular, arguing that the difficulty can be resolved and the precise nature of Kant's justification rendered intelligible by taking Kant's rationalist background into account. To see the difficulty, first recall Newton's formulation of the laws of motion as stated in his *Philosophiae Naturalis Principia Mathematica* (hereafter simply *Principia*):

Law I Every body continues in its state of rest, or of uniform motion in a right line, unless it is compelled to change that state by forces impressed upon it.
Law II The change of motion is proportional to the motive force impressed; and is made in the direction of the right line in which that force is impressed.
Law III To every action there is always opposed an equal reaction: or, the mutual actions of two bodies upon each other are always equal, and directed to contrary parts.[2]

Now consider Kant's formulation of the laws of mechanics in the Mechanics chapter of the *Metaphysical Foundations*:

First law of mechanics: With regard to all changes of corporeal nature, the quantity of matter taken as a whole remains the same, and is neither increased nor diminished.
Second law of mechanics: Every change of matter has an external cause. (Every body remains in its state of rest or motion in the same direction and

with the same velocity unless it is compelled by an external cause to forsake this state.)

Third law of mechanics: In all communication of motion, action and re-action are always equal to one another (4:541–44).[3]

Three points of contrast are immediately apparent. First, Kant does not even mention Newton's second law.[4] Second, Kant states a conservation law explicitly, whereas Newton is silent about whether any particular quantity must be conserved. Third, Kant provides a different formulation of Newton's law of inertia, citing change of matter and external causality rather than change of motion and forces. Kant does restate a principle very similar to Newton's law of inertia in parentheses following his own formulation, but such a principle may be simply an instance of his more general law rather than an equivalent formulation.[5] Only Kant's third law of the equality of action and reaction *seems* to be the same as Newton's. However, as shall be explained later, even in this case Kant's discussion following the proof of this law makes it clear that serious discrepancies arise as to the precise meaning of action and reaction (and their equality in cases of the communication of motion).[6] Accordingly, it would appear that none of Kant's laws of mechanics is identical to any of Newton's laws of motion. So we encounter a serious difficulty here, namely that Kant attempts to justify laws of motion that are not identical to Newton's.

How could this be? Did Kant not read Newton's *Principia*? Or was Kant not sufficiently impressed with Newton's achievement in the *Principia*? Did he sincerely doubt Newton's laws of motion? Since Kant repeatedly refers not only to Newton but also to specific passages from the *Principia*, one can safely infer that Kant did read at least significant portions of it. Further, it is clear that Kant does appreciate Newton's achievement, since his own account (in both his pre-Critical and Critical periods) employs many of Newton's main ideas. However, Kant thinks that Newton's account needs to be supplemented and at times even altered in important ways. For example, Kant criticizes Newton's treatment of the law of the equality of action and reaction by noting: "Newton did not at all trust himself to prove this law a priori, but appealed to experience to prove it" (4:449). More generally, in the preface to the *Metaphysical Foundations*, Kant states that in order to qualify as science proper a body of knowledge must be known (a) *a priori*, (b) with apodictic certainty, and (c) as a systematically ordered whole (4:468). Since Newton does not show (or even intend to show) that his principles satisfy such criteria despite the fact that Newton's achievement is clearly to be considered a scientific one, Kant would see Newton's account as standing in need of justification in order to qualify for its status as scientific knowledge.

However, the difficulty remains. Even if, by Kant's light, Newton's laws need more justification than Newton himself provides, this does not provide a reason for *changing* the laws of motion. One might naturally think that Kant's Critical epistemology and metaphysics explain the need for change. In fact, as we shall see, two of the more notable scholars of Kant's philosophy of science, Gerd Buchdahl and Michael Friedman, stress precisely such factors in explaining Kant's justification of his laws of mechanics.[7] While taking Kant's Critical epistemology and metaphysics into account in order to explain Kant's justification of the laws of mechanics is clearly important, such an appeal does not suffice for explaining the specific changes that they represent when compared to Newton's formulations. For, as I shall argue, it is essential to take into account the rationalistic, Leibnizian-Wolffian tradition in which Kant is trained and to which he is reacting in order to see how Newton's laws of motion are received. For taking this background into account reveals that Newton's laws of motion are a topic of considerable debate, not a set of dogmatic formulae that all accepted without question. Moreover, the kinds of considerations raised in this debate are of indispensable help in understanding some of the arguments Kant develops for his laws of mechanics.

1. THE STATUS OF THE LAWS OF MOTION IN EARLY EIGHTEENTH-CENTURY GERMANY

Before considering specific aspects of this debate, two criteria that are generally acknowledged by figures within the Leibnizian-Wolffian tradition as being of importance to the proper formulation of the laws of motion need to be explained. First, the Leibnizian-Wolffians attempt to provide nonempirical justifications of the laws of motion on the basis of either other laws of motion already established or more fundamental ontological principles. Second, the Leibnizian-Wolffians are interested in developing an adequate (i.e., Leibnizian-Wolffian) ontology by explaining how bodies or matter consist of simple substances, accidents, and forces.

In order to see how these two criteria are employed, consider very briefly some of the ways in which the laws of motion are treated in this period.[8] Christian Wolff discusses the laws of motion both in his main metaphysics textbook, *Vernünfftige Gedancken von Gott, der Welt und der Seele des Menschen, auch allen Dingen überhaupt* (1719–1720) and in much more detail in his *Cosmologia Generalis* (1731).[9] In the former work, Wolff, like Kant after him, does not explicitly state Newton's second law[10] and, while retaining what would appear to be Newton's third law, formulates the law of inertia as follows: "In this manner every body remains undisturbed either at rest or in its motion, and maintains the same direction in its motion until it is put into a different state by another."[11] Thus, in terms of their formulations Wolff's laws of motion in the *Vernünfftige Gedancken* differ from Newton's in ways that are very similar to the ways in which Kant's differ from Newton's.[12] For Wolff and Kant both omit Newton's second law and give a different characterization of Newton's law of inertia.

Two other aspects of Wolff's discussion of the laws of motion are also relevant here. First, Wolff attempts to derive these two laws of motion (the law of inertia

and the law of the equality of action and reaction) from more fundamental ontological principles. The law of inertia is based on the principle that no body can
move itself, whereas the law of the equality of action and reaction is justified in
part by his claim that there is no action without reaction. Second, even if Wolff
were attempting to justify Newton's laws of motion (as opposed to his own formulations of them), his clear emphasis throughout the course of the *Cosmologia
Generalis* is not on Newton's fundamental principles. Rather, after his discussion
of the laws of motion, he turns to a lengthy consideration of how active and passive
forces constitute bodies and are exercised in the collision of bodies, an issue that
stems from Leibniz (e.g., his *Specimen dynamicum*). Accordingly, Wolff's primary
intent is to show how bodies can be rendered intelligible in terms of forces, which,
in turn, require a certain conception of substance. In short, Wolff is attempting
to show how physics is intelligible on the basis of the particular ontology that he
has developed within the Leibnizian tradition.

Wolff is by no means the only eighteenth-century German interested in discovering the proper formulation and justification of the laws of motion. Many of
his followers, such as Ludwig Thümmig, Georg Bilfinger, Friedrich Baumeister,
and Johann Peter Reusch, devote considerable attention to this issue.[13] Reusch's
discussion in his metaphysics textbook, *Systema Metaphysicum*, published in 1735,
is particularly informative in this regard. He starts his discussion of the laws of
motion (§545) by recalling the account of action and reaction that he had developed in the ontology section of his metaphysics (§191) and then asserts (§549)
that action cannot occur without reaction.[14] It is only after defining the different
ways in which action and reaction can occur in bodies (namely through "naked
contact," impact, and pressure) that he derives a simplified law of inertia according
to which "there can be no motion of the elements without an external cause."[15]
Also, like Wolff (and Kant), nowhere does Reusch explicitly consider Newton's
second law. What Reusch's discussion makes clear, however, is the fact that he is
explicitly revising the laws of motion so that the law of inertia can be derived
(through a number of intermediary steps) from considerations pertaining to the
indispensability of reaction to action. Accordingly, Reusch's discussion reveals that,
like Wolff, he is concerned to show how the laws of motion can be derived from
sound metaphysical principles. Further, given that Reusch attempts to derive the
law of inertia from the law of the necessity of action and reaction, whereas Wolff
attempts to derive the law of inertia from the law that a body cannot act on itself,
it is clear that a number of different options for providing derivations of various
laws of motion are available in early to middle eighteenth century Germany.[16]

2. THE FIRST LAW OF MECHANICS

If one takes such general background information into consideration, the ways in
which Kant's laws of mechanics differ from Newton's laws of motion are much

less surprising. In fact, the differences are rather revealing when further, more specific background considerations are brought to light. Consider first Kant's first law of mechanics, which concerns the conservation of the quantity of matter. Newton himself is not particularly concerned with conservation laws when he attempts to state the fundamental laws of motion. At later stages in his project he does see the need to ensure that the universe is not depleted of all motion (and at one point he even invokes God in order to suffuse motion into the world whenever necessary), but even such a secondary concern is not tantamount to a conservation law per se. It is rather the rationalist tradition that is primarily concerned with and committed to the precise formulation of conservation laws.[17] Descartes suggests a conservation law according to which the quantity of motion (as measured by speed times volume) is conserved in the world due to divine immutability (see *Principles of Philosophy* II, art. 36). Leibniz reveals the inadequacy of Descartes's law by showing that the quantity of motion is not conserved, at least in the case of the free fall of bodies (see, e.g., §17 of the *Discourse on Metaphysics*). Leibniz counters by suggesting that what he calls living forces (as measured by mv^2) are conserved. Considerable debate ensues in the first half of the eighteenth century over whether Descartes's "dead forces" or Leibniz's "living forces" are conserved.[18]

In 1747 Kant takes up this issue in his first publication (*Thoughts on the True Estimation of Living Forces*) by arguing for a reconciliation between the two positions, holding that dead forces are adequate to the phenomena insofar as mathematical description is concerned, but that from a metaphysical perspective living forces are required as well. In enunciating his first law of mechanics (in the *Metaphysical Foundations* of 1786) Kant changes his position radically,[19] arguing that what is conserved is not the quantity of motion or living forces per se, but rather the quantity of matter, where matter is to be understood most generally as the movable in space, or alternately as spatial substance. In fact, at first glance such a conservation law must appear perplexing, since it seems to have nothing to do with motion as such; it does not seem to regulate the motions of bodies at all, claiming only that no spatial substance can arise or perish. However, it is important to note that in this work Kant is attempting to provide a metaphysical foundation of natural science, that is, in this case, of the communication of motion. Accordingly, Kant needs to develop principles that explain and justify the ontology underlying the communication of motion. The first law of mechanics in particular states that substances cannot arise or perish in the communication of motion. So even if motions or living forces were to arise or perish, the substances in which they inhere cannot. Thus, part of Kant's intent in formulating the laws of mechanics is to provide an ontological account that is justified in its own terms and that will explain the communication of motion in terms of substances, accidents, and the exercise of forces, concerns that stem from the Leibnizian-Wolffian tradition.

Since Kant shifts the focus of the debate on whether substances rather than motions or living forces are conserved, it might appear that the whole issue becomes trivial. For Newton, as a kind of atomist, could easily admit that the quantity of matter is conserved in the communication of motion (even if motion may not be). Indeed, it might appear that such a conservation law is so fundamental that it is implicitly presupposed by Newton's account.[20] However, such a claim is not trivial in the context of Kant's development, for such issues were not at all agreed upon in early to middle eighteenth century Germany.

Consider Kant's own pre-Critical position in his *Physical Monadology* published in 1756. In this work Kant maintains that simple substances, or monads as he calls them, adhering to the Leibnizian tradition, fill a space only through the exercise of attractive and repulsive forces. In other words, physical monads per se are not themselves extended, but fill space only through their sphere of activity. The advantage Kant hopes to reap from making physical monads nonextended, but their sphere of activity spatially extended, is the reconciliation of the infinite divisibility of space with the indivisibility of truly (i.e., metaphysically) simple substances or monads. While the effect of a monad's activity might be divided infinitely, the monad itself (including its activity) is indivisible. Further, what determines the amount of space that a given monad fills is the strength or degree of the forces that the monad possesses. Later, in the first *Critique*,[21] Kant will explicitly distinguish between extensive and intensive magnitudes in such a way that for an extensive magnitude the properties of the whole are determined by the properties of the parts, whereas for an intensive magnitude the properties of the whole are not determined by the properties of the parts, but are "apprehended only as unity" (A168/B210). For example, volume is an extensive magnitude, whereas a property like color is not. Accordingly, a monad must have an intensive, not an extensive magnitude; since a monad is not spatially extended and is thus simple (i.e., lacks parts), its magnitude cannot be extensive.

The consequence of the fact that monads proper (as opposed to the spaces they fill) have only intensive magnitudes is that they can perish through diminution. As Kant points out against Mendelssohn explicitly in the first *Critique* (and implicitly in his observation to the first law of mechanics in the *Metaphysical Foundations*), since the soul is constituted by a force with an intensive magnitude, just as a physical monad is (though the soul's intensive magnitude consists in the clarity of consciousness, which can vary without any change in the 'parts' of the soul), it might cease to exist. Although it could not perish through division because it has no spatially extended parts that could be divided, it could vanish through the gradual remission of its degree of consciousness, which Kant calls 'elanguescence' (B414).

Accordingly, the conservation of the quantity of matter is far from obvious. For Kant's own physical monads from the *Physical Monadology* or Mendelssohn's souls could perish by vanishing slowly over time. Why could matter not perish in precisely the same way? Even if one eliminated the possibility of vanishing matter by requiring that matter qua spatial substance necessarily be permanent, it would still not preclude the possibility that the quantity of matter might change. So how does Kant eliminate this possibility? Kant's solution to this problem in the *Metaphysical Foundations* is to argue that matter qua spatial substance is infinitely divisible into parts that are in turn spatial substances and that it thus has extensive magnitude. Accordingly, the quantity of a given spatial substance is determined by the number of its parts. However, Kant explicitly argues that the division of spatial substances into further spatial substances proceeds ad infinitum. Accordingly, one cannot *measure* the quantity of matter by counting up the number of parts into which a given substance can be divided. Rather, as Kant argues in proposition 1 of the Mechanics chapter of the *Metaphysical Foundations*, "the quantity of matter can be estimated in comparison with every other matter only by its quantity of motion at a given velocity."[22] Now given that matter or spatial substance has extensive magnitude, it is clear that its magnitude must be conserved over time, since qua extensive magnitude its magnitude is determined by the magnitude of the permanent parts into which it can be divided (and the magnitude of whose parts is also extensive).[23] No intensive magnitudes exist that could vanish over time. Only the relations among these parts can change. Since the relations among parts are not substantial, the quantity of matter (qua spatial substance) must be conserved.

The crucial step in Kant's argument for the conservation of the quantity of matter is thus his claim that matter is infinitely divisible into ever smaller spatial substances (and that therefore the quantity of matter is an extensive magnitude). What is Kant's justification for this claim? Michael Friedman[24] argues that matter must be infinitely divisible for Kant because "only infinitely divisible material substance, which is thereby spatial through and through, as it were, necessarily satisfies the principle of quantitative conservation and can thus play the role of 'the substratum of all time determination' (A183/B226). Substance can persist in this sense, therefore, only if it does *not* consist of ultimately simple parts." In short, Friedman argues that the infinite divisibility of matter (along with the extensive nature of its magnitude) is established by a constraint placed on matter by the first *Critique* (more specifically, by its First Analogy of Experience), namely that it must serve as "the substratum of time determination." However, Friedman's interpretation encounters a significant difficulty. In order to see the difficulty, it is important to note that Friedman is in fact making two main claims: (1) a conservation law can be demonstrated only if matter is infinitely divisible and thus has an extensive magnitude; (2) matter qua spatial substance can play the role of "the substratum of all time determination" only if a conservation law can be demonstrated.[25] Now the first claim agrees entirely with the results of the above analysis. However, the second claim simply begs the question against the possibility that substances have intensive magnitudes.[26] For even a substance that has an intensive magnitude could be the substratum of all time-determination. Of course, if such a substance were to perish through elanguescence, then it could not be the substratum of all time-determination. However, if that were to occur, then it would not be a substance in the first place, since substances are necessarily permanent.[27] Accordingly, the very real possibility of a permanent substance having intensive magnitude is inconsistent with Friedman's interpretation.

To put the point differently, Friedman's interpretation of the argument conflates two different senses of conservation. Substance is conserved in one, relatively weak sense simply if it cannot perish (i.e., if it is necessarily permanent). If something is conserved in this sense, it can be the substratum of all time-determination. Substance is conserved in another, much stronger sense if its *quantity* remains unchanged over time. Physical monads or substances having intensive magnitudes are conserved in the weak, but not the strong sense. Only substances with extensive magnitudes are necessarily conserved in the strong sense. However, since the weak sense of conservation is sufficient for substances to serve as the substratum of all time-determination, substances having either extensive or intensive magnitudes could fulfill that function. Accordingly, Friedman's interpretation of Kant's argument for the claim that matter is infinitely divisible and thus that the quantity of matter must be an extensive magnitude, an interpretation that stresses epistemological resources from the first *Critique*, is not satisfactory.

Kant's argument is rather to be found precisely where one would expect it, namely in the passage following his claim in the Dynamics chapter of the *Metaphysical Foundations* that matter is infinitely divisible. Kant first presents his formal proof of the infinite divisibility of matter:

Matter is impenetrable by its original force of extension (Proposition 3), but this force of extension is only the consequence of the repulsive forces of each point in a space filled with matter. Now, the space that matter fills is mathematically divisible to infinity, i.e., its parts can be differentiated to infinity, although they cannot be moved and, consequently, cannot be separated (according to the demonstrations of geometry). But in a space filled with matter every part of the space contains repulsive force to counteract on all sides all remaining parts, and hence to repel them and likewise be repelled by them, i.e., to be moved to a distance from them. Hence, every part of a space filled by matter is of itself movable and is therefore separable by physical division from the remaining parts, insofar as they are material substance. Consequently, as far as the mathematical divisibility of space filled by matter reaches, thus far does the possible physical division of the substance that fills the space likewise reach. But the mathematical divisibility extends to infinity, and consequently also the physical, i.e., all matter is divisible to infinity and indeed is divisible into parts each of which is itself in turn material substance (4:503–504).

In the first observation following this proof, Kant remarks that "by the proof of the infinite divisibility of space, that of matter has not by a long way been proved"[28] (4:504) and then raises the possibility of the physical monadologist who, as we saw above, admits infinite mathematical divisibility, but not infinite physical divisibility. Kant then explains how the above proof works against a physical monadologist:

> For from this proof it is clear that in a filled space there can be no point that does not on all sides repel in the same way that it is repelled, i.e., as a reacting subject, of itself movable, existing outside of every other repelling point; and it is clear that the hypothesis of a point filling a space by mere driving force and not by means of other likewise repelling forces is completely impossible (4:504).

Kant's argument in both passages is sufficiently obscure that one should not be surprised that Friedman (like many others before him) skips over it. However, it is clear that the intent of Kant's argument is to show not only that matter is infinitely divisible, but also that it must have extensive magnitude. But how does Kant's argument proceed? Again, Kant's rationalistic background provides the proper context. In the 1730s and 1740s one of the most important issues for Leibnizians and Wolffians is determining the precise relationship between monads and bodies. Leibniz's position on the issue is that bodies and their motions are well-founded phenomena, implying that monads are responsible for bodies and their motions without providing a detailed explanation of the specific ways in which they are responsible. Unfortunately, Wolff is no clearer on this point than is Leibniz. However, certain Wolffians, such as Kant's teacher, Martin Knutzen, pose a variety of critical questions about this relationship, at times coming to conclusions radically different from Leibniz's and Wolff's. For example, Knutzen argues that monads must be able to act on other monads because they have the power both to move their bodies and to resist the penetration of other bodies.[29] Given that this relationship underwent such careful scrutiny during Kant's formative years, it is natural that Kant would also be led to focus on such a relationship.

In light of this context, we can see that in the argument quoted above Kant is concerned with understanding how one body can be repulsed by another in virtue of monads and their forces. More specifically, his main point is to show that a physical monadologist cannot give an explanation of how a physical monad can fill a space through repulsion that is consistent with the infinite divisibility of space. The reason for the inconsistency in attempting to provide such an account lies in the fact that the physical monadologist is committed to three different claims about how a physical monad fills a space. First, for any space that any single monad fills, it fills this space through the exercise of its repulsive force. Second, a physical monad fills a space by exercising its repulsive force on all the physical monads that fill the spaces that immediately surround the space it fills. Third, it is impossible that a physical monad fill a determinate space unless it also fills the smaller spaces into which that determinate space can be divided. Of course, since space is infinitely divisible, there are infinitely many spaces that any given physical monad fills in virtue of filling any space at all. The inconsistency involved in the three claims can be revealed by considering how it is that a physical monad is to fill a subregion of its full space that does not border on any space filled by a different monad.[30] The third claim establishes that the physical monad is responsible for repulsion in this subregion, and the first claim establishes that it does so through the exercise of its repulsive force. The problem arises when one tries to incorporate the second claim's requirement that the physical monad fill this subregion by exercising its repulsive force on the monads that fill the space that surround the subregion. For in the case of the particular subregion chosen, the surrounding space is filled by the very same monad that fills the subregion.[31] This requirement causes an inconsistency because in this case it would necessitate that a physical monad exercise its repulsive force on itself, that is, that it repulse itself, which is conceptually incoherent.[32] Repulsion requires a plurality of monads that constitute repulsion through a specific kind of action and reaction. Accordingly, the physical monadologist cannot give a consistent account of how a physical monad can fill a space through the exercise of its repulsive force.

How does Kant's Critical position avoid such a problem? He simply makes substance as divisible as space is.[33] Accordingly, he can continue to hold that substances fill space through the exercise of their repulsive forces on other substances. However, he can avoid the problem created by the divisibility of space for the physical monadologist, because, unlike physical monads, substance can be divided whenever necessary.[34] In other words, a substance will never be required to repulse itself, because, as long as substance is divided just as space is, for any two spaces being filled there will be two distinct substances filling them. This solution has two important consequences. First, since the divisibility of substance is tied to the divisibility of space in this way, the infinite divisibility of space implies the infinite divisibility of substance. (Since each instance of filling space requires a distinct seat of repulsive forces and space is infinitely divisible, the seat of repulsive forces, that is, substance, must also be infinitely divisible.) Second, because space's magnitude is extensive,[35] substance's magnitude must be extensive as well.

Accordingly, it is clear that Kant's argument for the first law of mechanics is based not so much on Newtonian ideas,[36] but rather on the compatibility of a particular formulation of a conservation law with a certain conception of substance according to which repulsion and the forces that make repulsion possible are coherent. Therefore, Kant's first law of mechanics is unintelligible in any rich sense if one focuses only on its relation to Newton's laws of motion or on resources specific to Kant's Critical turn and does not also take Kant's rationalist background into account.

3. The Third Law of Mechanics

One might concede that Kant's first law of mechanics is concerned primarily with his Leibnizian-Wolffian predecessors, but argue that Kant's other laws are concerned with, and intelligible on the basis of, their relation to Newton or his own Critical epistemology. However, Kant's discussion of his third law of mechanics reveals that he is once again concerned in important ways with positions represented by Leibnizian-Wolffian figures from his rationalist background. Kant's formulation of the law of the equality of action and reaction is for all practical purposes identical to Newton's. However, Kant's goals extend well beyond Newton's insofar as he is explicitly concerned with providing (1) an a priori proof of the truth of this law and (2) a satisfactory ontological account of how action and reaction occur.

We need not concern ourselves with Kant's proof of the law of the equality of action and reaction in any detail.[38] In this context it is sufficient to note that in keeping with the Leibnizian-Wolffian tradition Kant thinks that all laws as such stand in need of some kind of derivation or proof. Kant even goes beyond Leibniz and Wolff by placing further requirements on *scientific* laws. In order to be scientific, they must be known to be true a priori and with apodictic certainty. Since Newton does not provide such a proof, but Kant's conception of science requires one, Newton's omission must be made good by providing such a proof.

Kant's rationalist metaphysical background is even more important for understanding the ontological account that Kant provides for the communication of motion and thus action and reaction. As is well known, Leibniz argues that finite substances do not stand in causal interaction with each other. Rather, each substance can act only on itself. Leibniz adopts this view for several reasons. In part, he is reacting against Descartes's position that the mind and the body can act on each other. For the mind and the body are too different in nature to be able to act on each other. How can something material, namely matter in motion, cause something immaterial, namely a thought in the mind (and vice versa)? In part Leibniz simply thinks that inter-substantial causation is unintelligible. For he rejects as absurd the claim that an accident could literally migrate or be transferred from one substance to another in inter-substantial causation. But if inter-substantial causation does not occur through the migration of accidents (which would at least explain how a new accident could arise in a distinct substance), then it seems inconceivable how one substance could cause an accident to appear ex nihilo in a distinct substance. Due to these (and other) difficulties, Leibniz claims that a substance can act only on itself, and, due to God's omnipotence, benevolence, and wisdom, all substances proceed in complete harmony with one another, appearing as if they acted on each other, although they do not in reality. Further, since God can foresee perfectly before the substances of the world begin acting on themselves how they will do so, there is a perfect "pre-established harmony" among all of creation.

Wolff adopts Leibniz's pre-established harmony and is, as a result, expelled from Prussia in 1723 since it allegedly leads to determinism, atheism, and Spinozism. To make the long story that ensues short,[38] suffice it to say that a number of Leibnizian-Wolffians (including Gottsched, Knutzen, Crusius, and the pre-Critical Kant) attempt to develop different versions of inter-substantial causation that could respond to some of Leibniz's main objections against inter-substantial causation, which was more commonly known as physical influx (*influxus physicus*). In this way the intelligibility of inter-substantial causation could be maintained without having to pay the price of relinquishing orthodoxy. While much of this development is purely metaphysical in nature, it is clear that at least Kant sees its application at the foundations of physics as well. For in his discussion of the equality of action and reaction, Kant explicitly argues against understanding the communication of motion as certain proponents of physical influx suggest.[39] For example, Gottsched can be read as suggesting that only one substance must exercise its force in order for inter-substantial causation to occur. The physical analog for such a model might be that one billiard ball in motion transfers all of its motion to a second billiard ball initially at rest. Kant calls proponents of such a model transfusionists (4:549).[40]

Kant has both metaphysical and physical reasons for rejecting the transfusionist's model. The metaphysical reason he cites (4:550) is that the transfusionist does not really provide an explanation of the communication of motion. Simply stating that motion is transferred does not explain *how* it is transferred or communicated. And all parties to the debate admit that *accidentia non migrant e substantiis in substantias*. Accordingly, the transfusionist position has no explanatory power at the level of ontology.

Kant presents three physical objections to understanding the communication of motion as the transfusionist suggests. First, he has of course provided an a priori proof that action and reaction are always equal in the communication of motion. Second, and more importantly, Kant raises the following objection:

> It is quite inconceivable to me how the transfusionists of motion intend to explain in their way the motion of elastic bodies by impact. For it is clear that the resting body does not insofar as it is merely resting receive motion which the hitting body loses, but that the resting body in impact exercises

actual force in the opposite direction against the hitting body, as though to compress a spring lying between them. To this end there is required on the part of the resting body just as much actual motion (but in the opposite direction) as the moving body on its part needs for this end (4:549).

In short, Kant's objection is that the transfusionist cannot explain how bodies behave in impact, because the transfusionist cannot account for the motion (or rather the change of motion) of the body which transfers its motion to another body. Why should the first body not continue to move as it did before? Presumably the transfusionist will say that the first body should stop because it has relinquished all of its own motion to the other body. However, according to the law of inertia (which Kant assumes the transfusionist will accept) a body will remain in its state of motion or rest unless *acted* upon by another body. If a body only transfers its motion to another body, it has not been acted upon by the other body and its motion should therefore not be changed. In order for the first body to stop, the second body must act on the first body. This reciprocal action is, however, precluded by the transfusionist's position.[41]

Third, Kant argues that the transfusionist position would render the law of the equality of action and reaction contingent, which is unacceptable given his conditions for scientific knowledge.[42] Kant argues that the transfusionist position implies the contingency of the law of the equality of action and reaction because the equality of action and reaction would hold only for bodies that are not absolutely hard. For only with bodies that are not absolutely hard will one body transfer all of its motion to another body. If the bodies are absolutely hard, then the transfusionist must admit that action is not equal to reaction. Accordingly, if action is to be equal to reaction, then no body can be absolutely hard. However, whether bodies are absolutely hard or not is a contingent matter.[43] Kant puts the point as follows: "This would be tantamount to admitting the contingency of this law, inasmuch as it is to depend on the *special quality* of the matter which moves one another" (4:549, emphasis added). Accordingly, if this law were true (and it would be true only if no bodies were absolutely hard), it would be only contingently true. But since Kant clearly holds that the fundamental principles of the *Metaphysical Foundations* (and of special metaphysics) are a priori and apodictically certain, he rejects the transfusionist's position.

In this same context Kant argues against a second ontological account of the communication of motion, an account he attributes to Kepler (but one which could apply to Newton as well). In order to explain the communication of motion, one might maintain not only an active force in the agent body (i.e., the body that causes the body acted upon to change its state), but also a passive force of inertia in the patient body which resists any change in its state. Action, according to this view, is the exercise of the active force, whereas reaction is the exercise of the corresponding passive force. Since this passive force is active only when another body attempts *via* its active force to change the first body's state, the resistance of the passive force 'uses up' some of the agent's active force. Kant objects to this account as follows:

> The designation force of inertia (*vis inertiae*) must, then, in spite of the famous name of its originator, be entirely dismissed from natural science. This must be done not only because this designation carries with it a contradiction in the expression itself, or because the law of inertia (lifelessness) might thereby be easily confused with the law of reaction in every communicated motion, but mainly because through this confusion the erroneous representation of those who are not correctly acquainted with the mechanical laws would be maintained and strengthened. According to this erroneous representation, the reaction of bodies, of which we are speaking under the name of the force of inertia, would result in the fact that motion in the world would be consumed, diminished, or destroyed. However, the mere communication of motion would not by such reaction be brought about, inasmuch as the moving body would have to expend a part of its motion merely to overcome the inertia of the resting one (such expense being pure loss), and with the remaining part alone could it set the latter in motion; but if no motion remained, then it would not by its impact bring the latter into motion because of the latter's great mass. Nothing but the opposite motion of another body can resist a motion, but this other's rest can in no way resist a motion. Here, then, inertia of matter, i.e., mere incapacity to move of itself, is not the cause of a resistance. A special and entirely peculiar force merely to resist, but without being able to move a body, would under the name of a force of inertia be a word without meaning (4:550–51).

Kant's main objection in this passage to the force of inertia understood in this way is twofold. First, if this account were correct, then motion would continually be lost in the communication of motion. Whether one accepts a strict conservation law or not, experience clearly contradicts such an account. Second, Kant makes the conceptual point that the mere incapacity of a body to move itself is distinct from its capacity to resist the actions of other bodies. To lump both of these functions together under the same name seems arbitrary and implies that the term 'inertia' does not apply to these two distinct functions in any univocal way.[44]

Given that Kant rejects the force of inertia understood in this way, he must develop his own ontological account of how bodies act in the communication of motion. According to Kant, action is to be understood as simply the exercise of a force that changes the state of a body distinct from the body exercising the active force. Reaction, however, is not a passive force, but rather simply the active force of the second body. In other words, at the same time that the first body acts on the second body, changing its state, the second body acts on the first body, changing its state. Action and reaction are not only equal, but they are of the same kind as well. Only such an ontology, Kant argues, can adequately account for the communication of motion.[45]

4. ACTION AT A DISTANCE

Of course, claiming that action and reaction are of the same kind does not settle all questions, not even all strictly ontological questions concerning the equality of action and reaction in the communication of motion. For both Newton and Kant consider the possibility of action at a distance as one particular instance of the communication of motion. Newton's own reservations about the ultimate causes of action at a distance are well documented, and it is perhaps fair to say that Newton does not ever arrive at a satisfactory resolution (or at least at any resolution that he himself finds satisfactory).[46] The nature of the difficulty of accounting for action at a distance is that it might seem occult or mysterious how a body can cause changes in another body that is not immediately contiguous to it. In short, how can a body act where it is not?[47] If the ontology Kant develops to account for the communication of motion is to be adequate, then it must also address the possibility of action at a distance.

Kant discusses the possibility of action at a distance not in the Mechanics chapter, but rather earlier in the Dynamics chapter of the *Metaphysical Foundations*, where he establishes the necessity of repulsive and attractive forces for our experience of matter as filling a determinate space. In his explanations of the force of attraction in particular, Kant both addresses the main objection generally raised against the idea of action at a distance and argues that action at a distance actually underlies and makes possible contact action! Kant explains this claim as follows:

> Attraction acts directly in a place where it is not—something that seems contradictory. But it is so far from being contradictory that one can say, rather, that everything in space acts on another only in a place where the acting thing is not. For if the thing should act in the same place where it is itself, then the thing upon which it acts would not be outside it; for 'outside' means presence in a place where the other thing is not (4:513).

Kant's line of reasoning can be reconstructed as follows. Either a body is acting at a distance or it is acting at no distance. If a body is acting at no distance, then it is not acting on a body outside or distinct from itself. However, in the case of contact action (e.g., impact), it is generally agreed that one body is acting on another.[48] In other words, contact action must be understood as the action of one body on another body that is distinct from it. Bodies can be distinct from each other only by occupying different spaces. If two bodies occupy different spaces, then they are at a distance from each other. Accordingly, contact action requires bodies acting on each other at a distance, that is, action at a distance.[49]

What leads Kant to this analysis of action at a distance and contact action is once again his rationalist background. As we saw above, Kant rejects pre-established harmony in favor of physical influx, that is, inter-substantial causation. Seen from this ontological perspective, there is no significant difference between action at a distance and contact action, because both are merely instances of inter-substantial causation. Further, if there is a difficulty with action at a distance, then there will also be a difficulty with contact action. From this ontological perspective, the difficulty of seeing how a body can cause changes so far away, as it were, in a distinct body is simply a more specific version of the general or ontological difficulty Leibniz had already raised for inter-substantial causation, namely how it is possible for one substance to cause a change in another (since accidents cannot migrate, whether between substances at a distance or those standing in contact). Since Kant has solved Leibniz's general or ontological difficulty by developing a concept of force (or perhaps by appropriating a concept of force from physics to be used in a metaphysical context) that makes possible inter-substantial causation, he can use the same concept of force to explain both contact action and action at a distance.

Given this explanation of Kant's background and of how it leads to his analysis of action at a distance, it would seem to be the case that his Critical turn is not the sole crucial factor in explaining action at a distance. Gerd Buchdahl claims that it is only in the *Metaphysical Foundations* that Kant develops "a more articulated methodological structure of scientific hypotheses"[50] which then allows for a more sophisticated attempt at rendering action at a distance intelligible. More specifically, Buchdahl argues that Kant's intent is to show that action at a distance is "an essential part of any 'possible construction' of the concept of matter,"[51] which, if successful, (1) would show how action at a distance is possible, (2) would render it intelligible in such a way that it is not occult, and (3) would show the actuality of action at a distance without any recourse to hypotheses. Though Kant does not, according to Buchdahl, meet with complete success in this project, given that attractive and repulsive forces have an empirical or material element which cannot be constructed in intuition a priori, his endeavors are still "not a total loss"[52] due to the greater methodological articulation he achieves (as compared both to the work of other figures in the eighteenth century and presumably to his own pre-Critical position).

However, I would argue that the Critical turn does not contain the essential key to explaining Kant's acceptance of action at a distance, though it does of course affect many other features of his philosophy of science in the *Metaphysical Foundations*. In particular, Kant does not rely on any special or Critical notion of possibility, namely construction in intuition a priori, in order to show that action at a distance can be conceived in such a way that the standard Newtonian and Leibnizian objections can be met. As I have argued above, the crucial notion is the concept of force he develops, according to which one substance or body can change the state of another substance or body through the exercise of its attractive or repulsive force. Further, if the Critical turn were essential to Kant's attempt at explaining action at a distance, then Kant would have been forced to reject action at a distance in his pre-Critical period (just as Leibniz, Wolff, and their followers do). However, Kant *accepts* action at a distance in his pre-Critical period, developing an explanation of action at a distance that is strikingly similar to the one presented in the *Metaphysical Foundations*. For in his *Physical Monadology* Kant argues first for the necessity of a force of impenetrability and then "in addition to the force of impenetrability, every element needs another force, that of attraction. If the force of attraction did not exist, then the bodies of nature would have no determinate magnitude" (1:484). Kant also makes clear (against Newton) that these two forces are inherent in matter and thus are not to be accepted on the basis of hypotheses. More clearly, in his *Inquiry Concerning the Distinctness of the Principles of Natural Theology and Morality*, published in 1763, Kant addresses action at a distance explicitly as follows:

> Thus, if I say that one body acts upon another immediately at a distance then this means that it acts on it immediately, but not by means of impenetrability. But it is by no means clear here why this should be impossible, unless, that is, someone shows either that impenetrability is the only force possessed by a body, or at least that a body cannot act on any other body immediately, without at the same time doing so by means of impenetrability. But this has never been proved, nor does it seem very likely that it ever will be. Accordingly, metaphysics, at least, has no sound reason to object to the idea of immediate attraction at a distance (2:288).

Given that he himself has argued for an intrinsic force of attraction, Kant is convinced that impenetrability is not the only force possessed by a body. Accordingly, Kant accepts action at a distance in his pre-Critical period on the basis of a certain conception of force, not on the basis of any Critical notion of possibility or construction in intuition a priori.[53] In fact, the reverse of Buchdahl's claim may be true, that is, Kant's notion of construction in intuition a priori seems to represent a significant obstacle to holding action at a distance, since, as Buchdahl rightly notes, the material element of forces upon which action at a distance depends cannot be constructed in intuition a priori.

5. CONCLUSION

In sum, Kant's justification of his laws of mechanics is intelligible only if one considers his rationalistic background (though not this background alone). His first law of mechanics, which states that the quantity of matter is conserved, is clearly not adopted from Newton, since Newton seems unconcerned with the conservation of matter. Nor is it intelligible on the basis of Kant's Critical resources, since Kant's argument for the claim that matter is an extensive magnitude is not based on arguments presented in the first *Critique*. Rather, Kant's argument stems from considerations pertaining to repulsion, considerations that were initially raised by Leibnizian-Wolffians who were trying to explain the relationship between monads and bodies (beyond stating merely that bodies are well founded by monads). Kant's second law is also distinct from Newton's law of inertia, though Kant may think that Newton's law can be derived from his own. Kant's version of the law of inertia takes the form it does because he, like many Leibnizian-Wolffians before him, is attempting to articulate an adequate ontology for the communication of motion, albeit now an ontology according to which a body cannot act on itself. Kant's law of the equality of action and reaction may be taken over from Newton in its letter, but not in its spirit. For Kant explicitly rejects a number of different models of action and reaction (one of which could be Newton's). Rather, Kant is again concerned to provide an adequate ontology for what physics may discover at the level of observation. The context of action and reaction also raises the possibility of action at a distance, revealing once again the importance of Kant's rationalistic background. For action at a distance is a notion that Kant endorses primarily on the basis of an analysis of force that stems from his rationalistic background.

NOTES

I would like to thank Karl Ameriks, Roger Ariew, Gerd Grasshoff, Don Howard, Dan Kolb, Wolfgang Lefevre, Wolfgang Malzkorn, Joe Miller, Eric Palmer, Joe Pitt, Bernd Thöle, Renate Wahsner, and Falk Wunderlich as well as the audience members of the first annual History of Philosophy of Science conference held in Roanoke, Virginia, for their helpful comments on an earlier and shorter version of this chapter. I would like to thank Michael Friedman and Martin Carrier for extensive and very helpful comments on the penultimate version of this chapter. I have also benefited from numerous discussions of these topics with Ernan McMullin. I would also like to thank the Max Planck Institut für Wissenschaftsgeschichte as well as the National Endowment for the Humanities for a fellowship during which part of this essay was written.

1. I address some of these issues in "The Argumentative Structure of Kant's *Metaphysical Foundations of Natural Science*," *Journal for the History of Philosophy* 36 (1998): 567–93.

2. Isaac Newton, *Mathematical Principles of Natural Philosophy and his System of the World*, trans. Andrew Mott (1729), rev. Florian Cajori (Berkeley: University of California Press, 1934), 13.

3. All translations are my own, though I have consulted James Ellington's translation of the *Metaphysical Foundations*, *Kant's Philosophy of Material Nature* (Indianapolis: Hackett Publishing, 1985), and Norman Kemp Smith's translation of the first *Critique*, *Immanuel Kant's Critique of Pure Reason*, 2d ed. (London: Macmillan, 1933).

4. Such an omission is of course quite significant, because some of the most fundamental aims of Newton's project require his second law. In particular, it would seem that the second

law is required in order to be able to correlate in a mathematical way (changes in) motions with forces, such as, ultimately, gravitational attraction. Accordingly, since Kant does not utilize this law, either his justification of Newtonian science is inadequate or his intent is different in significant ways. Although I shall not develop an argument for the latter alternative on the basis of Kant's omission of Newton's second law, I shall argue that the other differences between Newton's and Kant's formulations require the latter interpretation.

Michael Friedman suggests in *Kant and the Exact Sciences* (Cambridge: Harvard University Press, 1992) that Kant thinks that Newton's second law can be derived from the law of the equality of action and reaction. "However, since Kant formulates the equality of action and reaction in terms of equal and opposite *momenta*, and states that a 'dynamical law' of moving *forces* corresponds to his 'mechanical law' of the community of *motions* (note 2 to proposition 4 of the Mechanics: 548.13–29), Newton's second law appears to be contained in Kant's third law: in modern terms, Kant's third law states that any two interacting masses m_A, m_B have accelerations a_A, a_B such that $m_A a_A = -m_B a_B$; Kant's dynamical law then states that $F_{AB} = -F_{BA}$, where F_{AB}, F_{BA} are the forces exerted by A on B and by B on A respectively. It appears, then, that Kant is presupposing $F_{BA} = m_A a_A$ and $F_{AB} = m_B a_B$" (168, n.6). However, Friedman's interpretation encounters two difficulties. First, it does not fit Kant's text. For if Kant were presupposing F=ma, then, given his third law ($m_A a_A = -m_B a_B$), he would be in a position to infer immediately, and thus not have to provide an independent argument for, $F_{AB} = -F_{BA}$. However, Kant does provide an independent argument for the equality of $F_{AB} = -F_{BA}$ (and not through trivial substitution). Second, there is no independent reason to think that Kant must assume $F_{BA} = m_A a_A$ and $F_{AB} = m_B a_B$ in this derivation, since the derivation would work with many other laws relating force to changes in momentum. (For example, the derivation would work if $F^3_{BA} = m_A a_A$ and $F^3_{AB} = m_B a_B$, since substituting this principle into $m_A a_A = -m_B a_B$, would give $F^3_{BA} = -F^3_{AB}$, which of course entails $F_{BA} = -F_{AB}$.)

5. In note 11, I present some evidence that there is indeed a gap between the two claims that Kant would have been aware of. However, at the end of his proof of this law Kant adds "(d.i. ein Körper beharret, u.s.w.)" which does suggest that Kant wants the two claims to be understood to be equivalent.

6. Martin Carrier ("Kant's Relational Theory of Absolute Space," *Kant-Studien* 83 (1992): 399–416, esp. 405) identifies additional differences between Newton's and Kant's understandings of the law of the equality of action and reaction.

7. Buchdahl does not explicitly consider the differences between Newton's laws of motion and Kant's laws of mechanics and accordingly does not discuss in any general way how the reception of Newton's *Principia* might have influenced Kant's formulations of the laws of mechanics. Despite being interested in how action at a distance in particular comes to be accepted, Buchdahl discusses only Leibniz and then Locke and Hume very briefly in his explanation of the transition from Newton to Kant (cf. "Gravity and Intelligibility: Newton to Kant," in *The Methodological Heritage of Newton*, ed. Robert Butts and John Davis [Toronto: University of Toronto Press, 1970], 74–102). Friedman's position is more nuanced than the above characterization would suggest. His general approach (as expressed in the introduction to *Kant and the Exact Sciences*) is to argue that Kant is trying to synthesize and reconcile Newton with the Leibnizian-Wolffian tradition. Thus, in general he does not focus solely on Newton and the Critical Kant. However, his treatment of the relationship between Newton's laws of motion and Kant's laws of mechanics is somewhat different in character. For on this particular issue he does focus mainly on Newton by proceeding under the

assumption that what Kant needs for his argument to work can be adopted without change from Newton. As is already clear, Kant does not adopt Newton's second law. Now one might think that Kant's omission of Newton's second law presents no difficulty, since, as Friedman stresses, it is Newton's third law that is absolutely crucial to the success of Kant's argument for the law of universal gravitation. However, it is not clear that this line of response is completely satisfactory. First, on Friedman's interpretation Newton's third law is crucial to Kant's argument for the law of universal gravitation, not for the very definition of motion. (Friedman sometimes claims that Kant's laws of mechanics are a priori in virtue of their indispensability in defining motion.) Second, even granting the importance of Newton's third law, it is far from clear that one can derive the law of universal gravitation without Newton's second law (or without a law that identified the quantity of force in an empirical way). Thus, on this particular point (and unlike his general approach) Friedman does require Kant to be reacting directly to Newton. Accordingly, for very different reasons Buchdahl and Friedman do not appreciate fully the differences between Newton's and Kant's formulations of the laws of motion as well as the crucial role that is played by the rationalistic figures in Germany in the transition from the one to the other. Rather, on this point both Buchdahl's and Friedman's interpretations emphasize aspects of Kant's Critical turn rather than Kant's rationalistic background. Similar in nature are Kathleen Okruhlik ("Kant on the Foundations of Science," 251–68) and P. M. Harman ("Force and Inertia: Euler and Kant's *Metaphysical Foundations of Natural Science*," 229–49, both of which are published in *Nature Mathematized*, ed. William Shea [Dordrecht: Reidel, 1983]). Okruhlik tends to search for an explanation in Kant's Critical turn, while Harman, rightly emphasizing Euler's influence on Kant, does not (intend to) explain how Euler's work renders intelligible Kant's laws of mechanics in particular.

8. See my "The Laws of Motion from Newton to Kant," *Perspectives on Science* 5 (1997): 311–48.

9. Wolff considers specific laws of motion in great detail in his *Elementa Matheseos Universae* (Halle, 1733), reprinted in sec. 2, vol. 30 of *Christian Wolff's Gesammelte Werke* (Hildesheim: Olms, 1968). However, Wolff's concern in this work is precisely with the detailed laws of motion (e.g., concerning motions of bodies through resisting mediums, etc.) rather than with the fundamental laws of motion, which are of interest here.

10. Thomas Hankins, in "The Reception of Newton's Second Law of Motion in the Eighteenth Century," *Archives internationales d'histoire des sciences* 20 (1967), 43–65, argues that certain physical and philosophical problems caused many on the continent to reject Newton's second law. Accordingly, Wolff and Kant are hardly exceptions in omitting the second law. Again, see my "The Laws of Motion from Newton to Kant."

11. Christian Wolff, *Vernünfftige Gedancken von Gott, der Welt und der Seele, auch allen Dingen überhaupt*, reprint of the 1751 edition in sec. 1, vol. 2 of *Christian Wolff's Gesammelte Werke* (Hildesheim: Olms, 1983): "Auf solche Weise verharrt ein jeder Cörper unverrückt entweder in seiner Ruhe, oder in seiner Bewegung, und behält in seiner Bewegung einerley Richtung, bis er durch einen anderen in einen anderen Zustand gesetzet wird" (377).

In fact, Wolff and Kant explicitly argue for the claim that the only changes a body can undergo pertain to motion. Such a claim is necessary if Newton's law of inertia is to follow from their own formulations of the law of inertia, because Newton's law of inertia specifies in a way that their formulations do not that the changes to be explained by external causes must be changes in motion. Since Wolff explicitly addresses this issue, it is very likely that Kant is quite clear about the difference between Newton's and his own law of inertia and hence it is improbable that Kant would think that his second law of mechanics and the principle he states in parentheses after this law would be equivalent without further argument. Kant argues for the claim that the only changes that can be conceived of in matter are changes of motion at 4:524.

12. Taking Wolff's *Cosmologia Generalis* into account establishes that the differences between Wolff's and Newton's laws of motion are not accidental or unimportant, since this work's detailed discussion of the laws of motion does not disavow any significant point made in his *Vernünfftige Gedancken*.

13. This issue is discussed by Ludwig Thümmig in §§43–72, 88–97, of his *Institutiones philosophiae Wolfianae* (1725–26, Frankfurt), reprinted in sec. 3, vol. 19 of Christian Wolff's *Gesammelte Werke* (Hildesheim: Olms, 1982), Georg Bilfinger in §§167–84, 165–79, of his *Dilucidationes philosophicae de Deo, anima humana, mundo, et generalibus rerum affectionibus* (1725, Tübingen), reprinted in sec. 3, vol. 18 of Christian Wolff's *Gesammelte Werke* (Hildesheim: Olms, 1982), and Friedrich Baumeister in §§444–50, 295–301, of his *Institutiones Metaphysicae* (1738, Wittemberg), reprinted in sec. 3, vol. 25 of Christian Wolff's *Gesammelte Werke* (Hildesheim: Olms, 1988). It is also worth noting that those who do not quite fall into the Wolffian camp were also interested in this issue. For example, Christian A. Crusius discusses the issue in his *Entwurf der nothwendigen Vernunft-Wahrheiten* (Leipzig, 1745).

14. Reusch does not seem to consider in any explicit way the *equality* of action and reaction.

15. Johann Peter Reusch, *Systema Metaphysicum* (1735), reprinted in sec. 3, vol. 27 of Christian Wolff's *Gesammelte Werke* (Hildesheim: Olms, 1990): "nullus motus elementorum sine causa externa potest existere," 374 (§562).

16. The laws of motion are also discussed in Johann Peter Eberhard's *Erste Gründe der Naturlehre* (Halle, 1753), 47–51, one of the textbooks Kant used to lecture on physics. Thus, there is no question that Kant was familiar with this issue.

17. While Newton does argue that the quantity of motion (as measured by mass and velocity) is conserved, it does not seem to be essential to his view, since one can be a Newtonian and still argue for the conservation of living forces, as is shown by s'Gravesande's change of position between 1719 and 1722 (i.e., between the publication of *Physices Elementa Mathematica* and the "Essai d'une nouvelle theorie sur le choc des corps").

18. For extended discussion of the debate, see Ronald S. Calinger, "Frederick the Great and the Berlin Academy of Sciences (1740–1766)," *Annals of Science* 24 (1968): 239–49, "The Newtonian-Wolffian Controversy (1741–1759)," *Journal of the History of Ideas* 30 (1969): 319–30, and "The Newtonian-Woffian Confrontation in the St. Petersburg Academy of Sciences," *Cahiers d'histoire mondiale* 11 (1968): 417–35; Thomas Hankins, "Eighteenth Century Attempts to Resolve the Vis-viva Controversy," *Isis* 56 (1965): 281–97, "The Concept of Hard Bodies in the History of Physics," *History of Science* 9 (1970): 119–28, "The Influence of Malebranche on the Science of Mechanics during the 18th Century," *Journal of the History of Ideas* 28 (1967): 193–210, "The Reception of Newton's Second Law of Motion in the 18th Century," *Archives internationales d'histoire des sciences* 20 (1967): 43–65, and *Jean d'Alembert: Science and the Enlightenment* (New York: Gordon, 1990); Carolyn M. Iltis, "D'Alembert and the Vis Viva Controversy," *Studies in the History and Philosophy of Science* 1 (1970): 135–44, "Leibniz and the Vis Viva Controversy," *Isis* 62 (1971): 21–35, "Madame du Chatelet's Metaphysics and Mechanics," *Studies in the History and Philosophy of Science* 8 (1977): 29–48, "The Decline of Cartesian Mechanics: The Leibnizian-Cartesian Debates," *Isis* 64 (1973): 356–73, and "The Leibnizian-Newtonian Debates: Natural Philosophy

and Social Psychology," *British Journal for the History of Science* 6 (1972): 341–77; Larry Laudan, "The Vis Viva Controversy: A Post-Mortem," *Isis* 59 (1968): 131–43, and David Papineau, "The Vis Viva Controversy," *Studies in History and Philosophy of Science* 8 (1977): 111–42.
19. For Kant's Critical resolution of this controversy, see 4:539.
20. See J. E. McGuire, "Transmutation and Immutability: Newton's Doctrine of Physical Qualities," *Ambix* 14 (1967): 69–95, where it is claimed that "the very principle of transmutation presupposes the changelessness of the ultimate particles" (i.e., atoms) (83). Newton endorses atomism more explicitly in his *Optics* (with which Kant is also clearly familiar).
21. Baumgarten and Meier also distinguish between extensive and intensive magnitudes. Accordingly, even in his pre-Critical period Kant has such a distinction at his disposal.
22. 4:537. For a more detailed discussion of this issue, see my "Kant's Third Analogy of Experience" (Ph. D. diss., University of Notre Dame, 1994), 270–72.
23. In other words, what is crucial to Kant's argument is the conjunction of three claims. First, matter *qua* spatial substance is permanent. Second, matter is infinitely divisible into spatial substances. Third, the magnitude of matter is extensive. The third claim implies that the magnitude of matter is determined by the magnitude of its parts. The first and second claims imply that both matter and any parts into which matter can be divided ad infinitum are permanent. Thus, the magnitude of the matter cannot change since it is determined by the magnitude of its parts that are permanent. Now one might object that the fact that the parts are permanent does not establish that their magnitude does not change (for despite their permanence, their properties might change). However, the second claim is supposed to rule out the possibility that their magnitude might change because the magnitudes of the parts are in turn extensive, i.e., depend on the parts rather than any feature which could change over time.
24. In "Matter and Material Substance in Kant's Philosophy of Nature: The Problem of Infinite Divisibility," in *Proceedings of the Eighth International Kant Congress*, ed. H. Robinson, vol. 1, part 2 (Milwaukee: Marquette University Press, 1995), 595–610.
25. Such a claim is crucial to Friedman's interpretation of Kant's overall argument in the *Metaphysical Foundations*. For according to Friedman the first *Critique*'s principles have *meaning* only through their application to matter in the *Metaphysical Foundations*.
26. Gordon Brittan, in his comments on Friedman's paper, "The Continuity of Matter: Notes on Friedman," in *Proceedings of the Eighth International Kant Congress*, ed. H. Robinson, vol. 1, part 2 (Milwaukee: Marquette University Press, 1995), 611–18, attacks this same point, albeit in slightly different terms, noting that "the theory of physical monads renders a quantitative conservation law impossible by breaking the crucial link between substantiality and additivity" (612).
27. Kant explicitly argues for the permanence of substance in the First Analogy of Experience.
28. Although Kant does not explicitly note it in this passage, Descartes appears to be one of his targets when he distinguishes between mathematical and physical divisibility.
29. Such an argument is highly controversial, since Leibniz and Wolff both reject the claim that monads can act on each other. Nor could Leibniz and Wolff resolve the issue simply by denying that monads have the power of impenetrability, for that would make it difficult to see how it is that monads are responsible for the phenomena. For a more detailed discussion of the ways in which Knutzen and others discuss the relationship between monads and bodies, see my "The Development of Physical Influx in Early 18th Century Germany: Gottsched, Knutzen, and Crusius," *Review of Metaphysics* 49 (1995): 295–339.

30. That Kant makes precisely such a move is indicated in the text when, after reminding the reader of the infinite divisibility of space, he notes: "But in a space filled with matter *every part of the space* contains repulsive force to counteract on all sides all remaining parts" (4:503, emphasis added).

31. One might attempt to avoid this problem by reformulating the second claim as follows: a monad fills a space by exercising its repulsive force on any *other* monad that may attempt to penetrate into this space (cf. proposition VII of Kant's *Physical Monadology*). However, such a claim does not seem preferable since it cannot plausibly explain how a monad fills its internal spaces. One might think that a monad can fill external spaces only by first filling internal spaces, but Kant's model of causality is, I think, incompatible with such a suggestion.

32. It also violates Kant's claim that a substance cannot act on itself.

33. In order to distinguish Kant's position from that of the physical monadologist's, I shall use the term "substance" instead of "monad." Monads are necessarily simple, substances are not.

34. This difference allows Kant to avoid the inconsistency of the physical monadologist's three claims by rejecting the attributability of any space to any *single* monad, which is implicitly asserted in the first claim.

35. Kant argues for this claim in the first *Critique*'s Axioms of Intuition (A162–67/B202–207).

36. Since the first proposition of the Mechanics chapter links the conservation of matter with the conservation of momentum, which is an important Newtonian principle, there is a significant sense in which even in conservation issues Kant is attempting to reconcile different aspects of the Leibnizian and Newtonian traditions.

37. I consider this argument in my "The Argumentative Structure of Kant's *Metaphysical Foundations of Natural Science*."

38. For a fuller explanation, see my "The Development of Physical Influx in Early 18th Century Germany: Gottsched, Knutzen, and Crusius."

39. This background information also suggests that at least part of Kant's motivation for his second law of mechanics is his desire to be able to reject pre-established harmony.

40. I am not suggesting that Gottsched is in fact a transfusionist. Unfortunately, Kant does not identify any specific figure as a transfusionist. However, it is plausible to think that Kant might have read Gottsched in this way.

41. Even if the transfusionist does not assume the law of inertia per se, the reaction of the second body is required to explain the (lack of) motion of the first body by its own account.

42. Kant noticeably departs from Wolff on the issue of the contingency of the laws of nature. This issue was hotly contested both within and without the Wolffian camp. Part of the explanation for Kant's and Wolff's difference is that Kant has a different solution to the problem of freedom, a solution that does not require the contingency of the laws of nature.

43. In query 31 of the *Optics* Newton declares that the ultimate particles are hard, but it is not clear that this claim represents a necessary truth. Further, even if atoms are necessarily hard, one could still argue that the bodies that are composed of atoms are not perfectly elastic in collisions.

44. If Newton's account of the force of inertia is not sufficiently similar to the position described in the quotation above, then it is clear that Newton's *Principia* does not provide the crucial clue for explaining Kant's position. If Newton's account of the force of inertia is sufficiently similar, then Kant is attacking it, and thus his position is significantly different from Newton's.

45. For a fuller account of Kant's theory of causation, see my "Kant's Theory of Physical Influx," *Archiv für Geschichte der Philosophie* 77 (1995): 285–324, and "Kant's Third Analogy of Experience," *Kant-Studien* 88 (1997): 406–441.

46. See Ernan McMullin, *Newton on Matter and Activity* (Notre Dame: University of Notre Dame Press, 1978), esp. 106–109.

47. Kant is certainly aware of this objection, since he restates it in the *Metaphysical Foundations*, 4:513.

48. Alternately, Kant's criticisms of pre-established harmony also justify the claim that a body cannot act on itself (i.e., act, but not at a distance).

49. In response to the claim that bodies in contact with each other are not at a distance, Kant argues that they are separated by a point that is not a part of either body (4:513).

50. Buchdahl, "Gravity and Intelligibility: Newton to Kant," 74.

51. Ibid., 95.

52. Ibid., 101.

53. Of course this notion of force must be compatible with being constructed in a priori intuition (and thus Kant is of course attempting to reconcile Critical concerns with other considerations), but adopting construction in a priori intuition as a criterion of possibility occurs after his endorsement of action at a distance and the force necessary for its explanation. Accordingly, the crucial move (i.e., the development of a certain conception of force) lies in his pre-Critical period, although this crucial move must naturally be consistent with any changes pertaining to possibility that do occur in his Critical period.

PART III

Psychology and the Human Sciences

8

Kant on Empirical Psychology

How Not to Investigate the Human Mind

Thomas Sturm

KANT'S considered views on the aims and the philosophical value of psychology are quite critical, but it would be wrong to think that they are all of a piece. One is well advised to hold them apart and to discuss them separately. There is no single underlying idea that would unite his detailed rejection of rational psychology in the first *Critique* with his critical statement that it shows only intellectual confusion if one thinks it useful to insert psychological chapters into pure and transcendental logic (e.g., A54/B78, A87/B119). And neither of these claims is to be conflated with his further claim, made in the opening paragraphs of the *Metaphysical Foundations of Natural Science*, that "empirical psychology must always remain outside the rank of a natural science properly so-called" (4:471).[1] These claims all have different meanings and are supported by different kinds of arguments. Rational psychology is said to provide no knowledge at all, be it scientific or not, and Kant's argument for this claim is based on epistemological reasons developed earlier in the *Critique*. That psychology should not be mixed with logic is neither a claim about whether there can be psychological knowledge nor about whether there can be a science of psychology. It is, rather, the demand that one should not let empirical principles intrude into logic, since the latter is a purely formal and, therefore, strictly a priori discipline. Again, that empirical psychology cannot be a science "properly so-called" is argued for by requirements concerning the notion of a science "properly so-called." It is not meant as a general denial of psychological knowledge. Also, in this case the reasons Kant gives go beyond merely making use of the distinction between a priori and empirical knowledge. What the precise reasons are is a more complex and difficult matter.

The claim that empirical psychology can never become a science "properly so-called" I shall refer to as the 'impossibility claim'. This claim could easily seem embarrassing. It might seem as if this is merely another unfortunate instance of a philosopher attempting to predict the future development of a scientific discipline where one should rather let the future course of the science in question decide the issue. However, Kant provides an argument for his claim that has to be given due consideration. The argument builds upon Kant's requirement that "in every special doctrine of nature only so much science proper can be found as there is mathematics in it" (4:470). Kant also claims that empirical psychology is defective in that it cannot make use of certain empirical methods. But while that, for reasons that will become clear, is an important point in Kant's considerations, it is only the requirement of mathematizability that is crucial for the notion of a science "properly so-called." Against various interpretations, I shall argue that Kant does not claim that psychological phenomena cannot be mathematized at all, nor that causal laws governing psychological phenomena cannot be mathematized. What he means by the impossibility claim is, rather, that under a specific *conception* of empirical psychology—one shared by many of his contemporaries—one conceives of psychological phenomena in such a way that they cannot be mathematized appropriately or, more particularly, that geometry cannot be applied to them. While Kant's arguments are not without difficulties, one need not saddle him with an extreme and perhaps ultimately untenable position with regard to the scientific status of psychology. A proper understanding of the impossibility claim shows that psychologists who share a different conception of their own discipline do not necessarily have to be bothered by Kant's considerations.[2]

1. A Very Short Prehistory
of the Impossibility Claim

Only sometimes has it been noted that Kant's impossibility claim appears quite late within his philosophical development. To be sure, Kant discusses the status of empirical psychology much earlier than 1786. Beginning with his lectures on metaphysics and anthropology in the early 1770s, he repeatedly points out that empirical psychology does not belong to metaphysics. The reason he gives for this claim is a well-known epistemological one: The two disciplines use quite different methods of justification. Metaphysics is an a priori discipline, while empirical psychology is based upon observation (cf. 28:223–24, 28:542, 29:754–57). But nowhere prior to the publication of the *Metaphysical Foundations* in 1786 does Kant suggest that psychology cannot be a science at all. The only occurrence of such a doubt within the lectures can be found in the late manuscript *Metaphysik-Dohna* (1792–93; cf. 28:679–80, 20:285–86). In the first *Critique,* Kant still seems to think that there is such a doctrine (cf. A846/B874). In the *Prolegomena,* he alludes to the possibility of a "natural science in the strictest sense" of psychology, i.e. of a doctrine which brings its objects under "general laws" (4:295). And in a letter to Christian Gottfried Schütz, written in September 1785, Kant promises that the *Metaphysical Foundations* will treat the metaphysical foundations of the "doctrine of the soul" (*Seelenlehre*) in addition to that of matter (10:406). Admittedly, Kant remarks that this doctrine will be no longer than an appendix. But there is not the slightest suggestion that he calls into question the very possibility of a scientific psychology.[4] It is, therefore, clear that Kant changed his mind with regard to the scientific status of empirical psychology and that he did so between September 1785 and the appearance of the *Metaphysical Foundations* in 1786. However, why he changed his mind is another matter. Yet there is a connection here one should bear in mind: that Kant changed his mind so late and so suddenly should make one cautious with regard to the question of how convinced he was by his own arguments and, moreover, how strong an impossibility claim he really wished to make. I now turn to this question.

2. THE IMPOSSIBILITY OF MATHEMATIZATION, BUT WHAT KIND OF MATHEMATIZATION?

Kant claims that "in every special doctrine of nature only so much science proper can be found as there is mathematics in it" (4:470). This claim is itself the specification of a more general claim, namely that every science "properly so-called" cannot consist of empirical knowledge only. It must also possess a rational or a priori part as well. Kant often expresses this in a different manner. If, for any given subject matter, there is an empirical doctrine of it which deserves the title of a science "properly so-called," then there must also be an a priori doctrine—a systematized body of a priori principles or laws.[4] Kant does not claim that only a priori sciences are sciences "properly so-called." Rather, he claims that an a priori system of principles is a necessary condition for any science "properly so-called." He claims that an a priori counterpart to an empirical body of knowledge is a necessary, and indeed sufficient condition for a discipline deserving the—obviously honorific—title of a "science proper."[5]

The claim that the possibility of an a priori doctrine with regard to certain natural objects in turn depends on the possibility of a mathematical cognition of them is not a claim Kant would simply take for granted. Nor does he simply impose idealized standards of Newtonian physics upon psychology. He provides the following argument. To know an object a priori means to "know it from its possibility" (4:470). By this, Kant means not only that certain judgments about the objects in question are *logically* possible, since that alone does not provide us with knowledge of objects in a substantial sense of the word. For the same reason, he claims that one cannot know anything about the objects in question "from their concepts alone," or by means of an analysis of such concepts as 'material nature' or 'thinking nature'. When he says that to know an object a priori is to know it from its possibility, he means that we must know necessary conditions of the *real* possibility of certain kinds of knowledge of those objects (cf. A155/B194–95). More precisely, he thinks that one knows a specific natural object a priori only if one "constructs" concepts of that object in pure intuition. And this construction he identifies with giving a mathematical account of those things (4:470). The obvious point against psychology is that a mathematical construction cannot be given for "thinking nature"; so, psychology will never become a science "properly so-called." For our current purposes, it will be helpful to briefly sum up this argument in the following main steps:

1. Each science "properly so-called" must contain a system of laws that can be known a priori.
2. Natural doctrines can be sciences "properly so-called" only if they contain a system of laws that can be known a priori.
3. Natural doctrines contain a system of laws that can be known a priori only if these are mathematical laws.
4. Psychology, as the natural doctrine which treats of "thinking substances," cannot contain a system of mathematical laws.
5. Therefore, psychology cannot be a science "properly so-called."

Let us call this argument for the impossibility claim the 'argument from the impossibility of mathematization', and the impossibility claim as supported by this argument simply the 'mathematical impossibility claim'.

It is clear that the argument, stated this way, is hardly convincing. Scholars who discuss the mathematical impossibility claim typically concentrate upon (4), and this will be the main focus of the present discussion too. However, it should be pointed out that the argument is dubitable in other respects as well. I do not mean only the Kantian claims (1) or (2) here. One may find (1)—and its specific version for natural sciences, (2)—unnecessarily strong, namely too strong as a claim about the notion of science, even if it is safeguarded by the ubiquitous "properly so-called." Indeed, almost nowhere outside the *Metaphysical Foundations* does Kant use this qualification, and so it seems that he develops this notion of science ad hoc—only for the purpose of criticizing the pretensions of psychology.[6] But let us put these issues aside. Premises (1) and (2) clearly do express Kantian views. (3) may seem to be an unacceptably loose way of rendering Kant's views; but what he actually says is not helpful either. What he puts forward is not so much a principled claim but one of degree: In every natural doctrine there is only *so much* science "properly so-called" *as* there is mathematics to be found in it. Should we imagine that certain sciences deserve the honorific title to, say, 28 percent or 76.7 percent? Moreover, the argument underlying (3) is puzzling as well. Kant here does not refer to the relevance of mathematizability for the possibility of giving exact *explanations* and *predictions* of the phenomena under investigation, despite his emphasis upon the crucial role of *laws* for natural science. What he argues for, rather, is the claim that we can know natural things a priori or "from their possibility"— that is, we know certain necessary conditions for certain kinds of empirical knowledge. Which kinds? Kant merely states that in order to know things from their possibility it is necessary that "the intuition corresponding to the concepts is given a priori, i.e., that the concept is constructed. Now, rational knowledge through construction of concepts is mathematical" (4:470). This, one may grant, indicates something about the applicability of mathematics to natural phenomena. Kant's view is that mathematics is based upon pure intuition, and if we can, by reference to such pure intuition, construct concepts of specific objects of knowledge, then we can apply (certain kinds of) mathematics to them. That is an important point, but it is not what the argument requires. Kant does not show how from such a construction we can develop mathematical *laws* of specific natural objects. If one describes an object as a falling body, one presupposes that that object can be described in geometrical terms—say, that one describes its original position in space, its extension, its direction, and so on. To make a falling body as such subject to scientific investigation, one needs to have characterized it such that the relevant geometrical predicates can be applied to it. But the mathematical "construction" of objects is not yet the formulation of mathematically precise laws of those objects. It is one thing to give an interpretation for certain terms of pure geometry; it is quite another thing to state laws which make use of terms of geometry. It is not clear how we could, from the interpretation of geometrical terms alone, develop such laws. But premise (3) requires that there be such laws for a domain of objects to be the subject matter of science "properly so-called."

One might reply to this that Kant merely wants to show that we cannot have mathematical formulations of scientific laws of a given class of objects unless we have shown that mathematics is applicable to that class, and that, once we have shown that, there is no argument in principle against the possibility of adequate mathematical laws. Conversely, to show that mathematics cannot be applied to a class of objects means to show that there are arguments in principle against the possibility of mathematical laws of those objects. However, given the context of the argument against psychology, this does not suffice either. On the one hand, Kant makes the merely relative claim according to which there might be different degrees or ways in which mathematics is applicable to a given class of phenomena (and so different degrees or ways in which we are enabled to formulate precise laws about them). On the other hand, Kant does not completely exclude the idea that some sort of an a priori construction of psychological phenomena is possible. This brings us to premise (4).

The crucial premise (4) can be refuted if we are able to develop *some* sort of mathematical laws governing psychological events or processes. This point can neatly be connected with a consideration raised by Nayak and Sotnak in their insightful recent discussion of Kant's impossibility claim.[7] Nayak and Sotnak point out that it would be wrong to read Kant, as some scholars do,[8] as making an *unrestricted* mathematical impossibility claim—a claim with regard to all psychological phenomena. Such an interpretation would not cohere with a substantial, though often neglected, portion of Kant's system of principles of the pure understanding given within the first *Critique*. In the Anticipations of Perception, Kant develops arguments which purport to show the applicability of certain kinds of mathematics to certain phenomena, namely to our own perceptions (*Wahrneh-mungen*). These are said to have an "intensive magnitude," and Kant furthermore claims that the degrees of perceptions are always to be found on a continuous scale. What is meant here is the *content* of perceptions: the intensity of a color, a certain taste, and the like. Now, this qualitative content of perceptions can indeed be mathematized: briefly put, we can quantify the intensity of a color experience in that they are ordinally and cardinally measurable (see the example at A179/B221).[9] Psychologists in the nineteenth century, then, who hoped to refute Kant's pessimism by developing precise measurements of psychological phenomena of such a kind did not refute his mathematical impossibility claim in the first place.[10] Kant is not complaining vaguely that psychology is not a "hard" or "precise" science. It would seem to be an exaggeration to imagine him here as foreseeing the possibility of what came to be called "psychophysics" later on, because he does not conceive of the principles subsumed under the heading of the Anticipations as psychological laws. Still, what he argues there clearly might be used for the development of a kind of psychophysics.[11]

The unrestricted mathematical impossibility claim cannot be Kant's view for at least one further reason as well. When he rejects the pretensions of empirical psychology, he says that physics has made so much more progress than psychology because in physics we can construct concepts of objects in pure intuition in *all* dimensions of space and time. Psychology, however, is said to be restricted in its subject matter to purely temporal entities. Although interpreters frequently fail to point this out, this statement does not *completely* exclude psychological laws.[12] Kant actually says that one might state a "law of constancy of the succession of inner alterations" (4:471, cf. 20:237). It does not matter that this would hardly be a great achievement, compared to the mathematization embodied in Newtonian mechanics. Geometry is important and extremely fruitful for natural science in Kant's view, but it is surely not the only possible way to mathematize natural phenomena.

Nayak and Sotnak ascribe to Kant a *restricted* mathematical impossibility claim. But how exactly is the claim to be restricted? They suggest the following: Mathematics cannot be applied to psychological phenomena when the phenomena include a certain class of fundamental metaphysical properties, namely "attractive" and "repulsive forces." We can formulate a priori laws for these forces in physics, but in psychology we cannot. It will be useful to make this (substantial) qualification of premises (3) and (4) explicit again:

3a. Natural doctrines contain a system of laws that can be known *a priori* only if these are mathematical laws of attractive and repulsive forces.

4a. Psychology, as the natural doctrine which treats of "thinking substances," cannot contain a system of mathematical laws of attractive and repulsive forces.

There is, to be sure, a certain difficulty here in that Nayak and Sotnak do not clarify whether Kant holds, or should hold, that all and only causal laws are laws of "attractive and repulsive forces" or that the former can be reduced to the latter. We need not worry about this here, however. What Nayak and Sotnak wish to emphasize is a restriction that concerns causal properties. Let us call this the 'impossibility claim concerning mathematical causal laws' or simply, the 'causal impossibility claim'. What makes this reading quite plausible is an argument based upon two main steps. First, Nayak and Sotnak refer to Kant's claim that a science "properly so-called" has to fulfill an explanatory and predictive task, and laws of the "fundamental attractive or repulsive forces" of objects—that is, causal laws— are said to fulfill just that task. Measurement of the kind just mentioned might play an important role in the development of a science of psychology, but not every kind of mathematizability suffices for the development of explanatory and predictive laws. For Kant, it is obvious that the Analogies of Experience, as developed in the first *Critique*, are of direct relevance to this point. That the Analogies play a crucial role for natural science is stated in the *Prolegomena*, and repeated in the *Metaphysical Foundations* as well (4:307, 4:544). Kant also has them in mind when he claims that the concept of nature carries with it the notion of laws (4: 468). The three Analogies are held together by a principle according to which "experience is possible only through the representation of a necessary connection of perception" (B218). They state, more specifically, that in a (cognizable) change of an object, substance must be permanent; that every (cognizable) change has a cause or happens according to the "law of the connection of cause and effect"; and that substances, insofar as they are experienced at the same time, stand in continuous interaction (A182/B224, A189/B233, A211/B256).[13] There are thus two kinds of causal relations in Kant's view: causation as we ordinarily conceive of it, namely, as a relation between distinct events following upon another in time; and causal interaction between temporally coexisting events (cf. A177/B219). Laws concerning attractive and repulsive forces are specifications of those two kinds of causal principles. Also important, as will become clear, is that Kant assumes that both kinds of causal principles presuppose the First Analogy: no change in time and no interaction of co-temporally occurring events is possible without the permanence of the underlying substance.

The second step of Nayak's and Sotnak's argument, not surprisingly, is to deny the applicability of causal terms to psychological phenomena. They point out that Kant seems to imagine that chemistry might become a science if a law of the "approach and withdrawal of the parts of the matter can be stated according to which (as, say in proportion to their densities and suchlike) their motions together with consequences of these can be intuited and presented a priori in space" (4: 471).[14] Similarly, he could imagine that psychology can become a science if only we could develop such a law for the attractive and repulsive forces governing alterations of, say, our perceptions. But, as they write, he takes that to be impossible:

> The territory of psychology is forever restricted to inner sense (see MAN 471), to which the full range of categorical principles, most notably causality, is not cognitively applicable. For that causality be applicable to a set of phenomena, we must be able to distinguish objective from subjective successions of appearances (see A193/B238). But such a distinction requires the determination of objects of outer sense. It follows that genuine causal relations cannot be attributed to psychological phenomena.[15]

There can be no doubt that Kant thinks that causal laws have to play a crucial explanatory role in science. But are Nayak and Sotnak correct in saying that Kant also claims that causal notions cannot be applied to psychological phenomena? There is evidence of various sorts that this cannot be Kant's view. To begin, he accepts causal laws governing the alterations of perceptions and of other psychological phenomena as well. The law of association of ideas by spatiotemporal contiguity is just such a law (e.g., A100). In the *Anthropology from a Pragmatical Point of View*, he gives a somewhat more extensive list of three "laws of association" (7: 176)—different laws of association of representations according to relations of space, time, and resemblance. Kant also knows of other regularities governing psychological phenomena, and he does not hesitate to use causal vocabulary when he discusses them and their explanatory force for our experience, thought, and action. There are, for instance, principles governing the "causes that increase or decrease the degree [of intensity] of our sense impressions" (7:162). In the lectures on anthropology, discussion of these starts in the mid 1770s. The same holds for explanations of how representations can become more clear and distinct (25:501–502, 25:745–47, 25:936–43, 25:1248–53, 25:1455–56). The list can easily be extended by considering, for instance, Kant's remarks concerning phenomena of pleasure and pain, or of desire and inclination.

Of course, it might be the case that such passages are not to be taken seriously. It might be that, for important reasons, he would want to insist upon the impossibility of psychological causal laws. But what reasons could he invoke? Usually two such reasons are seen in Kant's writings, only one of which is invoked by Nayak and Sotnak. It is this: There are passages, especially in the B-edition of the *Critique*, in which Kant seems to reject the view that causal terms can be literally— as opposed to merely "analogously"—applied to psychological phenomena (B291–92). Given the almost parallel development of his criticism of the aspirations of empirical psychology to become a science "properly so-called," that may easily seem to be more than a mere coincidence.

This reading leads to various problems I shall return to soon. Let us first set aside the second kind of reason for doubt concerning whether Kant allows for the applicability of causal terms to psychological phenomena. It is not mentioned by

Nayak and Sotnak, but it is important to be clear about that issue too.[17] We have seen before that the applicability of causal terms to whatever they are applied to presupposes the applicability of the notion of permanence to the same entities. Both the Second and the Third Analogy presuppose the validity of the First Analogy. However, does not Kant argue in the Paralogism chapter that the soul, as subject matter of psychology, is not a permanent substance or thing—contrary to what rationalistic metaphysicians have claimed (see, e.g., A381–82)? What has to be said against such an interpretation is, very briefly, this. Whatever strength Kant's criticism of rational psychology is precisely supposed to have,[17] it is not meant as a denial of the permanence of the self "in life" or "as a human being." Kant clearly states this at B415:

> The permanence of the soul, therefore, as a mere object of inner sense, remains unproven, and unprovable, even though its permanence in life, where the thinking thing (as human being) is an object of outer sense as well, is evident; however, this does not suffice for the rational psychologist, who attempts to prove the absolute permanence of the soul beyond life from mere concept alone.

What is denied is that from the more or less unproblematic permanence of the self—which we presuppose when we ordinarily think about persons—we can draw conclusions about the "absolute" permanence of the soul, or that we can infer the immortality of the soul from it. Kant indicates that this is, at least in part, also due to the fact that we know of human beings qua thinking objects or conscious selves not through inner sense alone (see also 20:308–309). We also have outer experience of human beings in life, and what can be experienced by the outer senses, or what is spatially extended, is at least a candidate for the application of the category of permanence. So far, nothing stands in the way of the possibility of causal laws governing our lives as thinking beings.

Nayak and Sotnak defend their case as follows. As quoted earlier on, they say that Kant requires that, for the "cognitive applicability" of the category of causality to some set of phenomena, one must be able to distinguish between subjective and objective successions of appearances (with reference to A192/B237). That distinction is said to be impossible in the case of phenomena given through "inner sense." They infer that "genuine causal relations cannot be attributed to psychological phenomena."

However, Nayak and Sotnak do not really explain why they draw this connection or how they think that this claim might support the causal impossibility claim. It seems that, on their reading, what is introspectively accessible is identified with what is subjective (or known subjectively), and that what is known subjectively cannot be distinguished along the lines of subjective/objective. Presumably, they want to say that it is Kant's view that, in the case of our subjective experience, we cannot distinguish between what merely seems to be the case and what is objectively so. When we consider the contents of our consciousness, say, the experience of a certain beautiful noise, we cannot distinguish seeming to experience a beautiful noise from the objective fact of doing so. If we seem to have such an experience, then we are actually having it. But if that is their claim, then it is a highly questionable reading. It is inconsistent with what Kant actually argues for at A192/B237. His point there is that if we do not apply the principle of causality, we cannot order events in time; but we certainly do order events in time. Moreover, as various passages in the B-edition (again, B291–92) indicate, he thinks that we would not be able to *check* specific causal judgments if we did not have experience of outer objects against which to check them. That the subjective order presupposes the objective means not only that for ordering events in time we must make claims about which of them are causes and which effects, but also that we primarily do such checking with the help of "outer experience." When I see that the streets are wet and claim that it has probably been raining, I am making a claim not only about certain causes and effects. I am also prepared to test such a claim, not by introspection or by considering my subjective stream of experience, but by looking out the window, by going out on the street as soon as it starts to rain. At least, I cannot *always* check claims about the temporal order of events by looking into myself. That is hardly an argument for the claim that we cannot distinguish, with regard to phenomena of inner sense, between what is objective and what is subjective. Such an issue is not on Kant's mind in these passages. If his claims in the relevant passages are to be connected to—or imply—a further claim concerning the impossibility of drawing the distinction between what is objective and what is subjective within the psychological realm, Nayak and Sotnak have failed to explain and justify that connection.

How might such a connection be established? For Kant, the issue of a temporal order of events is connected to the issue of the validity of the principle of causality, and he does claim that the possibility of checking causal judgments depends upon reference to objects and events of outer experience—that we cannot *always* check them by means of introspection. Does that latter methodological claim not exclude the applicability of causal terms to phenomena of the inner sense? No. First, the additional passages in the B-edition are not without ambiguity. Perhaps Kant only makes the—weaker, and therefore more plausible—claim that the application of causal terms to objects of outer experience is merely a principled requirement, not one that has to be fulfilled in *every* particular case when we make a causal judgment. That would be consistent with what I have just explained. Stated differently, what is at stake is Nayak's and Sotnak's claim about the "cognitive applicability" of causal terms to psychological phenomena in general, not a methodological requirement for checking specific causal judgments. Of course, they might reply that none of this supports the positive claim that causal terms are indeed applicable to psychological phenomena. But that doesn't support their reading either. At A192/B237,

Kant does not exclude the applicability of causal terms to psychological phenomena. He simply leaves the issue open.

Nayak's and Sotnak's mistake can be expressed as follows. If causal terms cannot be applied to psychological phenomena, Kant would not merely have supported the premise

> 4a. Psychology, as the natural doctrine which treats of "thinking substances," cannot contain a system of mathematical laws of attractive and repulsive forces.

It would support a stronger premise, namely,

> 4a*. There can be no causal laws governing psychological phenomena.

Instead of an argument for the impossibility claim concerning mathematical causal laws of psychology, they have given an argument for a much stronger—unacceptably stronger—claim that may be termed an 'impossibility claim concerning causal laws governing psychological phenomena'. Their argument entirely focuses upon the "metaphysical" or "transcendental" issue of the applicability of causal terms to psychological phenomena. They have lost sight of the specific connection Kant wishes to draw between the a priority of genuine natural science and the mathematical construction of natural laws.

Nayak and Sotnak might reply that we should concentrate, not upon their reading of the argument for the Second Analogy, but upon this aspect of their claim: If we consider an experience of a certain beautiful noise as it is given through inner sense, we cannot distinguish the fact that we seem to experience a beautiful noise from the fact that we do experience such a noise. We cannot draw a line between the subjective and the objective in cases like these. Whether or not we cannot draw such a distinction, such a claim is both too general and it proves too much as well. First, it does not have anything to do with the inapplicability of *causal* terms in particular. Even if we grant that one cannot distinguish between the fact that one seems to hear a beautiful noise and the fact that one actually hears such a noise, this hardly shows that my hearing or my seeming to hear the noise cannot be causally explained. Nor does Kant try to argue for such a view. Second, if Kant really would deny the possibility of ever distinguishing between what is subjectively taken to be so and what is objectively the case with regard to psychological phenomena, then there would be no psychological knowledge at all. According to good Kantian doctrine, there can be no knowledge where we cannot draw that distinction. And that is inconsistent with the clear fact that Kant recognizes as a law of psychology the law of the continuity of alterations of our representations through time. Moreover, what Kant conceives to be possible and useful would become impossible: a "natural history of the soul," which he thinks psychology could still be (4:471).

That is psychological knowledge, even if not scientific knowledge "properly so-called."

3. EMPIRICAL PSYCHOLOGY IN HISTORICAL PERSPECTIVE

How could such misunderstandings have arisen in the first place? I think that, to a large extent, they are based upon a confusion concerning the crucial notion of 'psychological phenomena' and the related notion of 'inner sense.' It is useful to reflect on this for a moment. It will help to recognize the proper historical context of Kant's impossibility claim, and only if we understand that context can we evaluate his arguments adequately. Nayak and Sotnak say that the "territory of psychology is forever restricted to inner sense" and that "genuine causal relations cannot be attributed to psychological phenomena."[18] On the view under discussion, odd as it may seem, this "territory"—psychological phenomena—is accessed entirely through inner sense alone. But is that Kant's own view? Or is he discussing a conception of 'inner sense' advanced by other philosophers?

We can distinguish between *what* is given through inner sense and *how* it is given. Let us grant that Kant holds that what is, or what at least can be, given introspectively are features of our psychological lives: our perceptions, thoughts, beliefs, feelings, desires, inclinations, and so on. With regard to the question of how these features are given, or with regard to their epistemic accessibility, however, Kant might hold a different view altogether. He might say that our psychological states are given exclusively through inner sense alone, i.e., there is no other kind of epistemic access to them. Or he might hold that they can be given either through inner sense or in other ways as well. When commentators speak of 'psychological phenomena', they tend not to specify Kant's views on this point. Talk of 'psychological phenomena' might refer to what is given through inner sense and so mean that it is accessible in a certain way, namely introspectively—implying, perhaps, that he must mean that they cannot be accessed in other ways as well. Yet it might allow others modes of access, and it is clear that such an ambiguity could produce all sorts of confusion and faulty inferences.

Moreover, Kant does not think that what is given through inner sense possesses features that would make it inaccessible in principle to the obvious alternative—namely to "outer sense" observation. In his lectures on anthropology from as early as the 1770s, Kant warns against the fashionable desire for introspective self-observation of authors such as Pascal and Albrecht von Haller. He argues that too much self-observation and attention to one's own mind can easily lead to madness (e.g., 25:252, 25:477, 7:132). But more important than this is that, from at least the 1780s on, he advances a *methodological* claim against introspection as the primary method of knowing the human mind. He claims that one can experience "the state of one's own mind . . . through attention to one's own *actions* just as well," and he advises the physiognomist Johann Caspar Lavater—who published a *Geheimes Tagebuch: Von einem Beobachter seiner Selbst* in 1771—that if he aims to know his own soul or state of mind, he ought to take a look at what he is *doing* rather than observe his inner states (25:1220). Our vocabulary of representations, thoughts, feelings, passions, traits of personal character, and so on, is intimately connected to a careful observation of human action and human life as it occurs and as it can be observed, especially in society (7:119–20). 'Psychological phenomena' are open to public observation in Kant's view, contrary to what Nayak and Sotnak and others have claimed.[19]

It must be admitted that Kant's talk of "phenomena of inner sense" can lead to the ambiguity mentioned. But Kant's discussion of the issue in the *Metaphysical Foundations* should be seen as following a pattern which Kant frequently uses in order to show how one can develop a reasonable idea of a science. He argues against a specific *conception* of psychology, one which is characterized by reference to a certain view concerning (1) the subject matter of psychology and (2) the methods or "sources of knowledge" thought to be adequate for investigating that subject matter. This conception adheres to the idea that psychological states are given in their entirety to inner sense alone.

Kant thinks that one always has a more or less developed idea of a science, and that one cannot do without any such idea (A834/B863). In the *Prolegomena*, he claims that the "idea" of a possible science and its differences from other disciplines have to be explained by reference to "a difference in the object or in the sources of knowledge or in the mode of knowledge or also in several, if not all of these features together" (4:265). In the *Metaphysical Foundations*, he addresses a further feature as well, namely the aim or purpose of a science (4:477). Specification of the aims, methods, and subject matter of science provides the basic elements for explaining the definition or conception of a possible science. Further, the reasonableness of any given conception of science clearly depends upon whether the specification of its aims, subject matter, and methods are consistent and coherent. That is also how Kant discusses conceptions of various scientific disciplines—either by defending and improving his own conception or by criticizing competing conceptions.[20] For contemporary readers, it may not always be clear that Kant is not speaking in *personam propriam* when he discusses a certain conception; since he often merely alludes to certain widespread views without saying that they are held by this or that author. It may then happen that one ascribes to Kant views concerning some object or method or aim of scientific knowledge that he himself rejects. It seems that the second kind of mistake can happen when the first kind does not. Nayak and Sotnak recognize that there were different approaches to psychology available in Kant's times;[21] yet they do not clarify sufficiently Kant's views on the notion of the 'inner sense' and remain ambiguous in their talk of 'psychological phenomena'.

Not too surprisingly, the conception of psychology Kant attacks is that held by Wolff and Baumgarten, which also happens to have been Kant's own conception earlier in his career. Christian Wolff had introduced an influential epistemological distinction between two branches of psychology: namely, between a rational kind of knowledge of the mind, on the one hand, and an empirical kind, on the other.[22] He thought that empirical knowledge delivers certain facts, whereas rational knowledge provides the "ground" or the sufficient explanation of the possibility of those facts. In the case of psychology, empirical knowledge would supply certain facts about a specific subject matter, namely the soul (conceived of along Cartesian-Leibnizian lines as a spiritual substance, as opposed to material substance). Rational knowledge would then provide explanations, or the "reason of the possibility" for those facts—in the sense that it would explain the facts that "are possible through the human soul." This does not mean, however, that empirical psychology would merely deliver observational knowledge about what occurs in the soul. Wolff took empirical psychology to provide us with knowledge about certain habits and faculties of the mind as well. Such views were adopted by Alexander Baumgarten. It is not clear that Wolff was committed to the following, more specific methodological claim, namely, that empirical psychology has to be based upon the special source of knowledge called "internal sense" (*sensus internus*). However, Baumgarten was definitely of this opinion,[23] perhaps under the influence of Locke's notion of 'reflection' as "that notice which the Mind takes of its operations."[24] Baumgarten did place his "proof" of the existence of the soul within himself in a characteristically first-person form: "If there exists something in a thing which is conscious of itself, this is a soul. Something exists in me, §55, that can be conscious of itself, §57. There exists, therefore, a soul in me (I exist as a soul)."[25]

Baumgarten used first-person claims in virtually all of the "empirical" premises of his demonstrations of the "Psychologia Empirica."[26] Psychology, according to his conception, investigates "thinking nature," and in its empirical part, it does so *exclusively* through inner sense. Its cognitive aim, of course, is to systematize and explain the observations of these "inner" phenomena in terms of laws or of human faculties governed by laws.

Until the mid-1770s, Kant had accepted Baumgarten's conception of empirical psychology as an adequate and respectable one (see 2:397). In announcements of his lectures, for example, in 1756 and 1765/66, he praised Baumgarten's book for its precision and its richness (1:503, 2:308–309). He lectured on empirical psychology within his lectures on metaphysics, thus following Baumgarten's lead, whose *Metaphysica* (with its chapter on "Psychologia Empirica") he used as a standard textbook; and he used Baumgarten's chapter on empirical psychology for his lectures on anthropology as well. It is thus not at all surprising that he came to reflect upon the conception of psychology underlying that work. Empirical psychology, Kant continues to say in the *Anthropology from a Pragmatical Point of View*, is a "sum-total of inner perceptions under natural laws" (7:141). Kant frequently repeated this definition of empirical psychology and, even when he had become critical of the possibilities of such a kind of empirical psychology in his later years, he did not abandon it as a definition of that conception of psychology (28:223–25, 28:670, 29:754–56, 29:945, A347/B405, A381, 4:295, 4:337, 7:141).

Certainly the extreme introspectionism inherent in this conception is hardly a feasible methodological tool. It restricts the empirical basis of psychology to the observation of one's own mental states or processes, which is quite minimal. Is Kant fighting a strawman? It must be admitted that Wolff's and Baumgarten's work on empirical psychology was no longer viewed as being current in the 1780s.[27] Also, their *conception* of empirical psychology was not the only one available. For instance, Charles Bonnet, David Hartley, Ernst Platner and others took seriously the possibility of investigating the human mind by studying the human brain. The important point, however, is that such physiological or "anthropological" approaches soon came under attack, and objections against them were precisely what strengthened introspectionist psychology again. Johann Nicolas Tetens, whose work Kant knew well, vigorously defended introspectionism. Tetens did not deny that psychological states and properties might have a neural basis in the brain. His criticism of Bonnet's or Hartley's views was a twofold methodological one. First, so far their theories were "mere speculation," hypotheses without any serious empirical basis.[28] He took "Locke's method" of observing the "modifications of the soul as they are known through self-feeling [*Selbstgefühl*]"[29] as much safer methodological advice. Second, even if materialism were correct in some sense as an ontological thesis, one would nevertheless always have to *start* with introspection and "psychological analysis" based upon it—all materialistic hypotheses would always have to be tested by reference to "observational knowledge," and Tetens's only idea of what an observation of the mind could be is introspectionist, as his talk of knowing the mind through a "sense of self" clearly shows.[30] He admitted that observation through introspection did contain some sources of error, but he argued that there are no means at one's disposal other than to repeat the same observation under similar as well as under different circumstances. Whoever was not able to do so would not be an able "observer of the soul."[31] Tetens did *not* advocate the weak claim that introspection might be simply one source among others of knowing the mind. All mental states are alike in that we know them first and foremost through *Selbstgefühl* (literally, 'self-feeling' or introspection). That he holds even for dispositional terms of mental states, and he does not consider whether, say, the mental concepts that describe the intellectual and social capacities, or the characters and roles of human beings could be known in a different manner. Nor does he consider the possibility that introspective judgments might be corrected by other kinds of judgments or experiences—say, by psychophysical experiments which correlate, check, and possibly refine what subjects report about their mental life, or by a sufficiently reflective observation of human behavior.[32]

Setting Kant's considerations against the background of a methodological debate with extreme introspectionist conceptions of psychology shows that he is not denying the status of a science "properly so-called" to psychology under any conception whatsoever. Also, only if one reads him as attacking introspectionist psychology does a further group of objections he advances against empirical psychology make sense. In the *Metaphysical Foundations*, he argues that empirical psychology will not even become an "experimental doctrine" (4:471). He advances three considerations for this claim. First, as long as one observes one's own states through inner sense, these states cannot be subjected to *repeatable* experiments. As observed through introspection, psychological phenomena are not extended, have no shape, and are not objects of a constant or permanent kind. They appear *only* in time. Now if one conceives of psychological phenomena as a special class of objects (as Baumgarten does), then one is mistaken in thinking they could be subjected to experiments as physical bodies can. Kant's second consideration supports the first one: if psychological objects and events are conceived of as accessible only through introspection, all differentiation between them is performed only in *thought*. We think of the distinction of such events on the analogy of the distinction and separation of physical bodies, and our ability to do so in the case of the latter is due to our ability to literally "separate and store" them. However, we cannot "separately store" and "arbitrarily recombine" them if they are given introspectively only. Thus, the experiments we would perform with them would be nothing more than thought-experiments. Third, Kant claims that even the observation of one's own introspectively accessible psychological states is difficult, since introspective attention "alters and shifts the state of the object observed." To observe, even to observe introspectively, is more than to be merely conscious of mental states and events. It is to *focus* upon a certain area of one's own mind. Kant here indicates that it becomes questionable whether the psychological states or processes so observed function in the way they usually do—whether, say, my introspecting a certain state of passion, pleasure, or pain might not easily change that state so that it does not lead to its usual causal consequences in my reaction or in my beliefs about the causes of that state. These are surely fatal possibilities if one is trying to figure out how such states normally function in our lives.[33] Kant could not raise such arguments if they were not directed against part of the conception of psychology he was attacking all along.

4. The Impossibility of Mathematization Revisited

But how, then, should we understand Kant's impossibility claim? The result of our discussion above is that its real content is not,

> 4a. Psychology, as the natural doctrine which treats of "thinking substances," cannot contain a system of mathematical laws of attractive and repulsive forces.

It is rather a claim like this:

4b. Psychology, as the natural doctrine which treats of "thinking substances" insofar as these are given all and only through inner sense,
cannot contain mathematical laws of attractive and repulsive forces.

This is the case since, according to Baumgarten's conception of psychology, "thinking substances" as well as their psychological properties are thought of as strictly
nonspatial entities. It is only because of this assumption that *geometry*, as the
mathematical science concerning spatial relations, cannot be applied to them (4:
471; see also the very clear statement at 20:285–86). Premise (4b), of course, has
to be qualified insofar as Kant imagines a law of the "constancy of the succession
of inner alterations" as a mathematical synthetic a priori principle of psychology.

But why should (4b) be accepted? Kant's argument is based on the (limited)
impossibility of a mathematical "construction" of the subject matter of psychology
as conceived along the introspectionist conception of psychology—upon the difficulty of giving such a construction for "thinking substances" and the laws governing their modifications and alterations. But why is such construction required
in the first place? The crucial point is that Kant thinks that this is the only way to
develop an a priori *intuition* of the objects in question. For any kind of knowledge
of objects, Kant thinks that not only concepts, but also intuitions of those objects
are necessary; and for an a priori knowledge of those objects, not only a priori
concepts, but also a priori intuitions are necessary. And such a priori intuition, he
claims, is possible only through the mathematical construction of the objects in
pure intuition, be that space or time. That is just the positive way of raising one
of the crucial objections against Nayak and Sotnak: In their preoccupation with
the category of causality, they have neglected the fact that Kant is concerned with
the necessity of a priori intuitions for "specific kinds of objects of nature."

Kant's criticism of the introspectionist conception of psychology is a criticism
of a conception we don't share, but which was still influential at the time when
Kant discussed it. Given his arguments against pure introspectionism, Kant is
justified to point out that, from the very beginning, there is too deep a difference
between such an idea of psychology and, say, Newtonian physics for them ever to
become sciences in the same sense of the word. Philosophers and psychologists
did not realize that their hope that psychology as they conceived of it might, in
the course of ordinary scientific progress, become a science "properly so-called,"
is undermined by their own ontological and methodological views. Kant's way of
bringing this out is to reflect on the consistency and coherence of the specification
of the methods, subject matter, and aims which one accepts. We can surely learn
something from this procedure for philosophy of science and perhaps science as
well. Still, one has to realize that there is an important weakness in Kant's considerations. I do not mean the point indicated earlier on that the requirement of a
priority for the title of a science "properly so-called" is perhaps too strong, and
maybe even ad hoc. We can now say that it seems less ad hoc since now Kant's

substantial doctrine that knowledge of objects involves intuition is brought well into play. Why we should need an a priori intuition in order to have scientific knowledge "properly so-called" is another difficult issue, too difficult to be discussed here.[34] But even if we grant these points, we are faced with another weakness of his position.

Kant thinks that our psychological lives are open to outer experience as well. But he has given no argument for the claim that there can be no appropriate mathematical construction of the objects and events known in this way. It is at least an open question whether, to take Kant's favorite mathematical theory, geometry might not be applied to the principles governing the relevant events and entities. Kant never even considers the idea of a "mathematical construction" of, say, causal principles governing the "anthropological" features of our lives. Perhaps there might be arguments against such an idea; but they have to be brought to the fore first. And if they were considered, one would need to reflect on whether it is more our conception of the scientific disciplines investigating those objects and processes than the objects and processes themselves which exclude what Kant calls a 'mathematical construction' of them.

NOTES

I wish to thank Patricia Kitcher and Eric Watkins for many helpful discussions and suggestions.

1. Translations from Kant's lectures on metaphysics are from *Lectures on Metaphysics*, trans. and ed. Karl Ameriks and Steve Naragon (Cambridge: Cambridge University Press, 1997). All other translations are mine.

2. It might be suspected that the impossibility claim is part of Kant's reason for his (alleged) view that there can be no strict scientific explanation of human action (since human agents are free). Alternatively, one might suspect that Kant's claim that human beings are free agents is partially based upon his (again alleged) view that there can be no strict psychological laws. In at least one case, it has been argued that Kant's view is very close to Donald Davidson's "anomalous monism" according to which there can be no psychological laws and, hence, no strict science of psychology (see Hud Hudson, *Kant's Compatibilism* [Ithaca: Cornell University Press, 1994], 67, 70; and Donald Davidson, "Mental Events," in *Essays on Actions and Events* (Oxford: Oxford University Press, 1980), 201–25). Henry Allison makes similar suggestions, though he is less definitive about whether Kant held such a view, in *Kant's Theory of Freedom* (Cambridge: Cambridge University Press, 1990), 31–32, 33, 43. But the impossibility claim and Kant's views regarding human agency and its empirical description and explanation are really distinct issues. As will become clear below, Kant's reason for denying psychology the status of a science proper is not a complete denial of psychological laws (as it is on Hudson's view) nor that human beings are free agents. Rather, his impossibility claim is really directed at a conception of psychology too different from Davidson's (or Hudson's). More on this, as well as on other topics in this essay, in my "Kant und die Wissenschaften vom Menschen" (Ph. D. diss., Philipps-University of Marburg, forthcoming).

3. That passage is not revised in the B-edition of 1787, so one might see an incoherence between the *Metaphysical Foundations* and the *Critique*. However, the issue of what requirements there are for a science "properly so-called" is not being raised, so Kant might have thought that he didn't need to revise that passage. And there is at least one further possibility for dealing with the consistency of the A-and B-editions: since the issue of the status of psychology as a science does not affect the core of the project of transcendental philosophy, Kant could easily have overlooked that passage when reworking the *Critique*. It is perhaps significant that, in the rewritten introduction, Kant considers only physics when he asserts that one ought not to mistake certain principles of "pure natural science . . . which can be found in the beginning of (empirical) physics proper" for empirical ones (B20n.). There is an obvious contrast between this later passage and an earlier passage in the *Prolegomena*, where Kant draws a close parallel between "physics proper" and psychology (4:265).

4. Kant claims, first, that the notion of nature implies the concept of laws and, second, that the concept of laws in turn implies the "necessity of all determinations of an object which belong to its existence" (4:468). If one knows a certain judgment to be necessary, however, one knows it a priori (A2/B3–4). Of course, the first of these claims refers back to his well known claims concerning the lawfulness of experience in general (e.g., A108). But it must be noted that the idea that it is necessary that natural things obey laws (or are experienced as obeying them) hardly shows that specific natural laws are themselves necessary, nor that there must be such necessary laws. At best, it shows that there must be laws governing whatever phenomena are under consideration. One might even argue that the necessity in question is not an ontological but "merely" an epistemological one.

5. He speaks of empirical physics as "physics proper" (again, B20n., 4:265, 20:198).

6. Again, see nn. 3 and 5. The issue is further complicated by the fact that this is not Kant's only notion of science. He feels free on other occasions to speak of "historical sciences" as contrasted to "rational sciences" (*historische und Vernunftwissenschaften*; see 2:306, 5:137, 5:305, 7:28, 9:45, and 9:72). Historical sciences are historical in an older sense of the word: namely, they contain only factual claims which are based upon careful observation and experimentation, and the facts or objects are given some sort of systematic ordering, as in the classifications of objects developed by Linnaeus or Buffon in their natural histories. This notion, therefore, is more or less identical in meaning with the notion of an 'empirical' science. Hence the unhappy impression that it is only here that Kant, who alludes to the distinction between rational and historical sciences in the *Metaphysical Foundations* as well (4:468), requires historical sciences to have a rational counterpart in order to deserve the name of 'science'.

7. Abhaya C. Nayak and Eric Sotnak, "Kant on the Impossibility of the 'Soft Sciences,' " *Philosophy and Phenomenological Research* 55 (1995): 133–51.

8. They (Nayak and Sotnak, "Kant on the Impossibility," 145) mention Kathleen Okruhlik, "Kant on Realism and Methodology," in *Kant's Philosophy of Physical Science*, ed. Robert E. Butts (Dordrecht: D. Reidel, 1986), 307–29, and A. Wolf, *A History of Science, Technology and Philosophy in the 18th Century* (New York: MacMillan, 1939). The misinterpretation can also be found in, e.g., Charles Gouaux, "Kant's View on the Nature of Empirical Psychology," *Journal of the History of the Behavioral Sciences* 8 (1972): 237–42, esp. 241–42; David Leary, "Immanuel Kant and the Development of Modern Psychology," in *The Problematic Science: Psychology in the Nineteenth Century*, ed. William R. Woodward and Mitchell G. Ash (New York: Praeger, 1982), 17–42, esp. 22; Heiner Klemme, *Kants Philosophie des Subjekts* (Hamburg: Meiner, 1996), 236.

9. Nayak and Sotnak, "Kant on the Impossibility," 134–44.

10. See Leary, "Immanuel Kant and the Development of Modern Psychology," 35–36.

11. And that would apply to the Axioms of Intuition too. At least in the case of the Anticipations, Kant's foreshadowing of psychophysics may not happen by accident. Simple psychophysical experiments such as Lambert's photometer for the measurement of the varying intensity of the perception of light of different sources (described by Nayak and Sotnak, "Kant on the Impossibility," 140) were not uncommon in the eighteenth century. Kant may have known other examples from entries in Zedler's *Universal-Lexikon* (see Heiner Klemme, "Die mathematischen Grundsätze," in *Immanuel Kant, Die Kritik der reinen Vernunft*, ed. Georg Mohr and Marcus Willaschek [Berlin: Akademie, 1998], 245–64).

12. This qualification is overlooked by, e.g., Leary, "Immanuel Kant and the Development of Modern Psychology," 22; Klemme, *Kants Philosophie des Subjekts*, 236–37. The clearest exception to this rule is Gary Hatfield, "Empirical, Rational, and Transcendental Psychology: Psychology as Science and as Philosophy," in *The Cambridge Companion to Kant*, ed. Paul Guyer (Cambridge: Cambridge University Press, 1992), 218–19.

13. I cannot and, fortunately, need not enter here the complicated debates about the precise meaning and justification of the Analogies. But a remark concerning the question of how close a connection between the transcendental principles and their specific instantiations within natural science and its metaphysical foundations is in place. It is sometimes assumed that Kant takes the connection to be quite close: that the program of transcendental philosophy requires the *Metaphysical Foundations* for its full execution; that *physical laws*—say, Newton's laws of motion or the law of gravitation—are perhaps the *only* real instantiations of the transcendental Analogies; or that the sole function of the transcendental Analogies is their role in the justification of Newtonian physics. (See esp. Peter Plaass, *Kants Theorie der Naturwissenschaft* [Göttingen: Vandenhoeck and Ruprecht, 1965], 19–22, 68; Michael Friedman, *Kant and the Exact Sciences* [Cambridge: Harvard University Press, 1992], chap. 3, esp. 136–37; for a critique, see Henry Allison, "Causality and Causal Law in Kant: A Critique of Michael Friedman," in *Idealism and Freedom* [Cambridge: Cambridge University Press, 1996], 80–91.) While the transcendental principles can and indeed need to be given *some* scientific application, I do not see an argument in Kant for the claim that physical laws are the *only* possible specifications. Friedman, to be sure, does not make such a strong claim; but then one wonders what the point is of his—and Plaass's—claim that transcendental philosophy cannot fully be understood until a complete "investigation of the foundations of Newtonian science" has been carried out (Friedman, *Kant and the Exact Sciences*, 137). What Kant says is merely that transcendental philosophy needs "instances *in concreto*" or "examples" to explain the meaning of the transcendental principles, and that these typically come from our knowledge of physical nature (4:478). That is a rather weak claim. In any case, within the context of the argument over psychology the stronger claim should not be presupposed; it would be question-begging to exclude from the outset that psychological laws might be "instances *in concreto*" as well.

14. See Nayak and Sotnak, "Kant on the Impossibility," 148.

15. Nayak and Sotnak, "Kant on the Impossibility," 149.

16. This point is made, if with different emphasis and with qualifications, by Gouaux, "Kant's View on the Nature of Empirical Psychology," 239–40; Norman Kemp Smith, *Commentary on Kant's Critique of Pure Reason* (New York: Humanities Press, 1950), 311–12; Theodore Mischel, "Kant and the Possibility of a Science of Psychology," *The Monist* 51

(1967): 599–622, esp. 607–608; Richard McDonough, "Kant's Argument against the Possibility of Cognitive Science," in *Proceedings of the Eighth International Kant Congress,* Memphis 1995, ed. Hoke Robinson (Milwaukee: Marquette University Press, 1995), vol. 2/1: 37–45, esp. 38–41; Richard McDonough, "Kant's 'Historicist' Alternative to Cognitive Science," *Southern Journal of Philosophy* 22 (1995): 203–19, esp. 214; Kenneth Westphal, "Kant's Critique of Determinism in Empirical Psychology," in *Proceedings of the Eighth International Kant Congress,* Memphis 1995, ed. Hoke Robinson (Milwaukee: Marquette University Press, 1995), vol. 2/1: 357–70, esp. 358–61.

17. For a discussion of how strong Kant's arguments might be intended to be, see Karl Ameriks, *Kant's Theory of Mind* (Oxford: Oxford University Press), 1982.

18. Nayak and Sotnak, "Kant on the Impossibility," 149.

19. E.g., Jürgen Bona Meyer, *Kants Psychologie* (Berlin: Wilhelm Hertz, 1870), 295.

20. I develop this further in chap. 4 of my *Kant und die Wissenschaften vom Menschen.*

21. Nayak and Sotnak, "Kant on the Impossibility," 146.

22. See Charles Corr, "Christian Wolff's Distinction between Empirical and Rational Psychology," in *Akten des II. Internationalen Leibniz-Kongresses, Hannover 1972 (Studia Leibnitiana, suppl. vol. 14),* (Wiesbaden, 1975), 195–215, esp. 195–98.

23. See Alexander Baumgarten, *Metaphysica,* 7th ed. (Halle, 1757), §503 (17:130) and §535 (15:13).

24. John Locke, *An Essay Concerning Human Understanding,* ed. Peter H. Nidditch (Oxford: Oxford University Press, 1975), 105 (II.i.4); see also 104 (II.i.2).

25. Baumgarten, *Metaphysica,* §504 (15:5).

26. See Baumgarten, *Metaphysica,* §505 (15:6). Wolff, however, took the existence of a *plurality* of souls to be a basic experiential fact (*Psychologia Empirica,* §16). See Corr, "Christian Wolff's Distinction between Empirical and Rational Psychology," 199.

27. See Leary, "Immanuel Kant and the Development of Modern Psychology," 20.

28. Johann Nicolas Tetens, *Philosophische Versuche über die menschliche Natur und ihre Entwickelung,* 2 vols. (Leipzig: M. G. Weidmanns Erben und Reich, 1777; reprint Hildesheim: Georg Olms Verlag, 1979), 1: vi.

29. Ibid., 1: iii–iv.

30. Ibid., 1: xiii–xiv.

31. Ibid., 1: xvii.

32. Only a few psychologists seriously considered methodological alternatives, even though, for instance, certain psychophysical experiments were already available (Nayak and Sotnak, "Kant on the Impossibility," 140). Somewhat of an exception in the German discussion is Christian Gottfried Schütz, who had published a translation of Bonnet's *Essai analytique,* to which he had added an extended discussion of the methodological problems of psychology (Christian Gottfried Schütz, "Betrachtungen über die verschiednen Methoden der Psychologie; nebst einem kritischen Auszug aus des Hrn. Abt von Condillac *Trait des sensations,*" in *Karl Bonnets Analytischer Versuch über die Seelenkräfte,* trans. Christian Gottfried Schütz [Bremen and Leipzig: Johann Henrich Cramer, 1770–71], 2: 187–273, esp. 2: 187–206). Also, it is sometimes maintained that Hume belongs to the tradition of introspectionism as well. However, he explicitly points out the crucial relevance of the observation of human behavior and human social life for the "science of human nature" (David Hume, *A Treatise of Human Nature,* ed. L. A. Selby-Bigge [Oxford: Oxford University Press, 1978], xix). He was too much of an historian to focus exclusively upon introspection in the study of the mind.

33. Hatfield overlooks Kant's dialectical situation when he objects to these arguments by pointing out the possibility of controlling introspective reports with the help of psychophysical experiments (Hatfield, "Empirical, Rational, and Transcendental Psychology: Psychology as Science and as Philosophy," 222–23).

34. Hatfield is right to point out that there is need for further argument here (Hatfield, "Empirical, Rational, and Transcendental Psychology: Psychology as Science and as Philosophy," 220–21).

9

Kant on the Scientific Status of Psychology, Anthropology, and History

Rudolf A. Makkreel

KANT'S attitude to what we now call the human sciences seems to have fluctuated over the years. In the *Observations on the Feeling of the Beautiful and the Sublime* of 1764 Kant refers to the *Wissenschaft der Menschen* as a womanly occupation.[1] Yet in many of his lectures on anthropology he refers to it as a generally very important science. Then in 1781–82 his lectures on anthropology are labelled *Menschenkunde—Kunde*, suggesting a rather low informational level of knowledge about human beings that may not deserve the title of a science. Kant at times also utters rather dismissive comments about the sciences in general, which could lead us to the view that the scientific status of such disciplines as psychology, anthropology, and history is less important than their practical value.

To sort out these problems I will place Kant's views on the status of psychology and anthropology in the *Critique of Pure Reason* in the context of what he says about historical and other human knowledge in both his lectures on logic and anthropology over the years. Given the recent appearance of volume 25 of the Akademie edition, it is now possible to supplement the 1798 published version of the *Anthropology from a Pragmatic Point of View* with earlier versions and arrive at a much more nuanced understanding of Kant's views on the human sciences.

1. ACADEMIC, HISTORICAL, AND WORLDLY SCIENCES

Already in 1772 Kant holds the view later expressed in the *Critique of Pure Reason* that empirical psychology should be banished from metaphysics. In the Parow version of the lectures on anthropology Kant says that empirical psychology parallels physics. Both are based on observation and experience, one of inner sense, the other of outer sense. While it is obvious that physics as the science of observations based on outer sense is not part of metaphysics, it has traditionally been assumed that psychology as the science of the soul is a source of at least some pure concepts of metaphysics. For Kant psychology is problematic as such a source because the soul is obviously subject to influences from the body. Even the traditional doctrine of the temperaments reflects this somatic base of the psyche. It is difficult to be sure that the soul is autonomous, for the Cartesian thesis that the soul is a distinct substance goes beyond the limits of human knowledge.

The other reason why psychology is a problematic science according to Kant is that even as an empirical observational discipline it is subject to doubt. Already in the Parow anthropology lectures Kant speaks of the harm that self-observation can produce. The more attention one gives to oneself, the more hypochondriacal one becomes.[2] In the Friedländer anthropology lectures of 1775–76 we see Kant beginning to note that self-observation is much more difficult than the observation of things outside us: "Self-observation is difficult, unnatural, can lead to revision and must not last long" (25:478). The advantage of anthropology over psychology is that it can observe not merely the soul, but the whole human being. In fact, in these Friedländer lecture notes Kant indicates that anthropology is not so much a description of human beings, as it is "a description of human nature" (25:471). Anthropology is broader than psychology because it considers human beings as part of the world. In the context of psychology, inner sense is conceived as providing introspective access to feelings and other mental states. In the context of Kant's anthropology, inner sense refers to the whole human being as a participant in the world. Thus we read: "The world as an object of outer sense is nature, the world as an object of inner sense is the human being" (25:469). Just as we need physics and geography to explain and describe the world of nature, we need anthropology and history to study the full scope of the human world.

Insofar as anthropology studies not merely the private states of human beings, but also their public behavior and their interactions, it begins to encroach on the study of history. In the *Lectures on Logic* Kant distinguishes between two types of cognition (*Erkenntnis*): rational and historical. Starting with the *Blomberg Logic* of the early 1770s Kant argues that in rational cognition as found in mathematics and physics, the governing relation is that of subordination. In historical cognition, by contrast, the governing relation is one of coordination. "In history, namely, I enumerate one thing after another, be it as to space or to time. But in rational cognitions and sciences we always derive one thing from another."[3] Rational cognition based on the principle of subordination allows for a strong connectedness based on the relation of ground to consequence. The relation of coordination that characterizes historical cognition does not need to remain purely enumerative, however, as initially suggested by Kant. We will see that through the application of synthesis and analysis it becomes possible to organize historical data in terms of part-whole relations which allow the data to become coherent. If a discipline like history can be organized by an idea of the whole it can be considered a proper science according to Kant. We read, again in the *Blomberg Logic*, that "in historical sciences one has two methods, the *chronological* and the *geographical*. . . . The last is better than the first. In all cognitions that hang together one must first take into consideration the whole rather than its parts" (LL, 237, 24:292). One of the ways whereby history can be given coherence is to understand it in relation to geography. In this regard Kant observes that wars and competition have led people to disperse and to populate ever more remote regions of the earth. Geography provides the spatial coordinates of human history and can become the empirical base for historical cognition. Populations that are content to nourish themselves from native plants and wildlife are more free according to Kant than those that practice agriculture.[4] To cultivate land and grow crops on it is to make an investment there that militates against exploring new places. Kant seems to think that people willing to move elsewhere are more likely to overcome tyranny and preserve their freedom. In light of these comments one might wonder about Kant's own weddedness to Königsberg.

Like geography and history, anthropology is a historical science: They are historical both in the objective sense that their contents have an empirical origin and subjectively in that their contents are related to each other without the use of reason. Historical cognition is important, however, because it broadens our horizons. Geography is a useful starting point because it orients history to the world at large. But if history is to be a true science it needs a systematic idea to guide it.

Starting with his anthropology lectures in 1775, Kant begins to think that what really makes history and anthropology sciences in the sense of systematic disciplines that hang together is not some theoretical idea, but a practical idea. Whereas psychology is a theoretical science governed by the idea of the soul as a distinct substance, anthropology makes no such theoretical assumption. We read in the Friedländer anthropology of 1775–76: "He who has much theoretical knowledge ... but has no skill in making use of it, is learned in relation to the schools, but not in relation to the world" (25:469). Pragmatic anthropology relates our knowledge of human beings to their worldly tasks and ends. It provides not merely theoretical observations about human beings, but is also geared at developing "our judgment in making use of our skills" (25:469). In the 1781–82 *Menschenkunde*, we see Kant attacking certain scholastic or academic (*schulgerechte*) sciences for being of no use to human beings. They are dismissed as "brooding sciences" (25:853). He does not, however, tell us what is to count as a brooding science. As early as in his *Bemerkungen* on the *Observations of the Feeling of the Beautiful and Sublime*, Kant expresses the view that the sciences are often the product of luxury and leisure motivated by the desire for honor, and that they may be the source of evils. Despite this Rousseauean sentiment, Kant goes on to assert his confidence that whatever evils are produced by science, it can also cure them. Here Kant seems to have metaphysics in mind as a brooding science, because he clearly believes that the very illusions of reason exploited by speculative dialecticians can also be tamed by them through the critical method. Psychology based on the speculative idea of the soul as a distinct substance undoubtedly warrants the label "brooding science" as well. It is theoretical in an academic sense and when it proceeds to rely on

188 Psychology and the Human Sciences

introspection speculative brooding may even become morbid. To find a cure for such morbidity it will be necessary to transform psychology into a pragmatic anthropology.

It is important to note that Kant acknowledged the existence of legitimate academic sciences. Some of them such as physics do after all provide a model of rigor that even a pragmatic discipline such as anthropology can profit from. Kant's most characteristic criticism is of individuals who attempt to extend school learning beyond the limits within which it is appropriate. Thus someone who spouts general scholastic propositions in order to cope with a worldly situation is called a "pedant" by Kant. Such a pedant is unable to use his "power of judgment or discernment and fails to see what fits the situation" (25:853). A pedant fails to see that in situations where simple common sense or acquaintance with worldly affairs suffices for the solution of a problem, technical jargon should be avoided.

Beyond the academic sciences there are what Kant calls "worldly sciences" that can apply the general propositions of scholarly learning, but also must go on to produce their own general learning. Learning about the world is not just randomly picking up a series of useful specifics about human relations. In the Pillau anthropology lectures of 1777–78, Kant calls the latter "local world-knowledge (*Weltkenntniß*) possessed by merchants, which is empirical" (25:734). What Kant is aiming at is "a general world-knowledge . . . which is not empirical, but cosmological" (25:734).

In the *Menschenkunde* of 1781–82 Kant goes on to distinguish three kinds of learning:

> one kind makes us skillful or clever [*geschickt*], another prudential [*klug*], a third wise [*weise*]. All the academic sciences allow us to become skilled or clever. Thus one learns history to become well-versed about the things of experience. But if we want to step into the world then we must learn how to become prudent (25:855).

Being skilled or clever is conceived as merely having a theoretical knowledge of things; being prudential involves a "practical knowledge" (25:855) that enables us to make use of our skills and direct them to the worldly ends of human beings. We can distinguish here between the knowledge involved in having a skill and the prudential knowledge of what ends one wants to apply that skill to. More specifically, prudence is said to consist "in such knowledge of human beings as allows us to control others according to our intention" (25:855). Such practical worldly knowledge is pragmatic because it is directed at our actual purposes or ends. Practical worldly knowledge becomes moral when it aims at the ideals of wisdom. This latter kind of knowledge involves being able to judge what our final end should be and requires us to expand our horizon beyond that of our actual pragmatic concerns.

Geography and history are said to be useful in opening our eyes to the fact that other people in other regions of the world may have different judgments about things. But ultimately the expanded mode of thought that constitutes wisdom is a talent of reason, which cannot be taught. We read in the *Menschenkunde* that "through science we can add to the number of our concepts, but not to the scope of our concepts" (25:1039). No science, not even anthropology, can expand the scope of our concepts to grasp what is "best in the world [*das Weltbeste*]" (25: 1040). Only through the self-responsible use of our own reason in accordance with principles can we expand our thinking to reach such a cosmopolitan ideal of wisdom. This raises the question about the relation between science and wisdom. It is clear that no science can teach wisdom. The relation between science and wisdom can only proceed the other way, namely, moral ideals, whether of private virtue or of a cosmopolitan world-best, can be used to frame pragmatic sciences such as anthropology.

We can thus sum up by noting that there are academic sciences that teach us the skills needed to know nature, then there are the worldly sciences that teach us prudence and wisdom in human relations. Pragmatic anthropology arises at this second level, but insofar as it begins to broach a third kind of moral or properly practical consideration it must be framed by philosophical wisdom. We begin to see this aspect of anthropology develop beginning with the Pillau lectures (1777–78). Already there Kant formulates some of the theses of his "Idea for a Universal History from a Cosmopolitan Point of View" of 1784, namely, that only in the species as a whole can humans reach their destination, that the proper civil constitution which can make this realization possible must exhibit freedom, lawfulness, and power. When freedom is lacking we have despotic government, when lawfulness is lacking we have anarchy, and when power is deemed unnecessary we have wishful thinking that will never get us anywhere (see 25:847). In the last session of the *Menschenkunde*, given in 1782, Kant says: "Freedom under law and connected with power allows laws to be given as if they had arisen through the general voice of the people. These laws must apply to all, be valid for all, and be such that they could have been legislated by all; only then do they earn the title of just laws" (25:1201).

Kant considers it important that his anthropology be framed by the cosmopolitan moral ideal of the world-best. It is the task of reason to project such an overall framework, for without it our reason threatens to degrade into sophistical reasoning (*vernünfteln*). Accordingly, Kant warns in the *Menschenkunde* that "a judgment of reason is sophistical when we humans are not able to make a judgment about the whole" (25:1041).

Kant continues to distinguish three kinds of learning in later lectures. Thus in the 1788–89 Busolt lectures we read that academic theory is necessary to *cultivate* us, prudence to *civilize* us or make us social, and finally wisdom to *moralize* us or to enable us to value ourselves (see 25:1436). When it comes to cultivation we have made good progress according to Kant, in civilizing ourselves we have only achieved little, and in moralizing ourselves almost nothing (see 25:1198). Each of the kinds of learning seems to correspond to a phase of human development.

2. The Role of Description, Reflection, and Interpretation in Anthropology

We are now ready to begin our consideration of the final versions of the anthropology lectures based on Kant's own manuscripts and published in 1798 and 1800. Here again Kant classifies anthropology as a mode of world knowledge, but the three kinds of learning or phases of human development are reinterpreted. The cultivation of human skills is no longer dismissed as academic learning, but is redefined as a "technical disposition."[5] The pragmatic phase of civilizing ourselves is no longer defined in terms of practical prudence, but in terms of "culture" (see AP, 185). The last phase of moralization is now the only truly practical phase. The new terms "technical" and "culture" reflect the influence of the *Critique of Judgment*. There Kant came to realize that although technique and culture have practical consequences, they are still part of theoretical philosophy. Whereas in the *Menschenkunde* of 1781–82 Kant distinguished between skill as theoretical and prudence as practical, in the *Critique of Judgment* of 1790 prudence is mentioned as just another kind of theoretical skill. Technical skill is aimed at using things, whereas prudence is "skill in influencing people's volitions."[6] In the final *Anthropology* our pragmatic disposition is defined without reference to prudence as "using other men skillfully for one's purposes" (AP, 183; 7:322). Reconceived as a skill, our pragmatic disposition belongs to culture, and anthropology can be reconceived as theoretical without being academic.

In the *Critique of Judgment* Kant defined culture as the ultimate natural purpose of man (*letzter Zweck*) whereby he becomes prepared to freely assert his own final or moral purpose (*Endzweck*). It provides Kant with a theoretical language for reflecting on human beings as having a telos that is both natural and free. With this reflective turn in Kant's thinking, pragmatic anthropology must take theory more seriously than before. For this reason, Kant distinguishes in the preface to the *Anthropology* between "knowing (*kennen*) the world and having (*haben*) the world": "the former only understands (*versteht*)" (AP, 4; 7:120) the play of human forces, the latter participates in it. Kant has come to realize that unfortunately the real players in the world are defined by social status and form an inner circle that cannot always be fully known. Anthropology will have to content itself with general world-knowledge and must be oriented and guided by philosophy both theoretically and practically. Without the general ideas of philosophy anthropology would merely be a "fumbling about with fragments" (AP, 4) and could not become a science.

Kant is now more interested in the scientific status of anthropology again. Before determining what this is, we must consider certain developments in Kant's views about psychology beyond his already discussed position in the *Critique of Pure Reason*. In the *Metaphysical Foundations of Natural Science* (1786) Kant expressed doubts about psychology's ability to provide more than a "natural description (*Naturbeschreibung*) of the soul" (4:471). This is because mathematics is not applicable to the one-dimensional phenomena of the life of the soul. These temporal phenomena of inner sense have no spatial reference to make them determinate. They flow into each other and cannot be kept distinct. The inapplicability of mathematics is unfortunate, according to Kant, not only because it makes the analysis of psychic phenomena difficult, but also because it makes their a priori synthesis impossible. The assumption here is that any theory about phenomena can only be scientific insofar as it contains a priori knowledge and that the only a priori knowledge we can have about them is mathematical (4:470).

In the *First Introduction to the Critique of Judgment* of the late 1780s we read that "psychological explanations are in a wretched state compared with physical ones."[7] This is because psychological explanations are

> endlessly hypothetical [*hypothetisch*] so that given three different explanations a fourth, equally persuasive one can easily be conceived. . . . To make psychological observations, as Burke did in his treatise on the beautiful and the sublime, thus to collect material for a future systematic connection of empirical rules without striving for their comprehension [*begreifen*], is probably the sole true duty of empirical psychology, which can hardly even aspire to rank as a philosophical science.[8]

Psychology should dispense with hypothetical explanations, not because they are difficult to construct, or because they lack persuasive power, but rather because there is no way of testing the many alternate persuasive accounts that they produce. From the fact that no valid explanation of psychological processes is possible, Kant concludes that no definitive scientific comprehension of them is possible. All we can have are preliminary psychological descriptions.

However, when we move from the *First Introduction to the Critique of Judgment* to §78 of the *Critique of Judgment* itself, we find some grounds to take descriptive knowledge more seriously. This is where Kant explores the ideas of descriptive discussion (*Erörterung*) and exposition (*Exposition*) in relation to reflective judgment as a way of reconciling mechanism and teleology. Kant points out that mechanism and teleology each provides a mode of explanation of organic life. Although mechanistic explanations can be applied indefinitely—even to the movements of organisms—they will, given the limits of the human understanding, always leave something unaccounted for. We must, therefore, appeal to a principle of final causality as well. The relation of the principle of mechanical determinism and that of purposive activity cannot, however, itself be explained determinately, for the two principles mark out irreconcilable approaches to reality. Since "the two kinds of explanation exclude one another" (CJ, §78, 297), their interrelation is only understandable (*verständlich*) descriptively for reflective judgment (see 5:413).

Although reflective descriptions cannot rival the *Begreiflichkeit* (conceptual comprehensibility) of determinate explanations, they can nevertheless provide a kind of theoretical *Verständlichkeit* (understandability). Full conceptual comprehensibility gives way to a more limited understandability or intelligibility. This reflective reconciliation of mechanism and teleology works out what Kant proposed as his opening strategy in the *Critique of Judgment*, namely, to harmonize nature and freedom, not metaphysically, but for our mode of thinking (*Denkungsart*) (see 5:176). No matter how much human behavior can be explained physiologically, it will always be necessary for us humans to also reflect on and think about this behavior as free action. Kant provides no determinate metaphysical explanation reconciling natural causation and human freedom, yet he suggests that it is possible to think reflectively about the two so that we can interpret them as in principle reconcilable.[9]

Kant's position in the *Critique of Judgment* is that there are propositions, for example, about God, that cannot be known objectively, but which can nonetheless be cognized reflectively as subjectively valid "for us (humans in general) (*Menschen überhaupt*)" (CJ, §90, 354; 5:462). Such reflective cognition would seem to have its counterpart in what Kant calls a pragmatic science. As his anthropology becomes increasingly pragmatic it also is geared to us humans as "citizens of the world" (AP, 3). Before seeing how the themes of descriptive intelligibility, reflective judgment, and interpretive thought are applied pragmatically, it should be noted how they are theoretically relevant to the human sciences in general. They affect not only the empirical theorizing of psychologists, but also any human science insofar as it has historical content. It was pointed out earlier that historical cognition involves the coordination rather than subordination of data. As long as there is no general law to which historical data can be subordinated, we can only be descriptive. Reflective judgment can then attempt to generate something more general from particular descriptions either inductively or analogically (see LL, 626). That is, reflection can either generalize or define a generic framework. In the former case, it seeks a universal on the basis of partial descriptions (this is what Kant calls "synthesis of coordination," see LL, 236). In the latter case, it finds analogies aimed at an interpretive context or whole to which the data belong (this is what Kant calls "analysis of coordination," see LL, 236). We can now see that it is in order to generate a sense of an appropriate context for understanding human events that Kant places geography ahead of history. Geography and history can thus be added to psychology as theoretical or academic human sciences that provide the general empirical content of our world.

Although Kant wants to replace psychology as an academic natural science with anthropology as a pragmatic cultural science, he does so gradually. The Friedländer anthropology of 1775 for instance still contains many psychological discussions and goes into a fineness of detail concerning how to discriminate that in the soul which is called "mind [*Gemüth*]" from that which is called "spirit [*Geist*]." Mind is defined as "the mode in which the soul is affected by things," whereas spirit "is the subject that thinks, and is active" (25:474). Such speculative distinctions become less prominent in the later versions of the anthropology. But even in the Friedländer anthropology the contrast between a passive state of mind and an active spirit is complicated by some of Kant's examples. For instance, Kant points out that a physical pain can be located in the soul, but that sadness (*Betrübnis*) about it belongs to the mind (see 25:474). Mind as the capacity to feel what is felt is defined by Kant as "the capacity to reflect about one's state and to relate one's state to oneself and one's personality" (25:474). Here mind is no longer the passive aspect of the soul. The introspective reflection that characterizes mind seems to raise itself above the level of soul and is claimed in a manner reminiscent of Stoicism to distinguish us from animals who also have souls but no personality. Kant observes that we do not find it a weakness to feel pain in the soul about a setback, but that we take offense at people who allow themselves to be placed in a sad state of mind by it.

It is at this second psychological level of mind and introspective reflection that we speak of having it within our power to be happy or unhappy (see 25:474). However, a proper moral response to suffering is possible according to Kant only at the third level of spirit, which is truly active and free. This is the level of moral judgment and rationality. What Kant emphasizes about spirit is its capacity to make comparative anthropological judgments and relate to others. He defines moral judgment as "the capacity to transpose oneself into the standpoint and the place of other, so that one thinks with him and feels oneself in him" (25:475). Feeling oneself in the other might sound like a prefiguration of later conceptions of empathy or *Einfühlung*. But Kant makes it clear elsewhere that transposition also involves the inverse comparison that proceeds from the other to the self. On the basis of finding the other's character traits and actions objectionable I should examine whether I too may harbor such objectionable traits. Transposition as Kant applies it is meant to foster self-criticism.

We can see this contrast between reflection on the level of mind and comparative judgment on the level of spirit as part of the process of distinguishing psychology and anthropology. Fifteen years later in the *Critique of Judgment*, Kant renders reflection about our own state of mind inseparable from comparison with the states of mind of others through the idea of a *sensus communis* or *Gemeinsinn* that allows us to "a priori . . . compare our own judgment with human reason in general" (CJ, §40, 160, 5:293). Within the framework provided by the *Critique of Judgment*, reflection is itself judgmental and no longer simply psychologically introspective, as it was in the 1775 lectures on anthropology, but communal, cultural, and subject to confirmation by anthropological comparison. What aesthetic reflective judgment freely projects as a social and cultural ideal, anthropology must fill in empirically. This is a clear indication that pragmatic anthropology does not just stand outside the critical system, as is suggested in the editorial introduction to volume 25 (25:xlvii).

Kant's Stoical conception of the mind possessing reflective control over what we suffer continues to manifest itself in his final anthropology, but instead of being interwoven with academic psychological discussions about the soul and spirit, it is framed simply by a pragmatic comparison between people who do good to others on the basis of affects such as sympathy and those who have learned to do so on the basis of reason and the principle of apathy.[10]

3. Pragmatic Anthropology and the Characterization of What Humans Have in Common

In the published lectures of 1798 Kant states definitively that anthropology as a mode of knowledge of the human world should not be physiological and merely investigate "what nature makes of man" (AP, 3; 7:119), but should be pragmatic and investigate "what *man* as a free agent makes, or can and should make, of himself" (AP, 3). To show why anthropology should be pragmatic rather than physiological, Kant begins with an example. He points out that he is in no position to explain how he remembers things from the past. It may be that traces remain in the brain which are then revived, as some have speculated. But this is an untested hypothesis. Two centuries later, we might think that we are in a better position to make physiological observations about what parts of the brain are used when we remember. But even we are far from explaining why some people have better memories than others. Is it just a matter of reviving traces or are there repressive forces to be overcome as well? According to Kant, pragmatic anthropology must stay away from such explanatory speculation and focus on what our observations of human practices can teach us about the nature of memory and about ways to improve it.

Memory is located by Kant among our sensuous faculties. It is characterized as a form of reproductive imagination that is *voluntary*, as distinct from fantasy, which is not. Attempts to use our freedom to improve memory can be classified into three methodical kinds of memorizing: (1) through mechanical repetition, (2) through ingenious imaginative associations, and (3) through the judicious use of divisions. The only method that Kant fully approves of is the last and it is worth quoting him in some detail because it discloses much about Kant's general approach to anthropology:

> Memorizing *judiciously* is simply memorizing, in thought, the *outline* of the divisions of a system (Linné's, for example)—should we forget anything,

we can find it again by enumerating the members we have retained; or memorizing the *divisions* of a whole made visible (for example, the provinces of a country, as shown on a map, which lie north, west, etc.). . . . Most of all, the use of *topics*—that is, of a framework for general concepts, called *commonplaces* [*Gemeinplätze*] (*loci topici*)—makes remembering easier, by dividing the material into classes, as when we arrange the books in a library on shelves with different labels" (AP, 58; 7:184, translation amended).

Kant's appeal to a judicious use of memory and to a topics of commonplaces (*Gemeinplätze*) indicates that his pragmatic anthropology operates at the general theoretical level of common sense (*Gemeinsinn*) and of reflective judgment rather than that of determinant explanations. A pragmatic science serves to orient us in the world of fellow citizens by providing a kind of topological outline of it. The parallel with judicious memorization is that both build on our general feeling of orientation to the world and articulate it into a more specific mapping of this world where divisions can be made to systematically order things.

While admitting that there are many obstacles to pragmatic anthropology attaining "the rank of a formal science" (AP, 5; 7:121), it can be made systematic enough to become what Kant calls a "generally useful (*gemeinnützige*) science" (AP, 5; 7:122). Whereas the theoretical sciences in the academic sense are *allgemeingültig* (universally valid), pragmatic theoretical sciences have to content themselves with *Gemeingültigkeit* (common validity). Pragmatic anthropology should not merely observe and describe like a spectator, for it is also meant to be useful for us either as direct or indirect participants in the world (see AP, 4).[11] Description is not an end in itself because it must at the same time allow us to differentiate normal states from abnormal ones. Kant spends considerable time and skill differentiating healthy from unhealthy uses of our faculties. Mental difficulties can range from obtuseness and distraction to derangement. One can be deranged on the level of sense (*Wahnsinn*: deluded sense) where one's imagination is overactive and misinterprets things, or on the intermediate level of judgment (*Wahnwitz*: deluded wit) where one takes analogies literally, or finally on the level of reason (*Aberwitz*: excessive wit) where one snatches at principles that could never be tested by experience and claims to "comprehend the incomprehensible" (7:215). All these forms of derangement involve exceeding the limits of human finitude.

Because there is a normative aspect to Kant's descriptions of the mental faculties and their functioning we can see description and reflective judgment merging into evaluation. The task of a pragmatic anthropology is to help people restore a proper balance or equilibrium in the operation of their faculties: They must be neither under- nor overstimulated. But the proper coordination of the mental faculties is not a purely internal affair. As finite human beings we must also learn to coordinate our own private judgments with those of others. In the *Critique of Judgment* Kant appealed to common sense to compare our private aesthetic judgment with "the possible judgments of others" (CJ, §40, 180). Not making such comparative or reflective judgment makes our taste narrow or provincial. We may then fall prey to the illusion that the private conditions of our consciousness are objective and universal. Now in the *Anthropology* Kant goes on to suggest that the inability to orient oneself by common sense is the most general sign of insanity, as when one insists one hears a voice that no one else can hear. In the case of a provincial aesthetic judgment one can speak of an illusion, because here we merely generalize our own felt response to an object and naively attribute it to other subjects as well. The fact that we may be wrong about the taste of others does not mean that we are wrong to expect agreement, it just may not be on our own terms. In the case of insanity, however, we claim to experience objective properties in the world that no one else's experience can confirm. Here an innocuous aesthetic illusion becomes a dangerous logical delusion. Thus Kant speaks of the "loss of common sense" as producing a "logical private sense (*Eigensinn*)" that projects its own idiosyncrasies onto the world at large.

As useful as common sense is in broadening our own horizon, its contributions are only provisional. It is important to recognize that in the *Critique of Judgment* Kant defined the *Gemeinsinn* or *sensus communis* as an a priori sense that allows us to make formal reflective discriminations. It is not to be confused with the common understanding or vulgar common sense whose empirical content often conflicts with the scientific understanding of the world.[12] In light of Kant's position on common sense in the *Critique of Judgment*, we can say that anthropology's reliance on it does not detract from its scientific status. Kant's topological discriminations have a systematic import that can guide human life if only in outline.

Already in the preface of the *Anthropology* Kant points out that exact descriptions of human action are difficult to arrive at. For "if a man notices that we are observing him trying to study him, he will either be self-conscious (embarrassed), and *cannot* show himself as he really is, or he will *dissemble*, and not *want* to be known as he is" (AP, 4). Even if we are content to examine ourselves rather than others, it must be admitted that we are often too agitated to do so: "when our incentives are active, we are not observing ourselves; and when we are observing ourselves, our incentives are at rest" (AP, 4). That is, while we are doing things we attend to our object or goal, not to ourselves. And when we attend to ourselves we interrupt our normal engagement with life. While these problems stand in the way of a full descriptive account of anthropological behavior, they can of course be compensated for. One can try to observe other people without them becoming aware of it—whatever ethical problems that may eventually produce. And when introspecting one may have to wait for an activity or engagement with the world to subside before one can observe its main features. It is interesting to note that Kant turns to literature and history for portrayals of human nature that can help us to indirectly recognize things about our own mental life.

Kant seems to think that a complete description of our mental processes and our external behavior is not necessary. The observation that humans do not want to be observed is itself a significant descriptive fact that will be exploited in the conclusion of Kant's anthropology. What he promises at the beginning of this work is not an exhaustive description of human action and interaction but "an exhaustive account of the headings under which we can bring the practical human qualities we observe" (AP, 5). His anthropology will be complete in considering human practices in a systematic fashion and locating the appropriate typological divisions.

What Kant expects from a pragmatic anthropology in the final analysis is not pure description but characterization. To characterize is to go beyond description by pointing to more than what is directly given. In the context of Kant's theory of signs, a "character" is a letter that signals something other than itself. In the context of his theory of life, "the character of a living being is what enables us to know its destiny (*Bestimmung*) in advance" (AP, 189; 7:329). Characterization allows us to be prepared for the future and is thus more pragmatic than mere description.

The most important kind of knowledge that we demand about our life in this world concerns the future. Thus Kant writes: "Men are more interested in having foresight than any other power, because it is the necessary condition of all practical activity. . . . Any desire includes a (doubtful or certain) foresight of what we can do by our powers" (AP, 59). We already saw Kant discuss the imagination as a way of recalling the past, but he devotes much more space to the ways in which the imagination attempts to anticipate the future. There are two natural forms of such anticipation: (1) simple *praevisio*, which on the basis of simply remembering past sequences of events extrapolates similar sequences, and (2) *praesagitio*, which can predict (*hervorsagen*) the future events on the basis of knowledge of the laws of nature. Divination (*wahrsagen*) and prophecy (*weissagen*) are nonnatural and supernatural modes of imaginary anticipation respectively. They involve the interpretation of signs, which is the topic of the last two sections on the imagination.

Kant begins §38 of the *Anthropology* by declaring that "the ability to recognize the present as the means for connecting representations of what is foreseen with what is past is the *power of using signs*" (AP, 64). Thus on the basis of past experience we can make sense of a symptom like a skin rash and use it to diagnose a potential upcoming illness. Astronomical constellations can also be used to attempt to divine the future.

Prophecies tend to focus on extraordinary happenings like eclipses and pestilences to proclaim imminent doom. They constitute for Kant a separate class of "prodigious signs" in addition to the usual classification of "artificial" and "natural" signs" (AP, 65). There is clearly much room for misinterpreting such signs. The worst mistake here is to allow our imagination to confuse signs with things, or to attach a mystical significance to signs. Certain numbers like 7, 12, and 100 have received a special status so that unwarranted expectations about chronological sequences are aroused. Kant speaks here of a "would-be a priori" whereby history is made to "conform to chronology" (AP, 67; 7:195 translation amended). That is, we often arbitrarily impose a numerical order on historical data. There is no intrinsic reason why we should divide our historical narratives into periods of one hundred years. Certainly we cannot properly understand nineteenth-century political history without going back to the French Revolution of 1789.

Kant returns to the theory of signs again when introducing the final part of the *Anthropology* called "Anthropological Characterization." He writes: "From a pragmatic point of view, the universal, natural . . . theory of signs (*semiotica universalis*) uses the word *character* in two senses," to refer to "physical" and "moral" characters (AP, 151; 7:285). The first refers to character as man's way of sensing (*Sinnesart*), or to the temperament that nature has given him, the second to his mode of thinking (*Denkungsart*) (see AP, 151), or what he has made of himself morally. Whereas there are four physical ways of characterizing people by means of temperament, their moral character or mode of thinking according to Kant is "singular [*einziger*], a man either has it or has no character at all" (AP, 151; 7:285). Individuals have acquired character in the morally relevant sense if their mode of thinking is derived not from without, but from their own reason. Their actions will be principled and their speech honest. Since they will not dissemble (see AP, 151), their character will be like an open book.

The paradox about moral character is that it is open to scrutiny, and yet inscrutable. This is because character is "originality in one's mode of thinking" (AP, 158). It can no more be determined or imitated than can the greatness of a work of art. It manifests the incomparability of sublimity, which stands as a limit that challenges reflection or comparative judgment. To characterize someone's moral character is thus to project an interpretive idea through reflective judgment. Accordingly, the task of characterization, which is "to discern man's inner self from his exterior" (AP, 149) can only be approximated. There is no direct psychological introspective path to human understanding. We must understand ourselves indirectly by interpreting our expressions.

Kant is realistic enough to recognize that few if any individuals have attained his moral ideal of character.[13] He thus goes on to deal with the physiological counterpart of characterization, namely, physiognomy: "the art of detecting someone's inner life by means of certain external signs involuntarily given" (AP, 161). Whereas the moral ideal of the *ars characteristica* is to interpret people by their voluntary expressions, the physiological equivalent involves interpreting them by their involuntary expressions. Kant gets close to the heart of pragmatic interpretation when he speaks of "interpreting expressions that unintentionally betray one's inner life while intentionally lying about it" (AP, 165). What cannot be directly described about others because of their need for privacy, or directly communicated because of their urge to dissemble, may still be indirectly discerned because there is a limit to the ways in which they can be untrue to themselves.

Because we are imperfect as individuals we find it pragmatic to attempt to conceal at least some of our thoughts. Kant himself admits that men whose every thought were public would not get along peacefully unless they were "all as *pure as angels*" (AP, 192). Here again, however, we find Kant moving from the pragmatic to the moral. Sometimes it is not merely a question of self-interest that makes us want to dissemble, but rather moral shame. Then we find ourselves tempted to dissemble precisely because we see ourselves as falling short of what we should be. Kant is hopeful that this recognition of our imperfections ultimately "reveals a moral predisposition in us, an innate demand of reason to counteract this tendency" (AP, 192–93). On this basis, Kant characterizes the human species as striving "in the face of obstacles, to rise out of evil in constant progress toward the good" (AP, 193).

Moving from the level of the individual, where characterization still looks for something distinctive, to the level of the human species, characterization ends up becoming even more general. Kant ends with what he calls a "Delineation [*Schilderung*] of the Character of the Human Species" (AP, 190; 7:330). According to this delineation or sketch "we feel destined by nature" to associate with others in terms of national states governed by laws. These states in turn should form "a coalition in a cosmopolitan society . . . which though constantly threatened by dissension, makes progress on the whole" (AP, 191). This cosmopolitan ideal is acknowledged to be only a regulative principle (see AP, 191). Here we reach the level of moral reason or wisdom that provides a final practical systematic framework for anthropology.

4. CONCLUSIONS

I have analyzed the human sciences as Kant conceives them as nonexplanatory. To the extent that they are theoretical like psychology they should avoid speculative hypotheses that cannot be tested. Instead, they should settle for description. But even direct description is not always possible. Kant's approach to anthropology is often more indirect and involves normative evaluations and comparisons. This is why I have called it an approach that links description with reflective judgment. Pragmatically, description turns into characterization, through which reflective judgment becomes interpretive in a projective sense. Characterization constitutes an interpretive skill that allows us to reflectively bridge the theory-practice divide. Kant's response to the physiognomists of his age is to cast doubt on their promise to scientifically explain psychic states somatically. Physiognomy "can never become a science," according to Kant, "because the distinctiveness of a human form . . . cannot be understood [*verstanden*] through conceptual description [*Beschreibung*

nach Begriffen], but only by intuitive illustration and presentation [*Darstellung*]"
(AP, 161; 7:296). With this Kant is not denying the usefulness of conceptual description for human understanding, merely its ultimacy in exhausting our understanding of individuality. If physiognomy gives up its claim to be a determinant
or explanatory science, it can be reincorporated into the more generally reflective
science of anthropology as the art of interpreting or "judging what lies within a
man ... from his visible form" (AP, 160). This art of judging what is distinctive
about an individual brings out the aesthetic aspects of reflective judgment again.
Although reflective judgment is comparative and expansive in that it allows us to
transpose ourselves into the place of others, ultimately it is individuating in that
it aims to bring out what is distinctive or characteristic about human beings. The
search for the originality of moral character is analogous to the aesthetic search
for genius.

We have seen that ultimately Kant places pragmatic anthropology in a reflective
cultural context and delineates the character of the human species by means of
regulative cosmopolitan ideals. Just as teleological judgment pushes reflective judgment beyond its constitutive aesthetic employment for the human community
toward a regulative use of rational principles, so Kant ends his pragmatic *Anthropology* with a sketch of a practical ideal of wisdom. It is this delineation of a
cosmopolitan world-best that must orient or guide the more specific characterizations necessary for pragmatic cultural understanding. Whereas the regulative use
of reason stretches our available concepts beyond their theoretical limits to provide
an a priori practical orientation for pragmatic anthropology, reflective judgment
specifies our concepts to adapt them to new, more limited cultural contexts, as
when we differentiate character types.

NOTES

1. Immanuel Kant, *Observations on the Feeling of the Beautiful and the Sublime*, trans. John
T. Goldthwait (Berkeley: University of California Press, 1960), 79; 2:230.

2. Kant, *Vorlesungen über Anthropologie*, 25:252.

3. Kant, *Lectures on Logic* (hereafter LL), trans. and ed. J. Michael Young (Cambridge:
Cambridge University Press, 1992), 236, 24:291.

4. Kant, *Physische Geographie*, 9:244.

5. Kant, *Anthropology from a Pragmatic Point of View* (hereafter AP), trans. Mary J. Gregor
(The Hague: Martinus Nijhoff, 1974), 183.

6. Kant, *Critique of Judgment* (hereafter CJ), trans. Werner S. Pluhar (Indianapolis: Hackett
Publishing, 1987), 11.

7. Kant, *First Introduction to the Critique of Judgment*, trans. James Haden (Indianapolis:
Bobbs-Merrill, 1965), 42.

8. Kant, *First Introduction to the Critique of Judgment*, 42, translation amended.

9. For my thesis that reflective judgment involves a mode of thinking that is interpretive,
see Rudolf A. Makkreel, *Imagination and Interpretation in Kant: The Hermeneutical Import
of the 'Critique of Judgment'* (Chicago: University of Chicago Press, 1990), chap. 6.

10. See AP, §7, 121: "On the Government of the Mind [*Gemüth*] with Regard to Affects."
11. For a discussion of indirect participation, see Makkreel, *Imagination and Interpretation in Kant*, 149–51.
12. See Makkreel, *Imagination and Interpretation in Kant*, 163–66.
13. For an insightful treatment of the importance of character formation in Kant's moral thought, see Felicitas Munzel, *Kant's Conception of Moral Character: The 'Critical' Link of Morality, Anthropology, and Reflective Judgment* (Chicago: University of Chicago Press, 1999)

PART IV

Chemistry and Biology

10

Kant's Theory of Matter and His Views on Chemistry

Martin Carrier

KANT did not restrict his focus in the philosophy of science to physics and biology but also attended to matter theory in general and to chemistry in particular. The Dynamics chapter of the *Metaphysical Foundations of Natural Science* is devoted to an elaboration of his views on the structure of matter,[1] and on a number of occasions Kant reflected on chemical subjects or used examples from chemistry to clarify philosophical issues. I aim to show, perhaps contrary to what many working on Kant's philosophy of science implicitly presuppose, that Kant's thoughts on matter and chemistry constitute an important thread in his work.

The argument in this essay proceeds from the more general to the more specific. I begin by sketching in outline what I take to be the structure and objective of Kant's matter theory and I place this theory in the context of the period. Although Kant takes up Newtonian and Leibnizian motifs, he unites them in an original way. Section 2 is intended to clarify what Kant's account of the structure of matter precisely amounts to. My claim is that it involves a multiple overlap of material shells of different density. The relevant density differences can be explained by distinct intensity ratios of the fundamental forces, and their intensity is determined by universal, albeit variable, features, namely, mass and surface area. By taking recourse to features that are characteristic of matter in general yet differ in strength among different parts of matter, density can be accounted for in terms of forces that lie squarely within the context of Kant's transcendental analysis. In section 3, I go on to explain Kant's theory of the states of aggregation. This theory links Kant's transcendental account to more specific claims about empirical issues. The former entails the primacy of fluidity over rigidity, whereas traditional corpuscularianism advocated quite the reverse. As a result, Kant is faced with the challenge of deriving rigidity from fluidity. The account he develops for this purpose in the *Opus postumum* operates using heterogeneous substances and the matter of heat, and it bears all the marks of an ordinary theory in physical chemistry. In sections 4 and 5, I describe the essentials of Stahlian chemistry, which forms the background to Kant's views, and I sketch Kant's particular version of this theory. Kant adopts the chemistry of principles, which introduces abstract property-bearing elements for explaining the properties and reactions of chemical substances. In section 6, I present Kant's noncorpuscularian account of chemical combination, which fits with his basic approach to matter theory as explained in section 1. The final section, 7, is intended to clarify the connection Kant establishes between chemical elements and regulative ideas of reason. Elements in the principles tradition are nonoperationally conceived, and Kant's analysis rightly highlights this important feature.

1. FUNDAMENTALS OF KANT'S THEORY OF MATTER

Kant's theory of matter comprises a threefold commitment to a *dynamist*, a *plenist*, and a *continualist* thesis. The dynamist thesis says that extension and impenetrability are not primary properties of matter but derive from more fundamental forces. According to the plenist view, matter fills its space completely and without empty interstices. Finally, on the continualist position matter is infinitely divisible; there are no atoms.

To begin with the final thesis, one of the outstanding changes in Kant's views on matter was his rejection of the atomist position he had held in the *Physical Monadology* of 1756 and the corresponding adoption of the view that matter can be divided continually without ever reaching ultimate particles. This continualist position is rendered in proposition 4 of the Dynamics chapter (4:503); it is buttressed by a proof which starts from the infinite divisibility of space and draws on the plenist principle that matter fills each part of its space (4:503–504, 4:505–506). Kant is clearly aware of his invocation of the plenist premise in his argument for continualism (4:504) and aims to ground the former on a consideration of the relevant forces. "Monads" or centers of repulsive forces cannot be assumed, he argues, because each point between two such monads has to be taken as an origin of repulsive forces; otherwise the two monads would approach one another unhindered and finally converge. But only matter, not space, is the source of repulsive forces so that the space between the monads has to be filled with matter. This is the plenist conclusion of the argument (4:504–505). But the argument draws on the additional premise that repulsive forces cannot act at a distance. If forces of the latter kind were admitted, it would no longer be imperative that each point between the monads exert a force; rather, they could keep one another at a distance by virtue of their reciprocal repulsion and could thus be separated by empty space.[2] In fact, Kant stipulates that repulsion is a contact force, which only extends to the immediate vicinity of the corresponding material part (4:516). In sum, Kant's argument proceeds from dynamical principles and, in particular, from the premise that extension and impenetrability are grounded on repulsive contact forces originating from each part of matter. This dynamism constitutes the basis of Kant's plenist principle, which is in turn used as a foundation for his continualism.

This threefold conjunction of tenets uniquely characterizes Kant's matter theory—although each claim separately figures in the natural philosophy of the period. As to dynamism, it was Isaac Newton himself who had introduced forces into the theory of matter. Cohesion, chemical reactions, and the elastic properties of gases were supposed to arise from attractive and repulsive forces, conceived on analogy with gravitation and as acting between the particles of bodies. If a particle is attracted by particles of a different kind more strongly than by those that are similar chemically, a chemical compound is formed. That is, a chemical reaction takes place if the attractive forces of chemical affinity outweigh cohesive attraction. The expansion of gases or "airs" was supposed to arise from repulsive forces that become efficacious beyond the range of attractive powers. That is, Newton assumed that each chemically active particle of matter was surrounded by a force-filled sphere that comprised forces of different intensity and direction. Next to the particle, attractive forces of cohesion and affinity prevail, at larger distances repulsion grows stronger, and even further away universal gravitational attraction becomes the dominant force.[3] Following Newton, the distance dependence of the relevant forces was elaborated by John Keill, one of the leading early Newtonians. The range of a force was supposed to be captured by the corresponding force law. Newtonian force laws had the general structure $1/r^n$, and the larger the n, the shorter the range. Newton's force-based theory of matter grew into one of the leading traditions of eighteenth century chemistry.[4]

Working in the Newtonian tradition, in 1748 Gowin Knight had placed increased emphasis on forces. Knight regarded forces as the cause of impenetrability and thus considered them influential in bringing about matter.[5] Forces were held to be constitutive of matter. In the same vein, in 1758 Rudjer Boscovich argued that Newtonian forces between pointlike particles are responsible for the impenetrability of matter. Solidity is not a primitive property of matter but derives from the action of repulsive forces.[6] Accordingly, dynamical views can also be identified in parts of the Newtonian tradition.

By contrast, Kant's plenist theory stands in marked contrast to Newtonian matter theory. Following Robert Boyle, Newton assumed a complex, hierarchically ordered internal structure of matter. Several fundamental particles form one second-order aggregate, several of which in turn combine into one third-order particle and so forth. Chemical operations only involve a restructuring of higher-order particles and thus leave the more fundamental configurations unaffected. The assumption of a large number of particle levels suggested that gross matter contains only a small fraction of solid particles and consists mostly of empty interstices.[7] In the Newtonian tradition matter was supposed to be mostly void. Arnold Thackray called this tenet the "nutshell view" of matter, according to Joseph Priestley's phrase that "all the solid matter in the solar system might be contained within a nut-shell."[8] Kant was well aware of this received view of Newtonianism. Early in his career he mentioned it in general terms (1:486), and later on he explicitly referred to the idea of the universe in a nutshell (21:338, 21:501). The rejection of the nutshell view is among the invariants of Kant's thought. Over his entire career he attacked the assumption of empty spaces and advocated the view that matter fills space seamlessly.

This plenist position had been defended against Newton by Gottfried W. Leibniz. In the Leibniz-Clarke correspondence Leibniz contrasted the Newtonian nutshell theory with his own view, according to which the pores usually thought to prevail within bodies are actually filled with a weightless fluid. This fluid extends through the allegedly empty interstices with the result that all substances, regardless of possible differences in their specific weights, contain the same quantity of matter.[9] Whereas Leibniz accepts the usual corpuscularian reasoning in terms of particles and pores and merely assumes the latter filled with an all-pervasive, imponderable matter, Kant's position is more consistently plenist. Differences in the density of bodies are traced back to differences in the density of each material part, and the latter differences are thought to be reducible to the ratio of the attractive and repulsive fundamental force (see sec. 2). In contrast to Leibniz, Kant's account is no longer modeled on corpuscularian reasoning (4:521, 4:523–24, 4:533–34).

Third, Kant's continualism again agrees with the creed of a major Newtonian denomination. In spite of his commitment to atomism, Newton for polemical reasons advanced a claim to the infinite divisibility of matter. These reasons had to do with the quarrel between Newton and Leibniz over the invention of the calculus. Infinite divisibility was accepted in many Newtonian quarters, in particular by John Keill and Herman Boerhaave.[10] Kant approvingly refers to Keill's arguments in support of the infinite divisibility of matter (29:115).

The conclusion is that Kant conjoined Newtonian and Leibnizian ideas to form his own matter theory. The resulting amalgamation of tenets is unique and original—although each of its chief ingredients can be attributed to one of the traditions involved.

2. THE NATURE OF THE FUNDAMENTAL FORCES AND THE CAUSES OF DENSITY DIFFERENCES

Kant's dynamism invokes a fundamental repulsive contact force to explain impenetrability or solidity. This force is assumed to exhibit an inverse-cube dependence on distance, which, however, is thought to extend only to the immediate vicinity of the relevant material part. As just indicated, the use of force laws of the form $1/r^n$ was characteristic of the Newtonian tradition in chemistry. Within this framework, the short-range attractive forces of cohesion and affinity were supposed to exhibit an inverse-cube dependence or higher. Consequently, Kant's assumption of an inverse-cube law for his fundamental repulsion is at odds with the contact nature ascribed to it at the same time. Kant attempted to remove this tension by restricting the inverse-cube relation to infinitely small distances (4:520, 4:521–22).

That is, the range of the force is constrained by an independent condition, not by the force law itself. Kant's seemingly cumbersome rescue operation actually mimicked an example of Newton's (see later).

This fundamental repulsion, as the cause of solidity, is counterbalanced by an equally fundamental attraction, and the joint action of both forces generates matter of a "determinate extension" and density. Kant had already advocated the idea of two counteracting forces in his *Physical Monadology*. According to this earlier project, the differences in the distance dependence of the forces allowed for the determination of a unique point of equilibrium. This point was supposed to demarcate the extension of the "dynamic atoms" or spherical monads he had put forward at that time. The repulsive force, due to its inverse-cube relation to distance, increases more rapidly than the inverse-square attraction upon approaching the monad. By the same token, the intensity of repulsion decreases more quickly on receding from the monad. The result is an equilibrium extension where both forces compensate each other (1:483–85). Kant transferred this approach to his later, continualist understanding of matter, and, in particular, maintained his earlier attempt of explaining the density of bodies on the basis of the intensity ratio of both forces (1: 484–87). In spite of dropping the assumption of segregated, identifiable parts of matter, the equilibrium scheme is retained and differences in density are, at least in part, accounted for by different intensity ratios (4:521).

Although the principles of the dynamical approach are rather transparent, its consequences with respect to the internal constitution of matter remain largely opaque. Since Kant retains the dynamical construction from the *Physical Monadology*, the results should agree as well. That is, one should obtain spherical shells of matter that are constituted by the equilibrium of the two forces. However, in contradistinction to the earlier view and as a result of Kant's plenist stance, *each point* is taken as a source of both forces. That is, each point represents the center of a material shell. These shells penetrate one another and form an intricate array of multiple overlapping spheres. I take it that this is the picture Kant's approach is supposed to suggest. But one difficulty with this picture is that the action of the attractive force extends through space, so that the force originating at a particular point not only contributes to building up a material shell around this point; it affects the structure of other spheres as well. As a result, no undistorted superposition of the material shells will occur. It is hard to realize more distinctly what this approach precisely entails as to the internal constitution of matter.

Before I sketch a bit more clearly Kant's project of explaining density dynamically, let me add a few words about an empirical difficulty Kant encountered with his tenet of an inverse-cube repulsive force. One might plausibly expect that the expansion of gases would give empirical credence to Kant's thesis of fundamental repulsion. The relevant behavior of gases is governed by Boyle's law stating an inverse relationship between volume and pressure. Consequently, within Kant's framework, one might anticipate the action of an inverse-cube repulsion underlying this law. However, Newton had derived Boyle's law from the assumption of a repulsive force varying inversely with the distance and being restricted in its action to neighboring particles.[11] Newton's argument, just like Kant's treatment of fundamental repulsion, involved the explicit restriction of the range of a force. Newton introduced a long-range force law but cut off its domain with a separate condition.

In the eighteenth century, Newton's deduction was widely regarded as a mathematical demonstration that a $1/r$-repulsive force prevails between air particles. Obviously, this force law was at variance with Kant's inverse-cube law. In order to reconcile these contrasting tenets, Kant construed the elasticity of gases as resulting from the matter of heat or caloric. According to this expedient, the expansion of air is not a direct effect of fundamental repulsion. Rather, caloric, whose elasticity is "possibly original" and whose vibration drives the parts of air away from one another, plausibly gives rise to the $1/r$-force required by Newton's derivation (4:522, 4:530). Caloric as the material basis of heat was introduced by Boerhaave early in the eighteenth century. Boerhaave assumed repulsive forces between the parts of caloric as well as the existence of internal motions that were supposed to be transferred to the particles of bodies. The Newtonian Stephen Hales advanced a similar conception at the same time. In his *Vegetable Staticks* (1727), which Kant owned, Hales introduced the notion of an ether that was connected to heat phenomena and thus included caloric. Hales's ethereal caloric performed internal oscillations and set the parts of air in motion.[12]

These views comprised elements of the kinetic theory of heat but at the same time marked the beginning of the caloric theory, which was fully articulated by Antoine de Lavoisier at the end of the century. Lavoisier abandoned the vibrations of the matter of heat and consistently considered heat as the accumulation of caloric. The earlier hybrid conception of kinetic and material elements constitutes the basis of Kant's reasoning. Kant characteristically assumes vibrations of the matter of heat that are apt to displace the parts of air. Commitment to this conception was among the lifelong invariants of Kant's thought (2:184–85, 29:118, 29:119, 21:522). In the ultimate stage of his work, as embodied in the *Opus postumum*, caloric and its vibrations grew into one of Kant's favorite devices (see sec. 3).

Kant considers the explanation of density differences as one of the chief virtues of his dynamical conception. The corpuscularian account of such differences featured particles stacked together more or less densely. That is, the particles were supposed to be marshaled at varied distances or separated by diverse amounts of empty space. Kant felt that the explanation of bodily properties by microscopic particle configurations is too arbitrary to be acceptable. The invocation of empty spaces leaves the imagination unrestrained and opens up the floodgates to purely fictitious accounts—to the detriment of science (1:486, 4:523–24, 4:525, 4:532). Such accounts drew their credibility from the argument that the corpuscularian approach provided the only conceivable explanation of density differences. For this reason the assumption of empty spaces within bodies was supposed to be indispensable. Kant counters these allegations by attempting to reconstruct density differences on dynamical principles, without recourse to empty spaces. Thus, dynamism is thought to make the plenist approach coherent, which is in turn considered a chief distinction of the former (4:533).

Kant argues that the degree to which matter fills its space, i.e., its density (4: 525), arises from the intensity ratio of the two fundamental forces. Differences in density consequently result from the fact that this ratio may assume various values (4:523–44). The reason is that the intensity of both forces depends on distinct quantities so that their ratio may vary among different substances. The intensity of the fundamental attractive force is determined by the quantity of matter, that is, the relevant mass value, whereas the degree of repulsion is fixed otherwise. It follows that the resulting force may be different in pieces of matter of equal mass— which in turn allows for density differences (4:533–34).

One salient question in this context concerns which quantity is supposed to determine the intensity of repulsion. Kant's wording sometimes conveys the impression that this intensity is regarded as inherently substance-specific. As he says, repulsion displays an "originally varying degree" (4:523) or its degree "can be different in different matters" (4:533). In the same vein, Kant ascribes a particularly intensive repulsion to the ether—apparently due to its substantial nature (4:534). Likewise, Kant argues in his notes for a letter to Jacob S. Beck of September 9, 1792, that density differences need to be explained on the assumption that the given attraction a piece of matter exerts can "act against an infinitely different repulsion" which "can, however, be originally unequal in a certain volume" (11: 362, 11:365).

At the same time, adopting a substance-specific efficacy of forces would amount to abandoning the project of tracing density back to the action of fundamental forces. A fundamental quantity cannot plausibly be taken as varying with the specifics of the very substance it is thought to make possible in the first place. Regarding fundamental attraction, Kant admits this straightforwardly: "Now, inasmuch as this attractive force belongs to the possibility of matter as matter in general, and consequently precedes all distinctions of matter; so this force must not be attributed merely to a particular species of matter, but to every matter generally and originally" (4:509). Kant says that every part of matter is endowed with the force of attraction and that this force—by virtue of being fundamental and constitutive of matter—should precede any difference of matter. The natural conclusion is that repulsion—being a fundamental force as well—should likewise precede any such difference. This means that the intensity of neither force should depend on the nature of the substance involved. Introducing a dependence on the particulars of the case at hand would be tantamount to relinquishing the transcendental integration of the forces: What is dependent on variable properties of matter can hardly count as a condition of the possibility of gaining scientific knowledge of matter in general.

However, other passages suggest an interpretation that fits more harmoniously with Kant's transcendental approach. If the conditions of the possibility of cognizing matter are at issue, it is necessary to take recourse to only those properties that matter possesses without exception. Consequently, the intensity of the forces should exclusively depend on magnitudes that are characteristic of matter as matter. Mass is one such magnitude; it fixes the intensity of attraction (see above). And geometrical quantities constitute the other relevant set. In particular, it is the size of the relevant surface that determines the intensity of repulsion. Upon elaborating his equilibrium model of density, Kant draws on the contact nature of repulsion and argues that "by expansive force, only the parts [of matter] *in the surface of contact* act, and thereby it is all the same whether behind this surface much or little of this matter is found" (4:524). Consequently, the intensity of repulsion depends on the extension of the relevant area of contact.[13] Since attraction is dependent on mass, and repulsion on the relevant surface area, their ratio can be "thought of as infinitely diverse" (4:523–24).

On the proposed reconstruction, Kant's attempt at a transcendental specification of density differences proceeds by tying the intensity of both fundamental forces to different, albeit universal, properties of matter, namely, mass for one, and surface area for another. Although it is not fully transparent precisely which quantity is supposed to represent the relevant area, the picture emerging from these considerations displays distinct contours. Owing to the variegated intensity ratios between the attractive and repulsive fundamental forces, the overlapping spherical shells that constitute matter exhibit different density values. These density values rely on transcendentally accessible universal features of matter, and they allow for a reconstruction of macroscopic density gradients.[14]

3. The States of Matter and the Causes of Rigidity

Matter as an extended, space-filling entity is generated by the action of the two fundamental forces. However, these two forces do not suffice for holding bodies together. Kant introduces the force of cohesion, which is supposed to supplement the action of the fundamental attraction. Cohesion is not regarded as being constitutive of matter but as a derivative force (4:526). The reasons given are that the intensity of cohesion can be influenced by applying technical procedures, such as melting, and that its intensity bears no consistent relation to density (4:526). Clearly enough, if density or density differences can at least in part be accounted for on the basis of the fundamental forces, all likewise derivative properties of matter should be connected to density. Since no such connection exists, cohesion has to be taken as a force independent from and acting in addition to the fundamental force of attraction. In contradistinction to the latter, cohesion is a contact force like the fundamental force of repulsion (4:526).

Cohesion, along with the two fundamental forces, brings about the fluid state of matter. Kant characterizes fluids by the fact that their parts can be displaced easily. It is possible to exchange parts of the fluid without encountering any resistance due to internal friction. Cohesion is apt to generate a liquid since it is a central force, that is, a force acting along the straight line between the relevant parts and for this reason provides no obstacle to a lateral shift. Moreover, cohesion acts alike from all directions within a fluid so that no net force obtains which could hinder internal dislocation. So, in addition to characterizing fluids phenomenologically by frictionless displacement of the parts, Kant also distinguishes them by the equilibrium of internal forces. Although cohesion offers no resistance to displacement, it does counteract separation. As a result, cohesion is able to form segregated parts of matter, that is, bodies. But the essential property of solid bodies is the rigid connection among their parts, i.e., their resistance to internal displacement. It follows that the distinction between fluid and rigid bodies cannot be explained by recourse to different intensities of cohesion (4:526–29).

Wenceslaus Karsten, whose *Anleitung zur gemeinnützlichen Kenntniß der Natur* Kant used as textbook for his physics lectures in 1785, likewise attributed the cohesion and adhesion of fluid bodies to the action of attractive forces between relevant substances.[15] But Kant places heavy emphasis on the fact that the action of cohesion, along with the fundamental forces, is sufficient to produce fluid bodies, but not rigid ones. Kant's conclusion is that the property of fluidity is original (4:528). Among his contemporaries and early adherents it was widely received as one of Kant's chief tenets in natural philosophy that the fluid state of matter is more fundamental than the solid one. This involved a reversal of the corpuscularian view that hard particles represent the most basic constituents of matter.[16] However, it is at best suggested but in no way implied by Kant's dynamical account of fluidity that hard particles are to be renounced as basic. Boscovich, for instance, had advocated a similar explanation within a corpuscularian framework. According to Boscovich, the particles of fluids exert only central forces on one another and thus can be shifted easily, whereas the particles of rigid bodies are endowed with forces acting laterally and correspondingly resist displacement.[17] One might well stick with hard particles as the source of the relevant forces and thus integrate corpuscularianism into an overall dynamical approach.

By waiving hardness as a primary property of matter, Kant created for himself the challenge of accounting for the rigidity of bodies on dynamical principles. The derivation of density differences is not sufficient for this purpose. Different density values also obtain between fluid bodies such as water and oil. The distinction of solids cannot be grounded on density considerations alone. Kant resorts to internal friction. Friction resists the displacement of a body's parts and brings about solidity (4:527). But this approach brings with it the difficulty that only rigid parts of matter exert frictional forces on each other. That is, friction presupposes rigidity (4:529). In the *Metaphysical Foundations* Kant sees no way out of this circle and acknowledges defeat: "[H]ow rigid bodies are possible, is still an unsolved problem, in spite of the ease with which ordinary natural science believes itself capable of disposing of it" (4:529). "Ordinary natural science" refers to Kant's corpuscularian competitor, and the alleged solution of the latter is to advance rigidity as primary.[18]

Even if the corpuscularian approach is considered less than appealing, Kant's argument suffers from the defect that he first raised a problem and then had to admit that he was unable to solve it. Kant seems to have recognized this defect, since he continued working on the problem of rigid bodies throughout his career. Indeed, he offers a solution in the *Opus postumum*. In this work, he retains the account of the fluid state that he had developed in the *Metaphysical Foundations*. First, cohesion is regarded as an attractive contact force that acts in addition to fundamental attraction; second, fluidity is characterized by an equilibrium of cohesive forces; third, the intensity of cohesion is irrelevant for distinguishing rigid bodies from liquids (21:373–74, 21:385). But this earlier account is now supplemented with an attempt to explain rigidity. In this attempt caloric (or the ether) plays the key role. Caloric is conceived as an expansive substance, endowed with strongly repulsive and penetrating (i.e., long-range) forces. It constitutes a kind of counterpart to the fundamental contact force of repulsion, just as cohesion is introduced as the contact counterpart to the long-range fundamental force of attraction. The internal repulsive forces of caloric induce vibrating or oscillating motions among its parts. When caloric permeates material bodies, its vibrations intermix their parts. Second, fluids are now assumed to be of heterogeneous material; they include ingredients of distinct density. A sufficient amount of vibrating caloric contributes to an intermingling of the heterogeneous components so that a homogeneous mixture is generated. The parts of this uniform substance exert forces of equal intensity with the result of equally strong forces from all directions, a result that was formerly attributed to the action of cohesion alone. Solid bodies are produced when caloric is released from this mixture. The internal vibrations grow weaker, so that the heterogeneous components are intermingled less intensely, which means that they tend to be segregated. The formerly uniform fluid decomposes into its distinct ingredients. The fluid turns into a tissue of strata, plates, laminae, and fibers—separated by the residues of caloric—whose rigid texture resists the displacement of its parts. This segregation and ramification of distinct material parts constitute the basis of rigid bodies. Kant emphasizes, with explicit reference to the *Metaphysical Foundations*, that the mere decrease of caloric and the concomitant net increase of the attractive forces between the parts of matter could never produce rigid bodies. The existence of heterogeneous parts is essential to the formation of distinct aggregates whose concatenation interlocks parts of matter and brings about solidity (21:276–80, 21:374–75, 22:213–14).[19]

It appears, then, that in the *Opus postumum* Kant attributes important functions to ethereal caloric in physics and chemistry. Analogously, caloric is elevated to the ranks of transcendental philosophy. It is no longer considered a hypothetical substance that is introduced for the sake of making certain phenomena explicable; rather, its existence can be proven categorically and a priori. Kant's argument is that empty space is not an object of possible experience since it would involve the perception of the nonexistence of a real entity whereas only the nonperception of its existence would be possible. Caloric is a condition of the possibility of experiencing space, since the perception of space demands that it be continually filled with matter (21:218–24).

Accordingly, in the final period of his thought Kant shifts caloric to center stage. This contrasts markedly with attempts among his early disciples who were not familiar with the as yet unpublished ventures of the master. For instance, Georg Hildebrandt attempts to improve on Kant's system by dropping the matter of heat and by identifying heat with the fundamental force of repulsion. "Heat is nothing other than R [the repulsive force] itself; its only immediate effect is expansion and, doubtlessly, it is highly superfluous within the dynamical system to assume a matter of heat."[20] The idea is that a consistent dynamism should refrain from attributing forces to fundamental substances. Rather, such substances should be traced back to a configuration of forces, that is, to different intensity ratios of fundamental attraction and repulsion.[21] The upshot is that Kant's own project of developing the transition from the *Metaphysical Foundations* to physics proceeds along lines quite distinct from endeavors of his followers to elaborate the Kantian approach.[22]

4. THE CHEMISTRY OF PRINCIPLES AS BACKGROUND TO KANT'S THOUGHT

In Kant's taxonomy of the sciences at the time of the *Metaphysical Foundations*, chemistry is accorded the status of an "improper science" (4:468); its propositions are deductively ordered, to be sure, but its first principles lack necessity. In contrast to the fundamental laws of physics, the laws of chemistry are based on experience and cannot be known a priori (4:468, 29:97–98). The relevant laws are the force laws of chemical interaction as assumed within Newtonian chemistry. In order for chemistry to qualify as science proper (4:468), the dependence of chemical affinities on the relative distances among parts of matter would have to be established a priori.

So long, then, as . . . no law of the approach or withdrawal of the parts of matter can be stated according to which (as, say, in proportion to their densities and suchlike) their motions together with the consequences of these can be intuited and presented a priori in space . . . , chemistry can

become nothing more than a systematic art or experimental doctrine, but
never science proper (4:471).

As gleaned from the qualification "so long as," Kant's appraisal refers to the chemistry of the period, not to the structure of chemical phenomena in general. It is
conceivable, albeit unlikely (4:471), that chemistry will eventually be transformed
into science proper.

The background of Kant's concern is with Newtonian chemistry of short-range
forces (see sec. 1). His misgivings are obviously motivated by the room left for
adapting chemical force laws to the relevant experience. There is no way to recognize the necessity of a particular dependence of some affinity intensity on distance; experiment is the only source of this kind of knowledge (4:534). But tentative
hypotheses, or for that matter, any application of the method of trial and error,
goes against the grain of proper science. Chemical propositions in no way form
conditions of the possibility of experience.

Kant's unwillingness to accept chemistry as a proper science does not mean
that he placed little value on it. On the contrary, a number of remarks scattered
throughout his work show that Kant was familiar with the state of the art in
chemistry and interested in its development. In an obituary for Kant, published in
1804, the editor of *Neues allgemeines Journal der Chemie* underscored Kant's wide
knowledge in chemistry and the attention he devoted to chemical phenomena.[23]
Kant's high opinion of chemistry is revealed by, among other things, the fact that
he places the experiments of Georg E. Stahl, the founder of the phlogiston theory,
on a par with those of Galileo and Torricelli. All these experimenters, Kant argues,
exemplarily realized one salient aspect of scientific method, namely, the requirement to pose questions to nature actively, framed by reason according to the
principles of judgment, rather than passively following nature's lead. The latter
procedure only serves to collect accidental observations and fails to gain necessary
knowledge. What is mandatory, instead, is to design experiments by bringing to
bear the guidelines of reason (Bxii-xiii, B685). Stahl achieved this by transforming
"metals into calx and the latter back into metal by first removing something and
then putting it back again" (Bxii-xiii). Kant praises Stahl for having conceived
experiments such that they were apt to provide answers to theoretically significant
questions and did not merely serve to amass data. The experiment Kant mentions
is Stahl's reduction of metallic calxes to their corresponding metals using nonmetallic substances. The objective of this then famous experiment was the empirical test of a unified account of calcination and combustion.

The phlogiston theory, as formulated by Stahl, belongs to the tradition of the
so-called chemistry of principles, whose inception goes back to late antiquity. The
idea was to explain the properties of substances by assuming a number of abstract
elements or principles. These principles were supposed to bear properties such as
hardness, combustibility, or volatility. Ordinary substances gain their properties

by incorporating the corresponding principles, and it is the presence of these principles in the substances that accounts for the properties of the latter. The theory did not introduce one principle for each property, which would have made the approach somewhat pointless. By contrast, the number of principles was strongly restricted, and the challenge was to explain the multitude of chemical properties by a combination of these few property-bearing elements. Chemical reactions bring about a change in the properties of the substances and were thought to involve a transfer of principles.

Stahl elaborated this approach and introduced the term "phlogiston" for the principle of combustion. The mechanism of combustion accepted before Stahl (and by chemists such as Boerhaave even after Stahl) involved the release of a number of distinct but related elements from the burning body. First, fire and flames make it quite obvious that something is set free in burning; and the residue, that is, the ash, has lost the property of combustibility. These facts were taken to imply that an element of combustibility escaped in the process. Second, the relevant elements, however, were supposed to be distinct among different classes of substances and, in particular, among the various kingdoms of nature. The calcination or roasting of metals was thought to be produced by one such element, and the combustion of plants, for instance, by another. Stahl dropped this multitude of subprinciples and aimed to show that there is only one principle of combustion, namely, phlogiston. All combustion processes and all calcinations are brought about by the same mechanism of phlogiston release. Stahl intended to support this unifying account with his celebrated experiment. On this account, Stahl argued, it should be possible to invert the process of calcination, that is, to produce a metal from its calx, by supplying phlogiston from *nonmetallic* substances. For instance, Stahl managed to prepare metallic lead out of lead calx (PbO) by means of heating it with glowing charcoal (whose phlogiston is set free in burning). Charcoal is of organic origin and yet it is suitable for restoring the phlogiston to the lead calx and for transforming the latter into the metal. The conclusion was that phlogiston is alike in all the kingdoms of nature; there is only one kind of phlogiston.[24]

Stahl's experiment proceeded by first extracting phlogiston from the lead through calcination and by restoring it afterward using a different source. This experiment as well as Stahl's inference to the unity of phlogiston is accurately rendered in Karsten's *Anleitung* which was used by Kant for his physics lectures in 1785 (29:288); and this judgment is reproduced in the student transcripts of the lectures themselves, the so-called *Danziger Physik*. According to these transcripts, Kant taught: "Stahl was the first to bring phlogiston or pure elementary fire into chemistry. He proved it to be an element which is of the same kind in all combustible beings" (29:163). The methodological insight Kant credits Stahl with concerns his recognition that substances need to be subjected to a systematic procedure of analysis and synthesis in order to buttress claims in theoretical chemistry. Stahl was right indeed. Stripped to its essentials, Stahl had shown that a single substance is responsible for the entire realm of what were later called oxidation processes.

In addition to phlogiston or "sulfur," Stahl assumed two more "earthy principles," namely, "salt," chiefly responsible for solidity, density, and weight, and "mercury," the chief cause of metallic properties. Stahl's fourth principle was water. All these principles were taken to be distinct from the substances of the same name. They were conceived as abstract bearers of properties, not as ordinary chemicals. Moreover, Stahl distinguished *chemical elements* from *chemical instruments*. In contrast to the elements, instruments do not enter compounds; they rather contribute to initiating, continuing, stopping, or suppressing reactions. The two instruments Stahl considered are fire and air. Fire is not identical to phlogiston; it is rather constituted by whirling motion produced by the escape of phlogiston (a view strongly resembling Boerhaave's [see sec. 2]). The adoption of fire as an instrument reflects the fact that many chemical reactions occur only in intense heat. The instrumental efficacy of air can be gleaned from the fact that combustion processes in closed vessels come to a halt after a short time. The reason is that the phlogiston released from the burning body has to be carried away. Otherwise, the accumulation of phlogiston near the body would block the further escape of phlogiston so that combustion would stop. The surrounding air performs the task of taking up and carrying away the surplus phlogiston; air thus serves as an instrument for maintaining combustion.[25]

The eighteenth-century reception of Stahl's theory was strongly influenced by Johann Juncker's *Conspectus Chemiae theoretico-practicae* (1730–38). Juncker modified Stahl's approach in two respects. First, he identified phlogiston with the matter of fire—in contrast to Stahl's expressed views. The passage quoted earlier could be taken to suggest that Kant taught Juncker's version rather than Stahl's original position. But there is a contrary passage to the effect that phlogiston needs fire as an instrument, indicating the separation of the two: "combustible beings [i.e. phlogiston] need elementary fire as vehicle for dissolving earths" (29:161; see sec. 5). Second, as a consequence of this identification, phlogiston was construed as being *both* an element *and* an instrument. This theoretical route was pursued by Guillaume F. Rouelle who profoundly shaped French Stahlianism. Rouelle advanced a "dualist conception" according to which *each* element could serve as instrument as well.[26]

Gabriel F. Venel is one of the representatives of mid-century French Stahlianism and the author of the articles on chemical subjects in Denis Diderot's celebrated *Encyclopédie*. These articles constitute a noteworthy source about what was accepted as background knowledge in this tradition; for instance, Venel advocated Rouelle's dualist conception.[27] Further, Venel adopted five principles, namely, water, air, earth, fire (i.e., phlogiston), and acid and alkali (the latter counting as a single principle),[28] and he assumed four species of the earth principle while advancing the conjecture that they could be unified into a single one.[29]

One of the most important sources for Kant's substantive views on chemistry is his *Danziger Physik* lectures of 1785, based on Karsten's *Anleitung zur gemein-nützlichen Kenntniß der Natur* of 1783. Karsten's *Anleitung* indulges in chemical considerations and includes a number of recently made discoveries, in particular relating to different kinds of air and their properties. Karsten advances earth, water, salt, and phlogiston as his elements. Contrary to Stahl's terminology (see earlier), neither salt nor phlogiston count as earthy; in particular, salt is no longer connected to solidity but rather comprises acids and bases (denoted as "simple salts"); sub-stances we now call salts ("compound salts" in Karsten's terminology) are supposed to be composed of the two sorts of simple salts. In the mid-century, this is cus-tomary usage; the first German chemist to separate acids and bases from salts was Johann B. Trommsdorff in 1789.[30] Karsten distinguishes phlogiston from "ele-mentary fire," which he claims is likely identical to the matter of heat or the "fiery basis of heat." Karsten admits doubt as to the status and nature of air. Elementary air might exist, to be sure, but in light of recent discoveries this is uncertain. This latter qualification is due apparently to Karsten's recognition of a large number of airs exhibiting a wide variety of properties. Consequently, if there is elementary air, its characteristics are largely unknown (29:275–79, 29:316, 29:350–52).[31]

5. ELEMENTS AND INSTRUMENTS: KANT'S CONCEPTION OF CHEMISTRY

Kant accepts the chemistry of principles. As he argues, this approach grows out of an attempt to unify the multitude of chemical observations by integrating them into the scheme of a few property-bearing elements.

> [T]hus one reduces all materials to earths (mere weight, as it were), to salts and combustibles (as force), and finally to water and air as vehicles (ma-chines, as it were, by means of which the aforementioned operate), in order to explain the chemical effects of materials in accordance with the idea of a mechanism (B674).

This desire for conceptual unification pervades all chemistry. Legitimate as it is, chemists should be wary not to overshoot their goal and should proceed more cautiously.

> This unity, although it is a mere idea, has been pursued so eagerly in all ages that more often there has been cause to moderate than to encourage the desire for it. The chemists had already done much when they were able to reduce all salts to two main genera, acidic and alkaline, but they even attempt to regard this distinction as merely a variety or varied expression of one and the same fundamental material. They sought to get the several species of earths (the material of stone and even of metal) gradually down

to three, and finally to two; still not satisfied, they cannot dismiss from their thought the conjecture that behind these varieties there is a single genus or even indeed a common principle for both earths and salts (B680–81, translation amended).

Disregarding the details for the moment, what Kant approvingly refers to in these passages is the attempt, characteristic of the chemistry of principles, to account for the variety of chemical properties by assuming different combinations of fundamental, property-bearing elements. In this vein, the salts are rightly reduced to two, and the earths to either two or three fundamental substances.

In the first of the passages quoted here Kant gives his version of the chemistry of principles that takes up the Stahlian distinction between principles and instruments and thus follows Stahl's own approach rather than Juncker's or even Rouelle's dualist conception (see sec. 4). In particular, Kant assumes three elements and two instruments. The former comprise earth, salt, and phlogiston, a threefold distinction that is reproduced in the *Danziger Physik* (29:161). In conformity with the usage of the period and with Karsten's *Anleitung* (see sec. 4), Kant employs "salt" to refer to acid and alkaline substances (as can be gleaned from the second passage quoted above). Thus, salt contains the two subprinciples acid and base. Kant's earths comprise two or three varieties of unspecified nature, and he attacks attempts—as exemplified by Venel (see sec. 4)—to reduce them to one overarching earth principle.

In addition, Kant accepts water and air as chemical instruments or "vehicles" in the *Critique of Pure Reason* (as he describes them in the first passage quoted earlier). In the *Danziger Physik* water and fire are mentioned as instruments and, moreover, are coordinated with two of the elements. Salts need water as a vehicle for their activity, and phlogiston demands fire for this purpose; earths possess no relevant activity (29:161). The distinction between the element phlogiston and the instrument fire agrees with Stahl's views (see sec. 4), although it contrasts with the identification of the two Kant suggests two pages later (see sec. 4). The correlation between specific elements and instruments is found neither in Stahl nor in Karsten's *Anleitung*. As to air, the student notes only contain the statement: "air is not an element" (29:162), without repeating its status as an instrument, let alone giving a corresponding element. But earth as the only element left is denied activity anyway.

The passage on air as an instrument is already part of the first edition of the *Critique of Pure Reason*. In this passage Kant clearly follows Stahl in considering air a sort of catalyst incapable of combining with substances. But in the 1780s this view was completely out of date. Hales's *Vegetable Staticks* (1727), which was most probably known to Kant (see sec. 2), already entertained the contrary claim that air could enter solid bodies; this result was mentioned by Newton in his widely read *Opticks*. Moreover, Joseph Black, in 1756, had managed to release a specific kind of air (carbon dioxide) from what today is called magnesium carbonate. This air was regarded as being fixed in the substance before the experiment and was called "fixed air." Acknowledging the existence of fixed air was tantamount to abandoning air as a mere instrument. But in the *Danziger Physik* Kant does recognize fixed air (29:163, 29:166); retaining air as an instrument would thus be incoherent.

It seems plausible to attribute these conflicting views to different stages of Kant's thought. A suitable conjecture could run as follows. In composing the *Critique of Pure Reason* Kant had not been fully aware of the state of the art in chemistry and had resorted to obsolete views of Stahl. On the occasion of his physics lectures in 1785 Kant refamiliarized himself with the subject matter and adapted his earlier claims to the changed scientific situation. On this construal, Kant dropped air as an instrument in 1785 but failed to make the necessary alterations in preparing the second edition of the *Critique of Pure Reason* in 1787. That is, the *Danziger Physik* actually replaces the instrument air with fire (which is in agreement with Stahl as well). This interpretation implies that Kant's rejection of the elementary nature of air is not equivalent to accepting it as an instrument. Rather, it is the identification of different kinds of air, as reported by Karsten (29:341–61) and referred to by Kant in general terms (29:162–63), that prohibits considering air as an element.

This means, then, that Kant, following the mid-century received view of Stahlianism, initially assumed five chemical entities as elementary, namely, earth, salt, phlogiston, water, and air. Under the influence of Karsten's presentation of new discoveries in chemistry, Kant supplanted air with "elementary fire." Kant characterizes fire as material and as the cause of thermal expansion (29:118) so that he likely follows Karsten in identifying fire with caloric. Fire is claimed to "permeate" all bodies (29:118, 29:119), but nothing is said about the chemical combinations of caloric. This latter view had been proposed by Lavoisier, who featured caloric as an imponderable fluid endowed with chemical affinities like an ordinary substance. In particular, gases are construed as caloric compounds. Karsten is confused about this conception,[32] and it is clearly absent in the *Danziger Physik* (29:121, 29:123). Kant's failure to recognize the new conception of gases allows him to retain the traditional view of heat as an instrument rather than having to admit it as an element.

In addition to the correlation of particular elements and instruments, a second feature seems to be peculiar to Kant's views, namely the division of his three principles into active and passive elements (as contained in the first passage quoted earlier and in the *Danziger Physik*). Earth is a passive burden or "weight," and salt and phlogiston are active powers or "forces" (see earlier). The same idea is expressed in the *Danziger Physik*.

> The earths are the *onus* [the weight], the negative matter, which have no dissolving power but are to be dissolved. Salt and combustible things [i.e., phlogiston] are the two *potentiae* in nature that dissolve everything. . . . [Phlogiston] is the proper *potentia chymica*. Salts require water as a vehicle to act as powers, and combustible beings need elementary fire as a vehicle for dissolving earths (29:161).

"Dissolution" is Kant's term for chemical combination; the statement thus applies to chemical reactions in general. The distinction between active and passive substances was part of earlier versions of the chemistry of principles that had resorted to "vital agents" or "fermental virtues." But in the eighteenth century such entities had been largely abandoned. In the Newtonian tradition they had been replaced with "active principles," that is, forces or powers rather than substances. Active powers fit Kant's dynamism much better than active substances. So one might assume that Kant's distinction of active elements expresses his view that chemical principles are manifestations of some sort of force. On the whole, then, Kant assumes salt and phlogiston as two active elements, earth as a passive element, and water and caloric as instruments.

6. KANT'S CONTINUALIST UNDERSTANDING OF CHEMICAL COMPOUNDS

Kant was highly critical of the corpuscularian account of the structure of matter (see sec. 2). It gives free reign to the imagination and licenses fictitious constructions. In this connection Kant refers to *occult qualities* twice, which he says corpuscularianism invokes (4:502, 4:532). It deserves notice that Stahl had leveled the same criticism against corpuscularian explanations. This argument owes its rhetorical force to the fact that the mechanical philosophers had voiced this very objection against the "substantial forms" of the Scholastic tradition. Stahl and Kant thus turn the reproach against its authors.

It is true, Stahl adopted the corpuscularian stance at the ontological level. According to the so-called structural chemistry of the period, chemically significant properties derive from the shapes or figures of the relevant particles. Chemical bonds or chemical reactions occur according to the geometrical fit between the shapes of the particles involved. In this vein, Stahl accepted corpuscles endowed with "their own and definite shapes"[33] and required for reactions that "there is a proportion among the particles with respect to their shapes."[34] However, Stahl denied the corpuscularian approach any explanatory value. The principles are intimately related to chemical experience, whereas the shapes of the particles can be thought up arbitrarily. By recourse to the principles, substances can be labeled "with a much better known and more specific name . . . than by invoking incomprehensible definite shapes, that is, properties rightly considered occult qualities or hidden properties."[35] A chemist's statement that ordinary salt is composed of the principles salt and water has a clear empirical bearing.

> However, when I say salt is composed of pointed, twisted particles that are longer than they are wide, etc. and somebody asks me to identify salt in a substance, I will be at a loss to find it using these properties. Nor will anybody else be able to teach me how to get hold of this pointed, twisted, long but not wide thing.[36]

Accordingly, Stahl's argument against actually making use of the shapes of particles in chemistry is that such explanations always remain vague and arbitrary; they are too unspecified to possess tangible import.[37]

While Stahl saw nothing wrong in accepting the corpuscularian approach at the ontological level and at the same time rejecting it at the explanatory level, Kant is more consistent and tries to bring his ontology into harmony with his methodology. Methodology requires one to relinquish corpuscularian accounts; consequently chemical compounds should not be conceived ontologically as particle aggregates kept together by geometrical fit. Rather, they should be understood along the plenist and continualist lines characteristic of Kant's theory of matter. Borrowing from Aristotle's concept of "mixis," Kant assumes that a compound involves the complete reciprocal penetration of its ingredients. "The solution [i.e., the compound] of specifically different matters in one another in which no part of one matter is found not united with a part of the other matter in the same proportion as that of the whole solution is absolute solution, and may also be called chemical penetration" (4:530). That is, the reagents are not contained in the compound separately as they would be on the corpuscularian account. Each and every part of the compound, regardless of how small it might be, includes all the materials in the proportion of the whole. The compound is uniform at each stage of the analysis.

Aristotle had argued that the mixis is a uniform whole that is not composed of the substances from which it is generated. The latter are not part of the compound but can be recovered from it. The elements exist in the mixt not actually, but only potentially (as is shown by the possibility of obtaining them from the compound). Consequently, the original materials are not destroyed by forming a new substance; in particular, their "powers" or "virtues" are retained.[38] Stahl objects to Aristotle's view that if the reagents were not actually present in the compound, the properties of the former should not resemble those of the latter. In other words, the features of the initial substances should be quite distinct from those of the final product. But this, Stahl claims, is contrary to experience.[39] Stahl's argument is based on the chemistry of principles. Ordinary salt, for instance, is assumed to be composed of the principles salt and water. The former owes its solidity to the salt principle and its solubility to the water principle. The characteristics of the complex substance reflect the properties of its ingredients. But this retention of properties would be incomprehensible if the reacting materials were not really part of the compound, i.e., if they were not its components.

Kant follows Aristotelian lines in assuming the uniformity of the compound, but he refuses to accept the merely potential existence of the ingredients. Kant acknowledges that chemical compounds might represent a "complete division to infinity" (4:531) and thus come close to the "actual infinite multitude . . . in the object" (4:507) he had considered an "express contradiction" before (4:507). However, as he argues, this contradiction does not emerge in the case at hand since the process of compound formation and, correspondingly, the realization of the complete division to infinity take an infinite number of moments (4:531). The salient point is that this account entails that the reagents are actually part of the compound—if only infinitely dispersed. However intimate the penetration of the reacting materials may be, they do not disappear. In contradistinction to Aristotle, the reagents are components of the product. Consequently, Kant's concept of chemical combination is not affected by Stahl's anti-Aristotelian objection.

7. CHEMICAL ELEMENTS AS IDEAS OF REASON

Kant holds a nonoperational view of chemical elements, which contrasts with the commitment to the empirical identification of elements that was unanimously accepted in the wake of the Chemical Revolution. According to the operationalist understanding that would prevail later, chemical elements are those substances into which all other substances can eventually be resolved and which admit of no further resolution themselves. It follows that chemical elements should be accessible in the laboratory. By contrast, on Kant's dissenting position, elements are created by reason to order and unify the multitude of chemical phenomena; moreover, elements remain fictitious and can never be identified empirically. In the *Critique of Pure Reason* chemical elements provide Kant's chief example of regulative ideas of reason.

> Such concepts of reason are not created by nature, rather we question nature according to these ideas, and we take our cognition to be defective as long as it is not adequate to them. Admittedly, one hardly finds *pure earth, pure water, pure air*, etc. Nevertheless, concepts of them are required (though as far as their complete purity is concerned, have their origin only in reason) in order appropriately to determine the share that each of these natural causes has in appearance (B673–74, translation amended).[4]

The argument is likewise contained in the *Danziger Physik*:

> It is peculiar that although everybody talks of pure fire, water, air etc., one has to admit that nothing is pure. Thus we see [that] we merely encounter effects which we attribute to these matters, and we call them pure in light

of these effects. Our reason introduces certain divisions which precede experience and according to which we then order our experiences (29:161). The author says that pure water should in no way be required. It is an idea of our understanding since only such things are counted as pure water that are only *vehiculum* [vehicles] of dissolution (29:162–63).

The student who composed these lecture notes apparently intends "the author" to refer to Karsten, that is, the author of the textbook Kant's lectures were based on. But Karsten did not express any such view. He says that elements are not easily found in nature unless the art of chemistry is resorted to as well. The only element provided directly by nature is pure water; namely, in the form of rainwater (29: 275).

Kant holds a quite different view. He argues that in order to systematize the phenomena concepts are required. Pure water is introduced by its effect to act exclusively as a chemical instrument for the salt principle. In this way, the concept serves to structure the multifarious chemical phenomena that can be achieved without isolating a real counterpart of the concept. To give another example (that is not Kant's), such concepts resemble the axes of a coordinate system in that the pure cases do not need to be realized. The description of terrestrial motions using a system of degrees of longitude and latitude in no way demands the actual existence of, for instance, strictly northbound or purely westbound motion. The fictitious pure cases are employed to explicate the intricate real phenomena as a combination or superposition of these ideal factors. Nothing empirical corresponds to these pure cases; they precede experience and cannot be extracted from it.

Fictitious concepts that are indispensable for ordering the appearances and that, other than the axes of coordinate systems, necessarily fail to be realized in experience, represent Kant's regulative ideas of reason. Such ideas

> have an excellent and indispensably necessary regulative use, namely that of directing the understanding to a certain goal respecting which the lines of direction of all its rules converge at one point, which, although it is only an idea (*focus imaginarius*)—i.e., a point from which the concepts of the understanding do not really proceed, since it lies entirely outside the bounds of possible experience—nonetheless still serves to obtain for these concepts the greatest unity alongside the greatest extension (B672).

Chemical elements, as Kant's chief instances of regulative ideas of reason, are essentially nonempirical in kind. They transcend the boundaries of all possible experience and necessarily fail to be instantiated.

What Kant has in mind here are obviously not the operationally defined elements of late eighteenth-century, postrevolutionary chemistry. Rather, he refers to the chemical principles of the traditional approach. Once the scope of Kant's analysis is taken into account, it becomes clear that he excellently captures the deductive structure of the chemistry of principles. Clearly enough, principles are fictitious entities; and necessarily so, since they are supposed to explain the properties of ordinary substances and thus cannot be ordinary substances themselves. Any demand to the effect that principles be identifiable in the laboratory would have created a circularity in the theory. Principles are intended to account for the features of ordinary substances; thus it would do violence to the deductive structure of the entire principles approach to assume that principles are substances. The demand to isolate the principles empirically, that is, to identify pure earth, pure water etc., would amount to a category mistake. Kant's analysis shrewdly and accurately recognizes this feature.[41]

Stahl, by contrast, is far less consistent on this issue. On the one hand, he confirms that principles cannot be isolated empirically; on the other, he demands that phlogiston should be amenable to chemical analysis. Stahl's confusion is revealed by his "twofold definition" of a principle. "The entity which is essentially and primarily constitutive of its [a body's] nature is called a principle in a priori respect. Likewise, the entity into which the mixed body is eventually resolved is called a principle in *a posteriori* respect. Both descriptions are true."[42] Consequently, Stahl inconsistently requires that a principle account for the nature or the properties of a substance and at the same time be subject to chemical analysis and thus material itself. Stahl's second clause conflicts with the conceptual structure of the chemistry of principles. The emphasis on empirical isolation that underlies this clause is characteristic of a more empirical orientation of chemistry which went along with Stahl's own commitment to systematic experimentation and grew even stronger in the course of the eighteenth century. In the second half of the century it was widely required that principles, and phlogiston in particular, should be identifiable in the laboratory. Nothing of this later development is perceptible in Kant. He reconstructs the concept of element pertaining to the original chemistry of principles. In this respect Kant's reconstruction is much more appropriate than Stahl's "twofold definition." Kant captures the conceptual essentials characteristic of Stahlian principles more accurately than Stahl does himself.

Actually, Kant became aware of the Chemical Revolution later and adopted Lavoisier's new chemistry some time in the early 1790s.[43] Of course, this reorientation late in Kant's life necessitates a profound change regarding his conception of chemistry in general and regarding the nature of elements in particular.

8. CONCLUSION

As mentioned in the introduction, Kant's thoughts on matter range from transcendental arguments about what is constitutive of matter as such to the more tangible endeavor to take into account what the chemistry of his period had to say on matter and its transformations. But the two ends of the spectrum are linked with one another. The transcendental approach has ramifications for the realm of empirical chemistry. The point is that each of the three axioms of Kant's theory of matter involves the challenge to develop fitting pieces of substantive chemical theory. Accordingly, Kant elaborates his plenist principle to give a noncorpuscularian account of density differences. Dynamism needs to be supplemented with a derivation of rigidity from fluidity, a task acknowledged in the *Metaphysical Foundations* but addressed only in the *Opus postumum*. Finally, the continualist understanding of matter is to be translated into a viable construal of chemical combination and chemical compounds. In sum, Kant's theory of matter proceeds from transcendental arguments and extends into substantive chemical theorizing.

The chemistry of principles and the chemistry of interparticulate forces constitute the two chief threads of eighteenth century thought on matter and its transformations. Both approaches were widely regarded as complementary; they could be pursued indiscriminately by adopting abstract property bearers as well as short-range forces between particles. In fact, Newton's *Opticks* embodies this peaceful coexistence. For in addition to enunciating the chemistry of forces, Newton also advocated a version of the chemistry of principles—albeit one different from Stahl's.[44] Kant likewise adheres to both approaches, and his two chief meta-level considerations of chemistry are to be understood against this twofold background. The first one concerns Kant's judgment that chemistry is an improper science since its force laws remain empirical and fail to be derivable a priori (see sec. 4). This judgment can be fully appreciated only if it is connected to Newtonian force-based chemistry. Kant claims that this approach leaves too much room to adapt interparticulate forces to the observations. There is nothing inevitable or necessary about these laws as would be required for science proper; rather, they are read off from findings in the laboratory. Second, Kant's use of chemical elements as examples of ideas of reason is utterly incomprehensible unless the conceptual background of the chemistry of principles is taken into consideration (see sec. 7). In sum, it is Newtonian chemistry that is irremediably empirical, and it is Stahlian chemistry that invokes elements as regulative ideas. Being aware of the scientific context of the period allows one to appreciate properly the meaning and focus of these Kantian tenets.

NOTES

I am grateful to Eric Watkins for helpful suggestions that did much to improve the readability of the text.

1. All translations from the *Metaphysical Foundations* are from Immanuel Kant, *Philosophy of Material Nature*, trans. James W. Ellington (Indianapolis: Hackett Publishing, 1985). Translations from the *Opus postumum* are from *Opus postumum*, ed. Eckart Förster (Cambridge: Cambridge University Press, 1993). Translations from the *Critique of Pure Reason* are from *Critique of Pure Reason*, trans. and ed. Paul Guyer and Allen Wood (Cambridge: Cambridge University Press, 1998). All other translations are mine.

2. For a contrasting reconstruction of the argument, see chapter 7 here.

3. Isaac Newton, *Opticks or A Treatise of the Reflections, Refractions, Inflections & Colours of Light* (New York: Dover, 1979), 389–97.

4. See J. R. Partington, *A History of Chemistry*, 3 vols. (London: Macmillan, 1961–1970), 2:478–82; my "Newton's Ideas on the Structure of Matter and their Impact on Eighteenth Century Chemistry: Some Historical and Methodological Remarks," *International Studies in the Philosophy of Science* 1 (1986): 85–105, esp. 85–98; my "Die begriffliche Entwicklung der Affinitätstheorie im 18. Jahrhundert. Newtons Traum—und was daraus wurde," *Archive for History of Exact Sciences* 36 (1986): 327–89, esp. 327–28, 379–85.

5. See A. Thackray, *Atoms and Powers. An Essay on Newtonian Matter-Theory and the Development of Chemistry* (Cambridge: Harvard University Press, 1970), 141–47.

6. R. J. Boscovich, *Theoria philosophiae naturalis redacta ad unicam legem virium in natura existentium*, ed. and trans. J. M. Child (Venice, 1758), 58–77.

7. Newton, *Opticks*, 268–69.

8. See Thackray, *Atoms and Powers*, 54; see ibid., 54–65.

9. Leibniz, "Fifth Letter to Clarke," in *G. W. Leibniz Philosophical Essays*, ed. and trans. R. Ariew and D. Garber (Indianapolis: Hackett Publishing, 1989), 335–36.

10. See Thackray, *Atoms and Powers*, 56–59, 65, 109–110.

11. Isaac Newton, *Mathematical Principles of Natural Philosophy*, ed. and trans. A. Motte and F. Cajori (Berkeley: University of California Press, 1962), 300–302.

12. See H. J. Waschkies, "Wissenschaftliche Praxis und Erkenntnistheorie in Kants Opus postumum," in *Übergang: Untursuchungen zum Spätwerk Immanuel Kants*, ed. S. Blaschke (Frankfurt: Vittorio Klostermann, 1991), 185–207, esp. 190–91.

13. At first sight it appears likewise possible that Kant assumes a dependence of repulsion on the relevant volume (rather than the surface area). As he argues, through repulsion matter dynamically fills corporeal spaces (4:520–21). But he says in his notes mentioned earlier for the letter to Beck dating from 1792: "The degree of repulsion is not augmented by an equal increase in volume" (11:365). And similarly: "Repulsion can be originally unequal in a given volume" (11:365). Accordingly, at least some years after the completion of the *Metaphysical Foundations*, Kant explicitly denies that the intensity of repulsion is determined by the volume that matter occupies by means of its forces.

14. However, Kant apparently assumes that additional factors are influential in determining density. For eventually he restricts the scope of his equilibrium approach to the explanation of density differences of substances of the same chemical nature (4:526). This qualification might testify to Kant's recognition that the density of macroscopic bodies is affected by a host of causes other than fundamental forces.

15. 29:212–16.

16. F. Baader, "Ideen über Festigkeit und Flüssigkeit. Zur Prüfung der physikalischen Grundsätze des Hrn. Lavoisier," *Journal der Physik* 5 (1792): 222–47, esp. 225–27; F. W. J. Schelling, *Erster Entwurf eines Systems der Naturphilosophie*, in *Werke II*, ed. M. Schröter (München, 1927), 1–268, esp. 31; H. F. Link, "Ueber Festigkeit und Flüssigkeit," *Annalen der Physik* 25 (1807): 133–47, esp. 139.

17. Boscovich, *Theoria philosophiae naturalis*, 302–309.

18. See my "Kants Theorie der Materie und ihre Wirkung auf die zeitgenössische Chemie," *Kant-Studien* 81 (1990), 170–210, esp. 192–93, 204.

19. See also my "Kraft und Wirklichkeit. Kants späte Theorie der Materie," in *Übergang:*

Untursuchungen zum Spätwerk Immanuel Kants, ed. S. Blaschke (Frankfurt: Vittorio Klostermann, 1991), 218–21.

20. G. F. Hildebrandt, "Ueber die Modificationen der Materie," *Neues allgemeines Journal der Chemie* 5 (1805): 605–31, esp. 628.

21. Ibid., 605, 628–29.

22. See my "Kants Theorie der Materie und ihre Wirkung auf die zeitgenössische Chemie," 198–203, and my "Kraft und Wirklichkeit," 221–22.

23. See L. W. Gilbert, "Nekrolog [on Kant]," *Neues allgemeines Journal der Chemie* 2 (1804): 239–40.

24. See E. Ströker, *Theoriewandel in der Wissenschaftsgeschichte. Chemie im 18. Jahrhundert* (Frankfurt: Klostermann, 1982), 93–94, and my "What is Right with the Miracle-Argument: Establishing a Taxonomy of Natural Kinds," *Studies in History and Philosophy of Science* 24 (1993): 391–409, esp. 401–402.

25. See Partington, *A History of Chemistry*, 2: 664–77; Ströker, *Theoriewandel in der Wissenschaftsgeschichte*, 92–103, and my "Kants Theorie der Materie und ihre Wirkung auf die zeitgenössische Chemie," 195–97.

26. See Ströker, *Theoriewandel in der Wissenschaftsgeschichte*, 126–27, 154–57.

27. G. F. Venel, "chymie," in *Encyclopédie ou dictionnaire raisonnée des sciences, des arts et des métiers*, ed. M. Diderot and M. d'Alembert (Paris, 1751–1780; reprint Stuttgart: Frommann-Holzboog, 1966), 418.

28. G. F. Venel, "mixte," in *Encyclopédie ou dictionnaire raisonnée des sciences, des arts et des métiers*, ed. M. Diderot and M. d'Alembert (Paris, 1751–1780; reprint Stuttgart: Frommann-Holzboog, 1966), 585.

29. G. F. Venel, "principe," in *Encyclopédie ou dictionnaire raisonnée des sciences, des arts et des métiers*, ed. M. Diderot and M. d'Alembert (Paris, 1751–1780; reprint Stuttgart: Frommann-Holzboog, 1966), 376.

30. See Partington, *A History of Chemistry*, 3: 588.

31. See M. Friedman, *Kant and the Exact Sciences* (Cambridge: Harvard University Press, 1992), 282–83.

32. Ibid., 283.

33. G. E. Stahl, *Chymia rationalis et experimentalis; oder Gründliche der Natur und Vernunfft gemässe und mit Experimenten erwiesene Einleitung der Chymie* (Leipzig, 1720), 13.

34. G. E. Stahl, *Einleitung zur Grundmixtion Derer Unterirrdischen mineralischen und metallischen Cörper* (Leipzig, 1720), 34; analogously ibid., 27–34; Stahl, *Chymia rationalis et experimentalis*, 62–64, 69; see my "Zum korpuskularen Aufbau der Materie bei Stahl und Newton," *Sudhoffs Archiv* 70 (1986): 1–17, esp. 6.

35. Stahl, *Einleitung zur Grundmixtion*, 50.

36. Ibid., 50–51.

37. See Partington, *A History of Chemistry*, 2: 665, and my "Zum korpuskularen Aufbau," 5.

38. See Partington, *A History of Chemistry*, 1: 93–94.

39. Stahl, *Einleitung zur Grundmixtion*, 13.

40. The extant English translations render the second sentence to the effect that pure elements "are to be found with great difficulty," or that "it is hard to find" them. But this is misleading. The phrase contains the stronger claim that it is highly unlikely ever to find such elements, which means that one does not in fact find them.

41. See my "Newton's Ideas on the Structure of Matter," 86, and my "Kants Theorie der Materie und ihre Wirkung auf die zeitgenössische Chemie," 197–98.

42. Stahl, *Chymia rationalis et experimentalis*, 4.

43. See Friedman, *Kant and the Exact Sciences*, 288–89. For an account of Kant's later views on chemistry see ibid., 264–90.

44. See Newton, *Opticks*, 274–75, and my "Newton's Ideas on the Structure of Matter," 87–92.

11

Kant on Understanding Organisms as Natural Purposes

Hannah Ginsborg

Iᴛ is a central and often-repeated claim in Kant's Critique of Teleological Judgment that we must regard organisms as purposes. We cannot understand their possibility, Kant says, unless we invoke the notion of design. At the same time, however, he insists that we cannot assert that organisms are in fact the product of design. On the contrary, we both do, and must, regard them as natural products rather than as artifacts. Thus while the concept of purpose plays an indispensable role in our understanding of the organic world, its use is, in Kant's terminology, regulative rather than constitutive: It belongs to reflective judgment rather than to determining judgment. The concept of purpose plays a merely heuristic role, serving as a guiding thread in our observation and investigation of organisms without being invoked to explain directly how they come to be.

In this chapter I will consider two questions which arise from this conjunction of claims. The first bears on the issue of why we have to regard organisms as purposes. Ostensibly, Kant's argument turns on the idea that their origin cannot be mechanically explained. It is for this reason that we need to appeal to the notion of design in order to make sense of the organic world. However, this argument appears to contain a non sequitur. Why should the fact that the origin of organisms cannot be explained mechanically license the conclusion that we need the concept of purpose to guide our investigation into their structure and workings? It is clear how the mechanical inexplicability of organisms might be thought to warrant the conclusion that we need the concept of purpose to provide an alternative explanation of their origin. But this is not in fact Kant's conclusion, for he denies that the concept of purpose can play this explanatory role. What, then, *is* the role of the concept of purpose in our investigation of organisms, and how does it relate to our failure to explain their origin in mechanical terms?

While the main aim of this chapter is to answer this question, I shall defend my answer by showing that it also addresses a second and more fundamental question: What is it to regard an organism as a purpose, given that we must also regard it as a product of nature? To regard something as a purpose appears at first sight to be equivalent to regarding it as an artifact: something that is caused in virtue of a concept in the mind of a designer. But Kant denies that we either do, or should, regard organisms as artifacts: They are to be regarded instead as products of nature. How, then, can we regard them as purposes without falling into contradiction?

These questions have not, as far as I can tell, been discussed explicitly in the literature on Kant's teleology. So I begin in section 1 with an attempt to motivate them and to describe them more fully. In section 2, I approach my answer to the first question by trying to clarify the notion of mechanical inexplicability which figures in Kant's argument for the need to regard organisms as purposes. I go on in section 3 to argue that the mechanical inexplicability of organisms, as I have characterized it, not only concerns the origin of organisms, but also generates a difficulty for understanding their structure and behavior: specifically, a difficulty in subsuming biological phenomena under lawlike generalizations. It is in order to address this difficulty, I claim, that we need, on Kant's view, to regard organisms as purposes. I defend this claim in section 4 by invoking an interpretation of the notion of purpose on which to regard something as a purpose is to regard it as subject to normative rules or standards. This interpretation completes the answer to the first question by allowing us to see how the mechanical inexplicability of organisms makes it necessary for us to regard them as purposes. And, as I argue in its support, it also yields an answer to the second question by showing how we can regard organisms both as purposes and as products of nature.

1. REGARDING ORGANISMS AS PURPOSES: TWO QUESTIONS

In §10 of the *Critique of Judgment*, Kant defines a purpose as "the object of a concept, in so far as the concept is seen as the cause of the object" (5:220).[1] He goes on to say that "where an object is thought to be possible as an effect only through a concept [of the object], there we think a purpose." So far, it may look as though a purpose on his account is simply an artifact, that is, a product of design. But we soon find out that the concept of purpose applies more broadly: "An object . . . is called purposive, even if its possibility does not necessarily presuppose the representation of a purpose, merely because its possibility can only be explained and conceived by us in so far as we assume at its ground a causality according to purposes" (ibid.). Even if an object is not in fact intentionally produced, or produced in accordance with a design, it nonetheless can qualify as a purpose. All that is required is that we be unable to understand its possibility except on the assumption that it was produced according to design.

As the Critique of Teleological Judgment goes on to make clear, this is the case with certain products of nature, specifically organisms. Indeed, organisms are the "only beings in nature which, even when regarded in themselves and without relation to other things, must still be thought of as possible only as purposes of nature" (§65, 5:375). They are "singly and alone *explicable* according to natural laws which we can think to ourselves only under the idea of purposes as a principle, and indeed merely in this way are they so much as internally *cognizable* as regards their inner form" (§67, 383). Thus, as Kant goes on to assert in the Dialectic, "no cause other than an intentionally working one may be assumed for the possibility of organic beings in nature" (§78, 5:413); "such beings *must be regarded by us*, as regards their possibility, as produced intentionally and as purposes" (§77, 5:405).

Kant's argument for the claim that we need to regard organisms as purposes is based on the premise that we are incapable of explaining them by mechanical laws alone. The particular forms we encounter in the organic world are contingent with respect to the laws of inorganic nature, and hence these laws are not sufficient to account for them.[2] This is suggested by an example he gives in §61, which introduces the Critique of Teleological Judgment as a whole:

> If we cite, e.g., the construction of a bird, the hollowing in its bones, the position of its wings for movement and of the tail for steering, etc., we say that all this is in the highest degree contingent according to the mere *nexus effectivus* in nature, without appealing to a particular kind of causality, namely that of purposes (*nexus finalis*); i.e., that nature, regarded as mere mechanism, could have formed itself in a thousand ways without hitting precisely on the unity according to such a principle, and thus that only beyond the concept of nature, and not in that concept, may we hope to find a priori the least ground for that unity (§61, 5:360).

It appears from this that the appeal to purposes is intended to make good the inadequacy of mechanical laws in accounting for the origin of organisms.

Kant goes on to suggest the same line of argument by way of introduction to his exposition of the notion of a natural purpose at §§64–65.

> [The] *contingency* of [a thing's] form with respect to all empirical natural laws . . . is itself a ground for taking the causality of the thing in such a way as if it were precisely on that account possible only through reason . . . the object which is thought as possible only from this, would be represented as possible only as a purpose (5:370).

He illustrates the point with an example:

> If someone were to perceive in an apparently uninhabited land a geometrical figure, say a regular hexagon drawn in the sand . . . he would not judge the sand, the neighboring sea, the winds, or even animals with footprints known to him, or any other non-rational cause, to be a ground of the possibility of such a shape [*Gestalt*]; because the contingency of coinciding with such a concept, which is only possible in reason, would seem so infinitely great

that there might just as well be no natural law at all for it, and consequently that the causality for such an effect could not be contained in any cause in merely mechanically operative nature, but only in the concept of such an object, a concept which reason alone can provide and compare the object with; consequently this could be seen definitely as a purpose, but not as a natural purpose; i.e., it could be seen [only] as a product of *art* (*vestigium hominis video*) (5:370).

Now, as the last qualification indicates, this example is not intended to carry over unchanged to the case of organisms. In the example, we conclude from the contingency of the hexagon with respect to mechanical laws that it is, in fact, the product of design, and indeed human design: The land in which we found it was only "apparently" uninhabited. But in the case of an organism we do not draw that conclusion. In spite of its contingency with respect to the laws of inorganic nature, we continue to regard it as a product of nature. For it is caused, not by a rational agent external to it, but by its own nonrational powers or by those of another organism of the same species: It is, Kant says, "*cause and effect of itself*" (§64, 5:370). A new tree is naturally generated by a parent tree, which is identical with it with respect to species; a tree is the cause of its own growth and development in so far as it organizes externally given matter into its own form; the parts of a tree both maintain one another in existence and combine to produce replacement parts when old ones are lost. Thus, Kant continues in §65, we do not conclude that the organism is "merely an artifact, that is, the product of a rational cause distinct from the matter (the parts) [of the thing], whose causality (in procuring and connecting the parts) is determined through its idea of a whole that is thereby possible." Rather, we recognize that "the parts . . . connect themselves into the unity of a whole, in that they are reciprocally cause and effect of one another's form" (§65, 5:373).

However, the conclusion is apparently supposed to be parallel to that drawn in the case of the hexagon. For in the cases of both an artifact and an organism, Kant says, "the thing is a purpose, consequently grasped under a concept or an idea which must determine a priori everything which is to be contained in it" (ibid.). In both cases, the "idea of the whole . . . determines the form and connection of all the parts" (ibid.). The only difference is that, in the case of an organism, we do not conclude that the concept or idea plays a causal role in its production. The idea determines the form and connection of the parts "not as cause—for then [the thing] would be a product of art—but rather as ground of cognition of the systematic unity of the form and connection of everything manifold which is contained in the given material, for the person who judges it" (ibid.). It thus appears that, just as in the case of an artifact, the inadequacy of the laws of inorganic nature to account for the production of an organism requires us to invoke an alternative ground of its possibility: that is, an antecedent concept of the organism which determines how it is supposed to be. The difference is that we do not take the concept to be the cause or ground of the organism itself, but rather of our cognition of it. It is responsible, not for the unity of the organism itself, but for our ability to grasp the organism in a unified way.

But the fact that we do not regard the concept as the cause of the object—only as its "ground of cognition"—casts the whole argument into question. For its conclusion no longer seems to follow from its premise. The premise was that the origin of an organism cannot be ascribed to the workings of inorganic nature alone. From this premise it might be reasonable (given some further assumptions) to conclude that we must ascribe it to another cause, namely design. And this is indeed the conclusion Kant draws in the case of the hexagon. But it is not the conclusion he draws in the case of organisms. While he concludes that we must invoke the notion of purpose, it is in a different role: not as a hypothesis about the cause of the organism, but rather as a "ground" for "cognizing it." This conclusion is made clearer in several passages which emphasize that our use of the notion of purpose with respect to organisms is "heuristic" (§78, 5:411) rather than explanatory. We invoke a teleological mode of judging "to bring nature under principles of observation and investigation, without presuming to *explain* it accordingly" (§61, 5:360). We must judge organisms according to the concept of final causes "even only when we demand a guiding-thread in getting to know the constitution [of organisms] through observation, without aspiring [*versteigen*] to the investigation of their first origin" (§72, 5:389–90).

The rationale for our use of the concept of purpose is not, then, that it is needed to provide an alternative explanation for the origin of organisms where mechanical explanation fails. Any such explanation would, indeed, be inadequate: We are, Kant says, "far from satisfied with an explanation of products of nature through causality in accordance with purposes" (§77, 5:408). Rather, the concept of purpose is required to play a more fundamental role in our cognitive grasp of organisms. "Even the thought of them as organized beings is impossible without the thought of a production with intention" (§75, 5:398); "we cannot even begin to investigate [them] except under the concept of a purpose of reason" (§78, 5:415). Accordingly, the concept of purpose is required not only by researchers concerned with the origin of organisms, but also by those whose investigations are confined to their structure and workings. The principle of judging organisms in terms of the notion of purpose is relied upon by the "dissectors of plants and animals, to investigate their structure" (§66, 5:376); as Kant puts it in an earlier essay, "every anatomist as physiologist proceeds from this concept" ("On the Use of Teleological Principles in Philosophy," 8:181). But, we might now ask, why should the inadequacy of mechanical laws to account for the *origin* of organisms make it the case that such researchers need the concept of purpose to investigate how a given organism is *actually* constructed? Why should our inability to explain the origin of the dog now lying on the dissecting table have any bearing on what concepts are needed by the physiologist who is trying to describe its internal structure and determine the workings of its parts?[3]

The difficulty here is easily overlooked. For Kant often puts his conclusion by saying that we can "understand the possibility" of organisms only in terms of purposes (§10, 5:220; §61, 5:359; §81, 5:424) or that we must think the teleological principle as the "ground of their possibility" (§70, 5:388). This suggests a straight-forward move from the premise that it is impossible (at least as far as human beings can tell) for an organism to arise from merely mechanical causes, to the conclusion that we can regard the existence of organisms as possible only on the assumption of an intelligent cause. But this is not the move Kant is making. In saying that we need to regard an organism as a purpose in order to "understand its possibility," he does not mean that we need the notion of a purpose to account for its origin, but rather that we need it to understand its nature or essence: to form a determinate concept of it which allows us to grasp its structure and work-ings.[4] The question then arises of why the concept of purpose is necessary in this way. How does it follow from the insufficiency of mechanical laws to account for the origin of an organism, that we need to appeal to the concept of purpose to aid us in a quite different task: that of understanding its actual structure and the laws governing its actual behavior? And if it does not follow, then what entitles Kant to claim that we cannot carry out this task unless we regard organisms as purposes?

Reflection on the role of the concept of purpose in our understanding of or-ganisms raises a second and more fundamental question. As we have seen, Kant holds that we must regard organisms not only as purposes, but also as products of nature. But how are we supposed to regard them simultaneously in these two apparently opposed ways? To regard something as a purpose is, on the face of it, to regard it as produced by a causal process which involves a concept in the mind of an intelligent designer: in short, as caused by a concept. To regard something as a natural product is, on the face of it, to regard it as produced by a process which does not involve a concept in the mind of an intelligent designer: in short, as *not* caused by a concept. The conflict here cannot be resolved simply by pointing out that the concept of purpose is regulative rather than constitutive, or belongs to reflective judgment rather than determining judgment: In other words, it does not help to be reminded that we are not required actually to assert that the organ-ism is caused by a concept. For the question remains of how we can even coherently *regard* something both as a purpose and as natural. If it is inconsistent to assert that something is both natural and a purpose, how is there any less inconsistency in merely thinking of it as both natural and a purpose? It is true that we are not required to make contradictory claims about the object; but we seem nonetheless to be required to take up contradictory attitudes toward it.[5]

An alternative solution might be to grant that there is a conflict between re-garding organisms as purposes and regarding them as natural, but to deny that we are required to regard them as natural. According to this solution, Kant believes that we must regard organisms as designed by an intelligent being, and hence as artifacts rather than as natural: more specifically, we must regard them as divine artifacts. However, this fails to do justice to Kant's view that regarding organisms as natural is no less a methodological requirement than regarding them as purposes. We must not regard them as purposes at the expense of regarding them as natural: both ways of regarding them are necessary for biological investigation. This can be seen indirectly from §§64–65, where Kant emphasizes the contrast between organisms as self-causing and artifacts as caused by an external agent. His discussion there indicates that we *do* in fact regard organisms as products of nature; and nothing in those passages implies that we should give up regarding them as natural and treat them as artifacts instead. The point emerges more directly from a number of passages in which he criticizes various theories of organic development on the ground that they fail to do justice to the status of an organism as a natural product. For example, he says that we cannot regard the organization of the matter in an individual plant or animal as due to the operation of a soul, for in that case we "make the soul into the artisan of this structure (*Bauwerk*) and thus must remove the product from (corporeal) nature" (§65, 5:375). A similar consideration leads him to reject the theory of individual preformation, according to which each organism exists in miniature from the time of creation, so that its apparent embryological development is nothing more than an unfolding of parts that were antecedently formed and arranged by God. Kant objects to this account partly for empirical reasons (such as the difficulty of accounting for hybrids), but also on the ground that it relies excessively on the supernatural. In its place, he endorses the theory of epigenesis, on which nature is regarded "as itself producing organisms, not merely as unfolding [*entwickeln*] them" (§81, 5:424). This is an application of the more general view that we must invoke mechanical causality in accounting for organisms, because "without this kind of causality organized beings ... would not be products of nature" (§81, 5:422).[6] These passages take for granted that we must regard organisms as products of nature: Without this assumption Kant's criticisms would have no force.

This leaves unaddressed what is apparently the most straightforward resolution of the conflict: namely, that we regard organisms as purposes by regarding them, not as artifacts, but as *analogous* to artifacts. We thus regard them as natural products, yet natural products which are *as if* designed. As Kant puts it, "teleological judging brings nature under principles of observation and investigation according to the *analogy* of causality according to purposes" (§61, 5:360); in regarding natural products as purposive, we invoke "a kind of causality of nature according to an analogy with our own in the technical use of reason" (§68, 5:383). We regard natural purposes, then, "*as if* they were products of a cause whose causality could be determined only through a representation of the object" (FI IX, 20:232, my emphasis); in other words, as if they were artifacts.

However, the appeal to analogy does not overcome the difficulty. For we are now faced with the question of what it is to regard an organism as analogous to an artifact. Presumably, this is to regard it as possessing some, but not all, of the features that make it an artifact. But, at least on the face of it, the only feature that makes something an artifact is that it has been produced by an intelligent cause in accordance with a concept. And to regard an organism as having *this* feature conflicts, I have been arguing, with the need to regard it as a product of nature. So it remains unclear how an organism, *qua* natural, can be regarded as analogous to a product of art. That there is a lack of clarity here is conceded by Kant himself when he qualifies the analogy as "distant" and admits that the causality of organized beings is not "thinkable . . . according to the analogy of any physical or natural capacity known to us . . . not even through a precisely measured analogy with human art"; indeed, "strictly speaking, the organization of nature has nothing analogous with any causality that we know" (§65, 5:375). We are thus left with the question of how to regard an organism as a purpose while at the same time regarding it as natural: a question which casts suspicion on the very notion of a natural purpose.

I will offer an answer to this question in section 4. Before that, I turn to a discussion of the first of the two questions I have raised, beginning in section 2 with an attempt to clarify Kant's claim that organisms are mechanically inexplicable.

2. THE MECHANICAL INEXPLICABILITY OF ORGANISMS

We saw in section 1 that Kant takes the need for the concept of purpose in our investigation of organisms to be related to our inability to explain on merely mechanical laws how organisms come to be. Organisms are contingent with respect to mechanical laws: We recognize, in the case of any organism, that nature "could have formed itself in a thousand [other] ways" (§61, 5:360). Because of this contingency, it is impossible for human beings "to explain organized beings . . . according to merely mechanical principles of nature" (§75, 5:400); as Kant famously puts it: "It is absurd to hope that another Newton might one day arise who would make conceivable to us so much as the production of a blade of grass according to natural laws unordered by any intention" (§75, 5:400).

But there is much room for confusion regarding what Kant means by claiming that organisms are mechanically inexplicable, or inexplicable in accordance with mechanical laws. One source of confusion is that the term "mechanical" and its cognates are used in a variety of different ways throughout the Critical writings, and it is not obvious which sense Kant has in mind in the present context. The most specific sense of the term is to be found in the *Metaphysical Foundations of Natural Science*, where Kant identifies as mechanical the effects that moving bodies have on one another through the communication of their motion. Mechanical laws, paradigmatically Newton's laws of motion, are distinguished both from the more fundamental "dynamical" laws of matter according to which the parts of matter attract and repel one another, and from laws of chemical action; the ground for this distinction is that the parts of matter act mechanically only insofar as they are in motion, whereas chemical and dynamical powers belong to the parts of matter at rest (4:530, 4:536).

In other texts, including the *Critique of Judgment,* Kant uses the term "mechanical" more inclusively. Some passages from the Critique of Teleological Judgment associate it with the notions of matter and of motion: mechanism, sometimes referred to as the "mere mechanism of matter" (§73, 5:395; §78, 5:411), is identified as the "capacity of motion" (§65, 5:374) and described as being in accordance with "mere laws of motion" (§72, 5:390), and mechanical causality is characterized as the "causality of the natural laws of matter" (§78, 5:408). While these passages could perhaps be read as alluding to the sense of "mechanical" invoked in the *Metaphysical Foundations,* it seems more plausible to regard mechanical laws in this sense as including the dynamical laws (which are, after all, laws of moving forces) and perhaps even chemical laws. The third *Critique* also offers a more open-ended characterization of "mechanical" where it simply seems to mean "nonteleological": The mechanism of nature is defined as "a causal connection for which an understanding is not assumed as the only possible cause" (§77, 5:405), and mechanical laws are those in which "the idea of the effect must not be taken as the ground of the causality of the cause, but the other way around" (FI IX, 20:235). Even more broadly, the *Critique of Judgment* sometimes uses "mechanical" as a synonym for "natural" as opposed to "artificial," a usage on which a process can be both mechanical and teleological. Thus Kant equates "mechanical" with "physical" (§71, 5:389), a term which in turn is equated with "natural" (§65, 5:375). And his discussion of the subordination of mechanism to teleology at §§80–81 seems to allow that any process which does not involve the actual participation of an intelligent agent qualifies as mechanical, even if it can be understood only in teleological terms. For he cites the *Bildungstrieb* (the "formative drive" invoked by Blumenbach to account for such phenomena as organic growth and reproduction) as an example of "natural mechanism," even though it belongs only to organized matter and hence is distinct from what Kant calls the "merely mechanical" powers inhering in matter as such (§81, 5:424).

Finally, the broadest characterization of all is to be found in the *Critique of Practical Reason* and in the second-edition preface to the *Critique of Pure Reason.* Here Kant identifies the mechanism of nature with nature's conformity to the causal principle established in the Second Analogy: As such it is contrasted not with teleology, but with transcendental or noumenal freedom.[7] This sense is more inclusive than any of the others, since an object (say, a human artifact) can be produced according to a design, that is, in a way that is not mechanical in any of the senses mentioned previously, yet without the process of its production falling outside the universal mechanism of phenomenal nature.[8]

This means that there is, on the face of it, much ambiguity in the claim that organisms are not explicable in accordance with mechanical laws. Does Kant mean that they cannot be explained by the laws of mechanics? Or, more generally, that they cannot be explained by any laws that are nonteleological? Or, to make an even stronger claim, that organisms fall outside the phenomenal causal nexus altogether? And, even if this ambiguity is resolved, there remains a second source of confusion, this time due to an ambiguity in the notion of explanation that figures in the claim that organisms are mechanically inexplicable. On one possible understanding, to explain something in accordance with mechanical laws is to show how it follows, given those laws, from specified initial conditions. Thus we might say that a clock's striking on some particular occasion can be mechanically explained because we can show how it follows according to mechanical laws from the arrangement of the parts of the clock after it was wound up. But there is another possible understanding of mechanical explanation on which explaining something mechanically is a matter of showing how mechanical laws are sufficient to determine it even without any specific hypothesis about initial conditions. For example—supposing that we grant for the moment that chemical laws count as "mechanical"—we might say that the formation of regular crystals in a salt solution can be mechanically explained in so far as it follows solely from the laws governing the constituents of the solution. In contrast to the case of the clock's striking, no special arrangement of the matter in the solution needs to be appealed to in accounting for the formation of the crystals. No matter how much the solution is stirred, it will still produce crystals of the same regular shape.

The clue to a resolution of these ambiguities is to be found in two pre-Critical works that foreshadow the concerns of the Critique of Teleological Judgment. In one of Kant's earliest works, the *Universal Natural History and Theory of the Heavens* of 1755, he tries to show that the formation of the celestial system—both our solar system and the greater star system beyond—can be explained "through mechanical laws" (1:221), that is, "the universal laws of motion" (1:222) or the "universal laws of matter" (1:223). He describes his undertaking as follows:

> I assume the matter of the whole world to be universally scattered and make out of it a complete chaos. I see the material [*Stoff*] form itself according to the established laws of attraction and modify its motion through repulsion. I enjoy the satisfaction of seeing, without the help of arbitrary inventions, a well-ordered whole produce itself under the direction [*Veranlassung*] of established laws of motion, which seems so similar to that world system which we have before our eyes that I cannot prevent myself from holding it to be the same (1:225–26).

The account he goes on to give goes something like this: In the original chaos, there is variability in the degree of attractive force possessed by the particles of matter. The more strongly attracting (that is, heavier) particles attract lighter particles to them, resulting in the formation of large and massive bodies, one such body being the sun. At the same time, the repulsive force of matter causes the particles to move laterally, thus setting up a circular motion around the attracting bodies. The particles moving around bodies such as the sun are in turn subject to forces of attraction among themselves; these result in the formation of planets (1: 263–68). It is along these lines that Kant takes himself to be able to show, without appealing to anything but the forces of attraction and repulsion, how the system of stars and planets could come to be out of original chaos (1:234–35).

By way of contrast, Kant suggests that this kind of explanation cannot be given for organic systems, that is plants and animals. "We can say without presumption: *Give me matter, and I will make a world out of it* . . . But can we boast of such advantages concerning the smallest plant or insect? Are we in a position to say: *Give me matter, and I will show you how a caterpillar can be produced?*" (1:230). And he goes on, in a passage prefiguring his famous remark in the *Critique of Judgment* about the Newton of the blade of grass: "We will sooner understand the formation of all celestial bodies, the cause of their motions, in short, the origin of the entire present arrangement of the world-edifice, than we will come to know distinctly or completely the production of a single herb or of a caterpillar from mechanical grounds" (ibid.).

The contrast between the explicability of inorganic natural phenomena and that of organisms is taken up again in the *Only Possible Proof of the Existence of God* of 1763. Throughout section 2 of this work, Kant argues that many phenomena that might be thought to derive from divine artifice are in fact the necessary consequence of fundamental powers and corresponding universal laws. A variety of phenomena that are useful to human beings (for example, the possibility of respiration, of suction, of pumps; the existence of winds which have a favorable effect on climate; the slowing of the otherwise dangerously rapid fall of raindrops) follow of necessity from the fundamental nature of air. The rainbow depends on the cohesion of the parts of matter (a necessary consequence of the nature of matter in general) and hence is a product of the "very general laws of motion." The spherical rounding of the earth, the resistance of bodies on the earth to centrifugal force, and the retention of the planets in their orbits are all due to the "single force of gravity" (2:106–107; 2:113). But because of the composite character of organisms, the variety of their powers cannot in the same way be regarded as following from a single general ground: the human being "sees, hears, smells, tastes etc., but the properties that are the grounds of seeing are not the same as the grounds of tasting" (2:106).

The distinction is brought out sharply in a passage in which Kant emphasizes the range of different phenomena that he believes can in principle be explained in terms of general forces and laws. We have reason to believe, he says, that "the expansion of bodies through heat, light, electric force, thunder, perhaps even magnetic force are many kinds of appearance of one and the same effective [*wirksam*] matter which is spread out in all spaces, namely ether" (2:113). Snowflakes too, in spite of a regularity and delicacy which appears to be due to artifice, are rightly regarded as a consequence of "more general laws, which comprehend the formation of this product under themselves with necessary unity" (2:113–14). Even the "tree of Diana" (a chemical formation arising from the mixture of silver, mercury, nitric acid, and water) is most probably an effect of the "common laws of sublimation." By contrast, the "construction [*Bau*] of organisms shows a constitution [*Anstalt*] for which the universal and necessary laws of nature are insufficient . . . it would be absurd to regard the first production of a plant or animal as a mechanical consequence [*Nebenfolge*] of universal laws of nature" (2:114).

These passages speak directly to the two sources of ambiguity I pointed out in the notion of a mechanical explanation. The passage from the *Universal Natural History* suggests that the paradigm of a mechanical law is given by the laws of attraction and repulsion that are fundamental to matter as such. It is plausible to suppose that it is primarily these laws which Kant has in mind when he glosses mechanical laws in the third Critique as laws of matter and of motion. But the references in the *Only Possible Proof* to the "laws of sublimation" responsible for the tree of Diana, to the laws necessitating the formation of snowflakes, and to the laws governing "heat, light, electric force, thunder and magnetic force," suggest that the idea of a mechanical law can also be interpreted more broadly as including laws which govern the behavior of particular kinds of matter such as ether, water, and silver. For explaining a phenomenon as a consequence of these laws is assimilated to regarding it as a "mechanical consequence of universal laws of nature"— something that we cannot do in the case of the first production of organisms. And evidence of this broader conception of a mechanical law is to be found in the third *Critique* itself, in Kant's description of various kinds of crystal formation as brought about by the "mechanism of nature" (§58, 5:348–49), and in his identification of the formation of a maggot through the process of putrefaction (then thought to be chemical) with its being produced through "the mere mechanism of matter" (§78, 5:411).

Second, and more important for our purposes, the passages cited make clear that what is at issue is not the kind of explanation that presupposes a specific set of initial conditions. Rather, the issue is the sufficiency of mechanical laws alone to account for something's origin: whether we can explain it without appeal to any particular arrangement, but solely by appeal to the laws governing the (unorganized) matter out of which it comes to be. Thus the claim that organisms are inexplicable on mechanical laws—at least in the context we are considering—does not itself entail that we could never explain the origin of an individual bird as a lawlike consequence of the precise arrangement of matter to be found in an intact egg (as we might explain the ringing of an alarm clock as a lawlike consequence of its state just after having been wound up).[9] It entails only that we cannot explain the origin of a bird by appeal to the powers of unorganized matter, say the powers of the same egg after it has been beaten. As Kant puts it in the *Critique of Judgment*, it is "contrary to reason" that "raw material could have originally formed itself according to mechanical laws, that life could have originated from the nature of the lifeless, and that matter could have arranged (*fügen*) itself in the form of a self-maintaining purposiveness" (§81, 5:424). Rather, all explanation of the origin of organic formations must begin with "organized matter" (ibid.).[10]

3. THE PROBLEM OF BIOLOGICAL REGULARITY: HOW ARE WE TO REGARD IT AS LAWLIKE?

It is clear that the mechanical inexplicability of organisms, thus construed, presents a difficulty for explaining how organisms first came to be. But, as we saw in section 1, this is not the difficulty that the concept of purpose is supposed to help us address: we need to invoke final causes "even only . . . to get to know the constitution [of organisms] through observation, without aspiring to the investigation of their first origin" (§72, 5:389–90). If Kant's argument does not rest on a non sequitur, then there must be a further and more fundamental difficulty presented by the mechanical inexplicability of organisms, one which exists not only for the embryologist and the "archaeologist of nature" (§80, 5:419), but also for the anatomist and the physiologist.

In this section I shall try to say what the difficulty is. By way of approaching this task, I want first to note that the conception of mechanical explanation we identified in the previous section is extremely strong. Most particular things in nature do not admit of mechanical explanation in this sense, since they are not necessitated solely by the laws of matter, or even by the laws governing the particular kind of matter from which they originate. Consider, for example, a jagged fragment of limestone split off from a rock face by the impact of a falling stone loosened by an earthquake. It is contingent with respect to mechanical laws that there has come to be a fragment of precisely that shape, since neither the powers of limestone nor the powers of matter more generally are sufficient to determine that fragments of that particular shape must be formed. This does not mean that it could not be explained as a consequence, on mechanical laws, of the conditions that held just before the impact. For example, given an exact knowledge of the patterns of erosion on the rock face and the trajectory of the falling stone, we might be able to show how a fragment of that shape had to be produced given the laws of motion and the natures of the types of matter involved. But the point is that we need to have precise information about the antecedent conditions; simply knowing the natures of the kinds of matter involved does not put us in a position to deduce the shape of the fragment.[12]

This means that organisms are not unique in being contingent with respect to mechanical laws and hence in lacking explanations that are mechanical in the sense we have identified. On the contrary, most things in nature which we identify as particulars—stones, mountains, rivers, lakes and so forth—are not determined, so far as we can tell, either by the mere forces of matter as such, or by the forces inhering in matter of a particular kind. While we might be able to tell a causal story about why a granite mountain of a particular shape came to be in a certain location, we cannot say that the nature of granite determined that there should be a mountain of just that shape. It is only in a few cases, such as crystals and the solar system, that we can say that the formation of a thing is necessitated by the powers of the matter from which it comes to be. And even in those cases there remains a great deal of contingency: in the time and place that a crystal originates, say, or in the exact sizes, shapes, and locations of the planetary bodies.

If there is so much in nature that does not admit of mechanical explanation in this sense, why does the mechanical inexplicability of organisms deserve special attention? For we can say of the limestone fragment, no less than of the bird, that "nature could have formed itself in a thousand other ways": Things could have turned out so that the fragment had any number of different shapes, or that no fragment broke off at all, or indeed that there was no rock face there in the first place. On the face of it, the answer is obvious. The reason that we ascribe special significance to the mechanical inexplicability of the bird is that it displays an apparent order and regularity that are entirely lacking in the case of the stone fragment. At the most basic level of observation, the bird, unlike the stone fragment, is roughly symmetrical in form, with parts of matching shape and color on each side. Moreover it conforms to certain regular patterns of behavior of a kind not manifested by the stone fragment: for example it is consistently attracted to breadcrumbs and consistently repelled by loud noises. More extended observation and experimentation reveal further regularities in its internal structure and in the behavior of its parts: For example, it has a heart which beats at a rate which is roughly correlated with the levels of certain chemicals in its blood, and muscles which contract more or less predictably in response to certain neural stimuli. And a further level of regularity is manifested in the fact that, under certain circumstances, it produces other birds which come to have roughly the same shape, size, and coloration that it has, and which exhibit the same patterns of behavior. It is because of regularities such as these that organisms seem to call for an explanation: an explanation that mechanical laws alone do not provide. In the case of the stone fragment, by contrast, there does not seem to be anything that needs explaining. Because the fragment exhibits no more regularity than would be exhibited by any random fragment of the same material, we are not dissatisfied with the insufficiency of mechanical laws alone to account for its particular size and shape. The absence of a mechanical explanation in this instance does not constitute a failure that demands to be made good in some other way.

But this suggests that the failure of mechanical explanation in the case of an organism is not so much a failure to account for how that particular organism came to be, as a failure to account for the regularity which the organism exhibits. What calls (in vain) for explanation is not the particular historical event of a certain quantity of matter coming to be arranged in such-and-such a configuration at such-and-such a time; for if it were, the demand for explanation would apply, with no less force, to the case of the stone fragment. Rather, it is the order and regularity manifested by that and similar configurations, and by the processes through which they maintain and replicate themselves. Thus when Kant says that we cannot conceive how unorganized matter left to its own workings could spontaneously form itself into an organism, his point is that the regularities exhibited by organisms cannot be accounted for in terms of the fundamental regularities—those described by the laws of attraction and repulsion—that characterize the behavior of matter at the most general level.

Conversely, where mechanical explanation succeeds, what it succeeds in showing is that certain apparent regularities *can* be accounted for in terms of the fundamental regularities exhibited by matter as such, or at least in terms of regularities exhibited by some particular kind of matter. Thus to show that snowflakes can be mechanically explained is to show that the regularity of the form of a snowflake (in other words its symmetry) can be accounted for in terms of the regularities characterizing the behavior of water and air at freezing point. There is no need to appeal to a special ground of lawlike order over and above the lawlikeness we already ascribe to the basic interactions of the relevant chemical kinds. More fundamentally, in explaining the mechanical origin of the solar system, we are showing how the regularities exhibited by the behavior of the planets—their regular paths, the fact that they are all in the same plane, and so on—can be accounted for in terms of the regularity with which the parts of matter attract and repel one another. Again, no special ground of lawlike order need be invoked to account for the regularity of the planetary motions: Instead, we can view that regularity as a reflection or manifestation of the more fundamental laws governing the motion of bodies as such (planetary or otherwise).

These considerations allow us to reconstrue the mechanical inexplicability of organisms as relevant, not only to the historical question of how they came to be, but also to the investigation of their actual structure and workings. For in carrying out this kind of investigation—typified in Kant's time by natural history, anatomy, and physiology—we are concerned precisely with the regularities which organisms exhibit. Acorns grow into oaks, oaks produce acorns, tadpoles turn into frogs, plants grow toward the light, hearts beat, blood circulates: It is because of these and countless other characteristically biological regularities that the organic world first presents itself to us as a subject for scientific enquiry in its own right. Biological investigation is the attempt to understand the organic world by grasping these regularities and seeing how they are related to one another and to other regularities at a deeper level. We aim to describe and to codify the large-scale observable regularities in the morphology and behavior of organisms (for example in natural history, including taxonomy) and to reveal the less easily observable regularities on which they depend: regularities both in the structure of organisms (anatomy), and in the behavior of the elements of that structure (physiology). In claiming that organisms are mechanically inexplicable, Kant is denying that these regularities, whether on the surface or hidden, can be regarded by us as holding in virtue of the kinds of regularities studied in physics and chemistry. We have to view them as contingent with respect to the fundamental laws of inorganic nature.

At the same time, however, biological investigation of the kind we are considering presupposes that these regularities are genuine rather than apparent: that the patterns we observe do not hold as a matter of sheer coincidence but reflect some kind of necessity in the workings of nature. It presupposes, in effect, that there are laws governing the structure and functioning of organisms and their organic parts: laws that can be revealed either by unaided observation or with the help of dissection and experimentation. For without this presupposition, the investigation would have no point. While we might still formulate generalizations describing the apparent regularities presented to us, we could not regard these generalizations as having even the most limited predictive or counterfactual-supporting force. More importantly, we could not regard these regularities as capable of being understood or explained (as for example we regard the beating of the heart as explicable in terms of its pumping action, and that pumping action in turn as explicable in terms of the contraction of muscles in response to neural stimulus). It would make no more sense to seek an understanding of these regularities than it would to seek an understanding of an apparently regular pattern of heads and tails that came up during a random series of coin-tosses: If there are no underlying rules or principles to grasp, then there is nothing for this kind of understanding to consist in.

But now we can see the difficulty posed for biological investigation by the mechanical inexplicability of organisms. If biological regularities must be regarded as contingent with respect to the fundamental laws of inorganic nature, then how can we regard them as lawful or necessary in the way biological investigation requires?[12] What can we take as the ground of biological regularity, if not the regularity characteristic of matter and its basic kinds? It might be answered that this regularity needs no ground: We can simply take biological regularities to be primitive natural laws in their own right. But this possibility is ruled out for Kant by the principle of nature's purposiveness for our cognitive faculties, on which particular empirical laws must be seen as deriving from more general empirical laws in such a way that the totality of empirical natural laws constitutes an intelligible system.[13] Relatedly, it would entail the ascription of new and irreducible causal powers to each organic species (or at least, in view of Kant's acceptance of the possibility that higher species evolved from lower ones,[14] to the ur-species from which current organisms are descended). And this would violate Kant's prohibition on introducing new fundamental forces into our account of nature, a prohibition without which reason would find explanation too easy.[15] Moreover, irrespective of these Kantian considerations, it is clear that these regularities are poor candidates for basic natural laws, given that the generalizations expressing them are rife with exceptions. Any number of factors can prevent an acorn from developing into an oak or a heart from circulating blood, and there is no prospect of refining the corresponding generalizations in such a way as to rule them all out.

A more sophisticated proposal, one which might seem especially plausible in the light of the discoveries of molecular biology, would be to say that biological regularities do after all derive from the fundamental laws of matter: not *tout court*, as on the hypothesis Kant rejects, but rather in conjunction with the particular arrangement of matter which we find in each kind of organism. According to this answer, all acorns have in common a complex material structure of such a kind that—under appropriate conditions of heat, light, nutrition, and so forth—the laws of matter alone are sufficient to determine its transformation into the kind of complex material structure characteristic of an oak. An acorn or any other organic entity, on this view, is a machine like a clock: Its behavior and even its development can be seen, like the ringing of an alarm clock, as a lawlike consequence of the arrangement of its material parts.[16] As we saw in the previous section, Kant's claim that organisms are mechanically inexplicable is not intended to rule out that they or their states can be lawlike consequences of antecedent arrangements of matter. So it seems to be left open within the framework of Kant's argument that this type of necessity could serve to underwrite the lawlikeness of biological regularities.[17]

However, this proposal relies on the very strong assumption that organic entities such as acorns and hearts do in fact share common internal structures, so that the concept of an acorn is coextensive with the concept of a certain configuration of matter. For it shows the lawlikeness of the behavior of any given acorn, not *qua* acorn, but *qua* particular configuration of matter. And if, as seems plausible, biological classifications do not line up with classifications on the basis of physico-chemical structure, then the kinds of regularities that come out as lawlike on this proposal will cut across the regularities that are of interest to biology.[18]

Even if we accept the assumption, the proposal faces a deeper problem. Depending on the circumstances external to it, the presence of a given configuration of matter can have any number of outcomes, all of which are equally lawlike from the point of view of physics and chemistry. Although it is tempting to describe the ringing of an alarm clock at a given time as a lawlike consequence of its having earlier been set to ring at that time, the ringing follows as a matter of physical law only on the assumption that certain conditions have obtained in the meantime: that the clock has not been bathed in acid, subjected to extreme temperature changes, wired up to a bomb, and so on. If it has been wired up to a bomb after being set, then it may explode at the specified time instead of ringing, and this outcome under the circumstances will be just as much a lawlike consequence of its earlier state as its ringing would have been under other circumstances. The point is even clearer in the case of an acorn, which—although its internal structure might be said to determine that it will grow into an oak—will in fact do so only under very special circumstances. The laws of matter alone make it no less a lawlike outcome of the arrangement of matter in an acorn that it will rot, or be eaten and digested by an animal, or produce a shoot which dies for lack of light: and these consequences are in fact more probable than the acorn's growing into an oak. Yet from the point of view of biological investigation the outcomes are not regarded as equal. We privilege generalizations like "acorns grow into oaks" and "hearts circulate blood" over generalizations like "acorns rot" and "hearts fibrillate," taking the former but not the latter to reflect the lawlike order which biological investigation aims to reveal. The proposal we have been considering fails to recognize this distinction, and so cannot account for the kind of lawlikeness biology presupposes.[19] We are thus left with the difficulty of how to regard the relevant regularities as lawlike in the face of their contingency with respect to the laws of matter.[20]

4. The Notion of a Natural Purpose: Normative Lawlikeness without Design

We saw in the previous section how the mechanical inexplicability of organisms poses a difficulty, not only for explaining the origin of organisms, but also for investigating their structure and workings. It is in view of this difficulty, I now want to claim, that Kant takes the concept of purpose to be required for biological investigation. Initial support for this claim can be found in several passages indicating that it is precisely in order to understand organic phenomena as lawlike or necessary—despite their contingency with respect to mechanical laws—that we must regard organisms as purposes. We are "led to the concept of a purpose of nature" when we are presented with a cause-effect relation "which we find ourselves capable of understanding as lawlike" only by invoking this concept (§63, 5: 366); we need to regard organisms as purposes in order to satisfy reason's need to "recognize the necessity in each form of a natural product" in the case where that form is "contingent with respect to all empirical laws of nature" (§64, 5:370). Similarly, "the concept of connections and forms of nature according to purposes is . . . [a] principle for bringing nature's appearances under rules, where the laws of causality according to the mere mechanism of nature do not suffice" (§61, 5: 360).[21]

But how does the concept of purpose play the role described in these passages? How does it enable us to regard biological regularities as lawlike or necessary? To answer this, we need to look more deeply into what it means, for Kant, to regard something as a purpose. On the interpretation I shall go on to suggest, the concept of a purpose is closely associated with the concept of normativity: To regard something as a purpose is to regard it as subject to normative laws, standards, or constraints.[22] Regarding organisms as purposes thus opens the way to regarding the regularities they exhibit as lawlike in a way which does not conflict with their contingency in relation to mechanical laws: namely, as conforming to normative laws.

The main textual basis for this interpretation is section X of the First Introduction, where Kant draws a parallel between aesthetic and teleological judging. One of the distinguishing features of an aesthetic judgment is that it is "necessary": that is, that in claiming that something is beautiful, I claim that anyone else who judges the object ought to agree with me. Kant begins the section by emphasizing this feature of necessity, a feature that he characterizes in unambiguously normative terms. Aesthetic judgments "make claim to necessity and do not say that everyone judges thus—in that case their explanation would be a task for empirical psychology—but that we *ought* [*sollen*] to judge thus" (20:239). He then turns to teleological judgments, making it clear that they too involve an "ought": "A teleological judgment compares the concept of a natural product according to that which it is, with what it *ought to be*. Here a concept (of a purpose) is laid at the ground of the judging of its possibility, and precedes a priori." We think of the product of nature "that there is something it *ought to be* and we judge according to whether it actually is that way" (20:240).

Kant then goes on to give an example: "I judge of the eye that it *ought* to be suitable for seeing, and although the eye's shape and the constitution and composition of all its parts are, judged according to merely mechanical laws, quite contingent for my judgment, I still think in its form and construction a necessity to be formed in a certain way, that is according to a concept which precedes the formative causes of this organ, without which the possibility of this natural product is not conceivable for me according to any mechanical law of nature." And he then returns to the parallel between the necessity of aesthetic judgments and the necessity invoked in a teleological judgment: "This 'ought' contains a necessity which is sharply distinguished from the physical-mechanical necessity according to which a thing is possible according to mere laws of efficient causes (without a preceding idea of the thing) and can just as little be determined through merely physical . . . laws as can the necessity of the aesthetic judgment be determined through psychological laws" (20:240–41).

This passage makes clear that regarding an organism or one of its organic parts as a purpose is a matter of regarding it as subject to normative standards or constraints. In regarding something as a purpose we take it that there is a certain way it ought to be (or, equivalently, a certain way that it should be, or is meant to be, or is supposed to be). We regard an eye as a purpose because we take it that it ought to be constituted in such a way as to make sight possible: more specifically, that it ought to have a lens which refracts light in such-and-such a way, that it ought to adjust to different levels of illumination, and so on. An eye that does not meet these standards may be judged defective. A stone, by contrast, is not regarded as a purpose because we do not take it that there is any particular way a stone ought to be. Although it is possible to use a stone to bring about a certain effect, we cannot say that it ought to be such as to make that effect possible. This is indicated in the passage which introduces the example of the eye: "I can make use of a stone, in order to smash something on it, or for building . . . but I cannot on that account say that it ought to serve for building. Only of the eye do I judge that it *ought* to be suitable for seeing" (FI X, 20:240).

This seems at first sight to offer a different conception of "purpose" than the more familiar definition I cited at the beginning of section 1, where a purpose is "the object of a concept in so far as the concept is seen as the cause of the object" (§10, 5:220). From that definition, as we saw, it looks as though regarding something as a purpose is a matter of regarding it as having a certain causal history: that of being produced in accordance with a concept in the mind of an intelligent designer. And the question of whether or not something was or was not produced in accordance with design seems to be a very different matter from the question of whether or not it is to be regarded as subject to normative standards.

But in fact these two conceptions are closer than first appears. For (to take the simplest case) when we describe an artifact as a purpose on the ground that it was caused by a concept in the mind of its designer, the type of causation we have in mind already involves a normative element. If something is to qualify as designed and hence as a purpose, the concept of the thing must play, not just any causal role in its production, but a causal role of a specific kind: It must help bring about the object by serving as a normative rule or standard which determines how the object ought to be. It is not enough for the producer just to have the concept in mind while making the object, or even for his or her possession of the concept to be a necessary condition of the object's being produced. In addition, the concept must guide her actions in the production of the object, by specifying what the outcome of those actions should, or ought to, be. We can see this by considering cases in which the last condition is not satisfied. Imagine a portrait painter who is so obsessed with a certain woman that—in spite of his best efforts to represent faithfully the person he is painting—every portrait he paints ends up looking like her. In this case the concept of the woman is causally efficacious in producing her likeness, but we do not want to say that this likeness is produced as a result of design. What is missing is that the painter does not recognize the concept as having a normative bearing on his actions and their outcome. Only if he were to recognize the concept as a normative rule, representing how the outcome of his actions ought to be, would the concept exert the causality characteristic of design.

So far I have argued on textual grounds that to regard something as a purpose, for Kant, is to regard it as subject to normative constraints; and I have also argued that this interpretation can be reconciled with the more familiar conception of a purpose associated with the notion of design. But there is a third and philosophically deeper consideration in support of this interpretation, one that emerges when we recall the second of the two questions raised at the beginning of this paper. How can we consistently think of an object both as a purpose and as a natural product? If thinking of an organism as a purpose means thinking of it as a product of design, how can we think of it as a purpose without also thinking of it as an artifact, and hence ceasing to think of it as natural?

Much of the appeal of the interpretation I have suggested derives from the fact that it allows us to answer this question. To regard something as a purpose without regarding it as an artifact is to regard it as governed by normative rules without regarding those rules as concepts in the mind of a designer. It is thus to think— as we do of the eye in Kant's example—that there is a way it ought to be; yet without invoking the thought of an intelligent producer whose actions are governed by the idea that it ought to be that way. Thinking of an organism as a purpose, then, does not after all mean thinking of it as a product of design. It entails thinking of the organism *as if* designed, in that we regard it, like an actual product of design, as subject to normative constraints. But it does not entail thinking of the organism as *in fact* designed, since we do not think of those constraints as playing a causal role in the organism's coming to be.

Regarding an object in this way is not inconsistent with regarding it as a product of nature. It would be inconsistent only if the idea of production by nature excluded not only the idea of production by an intelligent cause, but also the idea of being subject to norms. But there is no reason to suppose that the one idea does exclude the other. By way of evidence to the contrary, we commonly speak of organisms and their parts as subject to norms, yet without any commitment to the idea that they have a supernatural or other nonnatural origin. We speak of what an organ should do, or is supposed to do, or will do if it works correctly. We also speak of organisms and their parts as defective or malformed, of organic processes as going wrong, and of external circumstances as interfering with this or that aspect of an organism's proper functioning or development. These ways of speaking imply a commitment to normative standards governing the structure and behavior of organisms, standards that may or may not be met in a given case. But they do not imply any commitment to the view that organisms are the product of design, or for that matter to any other view about how organisms came into existence. The question of whether or not we are entitled to apply normative standards to an object is, to all appearances at least, independent of questions about its historical origin.[23]

Now we are in a position to answer the main question with which this chapter is concerned: that of why Kant holds that we need to regard organisms as purposes in order to investigate their structure and workings. If biological investigation is to be possible, we must regard the apparent regularities displayed by organisms as lawlike. Yet organisms are mechanically inexplicable, which is to say that we cannot regard the lawlikeness of these regularities as deriving from the fundamental law-likeness displayed by the workings of inorganic matter. Our only alternative, therefore, is to regard the regularities manifested by the behavior as lawlike in the sense of conforming to *normative* law. The regularity with which an acorn grows into an oak, or a heart circulates blood, is lawlike in so far as these processes conform to laws saying that acorns ought to (are meant to, are supposed to) grow into oaks, or that the heart ought to circulate blood. Regarding organic regularities as lawlike in this way requires that we regard organisms and their parts as subject to normative standards or constraints: and this is just what it is to regard them as purposes.[24]

I claimed earlier that we do in fact commonly characterize organisms and their parts in normative terms. If the argument that I have ascribed to Kant is correct, then it should follow that this normative way of speaking is not a mere option for us, but a pervasive and ineliminable feature of biological discourse. And there is reason to think that this is indeed the case. For it is hard to see how we can make sense of the core generalizations of biology—the generalizations that enable us to grasp the structure and workings of individual living things—without recognizing in them an implicit reference to norms.

Consider, for example, the generalizations that in mammals, blood moves from the right ventricle of the heart into the lungs and then into the left ventricle; or that in the electron transport chain in the mitochondria of eukaryotic cells, the last cytochrome (cytochrome a3) passes its electrons to oxygen; or that in the replication of a DNA molecule, nucleotides line up along each template strand according to base-pairing rules and are linked by enzymes to form new comple-mentary strands. These generalizations are not strictly universal or necessary: they do not say what always happens or what must happen. The passage of the blood can be prevented by obstructions in the blood vessels, or it can be inhibited by defects in the valves; the passage of electrons from cytochrome a3 to oxygen can be blocked by the action of cyanide; ultraviolet radiation can cause covalent linking of adjacent thymine bases on the parent DNA strand, leading to mistakes in rep-lication. Nor is it plausible to regard them as merely statistical: as saying that the blood usually travels through the heart and lungs in the way described, or that DNA molecules are usually replicated according to the base-pairing rules. For— quite apart from the fact that some generalizations of this kind are not statistically born out—this view of them would fail to account for their capacity to yield not only predictions about, but also understanding of, biological processes. It would thus fail to distinguish them from the infinite number of statistical generalizations about organisms that we are capable of making but which lack any theoretical interest.[25]

How then are we to understand these generalizations? The most natural ap-proach is to take them as normative: as capturing not what always happens, nor what usually happens, but rather what is supposed to happen, or what will in fact happen if things go as they ought. They describe the regularities that we see manifested in properly functioning organisms (or other organic entities such as cells or organelles) when nothing interferes. Like the laws of physics and chemistry, they enable us to understand nature and its workings by grasping the regularities characteristic of observable natural processes. But understanding nature, in the context of biological investigation, is a matter of grasping not how things *must* be, but how they *should* be. In seeking to understand the structure and behavior of an organic entity we assume there is a way it is supposed to be and things it is supposed to do, and it is these which our investigation aims to discover.

This does not mean that we are not also interested in cases where organisms fail to function as they should. On the contrary, biological investigation relies heavily on the observation of pathological phenomena, whether naturally or experimentally induced. For example, much of our knowledge of where different cognitive functions are localized in the brain comes from the observation of brain-damaged patients, and (to recur to one example cited earlier) our understanding of the electron transport chain is due in part to research into the effects of cyanide and of other respiratory poisons which interfere with it. But, as these examples suggest, we are mostly interested in these cases not for their own sake, but for the light they shed on the corresponding normal cases: That is, we are interested in them insofar as they tell us what is supposed to happen. And even where we do have a more direct interest in cases of malfunction, the possibility of generalizing about such cases presupposes a grasp of the relevant proper functioning: for example, if we are concerned with what typically brings about the failure of a certain biological system, the generalizations through which we come to understand the conditions of failure are intelligible only if we already understand what the system is meant to do.

If this understanding of biological generalizations is correct, it lends plausibility to the line of argument I have ascribed to Kant. Conversely, Kant's line of argument offers an explanation of why biological generalizations are normative in the way I have described. If we are to regard biological phenomena as a target of scientific investigation, we must regard them as rule-governed, since otherwise they are not a potential object of understanding. But the only way we can regard them as rule-governed, given their contingency with respect to the laws of matter, is to regard them as governed by normative rules. This is what I think Kant has in mind when he says that the "concept of connections and forms of nature according to purposes" serves as a principle "for bringing nature's appearances under rules where the laws of causality according to the mere mechanism of nature do not suffice" (§61, 5:360). It is only by interpreting organic phenomena in normative terms— as conforming (or failing to conform) to rules of the proper functioning of organic beings—that we can bring lawlike order to the otherwise incomprehensible diversity of the organic world. This is why we need the concept of purpose as a heuristic principle or guiding thread for the observation and investigation of organisms, independently of any questions that might be asked about how organisms came to be.

NOTES

I am grateful to Karl Ameriks, Janet Broughton, John Carriero, Strefan Fauble, Michael Friedman, Paul Hoffman, Edwin McCann, and Calvin Normore for helpful comments and questions. I owe special thanks to Randall Amano for his detailed and valuable criticisms of earlier drafts, and to Daniel Warren for much illuminating discussion.

1. References to the *Critique of Judgment* will include section numbers in addition to Akademie edition volume and page numbers. References to the First Introduction of the *Critique of Judgment* are indicated by FI, and cite section number and page number from volume 20 of the Akademie edition. All translations are mine.

2. More precisely, they are not sufficient from the point of view of a discursive intellect, such as humans possess. For an intuitive intellect, the explanatory ground of organic and inorganic nature might coincide, so that the laws of inorganic nature would be sufficient for organisms (see §77, 5:406). Since I will be concerned in this chapter only with explanation from the point of view of a discursive intellect, I will omit this qualification in the rest of the chapter.

3. It should be noted that there is more than one question that can be asked about the origin of an organism: We can ask how a given individual organism originated from a seed or an embryo, how the first members of a given species evolved from earlier species, or how life itself originated from nonliving matter. In the case of the first of these questions, the distinction made in the text between understanding an organism's origin on the one hand, and understanding its structure and workings on the other, is not absolute, since understanding how an individual dog came to be formed in the womb is part of a complete understanding of how dogs "work." However, this does not undermine the central point that purposes are presupposed for Kant in all anatomical and physiological investigations, even those that are not directly concerned with an organism's embryological development.

4. Here I agree with Henry Allison that we must invoke the concept of purpose in regard to organisms "because only in this way can we even begin to conceptualize them" ("Kant's Antinomy of Teleological Judgment," in *The Southern Journal of Philosophy* 30 [1991]: 39). As he notes (ibid., 42 n.32), this view is of a piece with the more general view that an essential role of reflective judgment is the acquisition of empirical concepts. For this more general view, see my *The Role of Taste in Kant's Theory of Cognition* (New York: Garland Publishing, 1990), 182–92, and Allison, "Is the *Critique of Judgment* "Post-Critical"? (forthcoming). Allison maintains in the latter essay that reflective judgment aims, not just at any empirical concepts, but at empirical concepts which are "cognitively significant" (16). "Understanding the possibility" of an organism, as I interpret the phrase, is equivalent to arriving at what Allison calls a "cognitively significant" concept of it.

5. My point here is parallel to one made by Peter McLaughlin in his discussion of the Antinomy of Teleological Judgment, namely that the antinomy cannot be resolved simply by pointing out that the maxims are regulative rather than constitutive (*Kant's Critique of Teleology in Biological Explanation* [Lewiston: Edwin Mellen, 1990], 137–40). See also Allison, "Kant's Antinomy."

6. See also §74, 397 and §78, 413–14.

7. Uses of the term "mechanism" in this sense can be found at *Critique of Pure Reason* Bxxvii, Bxxix, and Bxxxii, and throughout the *Critique of Practical Reason*. The *Critique of Practical Reason* also uses the term "mechanical" in a narrower sense to mean (roughly) "nonpsychological," and it explicitly differentiates this sense from the broader sense borne by the term "mechanism" elsewhere in the work (5:96–7). The narrower use is akin, although not identical, to the third *Critique's* use of "mechanical" in contrast to "teleological."

8. See FI I, 20:173, where Kant describes the rules governing the various practical arts, in contrast to the law of a free will, as rules "for the production of an effect which is possible according to natural concepts of causes and effects." A related point is made in the *Critique of Practical Reason*, 5:96–97, where Kant makes clear that causality can be nonmechanical in the sense of nonpsychological, but still belong to the mechanism of nature in a broader sense. For more discussion see Christel Fricke, "Explaining the Inexplicable," *Noûs* 24 (March 1990): 51.

9. Here it might be objected that Kant holds organisms to be mechanically inexplicable in this stronger sense also. For he claims in the *Only Possible Proof* that we could never understand from the "inner mechanical constitution" of a tree how it could produce another tree (2:114). However, I do not take this kind of inexplicability to follow from the mechanical inexplicability of organisms in the sense with which we are concerned.

10. See also *Critique of Judgment*, 5:419n. and "On the Use of Teleological Principles in Philosophy," 8:179. It should be noted that the interpretation of mechanical inexplicability presented here differs from that of many commentators in that it does not take the mechanical inexplicability of organisms to stem from the "epigenetic" or self-forming character by which organisms are distinguished from machines. See McLaughlin, *Kant's Critique of Teleology*, 152–53, Allison, "Kant's Antinomy," 26–27, 35, Clark Zumbach, *The Transcendent Science* (The Hague: Nijhoff, 1984), 79–92; Paul Guyer, "Organisms and the Unity of Science" (chapter 12 in this volume). More specifically, it is at odds with the interpretation of mechanical explanation offered by McLaughlin and Allison, on which mechanical explanation consists in the reduction of a whole to the powers of its parts (as in the explanation of the workings of a machine in terms of its components). A full treatment of Kant's views on mechanical explanation would require discussion of this latter interpretation, but unfortunately I do not have the space for that here.

11. I take the conception of mechanical explanation here to be sufficiently strong as to exclude explanations of the origin of higher order forms of life by appeal to natural selection, even those which take as their starting point simple self-replicating structures such as crystals (see for example A. G. Cairns-Smith, *Genetic Takeover and the Mineral Origins of Life* [Cambridge: Cambridge University Press, 1982]). Explanations of this kind are excluded because they do not show that the powers of the available materials are sufficient to determine that organisms of the requisite level of complexity necessarily *had* to come into existence. Instead they treat the origin of any given species of organism—and indeed of higher level organisms *tout court*—as a contingent historical event. The contingency here has been emphasized by Stephen Jay Gould (see for example chap. 5 of *Wonderful Life* [New York: W. W. Norton, 1989]). Even Richard Dawkins, who emphasizes by contrast the nonrandomness of natural selection, allows that chance is an ingredient—albeit a minor one—in the Darwinian account (*The Blind Watchmaker* [New York: W. W. Norton, 1987]).

An account of the origin of organisms in terms of natural selection would still qualify for Kant as "mechanical" in the broader sense of not appealing to (conscious) purpose or design. Nonetheless, on the line of thought I am ascribing to him in this chapter, acceptance of such an account would not free us from having to invoke the concept of purpose in order to understand the structure and behavior of organisms. For even though we could dispense with the notion of conscious purpose in accounting for the historical fact of organisms' coming to be, we would still need it—as I argue in the text below—to regard biological regularities as lawlike in the way that anatomical and physiological investigation requires.

12. When I speak of "biological regularities" and of the "biological generalizations" which capture them, I have in mind primarily the kinds of regularities which are the focus of anatomy, physiology, natural history, and more recently of cell and molecular biology: roughly, those which we must grasp in order to understand the behavior of individual organisms and their organic parts. Present-day biologists are interested in regularities of other kinds too, e.g., regularities in processes of speciation or in the patterns of gene flow in populations. But these fall outside the scope of the argument I am ascribing to Kant.

13. See Introduction, IV-V, and FI II, IV-V.

14. See §80, 5:419.

15. See "On the Use of Teleological Principles in Philosophy," 8:179–81.

16. Here I have in mind what Ned Block calls "apparatus necessity" or "apparatus lawlikeness" ("Two Kind of Laws," in *The Philosophy of Psychology: Debates on Psychological Explanation,* ed. C. MacDonald and G. MacDonald [Blackwell: Oxford, 1994] and "Anti-Reductionism Strikes Back," *Philosophical Perspectives* 11 [1997]).

17. This might be contested in view of Kant's denials that organisms are machines (§65, 5: 374) and that the production of one tree from another can be mechanically understood (*The Only Possible Proof* 2:114). However, even though Kant was indeed committed to the nonmachinelike character of organisms, I take this commitment to be distinct from his view that they are mechanically inexplicable in the sense under discussion (see notes 9 and 10), and so I do not want to construe his argument as hinging on it.

18. This point echoes part of a familiar argument against reductionism formulated by Hilary Putnam and Jerry Fodor (see for example Fodor, "Special Sciences," *Synthese* 28 [1974]: 97–115). This kind of argument is often invoked in discussions of psychology, since there is a special plausibility to the claim that a mental concept can be instantiated by different types of physical state. For a similar claim about biological concepts see John Dupré, *The Disorder of Things: Metaphysical Foundations of the Disunity of Science* (Cambridge: Harvard University Press, 1993), chap. 6 (in particular the example of hemoglobin on 125–26).

19. It might be objected that the acorn example is misleading, since it is unlike most biological generalizations in not being borne out statistically. If we leave such examples aside, it might be claimed, we can interpret biological generalizations as expressing statistical laws, where the lawlikeness is ultimately underwritten, as on the original proposal, by the laws of physics and chemistry in conjunction with certain arrangements of matter. But this obscures the difference between those generalizations that are central to our understanding of biological phenomena—the "biological generalizations" invoked in the text—and those which are merely predictive, or which contribute only indirectly to our understanding of these phenomena. Compare the statement "if an infectious agent enters the blood, it is bound to an antibody" with the statement "if carbon monoxide enters the blood, it is bound to hemoglobin." These may be equally statistically likely, and, if so, they will serve equally well to predict what will happen in the organism's bloodstream under the specified circumstances. But we construe them quite differently. In particular, we take the former to be central to understanding the workings of the organism in a way that the second is not: to

the extent that the second helps us to understand something about the organism (e.g. why carbon monoxide is poisonous to it), it is only against the framework of generalizations like the first, which capture the laws according to which the organism operates. The point emerges more vividly when we consider that there are an infinite number of statistical generalizations that we could in principle make about organisms, most of which have no theoretical importance to biology (although some, e.g. generalizations about the effect of diet on the muscle-to-fat ratio of beef cattle, or the rate at which corn grows in various climates, might license predictions of practical value). If we interpret biological generalizations of the kind invoked in the text as merely statistical, then we have failed to capture whatever sets them apart from the vast majority of generalizations about organisms. Of course, it is open to the defender of the statistical interpretation to deny the significance of the distinction I am making, or to argue that it can be accounted for within the context of the interpretation. I do not take myself to have provided a conclusive argument against the interpretation, but simply to have drawn attention to a set of intuitions that prima facie tell against it.

20. Schopenhauer objects that the same difficulty arises for the phenomena of chemistry, electricity, magnetism, etc.: "we shall never succeed in explaining even the solution of a salt in water according to the laws of mechanics proper" (*The World as Will and Representation*, trans. E.J. Payne [New York: Dover, 1969], 533–34). A similar view is suggested by Kant himself in his emphasis on the empirical and contingent nature of chemistry (4: 469, 4:470–71). Why, then, is the concept of purpose not required in, say, chemistry as well as biology? While a full answer to this question lies outside the scope of this chapter, one possible response is that even if chemical regularities cannot be deduced a priori from the fundamental laws of matter, they can still—unlike biological regularities—be said to hold in virtue of these laws and the corresponding forces. We may need experience to know that table salt dissolves in water, or that silver dissolves in nitric acid, but this does not mean that we cannot take the regularity with which these interactions take place to derive from the regularity with which the parts of matter attract and repel one another. The possibility of so doing is in fact suggested by Kant's hypothesis that specific differences among kinds of matter consist in differences in their ratios of attractive to repulsive force (see *Metaphysical Foundations of Natural Science*, 4:533–34): presumably, granted this hypothesis, the regularity with which the kinds interact can be accounted for solely in terms of the regularity with which the operations of these basic forces produce their effects. By contrast, the difficulty presented by biological regularities is not just that they can be discovered only through experience, but that the fundamental forces are insufficient to account for their existence. The contrast here is related to the intuition that biological regularity is of a different order from chemical regularity. Regularity in the biological case does not lie merely in the fact that each kind behaves in a constant way, e.g., oaks always producing acorns and never pinecones, but also in the very existence of the members of the relevant kinds: Simply by positing the existence of an oak we are positing regularity in nature. In the chemical case, however, the regularity consists merely in the constant behavior of chemical kinds: e.g., the fact that silver always dissolves in nitric acid and never in water. The mere existence of, say, silver and nitric acid does not itself—unlike the existence of organisms—constitute a regularity in nature which needs to be accounted for.

21. Also relevant here is Kant's definition of purposiveness as the "lawlikeness of the contingent" (§76, 5:404; see also FI VI, 20:217 and FI VIII, 20:228).

22. For a more extended presentation of this interpretation, see my "Kant on Aesthetic and Biological Purposiveness," in *Reclaiming the History of Ethics*, ed. Andrews Reath, Barbara Herman, and Christine M. Korsgaard (Cambridge: Cambridge University Press, 1997).

23. It might be objected that normative discourse about organisms does depend on a view about their history, namely that they originated by natural selection (see, for example, Ruth Garrett Millikan, "In Defense of Proper Functions," *Philosophy of Science* 56 [1989]). However, it is intuitively implausible that a physiologist or molecular biologist should need to be committed to the theory of natural selection (or to any other theory about the origin of species) in order to be able to investigate what a given organ or system of enzymes is supposed to do, especially since such investigations are carried out largely without reference to the evolutionary history of the organisms or systems they study. Moreover, while in some circumstances knowledge of a species' selection history might help us to identify the norms which apply to organisms of that species, it is hard to see how natural selection on its own could be capable of licensing the application of norms to organisms in general. The historical fact that a trait contributed to the reproductive success of a species does not seem to me to entail that an organism of that species *ought* to have that trait unless it is already assumed that we are entitled to think of organisms in normative terms.

24. This is something of an oversimplification. As I have argued elsewhere, regarding organisms as purposes involves regarding them not only as *subject* to normative constraints, but also as by and large *conforming* to those constraints. For otherwise we could not take ourselves to be capable either of discovering biological laws, or of making predictions (even rough ones) about biological events. I discuss this point further in "Kant on Aesthetic and Biological Purposiveness," in Reath, Herman, and Korsgaard, eds., *Reclaiming the History of Ethics*, and "Lawfulness without a Law: Kant on the Free Play of Imagination and Understanding," *Philosophical Topics* 25 (1997), 37–81.

25. See note 19.

12

Organisms and the Unity of Science

Paul Guyer

1. ORGANISMS AND THE THREAT TO THE UNITY OF SCIENCE

In the appendix to the Transcendental Dialectic in the *Critique of Pure Reason,* Kant outlines his vision of the unity of our science of nature as a goal imposed upon us by the character of our own reason. "If we survey the cognitions of our understanding in their entire range," he says, "then we find that what reason quite uniquely prescribes and seeks to bring about concerning it is the *systematic* in cognition, i.e., its interconnection based on one principle" (A645/B673).[1] Kant illustrates the kind of unifying principle he has in mind with the concept of a "power," or the "causality of a substance" (A648/B677), and thus suggests that a systematic science of nature must ultimately be based on a single kind of causation, or a "fundamental power," presumably exerted by a single kind of substance, underlying what would initially seem to be the many kinds of causation and many kinds of substances we encounter in our experience of nature. To be sure, Kant stresses that the idea of such a power "is at least the problem set by a systematic representation of the manifoldness of [the] powers" of nature (A645/B573),[2] and a few pages later he stresses again that

> Systematic unity (as mere idea) is only a *projected* unity, which one must regard not as given in itself, but only as a problem; this unity, however, helps to find a principle for the manifold and particular uses of the understanding, thereby guiding it even in those cases that are not given and making it coherently connected (A647/B675).

Because no specific and determinate conception of the unifying principle for all knowledge of nature in the form of a single kind of causation or power is actually given by reason's mere idea of it, Kant calls it a "regulative" rather than "constitutive" principle for our conduct of scientific inquiry.

This designation suggests that this goal of a single principle explaining everything in nature may never be fully realized, but at the same time seems to assume
that we will never encounter anything in our experience which could conclusively
prove that this goal *cannot* be reached:

> What is strange about these principles . . . is this: . . . even though they con-
> tain mere ideas to be followed in the empirical use of reason, which reason
> can follow only asymptotically, as it were, i.e., merely by approximation,
> without ever reaching them, yet these principles, as synthetic propositions
> *a priori*, nevertheless have objective but indeterminate validity, and serve as
> a rule of possible experience, and can even be used with good success, as
> heuristic principles, in actually elaborating it (A663/B691).

The idea of a single type of matter, operating ultimately by means of a single type
of causation or power, Kant seems to suppose, is one that we can never reasonably
expect to be fully exemplified in our empirical science of nature, but yet at the
same time one that we can know a priori will never be conclusively falsified by it.

In the Critique of Teleological Judgment, however, the second half of the *Critique of Judgment* published nine years after the *Critique of Pure Reason*, Kant
appears to argue precisely what the first *Critique* had supposed never could be
shown, namely that we have good reason to suppose that we can never succeed in
bringing all of nature under a single principle attributing a single fundamental
power to a single kind of substance. The third *Critique* appears to argue that we
can never explain fundamental and indispensable properties of what Kant calls
"organized beings" and "physical ends," that is, what we now call organisms, by
means of the same mechanical laws of causation by which we can at least potentially
fully explain the behavior of inanimate matter in all of its myriad forms. Organisms, Kant argues, depend on "a causality that cannot be combined with the mere
concept of a nature without ascribing an end to nature" (§64, 5:371).[3] Kant argues
that it is only our experience of organisms that forces us to explain anything in
nature by means of final causes, thus teleologically rather than mechanically, so he
is not mounting an a priori argument that reason's idea of ultimately explaining
everything in nature by means of a single fundamental power is doomed. But his
position in the first *Critique* seemed to express an a priori assurance that the
possibility of approaching ever closer to such an explanatory ideal could not be
confuted by experience, thus even an empirical reason for assuming the necessity
of teleological explanation would conflict with that position. So the question naturally arises, does Kant's account of our teleological judgment of organisms in the
third *Critique* undermine his assurance in the first that we can always asymptoti-
cally approach the ideal of a single fundamental power and principle for all of our
knowledge of nature?

In the Critique of Teleological Judgment, Kant further argues that once we have
been forced to introduce teleological judgment in order to accommodate our ex-

perience of some objects in nature, namely organisms, it is natural for us to see whether the whole of nature, even including the vast array of inorganic materials and objects that would not of themselves force teleological judgment upon us, may not also be judged teleologically, as part of a single system in which the organic and inorganic are all related as means to some ultimate end. Thus Kant says:

> It is thus only matter, insofar as it is organized, which necessarily carries with it the concept of it as an end of nature, since its specific form is at the same time a product of nature. But this concept necessarily leads to the idea of the whole of nature as a system in accordance with the rule of ends, to which idea all mechanism of nature must be subordinated in accordance with principles of reason (at least to investigate the appearance of nature thereby) (§67, 5:378–79).

And indeed, Kant continues, once our experience of organisms has led us to consider whether all of nature may not be looked at as a system of means to some final end, it also becomes inevitable for us to consider whether there may not be a teleological explanation for the existence of natural beauty as well, although this is a question that Kant had explicitly abjured in the Critique of Aesthetic Judgment (see §31, 5:279–80):

> Also beauty of nature, i.e., its concordance with the free play of our cognitive faculties in the apprehension and the judging of its appearance, can be considered in this manner as an objective purposiveness of nature in its entirety, of which the human being is a member: when, that is, the teleological judging of it by means of natural ends, which has been provided to us by organized beings, has justified us in the idea of a great system of the ends of nature (§67, 5:380).

Thus Kant argues that our experience of organisms leads us to consider all of nature from a teleological point of view, and thus presumably to explain everything in it by reference to final as well as mechanical causation. And then our question about the first *Critique's* ideal of a systematic science unified by its single ultimate principle of explanation becomes even more pressing. Does Kant end up asserting not just that some objects in nature must be explained by one fundamental principle while others can only be explained by another, but rather that every object in nature must be susceptible of two radically different kinds of explanation?

If so, perhaps this would solve rather than exacerbate the conflict between Kant's account of organisms and his ideal of the unity of natural science, and do so in a manner continuous with one of Kant's earliest ideas. Early in his career, Kant had argued that it is not any contingency relative to the laws of nature, for example, miracles, that furnishes the basis for conceiving of an intelligent and purposive author of nature, but the very regularity of those laws, which can be conceived as the means through which the author of nature achieves his ends. This is the vision that Kant called "the revised method of physico-theology" (2:123) in *The Only Possible Basis for a Demonstration of the Existence of God* of 1763. Here Kant wrote that

> The spirit of true philosophy is most powerfully manifest in the following method of judging the perfect provisions of nature. . . . Above all, it allows neither nature's aiming at interest, nor all its harmoniousness, to hinder it from trying to discover their foundations in necessary and universal laws. And in the attempt to discover these grounds, it always pays careful attention to the preservation of unity, displaying a rational aversion to multiplying the number of natural causes in order to explain the benefits and harmony of nature. If, in addition to this, the physico-theological mode of judging also concentrates its attention on the universal rules which are capable of explaining the ground of the necessary connection, which holds between, on the one hand, that which occurs naturally without special provision, and, on the other hand, the rules relating to the advantage and convenience of rational beings, and if one then proceeds to ascend to the Divine Being—if all these conditions are satisfied, then this mode of judging will fulfill its obligations in a fitting fashion (2:136–37).

Kant's idea is that it is precisely a systematic explanation of all the phenomena of nature by some single, coherent sets of laws, presumably one conforming to the regulative ideal for a systematic cognition of nature subsequently outlined in the *Critique of Pure Reason,* that is the only basis for a successful inference from features of nature to the existence of God, who demonstrates both his wisdom and his power precisely by being able to accomplish all of his rational ends *through* the uniform and unified laws he has legislated for nature. Such a view would then suggest a model for the resolution between the regulative ideal of the unity of science on the one hand and the teleological view of the world as a whole to which we are led by our experience of organisms on the other: We could see a systematic cognition of nature ultimately aimed at the recognition of a single fundamental principle, as the only natural goal of our *theoretical* use of reason, while at the same time allowing that from a standpoint other than that of theoretical reason alone it might be natural for us to see this very systematic unity of natural laws as the means by which some higher purpose—of God or, as it may turn out, ourselves—is realized.

I believe that the *Critique of Judgment* was meant to be Kant's mature statement of such a vision, and that his basic reason for discussing organisms at all was precisely that these are the objects *within* our experience that can prompt us to take this twofold view of nature. But the special case of organisms also threatened the grand vision by threatening the assumption that there could be a single mode of explanation for all of nature within the theoretical point of view: the Critique of Teleological Judgment offers specific reasons why we cannot comprehend organisms by a mechanical model of causation and thus cannot use a single mode of explanation for all objects *in* nature. The material that has come down to us under the name of the *Opus postumum* indicates that Kant continued to struggle with this problem for the rest of his life. So we need to examine Kant's arguments about the exceptional status of organisms in both the third *Critique* and the *Opus postumum*. In doing so, we shall find the following. In the Critique of Teleological Judgment, Kant provides three different arguments for the necessity of judging organisms teleologically. First, we cannot comprehend the reciprocal causality demonstrated in various organic processes by means of our ordinary conception of causation, but can comprehend it only by conceiving of it as if it were the expression of purposive design. Second, our conception of life itself is inconsistent with the application of our ordinary conception of causation, in the form of the law of inertia, to all matter, so we have to view life as having a source outside of matter. Third, we cannot explain the complete determinacy of living organisms by means of the always merely general laws of nature that our ordinary science provides us. Each of these arguments is in fact problematic. The third argument proves too much, for it applies to all particular objects, not just organisms, and thus would not show that there is any fundamental difference between the laws that we can formulate for organisms and those we can formulate for the rest of nature. Kant does not explicitly acknowledge this objection, but he also does not seem to have repeated this argument after the third *Critique*, so perhaps he silently let it drop. By contrast, Kant himself rejects the second argument in the *Opus postumum*, by arguing that the law of inertia would render *all* motion inexplicable in a self-contained universe unless that universe includes an internal source of motion, to be found in an all-pervasive and self-moving ether which can also be considered as a *vis vivifica*, a life-force that is apparently sufficient to explain the phenomenon of organic life. Finally, in the *Opus postumum* Kant tries to refine rather than reject the initial argument of the Critique of Teleological Judgment: that we can only understand the reciprocal causality we observe in organisms by seeing it as if it were the product of purposive design. However, Kant's most explicit refinement of this argument, that the *unity* of the design of an organism implies an indivisible and hence immaterial substance as its cause, is a clear case of a paralogism of pure reason. This leaves standing what is perhaps only the passing suggestion that we must conceive of the purposiveness of organisms as an exception to the ordinary laws of nature because we can only conceive of purposiveness itself on the model of our own *free* purposiveness. But since our only reason for conceiving of our own purposiveness as free is our recognition of our obligation under the moral law, and Kant always argues that our own freedom as moral agents must be fully compatible with the complete determination of our behavior as natural beings by natural laws, he at least *should* conclude that organisms too, just like ourselves, can at least in principle be understood by viewing them from the two different standpoints of theoretical and practical reason, rather than by seeing two different kinds of law at work *within* nature. Thus Kant should have reached the position that although the distinction between the organic and the inorganic may be the most fundamental distinction to be drawn in the complete classification of matter, and our experience of organisms may play a special heuristic role in suggesting a teleological view of the whole of nature to us, it is only our awareness of the freedom of our own purposiveness that leads us to conceive of the purposiveness of organisms as necessitating a fundamental split between the teleological and mechanical views of nature—in which case, however, we should also conceive of the teleological view even of organisms as thoroughly compatible with the ideal of a complete mechanical explanation of their behavior. But there is no adequate evidence that Kant ever did reach such a settled view of what we learn from the case of organisms.

2. THE ARGUMENTS OF THE CRITIQUE OF TELEOLOGICAL JUDGMENT

2.1

The first argument of the Critique of Teleological Judgment, and the one to which Kant devotes the most space, is that paradigmatic organic processes cannot be understood by our ordinary, mechanical conception of causation. Kant does not define this ordinary conception, but seems to assume that it is both logically and temporally unidirectional: that is, the character of a composite whole is always explained by the character of its parts, which are in turn both logically independent of and temporally antecedent to the whole. His argument is then that we are incapable of explaining organic processes such as reproduction, growth, and self-preservation simply as processes of combining antecedently extant, fully formed parts into a subsequent whole or of adding such parts to an already existing whole and thereby changing its character, processes in which the (combination or addition of) antecedent parts would always be the cause and the subsequent whole or its modified state would always be the effect. Instead, on Kant's account, we can only conceive of an organism as "cause and effect of itself" (§64, 5:370). In the case of reproduction—the most opaque of Kant's examples—the idea seems to be that instead of one or two antecedent combinations of parts (the parents) producing a subsequent new combination of parts (the offspring)—a process that could be explained mechanically—reproduction actually involves a whole, namely a species, producing one of its own parts, namely a member of the species (§64, 5:371).[4] In the case of growth, the idea is that instead of simply adding pre-existing parts to itself, a growing organism "first processes the matter that it adds to itself into a specifically-distinct quality, which the mechanism of nature outside of it cannot provide, and develops itself further by means of a material which, in its composition, is its own product" (§64, 5:371). For example, a growing plant, instead of just adding bits of soil and water to itself, transforms the material that it takes in into its own characteristic form of cellulose; this is to be understood as the whole plant modifying what are to become its parts, rather than the converse. Finally, in the case of organic self-preservation or self-maintenance, parts are seen as having a reciprocal dependence on each other as well as upon the whole: In a deciduous tree, for instance, the continued life of the whole tree depends upon the proper functioning of such parts as its roots and leaves, but then again the emergence of a new set of leaves each spring depends upon the continued health of the whole tree; and while the growth of the roots each season depends upon the sugar produced by the leaves, at the same time the leaves can only function if they are supplied with water by the roots: In Kant's words, "the preservation of the one part" of the tree "is reciprocally dependent on the preservation of the other" (§64, 5:371). These various forms of reciprocal dependence—the dependence of a whole on its parts but at the same time of the parts on the whole, and the reciprocal dependence of parts on each other—Kant thinks of as cases of reciprocal causation: The whole is both effect and yet cause of its parts, and the parts are both cause and effect of each other. And this, Kant claims, cannot be understood by our ordinary model of causation, because "insofar as the causal combination is thought merely through the understanding, it is a connection that constitutes a series (of causes and effects) which always goes in one direction [*immer abwärts geht*]" (§65, 5:372).

To cope with this, Kant supposes, we need to conceive of the production and functioning of organisms by means of a conception of final *(nexus finalis)* rather than merely mechanical or efficient causation *(nexus effectivus)* (§65, 5:372), where final causes are understood on the model of our own intentional production of artifacts. "In the sphere of the practical," Kant says, "(namely of art), we readily find such a connection, as where, e.g., the house is, to be sure, the cause of the moneys that are taken in as rent, but yet, conversely, the representation of this possible income was the cause of the erection of the house" (§65, 5:372). That is, in a case of final causation such as our own intentional production of an artifact, the whole can be both cause and effect of itself without violating our unidirectional conception of efficient causation in this way: Our *representation* of the whole (and of its potential value) is the cause (a final cause) of our acquisition and/or fabrication of the necessary parts (as material cause), the ensuing combination of which in accordance with a plan (a formal cause) derived from that antecedent representation of the whole is the (efficient) cause of the subsequent actual existence of the intended whole. Thus, Kant proposes that we can reconcile the reciprocal causation that we observe in organisms with the only form of causation we actually understand, progressive or unidirectional causation, by thinking of organisms as if their complex organization is the product of an antecedent design for them which is part of an intelligible unidirectional causal sequence. And if this is so, then we must also think of there being some purpose that organisms serve, for an intelligent agent does not create a design (a formal cause) without some purpose (a final

cause) in mind: In Kant's words, the "causality" behind organisms "must be assumed as if it were possible only through reason; but this is then the faculty for
acting in accordance with ends (a will); and the object, which is represented as
possible only through this, will be represented as possible only as an end" (§64, 5:
370).[5]

Of course, the analogy between the human production of artifacts and the
natural functioning of organisms is only partial. In particular, while we conceive
of there being a variety of reciprocal relations among the parts of an artifact, such
as the parts of a complex watch, that can only be explained by reference to an
antecedent design, we do not conceive of a watch as being able to replace its own
parts as needed—"one wheel is not the efficient cause of the production of another" (§65, 5:374)—nor do we conceive of our artifacts as being able to reproduce
themselves.[6] In other words, though we appeal to our own artifacts to understand
organisms, in the case of artifacts our exercise of causation is external to the functioning of the object once we have produced it, while in the case of an organism
"its parts themselves combine into the unity of a whole by being reciprocally cause
and effect of its form" (§65, 5:373). More generally, the intricacy of organisms
exceeds our own capacity for design. So, Kant says, "we say far too little about
nature and its capacity in organized products when we call this an *analogue* of *art*"
(§65, 5:374), or at least of our art. Thus, although we must conceive of the agency
behind the design of organisms in analogy with our own voluntary production of
artifacts, we must also conceive this agency as possessing intellect and powers
greater than our own. Only thus can our conception of the causality behind organisms be that "of a being that possesses a causality according to concepts adequate for such a product" (§65, 5:373). And since we have neither empirical evidence nor theoretical proof of the existence of such an author of nature—though
later Kant will remind us that we have good grounds in practical reason for postulating such a thing—we can only use the notion of an organism as the product
of design as a regulative principle for heuristic purposes. In Kant's words,

> The concept of a thing, as an end of nature in itself, is thus not a constitutive
> concept of understanding or of reason, but it can still be a regulative concept
> for the reflective power of judgment, in accordance with a remote analogy
> with our causality in accordance with ends, for guiding the investigation of
> objects of this sort and reflecting on their supreme ground (§65, 5:375).

Kant's idea is that we can use the analogy between organisms and our own designed
artifacts to posit ends for particular parts of the organisms, which will in turn guide
us in our investigation of the mechanical causation manifested in those organs.

In spite of the limits that must restrict any analogy between ourselves and the
causality behind the existence of organic nature, in Kant's view this analogy suffices
to introduce a conception of not only internal but also external purposiveness for
organic nature: That is, we must not just represent the parts and the whole of

organisms as reciprocally related, but must also be able to conceive of some purpose for their very existence. Moreover, once we have conceived of an intelligent and purposive author of organic nature, it is inevitable for us to conceive of such a being as the author of all of nature, and as having a purpose in the creation of nature as a whole: "This concept necessarily leads to the idea of the whole of nature as a system in accordance with the rule of ends, to which idea all mechanism in nature must be subordinated in accordance with principles of reason (at least to investigate the appearance of nature thereby)" (§67, 5:379).[7] This feature of the analogy leads to the larger argument that is the chief point of the Critique of Teleological Judgment: Though we are driven to raise the question of the purpose of nature by (the limits of) our theoretical comprehension, only practical reason can furnish a candidate for this end, namely our own existence as moral agents. Thus reflection on nature leads us to the goal of our own morality, while at the same time, by means of the argument from the idea of the highest good that Kant restates in the final sections of the third *Critique*, morality itself also requires us to think of nature as a realm in which the ends that we set for ourselves as moral agents may be realized, and thus leads to the same postulate of the intelligent authorship of nature to which we are driven by the peculiarities of comprehending organisms. But a detailed discussion of this argument must be omitted here.[8]

2.2

Kant's second argument against a unified treatment of inorganic and organic matter comes in the course of the Dialectic of Teleological Judgment. In order to resolve an apparent antinomy between the maxims that everything in nature can be explained mechanically and some things in nature can only be explained by final causes (§70, 5:387), Kant considers different possible accounts of what might explain the appearance of purposiveness in nature. We might consider these to be alternative accounts of the ontological rather than the epistemological status of purposiveness in nature, since they are alternative accounts of what such purposiveness might be rather than accounts of how we might come to know it exists. The proposed accounts fall into two groups, each of which has two members. On one side is what Kant calls the "idealism" of natural ends, which would maintain that purposiveness in nature is "unintentional" and merely apparent and can be explained away by a proper understanding of the laws of nature; on the other side is the "realism" of natural ends, which maintains that purposiveness in nature is "intentional" and cannot be explained away—at least not by us, for we must remember that the epistemological status of this claim is regulative and heuristic (§72, 5:391). The two species of the idealism of natural ends are those of "casuality" *(Casualität)* or "accidentality," on the one hand, and "fatality" on the other. Casuality is the view of Democritus or Lucretius that all complexity in nature, a fortiori the appearance of purposiveness, is due to the utterly random collision of particles; fatality is the view of Spinoza that everything in nature can be explained as due to the inexorable laws of an original being but is not due to any intelligence in such a being (§72, 5:391). The two species of the realism of natural ends are the "physical" and the "hyperphysical": The first, or "hylozoism," is the view that life, and purposiveness, is "in matter, or, through an animating inner principle, in a world-soul"; the second, or "theism," is the view that the principle of organic life is not within the organisms themselves but is "a primordial ground of the world-all, as an intelligent being producing it with intention" (§72, 5:392). Kant then argues that the Lucretian view does not even explain the appearance of design in nature, while the Spinozist view explains too much, by leaving no room even for the appearance of contingency in nature (§73, 5:393). Then—and this is the argument we are interested in—he claims that "hylozoism" or physical realism with regard to natural ends must fail, because the idea that matter could contain in itself an originating life-force, let alone a principle of action in accordance with purposes, is incompatible with the law of inertia. As Kant puts it, "the possibility of a living matter" is contradictory because "lifelessness, *inertia,* constitutes the essential character of matter" (§73. 5:394); presumably the law of inertia implies that matter can never originate any change at all unless acted upon by an agent external to it.

Kant had stated this argument in his metaphysics lectures (Metaphysik L1) as early as the mid-1770s:

> Animals are not mere machines or matter, rather they have souls; for everything in the whole of nature is either inanimate or animate. All matter as matter (matter as such) is inanimate. From what do we know that? The concept we have of matter is this: Matter is an extended, impenetrable, inert thing. When, e.g., we perceive a mote on a paper, then we look to see whether it moves. If it does not move of itself, then we hold it to be inanimate matter, which is inert, and which would remain lying for all eternity if it were not moved by something else. But as soon as a matter moves, then we look to see whether it moved itself voluntarily. If we perceive that in the mote, then we see that it is *animate,* it is *an animal.* An animal is thus an animated matter, for life is the faculty for determining oneself from an inner principle according to the power of choice. But matter, as matter, has no inner principle of self-activity, no spontaneity to move itself, rather all matter that is animate has an inner principle which is separated from the object of outer sense, and is an object of inner sense. . . . Thus: All matter which lives is alive not as matter but rather has a principle of life and is animated. But to the extent matter is animated, to that extent it is *ensouled* (28:275).

Presumably Kant would have had to refine this argument to take care of the case of plants as well as animals: Plants would appear to have the power to generate motion from some internal principle, but not from the power of choice, and thus would not seem to be ensouled (even from a merely regulative point of view). So perhaps the noninertial principle of motion in plants could thus not be represented as an immaterial substance conjoined to lifeless matter like an animal's soul, but might instead have to be represented as the product of a soul-like substance that is not literally joined to its matter. But this would only mean that plants would draw us even more directly to the idea of an intelligent author of their design than animated organisms do.

In the Dialectic of Teleological Judgment, Kant does not expound the argument in such detail, let alone distinguish between its application to plants and to animals. But he does complete his discussion of the systems of purposiveness by arguing that although we can have no direct evidence for the truth of theism, that is, for the actual existence of a purposive and intelligent author of nature, at least this hypothesis is internally coherent, free of an outright contradiction like hylozoism, and can thus be adopted as a principle for reflective if not for determinant judgment (§73, 5:394). This conclusion, of course, paves the way for the larger objectives of the third *Critique*.

2.3

In the next part of the Dialectic, Kant gives an extended exposition of his third argument for the special status of natural ends. This is the argument that because of the discursive character of our understanding, that is, its restriction to the use of general concepts, there must always be much in the form of any particular entity in nature that cannot be regarded as determined by our general concepts for it: In cognition by means of our understanding "the particular is not determined by it through the general, and the former cannot therefore be derived from the latter alone" (§77, 5:406). Kant then interprets this to entail that much in the particular forms of nature remains contingent (*zufällig*) relative to all the general concepts of nature that we do or can ever possess. And this in turn he takes to mean that the *agreement* or *harmony (Zusammenstimmung)* of particular forms in nature with our general concepts must seem contingent to us. But this, he supposes, is incompatible with the very "possibility of an agreement of the things in nature with the power of judgment," and to make even this possibility intelligible to ourselves we must therefore "think of another understanding, in relation to which, and especially to the end that is ascribed to it, we can represent that agreement of natural laws with our power of judgment . . . as *necessary*" (§77, 5:407). That is, in order to explain even the possibility of our comprehension of particular things in nature, we have to postulate an intelligent author of nature whose concepts make necessary what appears merely contingent to us.

I am expounding this as a separate argument in Kant's thought about the distinctive character of organisms because it turns on neither the alleged reciprocal causality of organisms nor the supposedly self-contradictory concept of living matter. Kant himself does not draw a clear boundary between this argument and his original argument that the reciprocal causality characteristic of organisms is incompatible with our ordinary conception of causality. In fact, he intertwines these two arguments in his very first exposition of the argument about the special causality of organisms, taking that argument to imply the "*contingency* of the form [of an organism] in relation to reason given all the empirical laws of nature," and then arguing that because reason must nevertheless be able to "cognize the necessity in every form of a product of nature," it must therefore introduce at least the idea of a causality of nature, that is, a designer of it, for whom what appears contingent to us can be necessary (§64, 5:370). Yet there is at least one key difference between the arguments of §64 and §77: In the argument of §64, particular features of the forms of organisms will appear contingent relative to the *causal* concepts of our understanding because those concepts are incapable of representing reciprocal causality; in the argument of §77, the forms of organisms appear to be contingent relative to *any* concepts of our understanding just because those concepts are always general and therefore necessarily leave something in their particular objects indeterminate. So it seems worth considering the argument of §77 as a separate argument in the larger project of showing that our experience of organisms requires us to introduce a teleological conception of nature into the principles of reflective judgment.

3. THE FATE OF THESE ARGUMENTS

I now turn to the problems with these arguments and to Kant's further attempts to clarify the special status of organisms in the *Opus postumum*. I will consider the fate of these arguments in an order inverse to that in which I have just expounded them.

3.1

I begin with the argument from the contingency of natural forms to the need for a special principle of intelligent design to explain them (2.3) because of the obvious problem with this argument. By the obvious problem with this argument I do not mean to refer to the question it might well suggest: Why do we need to postulate an author of nature with concepts of its particular forms that make everything in them necessary in order to explain even the *possibility* of our successfully applying general concepts to them? This is indeed a question that can be raised about all of Kant's arguments for postulates, whether of reflective judgment or practical reason, but it is a difficult question that I will not pursue here.[9] Rather, the obvious problem is simply that the argument from contingency as separately stated in §77 has nothing special to do with *organisms*: It is a general argument that can be made about all particulars in nature, organic or inorganic, because any general concept leaves some thing undetermined about any particular object that falls under it. Any general concept of a kind of mineral, for example, will leave many things undetermined about any particular mineral sample that is subsumed under it, for example, its size or weight, perhaps its color or smell, perhaps even the number of neutrons in the atoms of its different isotopes. And if we are looking for a guarantee that our power of judgment will always be able to come up with even a general concept for any particular object we encounter, as Kant's argument about the conditions for even the possibility of harmony between our power of judgment and nature suggests, we will need that guarantee just as much for all the variegated minerals we encounter as well as for the immense diversity of organisms we experience.

Kant does not appear to make this objection to his own argument explicitly. But in the published introduction to the *Critique of Judgment*—the very last part of it to be written, as we know, extracted out of Kant by the publisher's constant pleading as the typesetting of the rest of the text approached completion—Kant deploys an argument of the same form in a way that presupposes its utter generality. This is his argument that because the categories of pure understanding that we are always able to impose upon our experience of nature in virtue of the constitution of our own minds furnish only the most general laws of nature, such as the general principles of causality or conservation, our confidence that we can succeed in discovering a system of particular laws of nature can only be based on the idea, valid of course for the reflective use of judgment only, that the particular laws of nature are also due to an understanding, but an understanding more powerful than our own. In Kant's words:

> There are such manifold forms of nature, as it were so many modifications of the general transcendental concepts of nature that are left undetermined by those laws that the pure understanding gives *a priori*, because these only pertain to the possibility of a nature (as an object of the senses), that there must also be laws, which, although they may certainly be contingent as empirical according to the insight of *our* understanding, must nevertheless, if they are to be called laws (as is also demanded by the concept of a nature), be regarded as necessary on the basis of a principle of the unity of the manifold, even if it is unknown to us. . . . Now this principle can be nothing other than that . . . the particular empirical laws, with regard to that which is left undetermined in them by [our general concepts of understanding], must be considered in accordance with such a unity as would be given to them by an understanding (even if not ours) for the sake of our faculty of cognition, in order to make possible a system of experience in accord with particular laws of nature (Introduction IV, 5:179–80).

At this point in the Introduction Kant has said nothing about the special status of organisms—that is not mentioned until section VIII of the Introduction, and then only barely. Instead, at this point he seems to assume that all of the particular laws of nature that we can discover can be unified into a single system, regardless of what particular objects in nature they deal with, and to be arguing that in order to overcome the appearance of contingency that appears to threaten our confidence in *that* possibility we must postulate the idea of a guiding intelligence behind the laws of nature. This argument would appear to apply to laws of geology and mineralogy just as well as to laws of biology and psychology and to imply that we could be led to the idea of an intelligent principle for nature by reflecting on the necessary conditions for the determinacy of any of these laws as well as on the condition of the possibility of unifying all such laws in a single system.

This argument in the Introduction is of the same form as the argument of §77, arguing that we can only ascribe necessity to something left contingent by the generality of our own concepts by postulating an understanding which does not suffer from this defect of our own. This at least implies that the argument of §77 has nothing to do with organisms in particular. Kant does not state this explicitly, but neither does he use this argument again in any of his discussions of the status of organisms after the *Critique of Judgment.*

3.2

I now turn to Kant's argument that organisms require a special mode of judgment because the law of inertia requires that matter be conceived as lifeless (2.2). Kant seems to undermine the premise of this argument in the *Opus postumum* by arguing that we cannot conceive of nature in general as a purely inertial system merely transmitting from one region or object to another the effects of some initial external impetus. Instead, he argues throughout this work, any conception of nature requires the postulation of an internal principle of motion that we can construe as the origin of all motion in nature. So at least insofar as the organic is that which contains its own internal principle of motion, the organic is not by that fact alone distinguished from inorganic matter. Kant's intentions in the mass of notes that have come down to us as the *Opus postumum* are notoriously obscure. Nevertheless, it seems reasonably clear that he wanted to make a transition from pure philosophy to an empirically applicable physics by constructing a system *of forces* that could ultimately be seen as deriving from some single elementary force, and that he wanted also to make a division of the fundamental types of *matter.* In the latter division, the distinction between organic and inorganic matter is always primary, and Kant often presents the purposiveness evident in the former but not the latter as the basis of this distinction. At the same time, it seems as if Kant also wanted to argue that both organic and inorganic matter can be joined in a single system of forces, because even inorganic matter cannot, contrary to the assumption underlying Kant's rejection of hylozoism in the *Critique of Judgment,* be understood as utterly lifeless, but is instead connected to a force that is also adequate to explain the mobility of living things.

This is, to be sure, not evident in everything that Kant writes in the *Opus postumum.* In an early passage, for instance, he writes that "*living* force (by impact) (*vis viva*) is different from the *vivifying* force (*vis vivifica*). The latter, in a separate world-system (and its generation) is perhaps the cause of *plants* and *animals*" (22: 210). This seems to suggest that there is a difference between the *vis viva* of inorganic matter and the *vis vivifica* of organic matter, and that the difference between these two forces is enough to entail that the organic and the inorganic constitute two separate world-systems.

Subsequently, however, Kant devotes many pages to arguing that motion in a system of even inorganic bodies cannot be understood as due to impact operating through the law of inertia alone, but that an internal and perpetual source of motion must be posited within nature itself, as the fundamental force of a fundamental matter that is never directly observed but is not a mere postulate (like God or the immortal soul) either—

> a matter, distributed in the whole universe as a continuum, uniformly penetrating all bodies, and filling [all space]. . . . Be it called ether, or caloric, or whatever, it is no *hypothetical material* . . . rather it can be recognized, and postulated *a priori,* as an element necessarily belonging to the transition from the metaphysical foundations of natural science to physics (21:218).

Kant gives a variety of reasons for this "*a priori* postulate," but it is important to note that none of them is restricted to any one kind of matter. Some of his arguments have to do with the conditions of the possibility of our perception of objects at a distance; others have to do with the very possibility of the existence of bodies, independent of the fact that we perceive them. One early passage argues for the ether for two reasons: first, to have a force even more fundamental than the opposed forces of attraction and repulsion which are necessary to explain how matter can coalesce, being neither infinitely dispersed nor infinitely condensed into a single point; second, to explain why motion does not cease in the universe.

> All matter must have repulsive forces, since otherwise it would fill no space; but attractive force must also be attributed to it, since otherwise it would disperse itself into the infinity of space—in both cases space would be empty. Consequently, one can think of such alternating impacts and counterimpacts [as existing] from the beginning of the world, as a trembling (oscillating, vibrating) motion of the matter which fills the entire universe, includes within itself all bodies, and is both elastic and at the same time attractive in itself. These pulsations constitute a living force. . . .
>
> An elastic fluid in the state of internal vibration necessarily occupies a greater space than in the state of rest. Thus is brought about, as the effect of a living force, the extension of matters in cosmic space. . . .
>
> The reason to assume such a hypothesis is that, in the absence of such a principle of the continual excitation of the world-material, a state of lifeless

stasis would come about from the exhaustion of the elastic forces in the unceasing universal attraction, and a complete cessation in the moving forces of matter would occur (21:310).

The vibration of an all-pervasive ether, Kant believes, can be understood as a single form of motion with both attractive and repulsive properties, and thus as the most fundamental force in a system of forces; and only the perpetuity of this motion can explain the continued extension as well as motion of the more obvious, visible bodies in the universe.

The details of such arguments as this for the ether are, of course, obscure, but we need not worry about them for my present point. This point is just this: In spite of Kant's distinction between *vis viva* and *vis vivifica*, the theory of force alone need not imply an essential contrast between organic and inorganic matter for the simple reason that even the motion of mere inorganic matter cannot be explained by the impact forces of *vis viva* alone. The very existence of inorganic matter alone is enough to entail the existence of an internal, noninertial source of motion in the physical world and thus undermines the argument of the *Critique of Judgment* that living matter is self-contradictory because the motion of matter is governed by inertia alone. And accordingly, Kant appears to drop this argument too from his search for the differentia between organic and inorganic matter in the *Opus postumum*.

3.3

This is not to say, however, that Kant eliminates all distinction between organic and inorganic matter in the *Opus postumum*. On the contrary, as I mentioned, he repeatedly presents the distinction between organic and inorganic as the most fundamental distinction in the system of matter—though at the same time he generally does portray this distinction, in contrast to the one passage cited above (22:210), as a distinction *within* a single system of matter rather than between two separate world-systems. Moreover, Kant also continues to portray the major ground for the distinction between the organic and the inorganic in the same terms he uses in his primary argument in the Critique of Teleological Judgment. Thus Kant writes:

> The definition of an organic body is that it is a body, every part of which is there *for the sake of the other* (reciprocally as end and, at the same time, means). . . . An organic (articulated) body is one in which each part, with its moving force, necessarily relates to the whole (to each part in its composition) (21:210–11).

At the same time, Kant clearly devotes much effort to trying to make more precise both why the reciprocal causality that defines the distinction between the organic and the inorganic should lead to the connection of the organic to an immaterial principle, and then how that immaterial principle is to be conceived as related to the matter of organisms as well as to the material world in general. Why are these still issues for him? What could he see as missing from the argument of the third *Critique*?

The argument of the third *Critique* is unstable. Kant starts by arguing that it is our experience of organisms that initially leads us to the thought of an intelligible purposiveness in nature because of particular organic processes which are resistant to any mechanical explanation given the resources of our own understanding (§65, 5:375–76). We then attempt to extend the idea of purposiveness to nature as a whole (§67, 5:379–80); Kant does not in fact say why we inevitably do this, but we can conjecture that the desire for universality that is the essence of reason makes such an attempt inevitable. Once we try this, however, a tension between mechanical and final explanation inevitably suggests itself, which is ultimately resolved by the suggestion that we conceive of these two forms of explanation as applying at two different levels, namely, the sensible and the supersensible, and that we further conceive of the supersensible purposiveness of nature as being fulfilled through the mechanical laws of sensible nature: "The principle which is to make possible the compatibility of the two [kinds of explanation] in judging nature in accordance with them must lie in that which lies outside of both (hence also outside the possible empirical representation of nature), but which contains the ground of these, i.e., in the supersensible" (§78, 5:412). But once this move is made, mechanical and teleological explanation are compatible everywhere in nature, and it is not clear whether there is any special reason why organisms need remain resistant to complete mechanical explanation at the level of sensible appearance; rather, the unique experience of organisms seems to be a ladder that can be thrown aside once we have ascended to the transcendental idealist reconciliation of mechanism and teleology. And indeed, Kant seems to shift from his original insistence that it is the specific structure of our understanding that sets an a priori limit to our possible success in explaining organic processes to a much vaguer suggestion that there is nothing particular in organic processes that necessarily defeats our ability to use mechanical explanation, though some general limit inherent in our understanding, perhaps its mere finitude, will prevent us from explaining everything about organisms. Thus, Kant begins his solution to the antinomy of teleological judgment by asserting that "[w]e can by no means prove the impossibility of the generation of organized products of nature through the mere mechanism of nature" (§71, 5: 388), and that we must therefore use the idea of the purposiveness of organic nature "only as a guide for reflection, which always remains open for all mechanical grounds of explanation" (5:389). And he concludes his entire discussion of the antinomy by emphasizing even more forcefully that we can set no a priori limit on how far we can progress in understanding everything in nature by means of mechanical principles alone:

Now since it is entirely indeterminate and always indeterminable for our reason, how much the mechanism of nature can do as means to its final end; and since it must always be assumed to be possible, on account of the above-mentioned intelligible principle of the possibility of a nature in general, that nature can be thoroughly explained in accordance with both generally harmonizing laws (the physical law and that of final causes): We therefore do not know how far the mechanical kind of explanation that is possible for us may go. . . .

On this is grounded the authority . . . and even the duty to explain all products and occurrences in nature, even the most purposive, mechanically, as far as stands within our power (whose limits within this kind of investigation we cannot state) (§78, 5:414–15).

But if, as this last remark suggests, there is in fact no particular a priori limit to our power to explain even organisms mechanically, what becomes of the special status of organisms that was supposed to force a teleological view of nature upon us in the first place? Is it just an empirical fact, a matter of empirical psychology rather than of transcendental psychology, that organisms suggest the idea of purposiveness to us? Is this enough to support the whole weight of Kant's teleology, in which he clearly wants to argue that science leads us to the same twofold conception of nature that morality also requires us to conceive?

As is typical of him, Kant never explicitly acknowledges that the argument of the Critique of Teleological Judgment might be in danger of collapsing in this way. But in the *Opus postumum* he does seem to be searching for a way in which to allow for unlimited mechanical explanation of organisms while still showing that they necessarily introduce the thought of an immaterial principle. What he now tries to argue is that organisms are genuinely material, and for that reason comprise a single system with inorganic matter, but that organisms, unlike other matter, *must* be linked to an immaterial cause, and for this reason do necessitate the thought of an immaterial ground for nature as more than a matter of empirical psychology. But since he can no longer use the argument from inertia for this end, he looks for a new reason to argue that the special complexity of organisms does not just test the extent of our cognitive powers, but specifically proves the necessity of an immaterial ground for themselves and then for nature as a whole.

One argument that Kant repeatedly tries is this: The thought of an antecedent design for the reciprocal causality of organisms does not force the thought of an immaterial cause of them on us just because of the temporal antecedence of the thought of design, but because the very thought of a design itself must have a kind of *unity* or *simplicity* that nothing material ever has; that is, it is not the temporal location of the idea of an organism that is a problem for mechanical explanation, but the very fact that such an idea is a *thought* at all. In one of its simplest versions, this argument is stated thus:

An organic body presupposes an organizing principle, whether inner or outer. The latter must be simple, for otherwise it would itself require an organization. As simple, it cannot be a part of matter (for each part of matter is always itself composite). So the organizing principle of the organic body must be outside space in general. It can, however, be internally active in one respect, while being external in another: that is, in another substance, the world-spirit (22:295).

In another passage, that might be thought to bring in a complicating factor by emphasizing that the organizing thought for an organized body is an intention, Kant writes thus:

An organic natural body is thus thought of as a *machine* (a body arranged *intentionally* as to its form). Under no circumstances can it be a property of matter to have an *intention* (since it is the absolute unity of a subject which *connects* the manifold of representation in one consciousness); for all matter (and every part of it) is composite (22:548).[10]

But the key claim is still that the reason why the design of an organism necessarily introduces the idea of an immaterial cause of it is the absolute incompatibility between the indivisible unity of a thought and the infinitely composite and divisible nature of matter. Thus Kant argues that while organisms are material machines, they must be designed and animated by something immaterial—not because matter is ruled by inertia, but because it is never a true unity.

This is certainly a new argument in the *Opus postumum*. Unfortunately, it is not an argument that the critical Kant of the previous decade would have tolerated, for it succumbs to the very error that Kant diagnosed in the first *Critique* in the Paralogism of Pure Reason: It confuses the *logical* unity or simplicity of a thought with the ontological indivisibility of the substance in which that thought inheres. As Kant said in the Paralogism, "The proposition 'A thought can only be the effect of the absolute unity of a thinking being' cannot be treated as analytic" (A353). This is because "Through the [representation] I, I always think an absolute but logical unity of the subject (simplicity), but I do not cognize the real simplicity of my subject" (A356–57). The argument of the Paralogism is just that one can never make a valid inference from the formal or logical properties of a thought to the structure of the substance that has that thought. Presumably the same would hold of the thought of a design: In whatever sense such a thought must be thought to be a unity, we just cannot automatically assume that the subject that thinks that thought must also be simple. Thus even conceding the unity of the thought of a design and a purpose for an organism does not seem to force us to posit an immaterial substance as its subject.

This new argument for the special nature of organisms in the *Opus postumum* clearly fails by the standards of the *Critique of Pure Reason*. However, although the last passage cited from the *Opus postumum* argued that it cannot "be a property of matter to have an *intention*" because of the contrast between the unity of an intention and the compositeness of matter, there are other passages in these texts where Kant asserts the dependence of organic matter on an immaterial principle because of the purposiveness or intentionality of organisms without saying anything about indivisibility. Here are several such passages:

> The first division of physical bodies is, thus, that into organic and inorganic. A physically organic body (in contrast to a mechanically organic body) is one, each of whose parts is by nature there in it for the sake of the other; in which, conversely, the concept of the *whole* also determines the form of the parts. . . . Such a formation indicates a natural cause, acting according to *purposes*. . . . One can seek the productive force of this inner form nowhere else than in a formative understanding—that is, seek it solely in a non-material cause . . . (22:283).

> Zoönomy contains three vital powers: *nervous power*, as a principle of excitability *[incitabilitas]*; *muscular power [irritabilitas Halleri]*; and a *third one*, which brings both forces into active and reactive, constantly alternating, play: one all-penetrating, all-moving etc. material, of which heat is one phenomenon. (4) The force of organization in space and time, which contains a *nonmaterial* higher principle, namely an effectivity according to purposes (22:301).

> In the latter part of physics, the highest division of *bodies* (not just matter) is [into organic] and inorganic. The division can emerge a priori from concepts. For, the possibility of an organic body (that is, a body each of whose parts is there for the sake of the other, or which is so formed that the possibility of the parts and the form of their inner relations emerge only from its concept—a body which is thus only possible through purposes, which presuppose an immaterial principle which forms this substance either mediately or immediately) produces a teleological principle (22:501).

The second of these passages confirms my claim that the *Opus postumum* rejects the third *Critique's* argument against hylozoism by treating a number of organic processes as forms of the self-moving force of the ether, and thus as features that organic bodies have in *common* with all forms of matter. Then this passage, like the other two, suggests that what clearly distinguishes organic from inorganic matter is the presence of purposes in the former, thus that there is an essential connection between purposiveness as such and the immaterial. What this connection is, however, is not made clear.

Several other passages make the essential connection to the immaterial even more obscure when they link the immaterial principle of organisms not to purposes in general but to *desire*. For instance,

> The principle of the spontaneity of the motion of the parts of our own body (as limbs), considering the latter as our own self, is a mechanism. Although this [spontaneity] is an absolute unity of the principle of motion from *desires* (thus not material), nevertheless, reason can do no other than to make general (if only problematically) the concept of a purposive mechanism of matter, under the name of organization, and to contrast it with inorganic matter (21:212).

> The idea of organic bodies is *indirectly* contained *a priori* in that of a composite of moving forces, in which the concept of a real *whole* necessarily precedes that of its parts—which can only be thought by the concept of a combination according to *purposes*. . . . How can we include such bodies with such moving forces in the general classification, according to *a priori* principles? Because man is conscious of himself as a self-moving machine, without being able to further understand such a possibility, he can, and is entitled to, introduce a priori organic moving forces of bodies into the classification of bodies in general. . . . He [must], however, generalize the concept of vital force and of the excitability of matter in his own self by the faculty of desire (21:213).

These passages only deepen the mystery, however. First Kant says that the mere presence of purposes in organisms implies their dependence on some immaterial substance, without explanation. Then he suggests that it is the evidence of motion from *desire*, an example of which we have in the spontaneity of our own motion, that implies the connection of organisms to a distinctive and immaterial principle. But given everything that we standardly assume about Kant's moral philosophy and moral anthropology, our *desires* are just the sort of thing for which we assume there can be, at least in principle, a completely physiological and, we should have thought, mechanical explanation. *Desires* are just those stimuli of our own actions that we can include in the phenomenal world, as part of the seamless causal nexus of that world. How is the presence of *desire* in ourselves supposed to prove the presence of any immaterial principle in or connected to our own organism, which we might then extend to the case of other organisms, and from there to nature as a whole?

One can only conjecture that a step is being omitted from Kant's argument. And what could this be? Perhaps it is precisely that reflection on our own desires is what reveals to us the difference between those desires, as what is merely passive in us, and our freely adopted *purposes*, which are the expressions of a kind of spontaneity that we do *not* directly experience in nature, namely our purposes as set for us by reason, and by means of which we can actually constrain our own desires. It is the *contrast* between our mere desires and our rational purposes that reveals to us the fact of our own freedom, as something that cannot be included in the seamless causal web of the phenomenal world but is an intimation of another aspect of our existence. Of course, we know well that it is Kant's view from the *Critique of Practical Reason* onward that it is only our recognition of our obligation under the moral law that leads us to realize that we are always free in the determination of our purposes, no matter how passively determined our mere desires may be. Then what is not explicitly stated in Kant's remarks on purposes in the *Opus postumum* would be the fact that we infer the freedom of our own purposes from our moral obligation, and so it is reflection on *morality* that requires us to think of purposes as free in a way that is not compatible with a purely mechanical explanation of the powers of matter. His argument would then have to be that it is our obligation under moral law that requires us to conceive of our *own* purposes as having a principle other than the mechanism of matter, so that when we impute an immaterial principle to organisms in general because of their purposiveness, it is our own model of purposiveness that we are using. The overall form of his argument would then have to be that it may be theoretical difficulties in comprehending organisms that require us to conceive of them as products of purpose, but that it is our morally grounded conception of our own purposiveness as free that leads us to the further thought that purposiveness entails immateriality, thus that organisms and ultimately all of nature must have an immaterial ground. In other words, only through the twofold stance that we need to take on our own purposes would our experience of organisms as purposive entities lead us to take a twofold view of nature as a whole.

Kant certainly does not make this argument explicit in the *Opus postumum*. But if, as we have seen, Kant himself has undermined the original arguments for the special nature of organisms offered in the *Critique of Judgment,* and if the explicit new argument in the *Opus postumum* falls victim to the original critique of any paralogism of pure reason, it is hard to see where Kant could turn for an argument for the special nature of organisms except to our own purposes, distinctive because they are under the legislation of morality. Of course, such an argument could never be considered theoretically constitutive; instead, the special status of organisms would be more like that of a postulate of practical reason such as that of our own freedom than like anything else. But since Kant had argued since the *Critique of Pure Reason* that it is only as postulates of practical reason that metaphysical claims can have any force for us at all, this is precisely the result we should have expected all along.

NOTES

1. Translations from the *Critique of Pure Reason* are from Immanuel Kant, *Critique of Pure Reason,* tr. and ed. Paul Guyer and Allen W. Wood (Cambridge: Cambridge University Press, 1998). Translations from the *Opus postumum* are from Immanuel Kant, *Opus postumum,* ed. Eckart Förster, trans. Eckart Förster and Michael Rosen (Cambridge: Cambridge University Press, 1993). Translations from Kant's pre-Critical writings are from Immanuel Kant, *Theoretical Philosophy, 1755–1770,* ed. and trans. David E. Walford (Cambridge: Cambridge University Press, 1992). Translations from Kant's metaphysics lectures are from Immanuel Kant, *Lectures on Metaphysics,* ed. and trans. Karl Ameriks and Steve Naragon (Cambridge: Cambridge University Press, 1997). Translations from the *Critique of Judgment* are mine.

2. Actually, in his first illustration of the application of the idea of a fundamental power, Kant is talking about the idea of a fundamental power underlying various *mental* capacities in human psychology, and the word "the" which I have interpolated in this citation replaces the pronoun "its," which refers to the mind as the seat of the powers being unified.

3. Citations to the *Critique of Judgment* include the section number, along with the volume and page numbers of the Akademie edition.

4. Kant actually uses the word *Gattung,* which in taxonomic contexts is ordinarily translated as "genus" in contrast to *Art,* translated as "species"; but since his example here does not depend on any contrast between levels of classification, his point may best be seen by taking *Gattung* to mean "species" in the ordinary contemporary sense of a population any of whose members are capable of combining to produce fertile offspring.

5. See also §84, 5:434.

6. Well, we didn't in Kant's time: Watches and Jacquard looms could not produce more of themselves. Perhaps computer-driven machine tools can or shortly will be able to make more computer-driven machine tools.

7. The suggestion that if it is inevitable for us to look at organisms as if they were products of design then it also becomes natural for us to look at all of nature as if it were in the service of an overarching end—at least for heuristic purposes—is repeatedly expounded; for other passages see §67, 5:380; §72, 5:391; §75, 5:398; §78, 5:414; and §82, 5:427.

8. I have explored this "master argument" of the Critique of Teleological Judgment in two essays: "The Unity of Nature and Freedom: Kant's Conception of the System of Nature and Freedom," in *The Reception of Kant's Critical Philosophy,* ed. Sally Sedgwick (Cambridge: Cambridge University Press, 2000), pp. 19–53, and "From Nature to Morality: Kant's new Argument in the 'Critique of Teleological Judgment'," in the proceedings of a conference on "The System of Reason in Kant and German Idealism," Vienna, October 1997 (to be published).

9. For some discussion of this general issue, see my "In praktischer Absicht: Kants Begriff eines Postulats der reinen praktischen Vernunft," *Philosophisches Jahrbuch* 104 (1997): 1–18, translated as "From a Practical Point of View: Kant's Conception of a Postulate of Pure Practical Reason," in my *Kant on Freedom, Law, and Happiness* (Cambridge: Cambridge University Press, 2000), 333–71.

10. See also 22:547.

Subject and Person Index

Index of Passages Quoted

References to the *Critique of Pure Reason* are located by A and B numbers. All other references are to the volume and page numbers of the Akademie edition, separated by a colon.